Introducing Philosophy through Pop Culture

From Socrates to *South Park*, Hume to *House*

Edited by William Irwin and
David Kyle Johnson

WILEY-BLACKWELL

A John Wiley & Sons, Ltd., Publication

Blackwell Publishing was acquired by John Wiley & Sons in February 2007. Blackwell's
publishing program has been merged with Wiley's global Scientific, Technical, and
Medical business to form Wiley-Blackwell.

Registered Office
John Wiley & Sons Ltd, The Atrium, Southern Gate, Chichester, West Sussex, PO19 8SQ,
United Kingdom

Editorial Offices
350 Main Street, Malden, MA 02148-5020, USA
9600 Garsington Road, Oxford, OX4 2DQ, UK
The Atrium, Southern Gate, Chichester, West Sussex, PO19 8SQ, UK

For details of our global editorial offices, for customer services, and for information about how
to apply for permission to reuse the copyright material in this book please see our website at
www.wiley.com/wiley-blackwell.

The right of William Irwin and David Kyle Johnson to be identified as the authors of the
editorial material in this work has been asserted in accordance with the UK Copyright,
Designs and Patents Act 1988.

Library of Congress Cataloging-in-Publication Data
Introducing philosophy through pop culture : from Socrates to South Park, Hume
to House / edited by William Irwin and David Kyle Johnson.
       p. cm.
   Includes bibliographical references and index.
   ISBN 978-1-4443-3453-1 (pbk.)
   1. Philosophy and civilization.   2. Popular culture–Philosophy.   I. Irwin, William, 1970–
II. Johnson, David Kyle.
   B59.I59 2010
   100–dc22
                                                                    2010016191

A catalogue record for this book is available from the British Library.

Set in 10.5/13pt Minion by Graphicraft Limited, Hong Kong
Printed in Singapore by Ho Printing Singapore Pte Ltd

01   2010

Contents

Acknowledgments   ix

Introduction   1

Part I: What is Philosophy?   3

Introduction   3

Socrates and the Spirit of Philosophy
1 Flatulence and Philosophy: A Lot of Hot Air, or the Corruption of Youth?   5
William W. Young III

Logic and Fallacies
2 The Chewbacca Defense: A *South Park* Logic Lesson   14
Robert Arp

Relativism and Truth
3 Wikiality, Truthiness, and Gut Thinking: Doing Philosophy Colbert-Style   25
David Kyle Johnson

Part II: Epistemology   37

Introduction   37

The Ethics of Belief
4 You Know, I Learned Something Today: Stan Marsh and the Ethics of Belief   39
Henry Jacoby

Skepticism
5   Tumbling Down the Rabbit Hole: Knowledge, Reality, and
    the Pit of Skepticism   46
    Matt Lawrence

*The Definition of Knowledge, the Gettier Problem,
and Faith*
6   Adama's True Lie: Earth and the Problem of Knowledge   57
    Eric J. Silverman

Part III: Metaphysics   67

    Introduction   67

Philosophy of Mind
7   Mind and Body in Zion   69
    Matt Lawrence

Personal Identity
8   Amnesia, Personal Identity, and the Many Lives of Wolverine 82
    Jason Southworth

Freedom and Determinism
9   Destiny in the Wizarding World   89
    Jeremy Pierce

Artificial Intelligence, The Turing Test, and the Chinese Room
10 The Terminator Wins: Is the Extinction of the Human Race
    the End of People, or Just the Beginning?   99
    Greg Littmann

Part IV: Philosophy of Religion   109

    Introduction   109

The Problem of Evil
11 Cartmanland and the Problem of Evil   111
    David Kyle Johnson

Faith Seeking Understanding
12 Aquinas and Rose on Faith and Reason   119
    Daniel B. Gallagher

Arguments for the Existence of God
13 "I Am an Instrument of God": Religious Belief, Atheism,
    and Meaning   128
    Jason T. Eberl and Jennifer A. Vines

Part V: Ethics   **139**

Introduction   139

Why Be Moral?
14 Plato on Gyges' Ring of Invisibility: The Power of *Heroes* and
    the Value of Virtue   141
    Don Adams

Virtue Ethics
15 The Virtues of Humor: What *The Office* Can Teach Us About
    Aristotle's Ethics   151
    Sean McAleer

Utilitarianism and Deontology
16 Why Doesn't Batman Kill the Joker?   163
    Mark D. White

17 Means, Ends, and the Critique of Pure Superheroes   172
    J. Robert Loftis

Part VI: Challenges to Traditional Ethics   **183**

Introduction   183

Nietzschean and Marxist Critique
18 Metallica, Nietzsche, and Marx: The Immorality of Morality   185
    Peter S. Fosl

19 When Machines Get Souls: Nietzsche on the Cylon Uprising   194
    Robert Sharp

Existentialist Ethics
20 Being-in-*The Office*: Sartre, the Look, and the Viewer   204
    Matthew P. Meyer and Greg J. Schneider

21 Batman's Confrontation with Death, Angst, and Freedom   213
    David M. Hart

Feminist Critique
22 "You Care for Everybody": Cameron's Ethics of Care   221
    Renee Kyle

23 Vampire Love: The Second Sex Negotiates the Twenty-First Century   228
    Bonnie Mann

Postmodern Critique
24 Killing the Griffins: A Murderous Exposition of Postmodernism   238
    J. Jeremy Wisnewski

Part VII: Social and Political Philosophy   247

    Introduction   247

    Social Contract Theory
25 *Lost*'s State of Nature   249
    Richard Davies

    Marxism
26 Laughter Between Distraction and Awakening: Marxist Themes
    in *The Office*   260
    Michael Bray

    Torture
27 The Ethics of Torture in *24*: Shockingly Banal   269
    Dónal P. O'Mathúna

    Race
28 Mutants and the Metaphysics of Race   280
    Jeremy Pierce

Part VIII: Eastern Views   287

    Introduction   287

    Zen
29 Zen and the Art of Cylon Maintenance   289
    James McRae

30 The Sound of One House Clapping: The Unmannerly Doctor as
    Zen Rhetorician   299
    Jeffrey C. Ruff and Jeremy Barris

    Taoism
31 The Tao of the Bat   308
    Mark D. White

Part IX: The Meaning of Life   317

    Introduction   317

    The Theistic View
32 Beyond Godric's Hollow: Life after Death and the Search for Meaning   319
    Jonathan L. Walls and Jerry L. Walls

    The Socratic View
33 Selfish, Base Animals Crawling Across the Earth: House and
    the Meaning of Life   327
    Henry Jacoby

Glossary   334
Notes on Contributors   338
Sources   343
Index   347

Acknowledgments

We would like to thank our friends and colleagues who offered feedback and advice in assembling this volume, especially Dave Baggett, Greg Bassham, and Jason Eberl. We would also like to thank Andrew Morton for permission to use his glossary definitions. Thanks are also due to Jeff Dean and a bevy of anonymous reviewers who helped us shape the volume. Kyle wishes to thank his wife Lori for her love and support. Bill wishes to thank his wife Megan and his children Daniel and Kate for making home so happy and philosophy-friendly.

Introduction

Philosophy has a public relations problem. Just the sound of the word "philosophy" scares a lot of people, conjuring images of long-dead Greeks and crusty old professors. But the stereotypes of philosophy are just that – stereotypes. They are mistaken exaggerations and overgeneralizations. Western Philosophy may have begun in Ancient Greece, but it is alive and well in contemporary America and around the globe. Some philosophy professors may be egg-headed, ivory tower intellectuals, but most are not. In fact, many philosophy professors like the same things you like: television, movies, music, and video games. We see connections between these elements of pop culture and philosophy. So this book, written by philosophy professors, takes you from pop culture to philosophy; we wade into the shallow water before swimming out deep. Each chapter focuses on a piece of pop culture, like *Harry Potter* or *The Office*, and teaches you about a particular issue in philosophy or the views of a particular philosopher. We think you'll agree that, to paraphrase a classic Disney truism, a spoonful of pop culture helps the philosophy go down.

The idea of using examples to facilitate learning is not new to philosophy. Famously, Plato (429–347 BCE) used the story of the ring of Gyges, and Descartes (1596–1650) imagined a deceitful demon. However, most examples in philosophy are rather dry – finding people with bland names like Jones and Brown in difficult to describe circumstances, such as those in which we are potentially justified in believing that "Jones owns a Ford, or Brown is in Barcelona." Thankfully, Hollywood writers do a much better job of creating engaging, imaginative scenarios than philosophers do. So why not use their creations to add spice to philosophy? As you'll discover in this book, *The Matrix* provides a vivid way of picturing Descartes' concerns about deception and knowledge, and *South Park* hilariously dramatizes the problem of evil by asking why good things (like inheriting a million dollars) happen to bad people (like Cartman). Indeed, many other insightful philosophical illustrations from pop culture await your reading.

Now, of course, you may be concerned that you're in trouble because in addition to being clueless about philosophy you're also clueless about *The Matrix* and *South Park*. There's no need to worry. You don't have to be an expert on Batman or to have seen every episode of *House* to benefit from this book. Even a passing acquaintance with the pop culture icon discussed in any given chapter will be enough for you to learn the philosophy to which it is connected. You can get that easily enough on the Internet. In fact, you can visit the website for this book at www.pop-philosophy.org for all kinds of helpful up-to-date links.

In sum, this book is intended to make initial connections between pop culture and philosophy that will pique your interest in the latter and lead you to study and appreciate the subject more deeply. Maybe you'll even decide to tell your friends that philosophy has gotten a bad rap. Certainly, we believe you'll find that philosophy is relevant, fun, and exciting.

How to Use this Book in a Philosophy Course

This book is intended to serve primarily as a supplementary text in Introduction to Philosophy courses. Introductory courses are structured in a variety of different ways depending on the professor. Some courses are questions and issues based, some are historically based. Some courses use a standard textbook; others rely on primary philosophical texts. Others mix it up and use a combination of approaches. This book is designed to go along with any of them. However, this book is not intended to cover all philosophical issues and figures in exhaustive detail. We leave that for the main text and the professor.

This book can be used in a variety of ways in the classroom. Its chapters can be used to introduce a philosophical topic unfamiliar to the student. Assigning a summary of the chapter can ensure the student reads it and is better prepared for a lecture on the topic of the chapter. Each chapter could also be used for philosophical reflection; you might consider having your students write reflection or argument papers in response to them. If you are worried about whether your students are familiar with the relevant pop culture phenomena, there is a wiki site for each pop culture phenomenon discussed (e.g., heroeswiki.com) that can provide a quick and easy summary. Other suggestions for professors on how to use this book in courses are available at www.pop-philosophy.org.

Part I

What is Philosophy?

Introduction

The word "philosophy" is often confused with the words "opinion," "theory" or "approach" – as in, "What is your philosophy of life?" or "Our philosophy is never to be undersold!" As a result, some students have mistaken ideas about what a philosophy class is. "Can you even give a wrong answer in a philosophy class? Isn't it just whatever you think?" Well, yes you can, and no it's not.

The word "philosophy" comes from the Greek language and means "love of wisdom." Philosophers seek truth and wisdom above all else. The questions for which true answers are most important, but most elusive, form the core of philosophy. What is the nature of reality? What is knowledge, and how can one attain it? Is there a God? What is the nature of good and evil? How can I live a good life? How should we govern ourselves? What is the meaning of life? So how do philosophers seek answers these questions? Are there really answers? Or is whatever anyone thinks just "true for them" because they have a "right to their opinion"? What role does philosophy play in society? And, what attitude does philosophy require?

In his chapter, William Young argues that philosophy and the TV show *South Park* share some common aims. Like the philosopher Socrates (469–399 BCE), *South Park* is charged with corrupting the youth, inappropriately challenging moral norms, and being a social nuisance. But, the accusations are unfounded for both Socrates and *South Park*. The accusers are actually the corruptors; for example, parents corrupt the youth when they leave their kids to be raised by television without educating them about what they are seeing. Thankfully *South Park*, like Socrates, teaches us to draw our own conclusions – not merely accept the consensus of the crowd – and to reach those conclusions by considering the perspectives of others. Clearly, Young argues, *South Park* is not mindless and harmful; the show, like philosophy, is a gadfly, "an annoying pest that goes around 'stinging people' with . . . challenging questions and critical reflections so as to keep them intellectually awake and on their toes."

Philosophers' appetite for truth is insatiable, but they do not always agree. To solve their disputes they use logic. In his chapter, Robert Arp takes examples from *South Park* to teach some of the basics of logic including the structure of arguments, the differences between good and bad arguments, and the distinction between inductive and deductive arguments. The lesson concludes with common logical fallacies, illustrated by *South Park* for comedic effect. In one classic episode, for example, the cartoon version of Johnnie Cochran commits the red-herring fallacy by suggesting that Chef must not have written the Alanis Morissette song "Stinky Britches" because Chewbacca spent most of his time on Endor: "If Chewbacca lives on Endor, you must acquit."

South Park is not the only show that plays philosopher. Late night political talk shows, like *The Daily Show* and *The Colbert Report*, are gadflies as well. In his chapter, David Kyle Johnson uses Stephen Colbert to teach us about the philosophical attitude. Relativism (what Colbert calls "wikiality") and intuitionism (what Colbert calls "truthiness") are contrary to the endeavor of philosophy. More importantly, Johnson enlists Colbert to dispel a myth that holds back almost every philosophy course – the myth that everyone has a right to their opinion. Attempts to end philosophical discussion with appeals to "a right to my opinion" only reveal a disregard for truth and a desire to protect entrenched beliefs. Real philosophers must be willing to give up disproven beliefs and embrace the truth.

1

Flatulence and Philosophy

A Lot of Hot Air, or the Corruption of Youth?

William W. Young III

Summary

Though Trey Parker and Matt Stone haven't been killed for it yet (they did receive death threats after their 200th episode) the creators of *South Park* have faced accusations much like those that led to Socrates' execution: the corruption of youth and the teaching of vulgar, irreligious behavior. A closer examination, however, reveals that *South Park* is very much within the Platonic tradition, as Kyle and Stan engage in questioning and dialogue in order to "learn something today." Moreover, the mob mentality of the parents, along with the malicious yet mimetic evil of Cartman, demonstrates how evil emerges from thoughtlessness: a failure to ask if one can live with oneself, and a failure to put oneself in the place of others. Through its different characters, and even in its apparently mindless vulgarity, *South Park* shows the need for engaging in dialogue, and thinking from others' perspectives, in order to pursue wisdom, examine life, and make it worth living.

The "Danger" of *South Park*

In the episode "Death," Kyle's mother leads a boycott of the boys' favorite cartoon show – *Terrance and Philip* – because of its continuous farting, name-calling, and general "potty humor." While the parents are up in arms over this "moral" issue, the boys wrestle with the problem of euthanasia for Stan's grandfather, something none of the parents will discuss with them. "Death" brings together many of the central issues that have made *South Park* successful and controversial: vulgarity, the misplaced moral concerns of American culture, the discussion of controversial moral topics, and the criticism that *South Park* itself is a "disgusting" show. Since "Death" the criticism of the show has only grown – getting even bigger than Cartman's fat ass – drawing fire for its obscene language, criticisms of religion, and emphasis upon freedom of speech.

Like the parents protesting *The Terrance and Philip Show*, critics of *South Park* make claims that are strikingly similar to those that have been leveled against Western philosophy since its beginnings. It mocks religious **beliefs**, leads younger folks to question accepted authority and values, and corrupts our children and culture. The "it" in the previous sentence refers to *South Park*, but in fact, the same criticisms formed the basis for Socrates' (470–399 BCE) trial and execution in Athens, Greece in 399 BCE.[1] So in this chapter we'll explore the heretical possibility that people perceive *South Park* as dangerous precisely because it is a form of philosophy. The "danger" that *South Park* poses has to do with its depiction of dialogue and free thinking. In the end we will have learned something: like Socrates, *South Park* harms no one. Philosophy and *South Park* actually instruct people and provide them with the intellectual tools they need to become wise, free, and good.

Oh My God! They Killed Socrates! You Bastards!

In Plato's (427–327 BCE) *Apology*, Socrates defends himself against two charges: (1) impiety (false teachings about the gods, possibly that they don't exist) and (2) corrupting the youth of Athens. In reality, Socrates probably had as much chance of winning his case as Chef did against Johnny Cochran's "Chewbacca" defense! What is most important about Socrates' defense, however, is not so much what he says as *how* he says it. He defends himself by questioning his accuser, Meletus, leading him through a process of **reasoning**. For example, Socrates refutes the charge of corrupting the youth as follows:

> SOCRATES: You say you have discovered the one who corrupts them, namely me, and you bring me here and accuse me to the jury . . . All the Athenians, it seems, make the young into fine good men, except me, and I alone corrupt them. Is that what you mean?
>
> MELETUS: That is most definitely what I mean.
>
> SOCRATES: You condemn me to a great misfortune. Tell me: does this also apply to horses do you think? That all men improve them and one individual corrupts them? Or is quite the contrary true, one individual is able to improve them, or very few, namely the horse breeders, whereas the majority, if they have horses and use them, corrupt them? Is that not the case, Meletus, both with horses and all other animals? . . . It would be a happy state of affairs if only one person corrupted our youth, while the others improved them. You have made it sufficiently obvious, Meletus, that you have never had any concern for our youth; you show your indifference clearly; that you have given no thought to the subjects about which you bring me to trial. (*Apology*, p. 30)

---

[1] Plato, *Apology*, in *Five Dialogues: Euthyphro, Apology, Crito, Meno, Phaedo*, trans. by G. M. A. Grube (Indianapolis: Hackett Publishing, 1981). Hereafter noted as (*Apology*, p. "x") in the text. Also see Xenophon, *Recollections of Socrates, and Socrates' Defense Before the Jury*, trans. by Anna Benjamin (Indianapolis: Bobbs-Merrill, 1965).

Through the analogy with horse training, Socrates shows how illogical the accusations against him really are. Just as a majority of people would injure horses by training them, and only a few good trainers improve them, so too it is likely that a few teachers improve the virtue of the youth, while many others corrupt them. Socrates argues, further, that he is in fact the one who is teaching Athens' youth what virtue involves, while many others – including the idiots sitting before him – corrupt them. (As you can imagine, this did not go over well with the jury.)

While showing that the accusations are groundless, this "apology" – a word that also can mean *defense* – demonstrates why Socrates got a death sentence of hemlock. Socrates is famous for saying "I know that I don't know" and, actually, this is a wise insight. For Socrates, philosophy was the love and pursuit of wisdom, and this required questioning others to find out what they do or don't know. Unfortunately, people often believe they are wiser than they are. By questioning them, Socrates would show them that they don't know what they believe they know: "I go around seeking out anyone, citizen or stranger, whom I think wise. Then if I do not think he is, I come to the assistance of the god and show him that he is not wise" (*Apology*, pp. 28–9). What makes Socrates wise is his recognition of his own ignorance, through continuous questioning of himself and others. Many powerful people in Athens saw him as dangerous because his questioning and debate would undermine their bases for power.

In the town of South Park, people in positions of power believe they are teaching the children wisdom and virtue. However, as in Athens, the many people of South Park seem to make the children worse, not better. For example, Mr. Garrison "teaches" the children life lessons from re-runs of *Barnaby Jones*, Mrs. Broflovski always goes to crazy extremes with her "moral" outrage, Uncle Jim and Ned teach the boys to kill harmless bunnies and squirrels in "self-defense," and the mayor panders shamelessly to voters. None of the townsfolk really *talk* to the children, except Chef (God rest his soul), who taught the art of making sweet, sweet love to a woman. Blindly following the crowd, from protesting *The Terrance and Philip Show* to boycotting Harbucks, to – yes – burying their heads in the sand to avoid watching *Family Guy*, the parents of South Park corrupt the children far more than a television show ever could. Like the Athenians, the adults don't know as much as they believe they know. Ultimately, if television does corrupt them, it does so because they are left to it by their parents, with no one to educate them about what they are seeing. Of course, there are also cases where parents and people in powerful positions *do* try to discuss issues and **ideas** with the children. These discussions, though, support the same point, as the adult usually sounds like a bumbling idiot.

Cartman Gets a Banal Probe

One of the most significant philosophical reflections on evil in the twentieth century is Hannah Arendt's *Eichmann in Jerusalem: A Report on the Banality of Evil*, a study of the trial of Adolf Eichmann for his role in the deportations of millions of European Jews to concentration camps during the Jewish Holocaust. Eichmann just followed the law of the land, whatever it happened to be, and when Hitler was making the laws, Eichmann simply carried them out.[2] In the words of Arendt, Eichmann was an unreflective person, unable to think for himself and *definitely* unable "to think from the standpoint of somebody else" (Arendt, p. 49). What was really monstrous about Eichmann was not his vicious cruelty, but rather the way that he was not that different from so many Germans who, under Hitler, accepted and supported laws that were obviously evil and believed that they were doing what was right. Eichmann's banality – the fact that there is nothing distinctive or exceptional about him – is *precisely* what makes him evil. He was one of the "crowd" who *didn't* walk to the beat of a different drummer and *didn't* rock the boat. He embodied complicit citizenship under a dictatorship, which speaks *for* its subjects and, thus, cuts off their reflective and critical thought.

Thoughtlessness leads to evil, as Arendt says, because it doesn't let us see things from others' perspectives. By blindly following orders, Eichmann didn't think about what his actions were doing to others, or even what they were doing to himself. By saying he was "following the law" and "doing his duty," he ignored how his actions sent millions to their deaths and, despite his protests, made him a murderer. Thinking, according to Arendt, requires taking another's standpoint, reflecting on how you might be harming others, and asking if you can live with what you are doing.

While the adults in South Park blindly follow the latest fad, or what they are told, it is the children who bring out the absurdity and potential harm that lurks in such thoughtlessness. To be more accurate, it's usually Kyle or Stan who are the reflective ones, while Cartman's mind is as empty as the Cheesypoofs he devours daily. He is often sadistic, cruel, and evil. Like Eichmann, Cartman is probably evil because, when it comes to "authorita," he lacks reflection and critical analysis. (And like Eichmann, he has a Nazi uniform that he has sported on occasion.) Cartman sings the Cheesypoofs song so well because all he can do is imitate what he hears on television. His evil is an imitation of the evil characters of our culture, as prepackaged as his afternoon snacks. Cartman consumes evil and imitates it as blindly and thoughtlessly as Eichmann. Most importantly, because of this thoughtlessness, Cartman is unable to see things from anyone else's viewpoint (as illustrated most clearly in his manipulation of his mother). As Arendt says, such thoughtlessness is precisely what allows evil to emerge in modern society, and Cartman's mindless consumption is as thoughtless as it gets.

Friendship Kicks Ass! The Dialogues of Kyle and Stan

Part of what makes *South Park* philosophically interesting is the contrast between Cartman's evil stupidity and the non-conformist, reflective virtue of Kyle and Stan. Philosophers like Plato and Aristotle (384–322 BCE) have noted the importance of

---

[2]   Hannah Arendt, *Eichmann in Jerusalem: A Report on the Banality of Evil* (New York: Viking Press, 1964), pp. 135–50. Hereafter cited as (Arendt, p. "x") in the text.

how critical reflection leads to harmony or balance and helps us to avoid extremes. After all, the "extremes" of thinking and acting often lead to mistaken beliefs and harmful behavior. In fact, following Plato's lead, Aristotle put forward the idea that *virtue* is concerned with striking a balance or hitting the mark between two extreme viewpoints, ideas, beliefs, emotions, or actions.[3] *South Park* addresses moral issues through a discussion and criticism of established "moral" positions, both conservative and liberal, which are found to be inadequate. Kyle and Stan come to a virtuous position, in part, by negotiating and listening to these views before reaching their own conclusion through questioning and reason. Frequently, their conclusion recognizes that there is some truth to each position, but that its limited perspective is still dangerous. For example, it's true that hybrid cars are more environmentally responsible than gas-guzzling SUVs. But when an air of moral superiority clouds one's judgment, this "smug cloud" creates hostility and pollutes society in other ways.

How Stan and Kyle reach their conclusions is more significant than the conclusions themselves. Think of how they discuss whether it's wrong to kill Stan's grandpa, who wants to die. They, like Socrates, question those around them, seeking to know if the people are as wise as they believe. Their parents, Mr. Garrison, and Jesus won't discuss or touch this issue "with a 60-foot pole." What Kyle and Stan ultimately realize – with the help of Stan's great-great-grandfather's ghost – is that they shouldn't kill his grandfather because the action would change and harm them. As it turns out, Stan's grandfather is wrong in asking them to do this vicious action. Note that the boys reach this conclusion through living with each other, recognizing their differences, and engaging in debate. Stan and Kyle – unlike Eichmann and Cartman – learn to see things from others' perspectives, through their ongoing conversation.

In the *Apology* Socrates makes the claim that a good person cannot be harmed by the actions of others. This seems false. After all, aside from being a cartoon character, what could prevent Cartman from punching out the Dalai Lama? But what Socrates means by "good" is something different than we often realize. Goodness means reflectively thinking about one's actions and *being able to live with what one has done*. Despite any *physical* harm – torture, imprisonment, exile, or death – that may come a person's way, no one can "hurt" a virtuous person by making him/her *do* something bad. Cartman, for example, couldn't make the Dalai Lama punch *him*. Socrates, for his part, refused to execute an innocent person, or to try generals for "crimes" beyond the laws of the city. And, significantly, Socrates would rather die than give up the thinking and questioning that he sees as central to philosophy:

> Perhaps someone might say: But Socrates, if you leave us will you not be able to live quietly, without talking? Now this is the most difficult point on which to convince some of you. If I say that it is impossible for me to keep quiet because that means

---

3   See Plato, *The Republic of Plato*, trans. by David Bloom (New York: Basic Books, 1991); Aristotle, *Nicomachean Ethics*, trans. by Terence Irwin (Indianapolis: Hackett Publishing, 1999).

disobeying the god, you will not believe me . . . On the other hand, if I say that it is the greatest good for a man to discuss virtue every day and those other things about which you hear me conversing and testing myself and others, for the unexamined life is not worth living for man, you will believe me even less. (*Apology*, p. 41)

Arendt has a similar **conception** of goodness. Ethics, for those (unlike Eichmann) who resisted the Nazis, was being able to look back on one's life without shame, rather than adhering to a set of rules. Her description deserves quoting:

Their criterion [for goodness], I think, was a different one; they asked themselves to what extent they would still be able to live in peace with themselves after having committed certain deeds; and they decided that it would be better to do nothing, not because the world would then be changed for the better, but simply because only on this condition could they go on living with themselves at all. Hence, they also chose to die when they were forced to participate. To put it crudely, they refused to murder . . . because they were unwilling to live together with a murderer – themselves. The precondition for this kind of judging is not a highly developed intelligence or sophistication in moral matters, but rather the disposition to live together explicitly with oneself, to have intercourse with oneself, that is, to be engaged in that silent dialogue between me and myself which, since Socrates and Plato, we usually call thinking.[4]

Thinking, for Arendt, is a twofold process: it involves seeing things through another's eyes, in dialogue and reflection, as well as determining whether you can live with your own actions. It is, then, both an internal and an external dialogue, and it is only through this dialogue that critical reflection and goodness become possible. Whereas Eichmann and Cartman do not critically reflect upon the consequences of actions, nor put themselves in another's shoes, thoughtful dialogue makes us attentive to others around us, lets us live with them, and helps us attend to our own goodness. Such dialogue allows us to live with ourselves – even when, like Socrates or those who resisted the Nazis, this means we must die.

Of course, in *South Park* there is no Socrates to teach philosophy or help us engage in dialogue. Surrounded by ignorance and violence, the boys are on their own. While the four are friends, *South Park* makes a compelling point about philosophy and ethics through the particulars of the friendship of Kyle and Stan. For instance, in "Spooky Fish," where the "evil" Cartman (who is good) arrives from a parallel universe, an evil Kyle and Stan arrive *together*. Their friendship – thinking from one another's perspective – is what helps them to be good, both for themselves and for others. In Arendt's words, to live well is to "be plural," so that the good life is never simply one's own.[5] This probably is why Plato wrote about important philosophical issues in a dialogue format, so that it becomes clear that debate and discussion of ideas are essential to any intellectual and moral growth.

---

[4] Hannah Arendt, "Personal Responsibility Under Dictatorship," in *Responsibility and Judgment* (New York: Schocken, 2003), pp. 40–1.

[5] Arendt, "Some Questions of Moral Philosophy," in *Responsibility and Judgment*, pp. 96–7.

For all their faults, Kyle and Stan still debate and discuss whether certain actions are wrong. On his own, Stan will sometimes just go along with the crowd (an important exception is his refusal to kill). Through their conversations they learn goodness and engage in the "thinking" Arendt describes. Friendship, then, helps us to examine our lives. In the episode "Prehistoric Ice Man" Larry says that "living is about sharing our ups and downs with our friends," and when we fail to do this we aren't really living at all. If thinking and goodness only arise through real dialogue with others – through critically questioning and examining *our own* views – then we need more friendships like the one Kyle and Stan share.

An Apology for *South Park*:
Getting in Touch with Your Inner Cartman

If friendships help us to critically examine the lives that we lead, then perhaps it's no accident that the critical voice of *South Park* has been created by two friends – Trey Parker and Matt Stone. In the *Apology* Socrates likens himself to a gadfly, an annoying pest that goes around "stinging" people with his challenging questions and critical reflections so as to keep them intellectually awake and on their toes. *South Park*, too, serves as a gadfly, trying to wake American culture from its thoughtlessness and ignorance. The show generates discussion and debate and leads many people into discussions of ethical issues that would otherwise be passed over in silence. For a show that supposedly corrupts, it has far more of a focus on religion, ethics, and democracy than its critics would like to admit. But of course we could still ask if the *way* that *South Park* presents these issues is really necessary. For example, is it philosophically wise and necessary to use the word *shit* 163 times in one show? Or to have so much farting, vomiting, and violence? What philosophical goal can such vulgarity serve?

The vulgarity and crudeness of *South Park* are often defended on the grounds of free speech. However, a different issue is also in play. *South Park* often says what is not socially or morally acceptable to say – what, in Freudian terms, must be repressed. According to Freud, our thoughts and actions are shaped by what he calls "drives," examples of which include emotions, desires, and energy that can be aggressive, hostile, and consumptive. (Freud would have a field day with Cartman's twisted little mind, on this score.) These drives are part of our embodied being, yet, since they are dangerous and often violent, we try to control or even silence them. This control is a form of repression, but it can often have unintended consequences. Repression of a drive can lead to other sorts of unconscious, violent behavior, and such suppressed wishes form the content of dreams – our "unconscious" life.[6] Repression, as a form of internal censorship, redirects but does not diminish our aggression. In spite of our intentions, this unconscious aggression often shapes who we are, how we think, and what we do.

[6] See Sigmund Freud, *The Interpretation of Dreams* (New York: Avon Books, 1965), pp. 156–66.

What Freud discovered with psychoanalysis was that talking out and interpreting our dreams may serve as a way to address this repression and its associated violence. When we talk these ideas and feelings out, the repression is broken and, through the realization, we can come to terms with the desire and shape it through thinking. Representing desires lets them be *expressed*, and this helps us to integrate them into the structure of our lives.[7] By bringing to light what had been unconscious, dream-interpretation lets us think through these aspects of ourselves.

Freud thought that jokes work much like dreams. When one person tells a joke, its spontaneous and unexpected word-form breaks through another person's repression. Laughter is a "release of energy" that has been blocked, because we have tried to repress the wish or drive; this is why many jokes have a vulgar or obscene dimension. As Freud points out, the one who supplies it has to deny it – jokes only really work when the person telling them doesn't laugh, so that the surprise can make others laugh.[8] There is pleasure in laughing at the joke, and in telling it, as well as pleasure in freeing others from their repression.

Through its vulgarity, *South Park* verbalizes the drives and desires that we often repress; and, it allows us to laugh so as to reveal these inhibitions. This is what makes the show's crudeness essential. By showing us "Token" or the conjoined fetus nurse, or saying *shit* over and over, it brings out the aggression and desire that we feel we cannot express. And, for things that really *shouldn't* be said, Kenny says them in a muffled way, and the other boys comment on it. By verbalizing these drives, the show lets us begin to think these through – it makes it possible to analyze them, and thereby distance ourselves from them. For instance, many episodes address how outsiders are berated and subjected to racist or xenophobic slander. However, by working through these statements, the show argues that in many cases, such slander is used among friends as well – and that such verbal sparring, when so understood, need not lead to violence or exclusion. It doesn't justify such speech, but it does create a space in which the hostility can be interpreted and analyzed.

Likewise, one can analyze all of the farting on *Terrance and Philip*. At least two interpretations of this show-within-the-show are possible. First, there is the issue of why the boys love such a stupid show so much. It's not that they wish they could fart all the time. Rather, when they fart, Terrance and Philip do what is forbidden: they transgress the parents' social prohibition. This appeals to the boys, because they wish they too could be free from parental control and regulation.

Second, regular viewers (mostly my students) have noted that *Terrance and Philip* is self-referential, a way for *South Park* to comment on itself. The opening of *South Park* tells us that, like *Terrance and Philip*, the show has no redeeming value and should be watched by no one. The stupidity and vulgarity of the cartoon is better understood, however, if we look beyond *South Park*. Is *Terrance and Philip* really more vapid, crude, and pointless than *Jerry Springer* or *Wife Swap*? Is it more mindless

---

[7] For more on this issue, see Jonathan Lear, *Love and Its Place in Nature: A Philosophical Interpretation of Freudian Psychoanalysis* (New York: Farrar, Strauss, and Giroux, 1990).

[8] Freud, *Wit and Its Relation to the Unconscious*, trans. by A. A. Brill (New York: Dover, 1993), pp. 261–73.

than *Fox News*, *The 700 Club*, or *Law and Order*? The answer is no. When we see Kyle, Cartman, Kenny, and Stan watching *The Terrance and Philip Show*, it shows us that television fulfills our wish for mindlessness. What offends the parents in South Park, and the critics of *South Park*, is not that the show is vulgar and pointless, but that it highlights the mindlessness of television in general.

What both of these interpretations show is that there are multiple levels of censorship that need to be questioned. On the one hand, there is the censorship that simply looks at vulgarity, and decides what can and cannot be seen, based upon social norms. *South Park* clearly questions this sort of censorship, saying so often what cannot be said and challenging social forms of repression. But, if part of *South Park*'s message is the need for thinking, then it also questions how television, by fulfilling our wish for mindlessness, supposedly represses thinking. Of course, such mindlessness can't simply be blamed on one's parents, or television corporations, or two doofusses from Colorado who can't draw straight. Like the mindless Athenians who were to blame for their own ignorance, or Eichmann's responsibility when he thought he was just obeying the law, the mindlessness that prevents thinking is ultimately our own doing. Like Socrates, perhaps *South Park* – and Kyle and Stan more specifically – presents us with a way to think about what *we think* we really know, and through reflection move beyond our mindlessness.

The Talking Cure for Our Culture

By ceaselessly testing the limits of our culture's tolerance, *South Park* asks us to examine the things we think we know, why certain words and actions are prohibited, what we desire, and what we are teaching our children. Through its provocation, it asks us to think about what is truly harmful, and what issues we really should be outraged about. Breaking the silence of our culture's repressions could be the starting point for a Socratic dialogue that helps us to think, analyze our desires and aggression, and become good. If we take the opportunity to discuss the show, why it is funny, and what it tells us about our culture and our own desires, then the show need not be mindless, vulgar, or corrupting, but rather a path to thinking that helps us to live with one another, and with ourselves.

2

The Chewbacca Defense

A South Park *Logic Lesson*

Robert Arp

Summary

The creators of *South Park* are aware of logical principles and purposely violate them to show the absurdities associated with certain beliefs, opinions, ideas, and arguments. In fact, much of *South Park*'s humor concerns logical violations and the contradictions and problems that result. Logic is the study of the principles of correct reasoning associated with the formation and analysis of arguments. Using examples from *South Park*, this chapter offers a short logic lesson as an introduction to what philosophers do when they put forward and critique arguments. Topics covered include the parts of an argument (premise and conclusion), premise- and conclusion-indicating words, deductive versus inductive arguments, good versus bad arguments, and a few common fallacies such as the famous Chewbacca Defense utilized by the cartoon Johnny Cochran in the episode "Chef Aid."

It Does Not Make Sense!

The episode "Chef Aid" is classic *South Park* with its cartoon Johnnie Cochran's "Chewbacca Defense," a satire of Cochran's actual closing arguments in the O. J. Simpson case. In the episode, Alanis Morissette comes out with a hit song "Stinky Britches," which, it turns out, Chef had written some twenty years ago. Chef produces a tape of himself performing the song, and takes the record company to court, asking only that he be credited for writing the hit. The record company executives then hire Cochran. In his defense of the record company, Cochran shows the jury a picture of Chewbacca and claims that, because Chewbacca is from Kashyyyk and lives on Endor with the Ewoks, "It does not make sense." Cochran continues: "Why would a Wookie, an eight-foot tall Wookie, want to live on Endor with a bunch of two-foot tall Ewoks? That does not make sense. If Chewbacca lives on Endor, you must acquit! The defense rests." The jury is so convinced by

Cochran's "argument," that not only do they apparently deny Chef's request for credit recognition, but they also find Chef guilty of harassing a major record label, fining him two million dollars to be paid within twenty-four hours. Friends of Chef then organize "Chef Aid" to pay his fine.

We laugh at Cochran's defense because it has absolutely nothing to do with the actual case. We laugh all the more at the absurdity when the Chewbacca Defense is also used to find Chef guilty of harassing the very record company that had produced a stolen song. The issue of Chewbacca living on Endor has absolutely nothing to do with, and is in no way **logically** related to, the issues of whether Chef should receive credit for the song, or whether he has harassed the record company. As rational thinkers, we recognize this, laugh at the absurdities, and wonder why anyone in their right mind would be convinced that the Chewbacca Defense and the other issues are related. In fact, logicians (people who study the principles of correct **reasoning**) have a term for the kind of bad thinking involved in the Chewbacca Defense. They call it a *fallacy*. A fallacy is faulty reasoning that inappropriately or incorrectly draws a conclusion from evidence that does not support the conclusion. To draw the conclusions that the record company is not liable for crediting Chef with writing the song *and* that Chef has harassed the record company based upon reasons that have to do with the Chewbacca Defense is fallacious reasoning.

Fallacious reasoning, some of it not too different from the Chewbacca Defense, is quite common. For example, suppose Principal Victoria thinks that, just because she had a bad experience with a person of a particular sex, race, creed, or color, "they must all be like that." Or she believes since a celebrity has endorsed a particular product, then it must necessarily be good for us. Instead of seeking to become an authority in a particular matter, she blindly accepts what some tells us as "The Gospel Truth." Or, she concludes that "there must be no true or false, right or wrong, good or bad **beliefs**" because "people have so many different beliefs." However, on reflection, we can see why she's not justified in any of these conclusions.

This chapter offers a short logic lesson as an introduction to what philosophers do when they put forward and critique arguments.[1] Logic is the study of the principles of correct reasoning associated with the formation and analysis of arguments. As we've seen already, people don't always abide by these principles. The creators of *South Park*, for the most part, are aware of these logical principles, and purposely violate them to show the absurdities associated with certain beliefs, opinions, **ideas**, and arguments. In fact, much of *South Park*'s humor concerns logical violations and the absurdities, contradictions, and problems that result. The way people reason correctly, or incorrectly, has real consequences. It affects the policies they adhere

---

[1]   For more extensive discussions of logic see Gregory Bassham, William Irwin, Henry Nardone, and James M. Wallace, *Critical Thinking: A Student's Introduction* (New York: McGraw-Hill, 2004); Patrick Hurley, *A Concise Introduction to Logic* (Belmont, CA: Wadsworth Publishing, 2006); Robert Johnson, *Fundamentals of Reasoning: A Logic Book* (Belmont, CA: Wadsworth Publishing, 2002); Anthony Weston, *A Rulebook for Arguments* (Indianapolis: Hackett Publishing, 2000).

to, the laws they make, the beliefs they are willing to die for, and the general way in which they live their lives.

For example, because of Mrs. Broflovski and the town's belief that *The Terrance and Philip Show* promotes immorality, the entire community not only boycotts the show, but also sacrifices members of the community to get the producers of the show to take it off the air. This fictional morality tale parallels parts of reality, and raises questions as to whether TV promotes immorality, as well as what people are willing to do based upon their perceived connection between TV and immorality. Can we draw the general conclusion that a show like *South Park*, even if viewed by children, is bad for *all* children, from evidence that supports the fact that it's bad for *some* children? Further, even if it does promote immorality, is that the kind of thing we are willing to die for? This may seem like a silly question, but the actions of the South Park townspeople get us to think about what kinds of things people are willing to believe or do based upon their faulty reasoning. Consider a somewhat parallel case. Are all Americans immoral? And even if so, should we sacrifice people so as to make our point about them being immoral by flying planes into a skyscraper? Again, how we live our lives, as well as how we affect others' lives, depends upon whether we reason correctly or incorrectly. (You, the reader, may even find what I have said in this paragraph to be logically questionable.) In what follows, we'll consider some basics of logic and, using examples from *South Park* episodes, show some differences between correct and incorrect reasoning.

Dude, Listen to Reason

Logic is the study of the principles of correct reasoning associated with the formation and analysis of arguments. So let's define the word **argument**, and describe its basic components and types. Then, we can talk about correct argument formation and analysis.

An argument consists of two or more claims, one of which is called the *conclusion*. The conclusion is the claim in the argument that is supposed to be supported by, shown to be the case by, demonstrated by, justified by, warranted by, or proved to be the case by the premise or premises. A *premise* is a claim in the argument that is supposed to support, show, demonstrate, justify, warrant, or prove the conclusion. The fundamental purpose of an argument is to persuade or convince someone of the truth of one's concluding claim. In other words, when we put forward an argument, we want others to be persuaded or convinced of the conclusion we arrived at and believe to be true, and we use another claim, or other claims, as supposed support for the truth of that conclusion.

Cochran's fallacious argument can be rephrased, simply, like this: "Because Chewbacca lives on Endor (the premise of the argument), therefore you should acquit my client (the conclusion of the argument)." A complete argument has at least one premise and only one conclusion, but arguments usually have two or more premises. So for example, I was watching a *South Park* re-run last night called "Ike's Wee Wee," and Cartman put forward an argument for why we should be convinced drugs are bad that could be paraphrased like this: "If you do drugs, then you're a hippie; if you're a hippie, then you suck; if you suck, then that's bad (all premises); So, if you do drugs, then that's bad (conclusion)."

Arguments are composed of claims, a concluding claim (the conclusion), and at least one supporting claim (the premise). A *claim* is a statement, proposition, assertion, judgment, declarative sentence, or part of a declarative sentence, result-ing from a person's beliefs or opinions, which communicates that something is or is not the case about the self, the world, states of affairs, or reality in general. Claims are either true or false, and again, are the results of beliefs or opinions that people have concerning any part of what they perceive to be reality. We make our beliefs and opinions known through claims. For example, the claims "I am typing this chapter on a laptop" and "Chewbacca is a Wookie" are true, whereas the claims "I was the 40th president of the United States" and "The sun revolves around the earth" are false.

A claim is shown to be true or false as a result of *evidence*, which can take the forms of either direct or indirect testimony of your senses, explanations, the testimony of others, appeal to well-established theories, appeal to appropriate authority, appeal to definitions, and good arguments, among others. So, that I am typing on a laptop is shown to be true by the direct testimony of my own senses, that Chewbacca is a Wookie is true by definition of "Chewbacca," that I was president of the US is false because of the testimony of the senses of others and authorities, and that the sun revolves around the earth is false because of indirect sensory evidence as well as the well-established heliocentric theory. Some claims are difficult, or impossible, to show true or false with evidence. Claims like "God exists," "Abortion is always immoral," and "I have an immortal soul" would fall into this ambiguous category. That is probably why ideas, issues, and arguments surrounding these claims are considered to be "philosophical."

As rational, adult critical thinkers, we have beliefs or opinions that we think are true about reality as we perceive it, and we express those beliefs or opinions in written or spoken claims. But, we can't stop there. We must convince or persuade others as to why we hold these beliefs, and when we do so, we must give a reason or set of reasons (the premises of our argument) for why we hold to a particular belief (the conclusion of our argument). So, for example, in the episode "The Passion of the Jew" Kyle believes strongly that the Jewish community in his hometown should apologize for Jesus' death. If asked why the Jewish community in his hometown, or anyone, should be convinced or persuaded to apologize, Kyle's argument might look like this:

Premise 1: Since Jews are known to have been partly responsible for the death of Jesus
Premise 2: And, since an action like this requires that one should apologize
Premise 3: And, since the Jews in South Park are part of the Jewish community

Conclusion: Therefore, the Jews in South Park should apologize for Jesus' death

Let's note a few things about this argument. First, it has been placed into *standard form*. Putting an argument in standard form means placing the premises of the argument first, the conclusion last, and clearly dividing the premise(s) and conclusion with a horizontal line. This is a handy tool because it helps make the logical form and parts of the argument clear. And, as we'll see later, standard form makes the argument easier to analyze in terms of whether the conclusion follows from the premises as well as whether all the premises are true.

Notice the word *since* at the beginning of the premises and the word *therefore* at the beginning of the conclusion. The word *since* is an example of a premise-indicating word, along with words like *because, for, for the reason that,* and *as,* among others. The word *therefore* is an example of a conclusion-indicating word, along with words like *hence, so, thus, this shows us that, we can conclude that,* and *we can reason/deduce/infer that,* among others. Premise-indicating and conclusion-indicating words are important because they usually let us know that premises and a conclusion are coming in an argument. At times, it can be incredibly difficult to tell if someone is putting forward an argument, so you can look for these indicating words to see if there's an argument in front of you and, further, you can identify what the conclusion and the premise(s) of the argument are. Unfortunately, these indicating words are not always present, and people sometimes place the conclusion anywhere in their argument (sometimes it'll be the first claim, sometimes the second, sometimes the last). In such cases you must supply these words to make the structure and parts of the argument crystal clear.

You're Not Asleep Yet, Are You?

Broadly speaking, there are two different kinds of arguments, *deductive arguments* and **inductive** *arguments*. In deductive arguments, the speaker intends the conclusion to follow from the premises with absolute certainty such that, if all of the premises are true, then the conclusion must be true without any doubt whatsoever. To say that a conclusion *follows* from a premise means that we are justified in having reasoned appropriately from one claim (the premise) to another claim (the conclusion). Cartman puts forward a deductive argument in "The Tooth Fairy Tats 2000" episode that goes something like this:

Premise 1: If the boys combine their lost teeth, then they'll get money from the Tooth Fairy

Premise 2: If they get money from the Tooth Fairy, then they can buy a Sega Dreamcast

Conclusion: Hence, if the boys combine their lost teeth, then they can buy a Sega Dreamcast

We can see that, provided that the two premises are true, the conclusion absolutely must be true. We can also see that there is no other conclusion that could correctly be drawn from these premises. In fact, from looking at the premises alone you know the conclusion before even seeing it. The previous argument about Jews apologizing for Jesus' death is also a deductive argument. Just like with the Tooth Fairy argument, if all the premises are true then the conclusion must be true, there is no other conclusion that possibly could be drawn from the premises, and you know exactly what the conclusion is without even seeing it.

In inductive arguments, the speaker intends the conclusion to follow from the premises with a degree of probability or likelihood such that, if all of the premises are true, then the conclusion probably or likely is true, but it is still possible that the conclusion is false. In the "Towelie" episode, the boys notice that when they speak about anything having to do with towels, Towelie shows up, and so they reason like this:

> Premise 1: Because in the past, when we mentioned towel-related things, Towelie showed up
> Premise 2: And because we will mention something towel-related now
>
> Conclusion: We can conclude that Towelie will show up

We can see that, provided the premises are true, the conclusion is probably or likely true, but not definitely true. It makes sense to conclude that Towelie will show up, given past experience. But the truth of Towelie showing up in the past does not guarantee that, with absolute certainty or without a doubt, Towelie *will* show up. It is still possible that Towelie won't show up, so the conclusion is merely probable or likely. In the episode, Towelie does show up, but he need not necessarily have shown up.

Consider Stan's reasoning at the end of the episode "Scott Tenorman Must Die" after it has been revealed that Cartman orchestrated the death of Scott's parents, the subsequent addition of their bodies to the chili, and Radiohead's witnessing the entire event so as to make fun of Scott for being a woossie.

> Premise 1: Since Cartman does horrible things to people for minor offenses (like being cheated out of $16.12)
> Premise 2: And since we (the boys) commit, at least, minor offenses against Cartman frequently, and he may retaliate like he did with Scott
>
> Conclusion: Therefore, we had better not piss Cartman off in the future, for fear of retaliation

Again, even if both of the premises are true, it doesn't follow with absolute certainty that the boys had better not piss off Cartman in the future. In fact, as it turns out, the boys piss off Cartman numerous times without receiving the kind of retaliation given poor Scott Tenorman. So, the conclusion is false.

Our goal is not just to form arguments. We need to form *good arguments*, and we need to evaluate the arguments of others. There are good arguments and there are bad arguments in both the deductive and inductive realms. A good argument, in either realm, is one in which the conclusion logically follows from the premises and all of the premises are true. If either one of these conditions is absent, then the argument is bad and should be rejected.

In the deductive realm, that a conclusion follows from premises means that the argument is *valid* (and *invalid* if the conclusion does not follow). When an argument is valid and all the premises are true, the argument is said to be a good, *sound argument*. The conclusion absolutely, positively, without a doubt, is true, and this is a good thing! In the inductive realm, that a conclusion likely will follow from premises means that the argument is *strong* (and *weak* if the conclusion likely does not follow). When an argument is strong and all the premises are true, the argument is said to be a good, *cogent argument*. The conclusion most likely or probably is true, and this is a good thing too!

So, as rational, adult critical thinkers we must always go through this two-step procedure of checking our own arguments and the arguments of others to see if (a) the conclusion follows from the premises (is the argument deductively valid or inductively strong?) and (b) all of the premises are true. If the argument fails to meet either (a) or (b) or both, then we should reject it, thereby rejecting the person's conclusion as either absolutely false or probably false.

For example, Cartman's argument for pooling together the boys' teeth probably is a bad one because Premise 2 seems false, given the information. It is not true that if they get money from the Tooth Fairy then they will be able to buy a Sega Dreamcast, because the Tooth Fairy only gave Cartman $2.00. $2.00 × 4 boys is $8.00 and, provided we are talking about a new one from the store, that is not enough to buy a Sega Dreamcast. So in the case of this particular deductive argument, the conclusion "If the boys combine their teeth, then they can get a Sega Dreamcast" is false.

On the other hand, the Towelie argument was a good one. It was true that the few times they mentioned towel-related things, Towelie showed up. And given this fact, they had a strong case for drawing the conclusion that he would show up again, asking, of course, "Wanna get high?"

If Chewbacca Lives on Endor, You Must Acquit

At times, checking to see if conclusions follow from premises and if premises are true can be very difficult. Some words have multi-level meanings. And some people will try to convince us of the truth of claims in order to deceive us, sell us something, get us to vote for them, become part of their group, or share their ideology. Often, people will try to convince us that a conclusion follows from a premise or premises when, in fact, it does not, kind of like what the cartoon Cochran does with the Chewbacca Defense.

As we have seen in the first section of this chapter, logicians have a special term for these bad arguments in which the conclusion does not follow from a premise. They call it a *fallacy*, and a fallacy occurs when we inappropriately or incorrectly draw a conclusion from reasons that don't support the conclusion. Fallacies are so common that logicians have names for different types of fallacies.

The Chewbacca Defense is an example of a *red herring* fallacy, which gets its name from a police dog exercise in which policemen, while trying to discern the best trail-hunters, use strong-smelling red herring fishes in an attempt to throw dogs off the trail of a scent. In a red herring fallacy, someone uses claims and arguments that have nothing to do with the issue at hand in order to get someone to draw a conclusion that they believe to be true. So, the claims and arguments are the "red herrings" they use to throw you off the "trail" of reasoning that would lead to another, probably more appropriate, conclusion altogether.

In the episode "Weight Gain 4000," Wendy seems to have a legitimate complaint that Cartman cheated to win the essay contest, but people refuse to draw that conclusion given that they are diverted by the idea of Kathy Lee Gifford coming to town. Even after Wendy produces the evidence that Cartman had really handed in a copy of *Walden* as his essay, they simply don't care about drawing the conclusion that Cartman had cheated. In a lot of *South Park* episodes, people are thrown off the track of issues or arguments by other circumstances or events that capture their attention. This is a humorous way for Trey and Matt to make their points about people's faulty and crazy reasoning.

Hasty generalization is a common fallacy often lampooned on *South Park*. In a hasty generalization, a person fallaciously draws a conclusion about characteristics of a whole group based upon premises concerning characteristics of a small sample of the group. Most times, when we think to ourselves "they're all like that" in talking about anything – people, cars, movies, Kenny's extended family – based upon a small sample of the group we're talking about, we commit a hasty generalization. There is usually no way *definitely* to conclude something about the characteristics of an entire group since we have no knowledge of the entire group. The next member of the group we encounter may turn out to have different characteristics from members of the group we know thus far. Any form of prejudice and stereotyping, by definition, constitutes a hasty generalization.

Consider the way Kyle's Jewish cousin, Kyle 2, is stereotyped in the episode "The Entity," or how Mexicans are typecast as lazy, gays are *all* flamboyant like Big Gay Al or Mr. Slave, and African Americans are reverse typecasted as "richers" in "Here Comes the Neighborhood." Even Officer Barbrady commits the fallacy of hasty generalization in the episode "Chickenlover" when, after reading a copy of Ayn Rand's *Atlas Shrugged*, he concludes that all books must be this bad, and reading "totally sucks ass." The creators of *South Park* play on people's hasty generalizations to make their points in episode after episode, probably because not only is prejudice something that *morally* harms people, but it also *logically* "harms" people's thinking as well.

The *slippery slope* is another fallacy often lampooned on *South Park*. This fallacy occurs when one inappropriately concludes that some further chain of events, ideas, or beliefs will follow from some initial event, idea, or belief and, thus, we should reject the initial event, idea, or belief. It is as if there is an unavoidable "slippery" slope that one is on, and there is no way to avoid sliding down it. Mrs. Broflovski's reasoning about the *The Terrance and Philip Show* being taken off the air might go something like this: "If we allow a show like *The Terrance and Philip Show* on the air, then it'll corrupt my kid, then it'll corrupt your kid, then it'll corrupt all of our kids, then shows like this one will crop up all over the TV, then more and more kids will be corrupted, then all of TV will be corrupted, then the corrupt TV producers will corrupt other areas of our life, etc., etc., etc. So, we must take the *The Terrance and Philip Show* off the air; otherwise, it will lead to all of these other corruptions!!!" If I have accurately characterized Mrs. Broflovski's reasoning here, then we can see the slippery slope. It doesn't follow that the corrupt TV producers will corrupt other areas of our life. All of a sudden we're at the bottom of the slope! What the heck just happened!

In the episode "Clubhouses," Mrs. Marsh uses a kind of slippery slope fallacy in combination with a hasty generalization in response to Stan's grabbing a cookie. Here, we can see the obvious humor involved, as she is going through a rough separation time with her husband: "You men are all alike. First you get a cookie and then you criticize the way I dress, and then it's the way I cook! Next you'll be telling me that you need your space, and that I'm sabotaging your creativity! Go ahead Stanley, get your damn cookie!" Her conclusion is obviously that Stan should not grab a cookie because, otherwise, all of these other things will happen. Further, the "you men are all alike" comment is the result of a hasty generalization.

A *false dilemma* is the fallacy of concluding something based upon premises that include only *two* options, when, in fact, there are three or more options. People are inclined to an "all or nothing" approach to matters, and this usually is reflective of a false dilemma in their thinking. In some situation, could it be that we have a little bit of both, so that we get a both-and, rather than an either-or as our conclusion? In the episode "Mr. Hankey, The Christmas Poo" the people of *South Park* have an all-or-nothing kind of thinking when they conclude that the only way not to offend anyone is to rid the Christmas show of any and all Christmas references. This kind of logic has disastrous consequences, as the show is ruined and people wind up fighting over it. Could they have *included* a few other religious traditions, instead of *excluding* all of them?

Now the both-and strategy, which can avoid a false dilemma, might not always have the best consequences. Consider the episode "Chef Goes Nanners" where, in the end, even though a both-and solution is reached and supposed "ethnic diversity" is added to the South Park flag, it is obviously questionable whether such an addition is good, let alone right, for the townsfolk.

An *argument from inappropriate authority* is a fallacy that sounds like what it is, incorrectly drawing a conclusion from premises based upon a non-credible, non-qualified, or illegitimate authority figure. The best way to avoid this fallacy altogether is to become an authority concerning some matter yourself by getting all of the relevant facts, understanding issues, doing research, checking and double-checking your sources, dialoguing with people, having your ideas challenged, defending your position, being open to revise your position, and the like. However, since we can't become authorities on everything, we need to rely upon others.

In the episode "Do the Handicapped Go to Hell?" Fr. Maxi claims that Kyle (who is Jewish) and Timmy (who is limited in his verbal communication) will both go to hell if they don't confess their sins and, apparently, accept Christ as their savior. At first glance, the boys' conclusion that Kyle and Timmy will go to hell if they don't confess and convert seems not to be a case of the fallacy of appeal to inappropriate authority. After all, Fr. Maxi is an authority of the Church. However, if one investigates Church doctrine, one can see that no human being – pope, priest, or layperson – can make pronouncements about who will go to hell or who will not go to hell.

In an *ad hominem* fallacy someone concludes that a person's claims or arguments are false or not worth listening to because of premises that concern an attack on the actions, personality, or ideology of the person putting forward the claim or argument. In other words, instead of focusing on the person's issue, claims, or argument, one attacks the person (*ad hominem* is Latin for *to the man*). This strategy of discrediting a person's argument by discrediting the person is common. But notice, the person and the person's arguments are two distinct things, and they are not logically related to one another.

For example, in the episode "Butt Out" a cartoon Rob Reiner puts forward an argument for why kids in South Park should not smoke, and he goes on a campaign to get a law enacted to ban smoking in the town. However, not only is he portrayed as having a junk food vice, but he wants to use the boys – quite deceptively – to get the law passed. Now, even if Reiner does have a junk food problem and even if he does something immoral in trying to get the boys to help him, what does this have to do with the arguments concerning whether kids should smoke or whether laws against smoking should be passed in South Park? The answer is, absolutely nothing! Yet, we could be led to the conclusion that no law should be set up in South Park against smoking based upon premises that portray Reiner's apparent hypocrisy and deviance. Again, Reiner's hypocrisy and deviance have nothing to do with the arguments for or against smoking.

The Defense Rests

At least part of the appeal of *South Park* has to do with pointing out the flaws in our thinking, and no one is free from blame. We all occasionally forget to check if all of our premises are true, or believe that a conclusion follows from premises when it doesn't. But the biggest logical problem we have has to do with our staunchly held emotional beliefs, the ones that we just can't let go of no matter what evidence and arguments are presented to us. Often times, this logical problem turns into a factual problem, and people suffer as a result. Some people are almost phobic in their fear of letting go of some belief. I am actually afraid to fly, and no amount of evidence or reasoning will get me to feel good about it, period. People can hold to their ideologies in the same crazy way that I hold to the belief that the plane *will* crash when I am 35,000 feet in the air.

In the episode "All About the Mormons," Stan yells at the Mormons for believing in their religion without any **proof,** and they smile and explain that it's a matter of faith. Without insulting the Mormons, or any religion for that matter, in that moment Stan is hinting at part of what a rational, adult critical thinker should constantly do. As you read the chapters in this book, I ask you to be mindful of claims, arguments, deductive arguments vs. inductive arguments, good vs. bad arguments, and fallacies that are spoken about by the authors. And, hopefully, the authors have avoided fallacies and bad arguments in putting forward their own positions! With this logic lesson in mind, you can be the judge of that.

3

Wikiality, Truthiness, and Gut Thinking

Doing Philosophy Colbert-Style

David Kyle Johnson

Summary

Against Stephen Colbert's concept of "Wikiality," this chapter argues that truth is not relative to individuals or cultures. You can't change the truth by changing a Wikipedia entry. Likewise, you can't justify your beliefs with "your gut." Such gut thinking – what Colbert calls "truthiness" – is at best equivalent to a guess; at worst it employs circular reasoning.

Every night on my show, The Colbert Report, *I speak straight from the gut . . .*
I give people the truth, unfiltered by rational argument.
  – Stephen Colbert, White House Correspondents' Dinner April 29, 2006

Nation, Stephen Colbert is hard to figure out. An Irish Catholic, born in Washington DC and raised in South Carolina as the youngest of 11 children, he hosts Comedy Central's fake news show *The Colbert Report*.[1] To confuse things, he also plays a character named "Stephen Colbert" who is an Irish Catholic born in Washington DC, raised in South Carolina as the youngest of 11 children. Needless to say, it's hard to tell where the character stops and the actor starts. Colbert, as his character, mirrors the attitude and approach of super conservative pundits, stating ridiculous positions backed by illogical **arguments** (if any). For example, in an interview about Global Warming, Colbert asks CNN News Anchor Anderson Cooper "What's wrong with the ice melting . . . maybe now Greenland will actually turn green."[2] The idea is to reveal the stupidity of the argument, and those who promote it (like Rush Limbaugh) by mocking it.[3]

---

[1] Don't pronounce the "t"s – "Cole-bear, re-pore".
[2] *The Colbert Report*, October 18, 2007.
[3] Ironically, Rush Limbaugh made this argument after Colbert did. (RushLimbaugh.com, 2008).

Colbert delivers his lines in "dead pan style" – never breaking character. That's what makes it so funny, but that's also why it is so hard for those unfamiliar with Colbert to realize he is joking – that he is offering satire. Studies – real, honest to God, studies – have shown that most conservatives seeing Colbert for the first time fail to recognize the satire and think Colbert is serious and defending the conservative positions he is mocking – the positions they agree with. Of course, the studies also show that most liberals seeing Colbert for the first time think that he agrees with them (that he is mocking the conservative positions he espouses). So the studies reveal the human propensity to "see what you want" more than anything else.[4] But they raise an interesting question. If there is a human propensity to see what we want in Colbert, how can anyone know that they are reading Colbert correctly? For instance, I have said that Colbert is offering satire of conservative pundits. But I consider myself fairly liberal (at least on the issues Colbert talks about . . . and free health care for philosophers). How do we know that I'm not just seeing what I want in Colbert? How can we know that he is satirical instead of deadly serious?

If you watch the show long enough, you'll just know. It's one of those things that's obvious when you see it, but hard to explain. But can we explain it? Fortunately, philosophy can help us out with something called "the principle of charity." When it is unclear what someone means, we should always choose the most charitable interpretation – the one that makes them look least dimwitted. Such interpretations are usually right because, usually, people aren't that stupid. This helps us discover that Colbert is offering satire because, if he really meant most of the things he said, he would be idiotic beyond all comprehension. For instance, after scientists unveiled a 47 million year old "missing link" fossil,[5] Colbert's replied "Wrong! The Earth is 6,000 years old. Always has been, always will be."[6] We know he can't be serious because not only is the idea that the earth is 6,000 years old contrary to all relevant modern scientific findings, but the idea that the Earth doesn't age – that it has *always* been 6000 years old – is absurd. Colbert can't be that dumb, so we know he's kidding.

But this is only one example. Maybe it's the exception to the rule. So let's consider some more examples that show Colbert has "got to be kidding."

[4] Heather L. LaMarre, Kristen D. Landreville, and Michael A. Beam "The Irony of Satire: Political Ideology and the Motivation to See What You Want to See in *The Colbert Report*," *The International Journal of Press/Politics*, 2009, vol. 14, p. 212.

[5] Samantha Strong and Rich Schapiro "Missing Link Found? Scientists Unveil Fossil of 47 Million-Year-Old Primate, Darwinius Masillae" (*New York Daily News*, May 19, 2009). http://www.nydailynews.com/news/us_world/2009/05/19/2009-05-19_missing_link_found_fossil_of_47_millionyearold_primate_sheds_light_on_.html

[6] May 21, 2009.

My Truth (Individual Relativism)

[My book is] not just some collection of reasoned arguments supported by facts. That is the coward's way out. This book is Truth. *My Truth.*
> – Stephen Colbert, *I Am America (And So Can You!)*[7]

The phrase "My Truth" is the first clue that Colbert is kidding. He is suggesting that, somehow, truth belongs to him and can be determined by him. Colbert is espousing a naive "individual relativism." In general, **relativism** says that there are no truths in a universal sense; truth is relative. More specifically, individual relativism says that truth is relative to individuals. But to understand what this means, and why Colbert can't possibly be an individual relativist, some questions need answering.

If truth is relative, what is truth? Truth is a property of **beliefs** and propositions. ("Proposition" is a term the wordinistas came up with because "sentence" wasn't good enough.) A belief or proposition is true if it corresponds to the way the world is; it is false if it doesn't. Philosophers call this "the correspondence theory of truth." The part of the world that a true belief or proposition corresponds to is called that proposition's "truthmaker" – it is the part of the world that makes that proposition or belief true.

What does it mean for a truth to be relative? This is a question best answered by example. "You should drive on the right side of the road." This truth is relative to culture; it is true in the USA but false in the UK. There is no universal truth about what side of the road you should drive on – it's a matter of convention. The truth of "Baconnaise tastes great" is relative to individuals; one person thinks it's true, and another thinks it's false, but neither one is right or wrong because there is no universal fact of the matter about it. Or consider whether Colbert is funny. You think he's hilarious; your mother doesn't get it: but neither of you is wrong or right (but, between you and me, your mom is wrong).[8]

The individual relativist thinks all truths are like this, but obviously this cannot be the case. For example, whether or not you exist is not a matter of convention or taste. If someone believes that you don't exist, it is not "true for them." Your existence is a matter of fact. They may believe you don't exist, but their belief is false. In addition, individual relativism in this form is self-contradictory. It says there are no universal truths. But isn't the individual relativist trying to establish that individual relativism is universally true? How can it be universally true that there are no universal truths? And, since something is true if it corresponds to the way the world is, if there were no universal truths there would be no world. The only way *everything* can be relative is if nothing exists to make any proposition universally true. And that's crazy!

---

[7] Introduction (Grand Central Publishing, New York, 2007).

[8] Of course, you can find philosophers who disagree about whether there are facts about the taste of Baconnaise and whether Colbert is funny. If they are right, my point is all the stronger – for even these things are not relative.

Some individual relativists don't think everything is relative, just some things. For example, some people think that moral truths are relative to individuals. Is abortion immoral? The individual relativist would say that, for people who believe abortion is wrong, it is wrong – "wrong for them." For people who don't think abortion is wrong, it is right – "right for them." Because moral questions, like the abortion issue, are often very hard to answer, this is a very tempting line to take. Whatever each person thinks is the right answer, is the right answer for that person.

But individual relativism has unwelcome consequences if true. If individual relativism was true, being racist would be the morally acceptable attitude for a neo-Nazi skinhead to take. Killing people and eating them would be morally acceptable for Jeffery Dahmer. That such things are morally acceptable would be "true for them." But, as most people would agree, that's ridiculous. Disagreements from racists and the cannibals can't make racism and murderous cannibalism right.

Colbert can't really believe that his book is "his Truth." It might be a collection of opinions he thinks are true, but that does not make those opinions "Truth."

Wikiality (Cultural Relativism)

> I love Wikipedia. Any site that's got a longer entry on Truthiness than on Lutherans has its priorities straight . . . any user can change any entry, and if enough other users agree with him it becomes true. . . . If only the entire body of human knowledge worked this way. And it can, thanks to tonight's word: wikiality. . . . We should apply these principles to all information. All we need to do is convince a majority of people that some factoid is true. . . . what we're doing is bringing democracy to knowledge.
> – Stephen Colbert, *The Colbert Report*, July 31, 2006

Wikipedia is an online encyclopedia. It's great because it has an entry on almost everything; the catch is, anyone can edit it. (This is one of the many reasons that Wikipedia should not be cited in research papers; you never know if what you are getting is right.) Wikiality is the "reality" created by majority consensus. Stephen tells us that if someone writes something on Wikipedia and enough people believe it, it "becomes true." With Wikiality, Colbert espouses a naive "Cultural Relativism." The cultural relativist, like the individual relativist, says that truth is relative. However, the cultural relativist says truth is relative to whole cultures, rather than to individuals. In the moral realm, the cultural relativist says that the majority consensus on morality in a culture defines morality for that culture. For example, if the majority of the people in a culture agree that abortion is moral, then abortion is moral for the members of that culture.

Cultural relativism is tempting because it appears to resolve cultural conflicts. In America, people marry for love. However, for most of human history, marriage was socially motivated and arranged by family. Until recently, for example, nearly all Hindu marriages were arranged by the parents of the couple. As Colbert himself says, "They [don't] fall in love, they [learn] to love. It's a wonderful system."[9] Unlike Colbert, most Americans would think it morally wrong for Indian parents to determine their child's marriage partner. However, the cultural moral relativist would say that it is "true for them" that arranged marriage is morally right since it is the custom of the majority in their culture. This seems to have some intuitive appeal, because there doesn't seem to be a universal "right answer" to the question, "What is the correct motivation for marriage?"[10] Embracing this view would seem to promote tolerance between the two cultures.

So the morality of some things is relative to culture. For another example, consider the many parts of Europe where men and women share the same public toilet facilities. This isn't morally wrong, but it would be morally wrong of a European to use the opposite sex's bathroom in America (as long as s/he was aware of the American custom.) It can't be, however, that the answers to all moral questions are relative to culture. Consider female circumcision – where the clitoris of a nine year old girl is cut off without anesthetic and her vagina is sewn shut. Since this practice is culturally accepted in many parts of Africa, cultural relativism would say it's morally acceptable in those parts of Africa. Most people will disagree, appealing to moral facts that transcend culture and insist that female circumcision is wrong in any culture.

Contrary to its aims, cultural **moral relativism** can actually promote intolerance between cultures. For example, during the Third Reich in Germany, the oppression of Jews was accepted as moral by the majority. Thus, according to cultural moral relativism, the intolerance of the Nazi party was morally justified. Of course, you probably don't agree despite what Colbert's "child-safe Nazi" video might make some think,[11] and the fact that *Valkyrie* taught us that there were "some good Nazis."[12] Clearly, cultural moral relativism is hard to swallow.[13]

The follies of cultural moral relativism do not stop there. Consider America before the civil war. Slavery was a culturally accepted practice. According to cultural relativism that means, before the civil war, slavery was not morally wrong. They're not just saying that it was not *seen* as morally wrong. That's obvious, since the majority accepted it. More dramatically, the cultural relativist would say that slavery actually *was not* morally wrong. Not only is this contrary to intuition – slavery was

---

[9]   *The Colbert Report*, October 26, 2005.

[10]   In case you think there is a universal truth in this matter, keep in mind that "love marriages" end in divorce more often than "arranged marriages." Of course, this might be due to social pressures instead of marital bliss – such things are hard to tell. That one kind of marriage is more moral than another is far from clear.

[11]   *The Colbert Report*, April 27, 2009.

[12]   *The Colbert Report*, May 27, 2008.

[13]   My examples here are all applying American moral intuitions to practices outside its borders. That is because I am writing to Americans. I do not mean to imply that American moral values are somehow superior to the rest of the world. We do plenty of things wrong. For example, my guess is, in the near future, the American banning of gay marriage will be used as an example of something that was clearly morally wrong despite the majority consensus.

wrong even before we figured out it was wrong – but it means that the abolition of slavery was not a real step forward in moral progress for the nation. To progress morally, one must stop doing something wrong and start doing something right. But, according to the cultural moral relativist, when America abolished slavery it went from doing something right (majority approved slavery) to something else right (majority approved abolition). It didn't progress morally; it just changed its definition of moral. *Obviously* most people will think this absurd because *obviously* most people think slavery was wrong and that we *obviously* made moral progress as a nation by abolishing it. If we hadn't, Colbert wouldn't have sung Honest Abe – our greatest non-Reagan president – "Happy Birthday" on his 200th.[14]

So, the principle of charity demands we conclude that Colbert is not a cultural relativist. He doesn't really think that the entire body of human knowledge works like Wikipedia. He doesn't really think that "[t]ogether we can create a reality that we can all agree on – the reality we just agreed on."[15] Wikialty is just one of his "WØRDs."[16]

Truthiness (Intuitionism)

Like our Founding Fathers, I hold my Truths to be self-evident, which is why I did absolutely no research. I didn't need to. The only research I needed was a long hard look in the mirror.

– Stephen Colbert, from the Introduction of *I Am America (And So Can You)*

[They] cannot be mistaken in what they feel. [This is how] they support themselves and are sure reason hath nothing to do with what they see and feel in themselves: what they have a sensible experience of admits no doubt, needs no probation . . . It is its own proof and can have no other.

– John Locke, *An Essay Concerning Human Understanding*[17]

Speaking of WØRDs, on his very first show, Colbert coined a new word in his segment "THE WØRD." That word, of course, was "Truthiness."[18] Thanks to our humble correspondent, "truthiness" is now an official English word; in fact it was Merriam-Webster's Word of the Year in 2006.[19] Something has truthiness if your gut tells you it's true. To *think with the gut* is to accept something's truthiness as evidence that it is, in fact, true. Colbert constantly professes to be a gut thinker. But, we know he can't be serious because gut thinking is ridiculous.

[14] *The Colbert Report*, February 12, 2009.
[15] *The Colbert Report*, July 31, 2006.
[16] To be fair, there are non-naive versions of relativism out there defended by very smart people – Gilbert Harman of Princeton, for one. For example, see "Moral Relativism Defended," *Philosophical Review*, 1975, vol. 84, pp. 3–22.
[17] (Dutton, New York, 1978), p. 291.
[18] October 17, 2005.
[19] Merriam-Webster online. http://www.merriam-webster.com/info/06words.htm.

John Locke (1632–1704) called gut thinkers "*enthusiastic.*" The problem with gut thinking is that it provides insufficient evidence. People's intuitions vary widely and no one has reason to think their gut gets things right more often than anyone else's. Locke points out that gut thinkers are essentially arguing in a circle. "This is the way of talking of these men: they are sure because they are sure, and their persuasions are right only because they are strong in them."[20] In other words, they trust what comes from their gut because they think it gives them the truth, but they think it is true because it comes from their gut. This is like pulling yourself up by your own bootstraps – it doesn't work.

Locke argues that, if something is really true, it can stand up to rational inquiry and should be subjected to it. So one's gut should be tested. If it happens to get things right, it will be proven and then can be justifiably believed. If it gets things wrong, it should be abandoned. Locke points out that even the prophets of the Old Testament knew this, for when they received a revelation from God, they didn't merely trust their gut instinct that it was God, but asked for signs to verify the revelation's source. For example, Gideon in *Judges 6* asks a voice to prevent a fleece from getting wet in the morning dew to verify that it is God's voice. God sometimes even provided the sign without asking, like with Moses and the burning bush. You may not be like Colbert, who thinks science should aim to make the world more like the Old Testament (by strapping rockets onto the sun to make it orbit the earth)[21] – but the lesson remains the same; gut feeling is not good enough to justify beliefs on its own.

Thinking from the gut should not be confused with "appealing to intuition." Philosophers will sometimes use their own intuition as a litmus test; if an argument or position is contrary to the intuition, then the argument or position is thought to be faulty. But the intuitions in these cases are almost universally accepted and thus are thought to point to facts. For example, a philosopher might argue, "Jimmy's (Colbert's director's) ethical theory can't be right because if it is, that would mean that it can be acceptable to torture babies just for fun – and that can't be right."

If the intuition is not as universally accepted as "baby torture = wrong," the philosopher will not think the theory is refuted, but merely point out the theory's cost. "Esteban Colberto's (Colbert's Cuban alter ego) ethical theory implies that discrimination can be okay; so if you accept that theory you will have to abandon your intuition that discrimination is always wrong." (This might be said in a debate about affirmative action – which, of course, Colbert would never take part in since he is colorblind and literally can't tell the difference between the colors black and white – although he does still discriminate against bears.) Philosophers sometimes defend gut feelings with argument. Good philosophers will never let their gut be the last word. If their argument fails and their gut is disproven, they reject what it says in favor of the truth.

[20]   Locke, p. 291.
[21]   *The Colbert Report*, March 20, 2007.

In his bestseller *Blink*, Malcolm Gladwell argues that when it comes to recognizing danger and "reading people," our gut is actually more trustworthy than our intellect.[22] However, Colbert is suggesting gut thinking can justify beliefs about issues as cerebral as those in politics and philosophy, so Gladwell can't be used to defend Colbert's suggestion. I was surprised to discover, though, that some philosophers think that gut thinking can be acceptable, even in politics and philosophy.

In "Truth, Truthiness, and Bullshit for the American Voter,"[23] Matthew Peirlott argues that, even when it comes to important political and philosophical issues, one can be allowed to think with one's gut to draw a conclusion. Regarding major political matters, there is a large amount of information one has to process and verify before one comes to a truly informed decision. Peirlott argues that because so many different people are giving us this information, and because it's hard to determine "which facts are facts,"[24] we are allowed to choose who to listen to with our gut.

> It's not that we ignore facts; it's that we select which "facts" presented to us we will accept as facts . . . we follow our guts and trust the people whose hearts we think we know . . . When there are too many "facts" to be accessed, and the situation is too complicated for an individual to understand fully without dedicating his whole waking life to that issue, truthiness seems to be the only thing we have to go on.[25]

He does have a point about conflicting "facts" and the difficulty of determining the truth, but I don't think "I'll just trust my gut to tell me who to believe" is the correct response to this difficulty. If it was, the guy who only relies on *Fox and Friends* for his "facts" because he likes what his gut says about them would be justified in believing all the stories they report, including that beer pong causes herpes – a hoax news story they reported as genuine without checking it.[26]

Instead, one should try to determine which facts to believe despite the difficulty. It may take a little time, but if the issue is important the time is worth it. What if one simply doesn't have the time to do the proper research, as Peirlott suggests? Regardless of why one hasn't done the research, if one hasn't done it, one shouldn't pretend one has. Instead, one should admit that one doesn't know what facts to accept. A better response to the difficulty is agnosticism – the suspension of belief and admission of ignorance.[27] If you don't know, admit it.

By admitting our ignorance we emulate Socrates (469–399 BCE), about whom the Oracle at Delphi said "no one is wiser," not because he knew everything, but because he was the only one to admit when he knew nothing. Socrates spent his entire life trying to find someone who had knowledge – because he believed he lacked it – but only found supposed "experts" who professed to have knowledge,

---

[22]   (Back Bay Books, New York, 2007).

[23]   Chapter 6 in *Stephen Colbert and Philosophy: I Am Philosophy (And So Can You)*, ed. Aaron Schiller (Chicago: Open Court, 2009).

[24]   Schiller, p. 83.

[25]   Schiller, p. 91.

[26]   Colbert called them out on this, March 3, 2009.

[27]   This is Ethan Mills' conclusion in "Truthiness and the Appearances," ch. 7 of Schiller's book.

but in fact had none. Not only does Socrates give us a good belief forming model, but he give us good reason not to trust experts simply because our gut tells us to; they often don't know nearly as much as they think they do.

So, again, the principle of charity dictates that Colbert can't be serious – he can't really be a gut thinker. That is not, however, the only way he defends his positions.

A Right to Your Opinion

> Now Folks, I'm no fan of reality [It Has a Liberal Bias] and I am no fan of encyclopedias [Just Fat-Ass Dictionaries]. I've said it before: "Who is Britannica to tell me George Washington had slaves?" If I want to say he didn't, that's my right.
> – Stephen Colbert, *The Colbert Report*, July 31, 2006

Suppose you're arguing with Colbert about whether George Washington owned slaves. You present evidence and argument that he did, but Colbert simply says "Doesn't it feel like he wouldn't own slaves?" When you point out to Colbert that he is thinking with his gut, and explain why gut thinking is wrong, he will respond "I have a right to my opinion." This is a common thing for people to say, so Colbert may actually mean it. But, do people really have a right to their opinion? Before answering, we need to figure out what Colbert means when he claims this alleged right.

Colbert might mean he has a legal right to his opinion. If this is what he means, he is correct. No one can haul him away for just thinking or speaking his opinion. But I doubt this is what he had in mind. Was he actually thinking you were about to call the cops to haul him off? No. Instead, Colbert might mean that he has an epistemic right to his opinion. "Epistemic" comes from "epistemology," which is the study of knowledge and how knowledge is justified (obviously Colbert missed that day of philosophy class). A belief to which one has an epistemic right is a belief that is justified by rational defense and argument. Given that we have already established he is just thinking with his gut, it's obvious that he has no rational defense or argument. Thus, he is mistaken if he thinks he has an epistemic right to his opinion.

What Colbert probably means is that he has a moral right to his opinion. Moral rights create moral duties in others.[28] For example, people's moral right to freedom gives Colbert the moral duty to free the Jews living under his desk on Birkat Hachama.[29] If Colbert has a moral right to his opinion, then you have a corresponding moral duty to treat that opinion in a certain way. What way?[30]

Maybe Colbert thinks you have a moral duty to agree with his opinion. But, if he has a right to his opinion, you have a right to yours, and that would mean that he

---

[28] Do moral rights always create moral duties? There are those who contest the issue. See Joel Feinberg, *Social Philosophy* (Prentice-Hall, Inc., Englewood Cliffs, New Jersey, 1973), pp. 61–4.

[29] April 8, 2009.

[30] Jamie Whyte makes three suggestions in *Crimes against Logic* (McGraw-Hill, New York, 2004), ch. 1. I have borrowed heavily from him here.

is obligated to agree with you. Not only would Colbert never agree with anyone but himself, but given that the two of you disagree, that doesn't make any sense. So maybe he thinks you have a duty to listen to his opinion. He may want that, but that can't be right either. Everyone has a right to his/her opinion if Colbert does, so we would be obligated to listen to everyone's opinion, and that is impossible. There is just not enough time. And we can't be obligated to do the impossible. (Besides, Colbert would have that duty too and to "hear" everyone's opinion would require a lot of reading – and we know Colbert is no fan of reading.)

Given that Colbert is trying to end the discussion without changing his mind, what he probably means is that you have a duty to let him keep his opinion – you should stop arguing with him and looking stuff up in books and just let him think what he wants to think. He thinks he has a right to believe whatever he wants, and thus you have a duty to let him. But your possession of such a duty is far from obvious. Suppose Colbert is about to cross the street in Bagdad, to go to Saddam's Water Palace to do a week of shows in Iraq.[31] He believes there are no insurgents around, poised to shoot him, but his escort corrects him, points out the insurgents, and tells him to wait until they are dealt with. Does his escort violate Colbert's right by curing Colbert of his ignorance? Of course not – Colbert would agree; he would rather not be shot. "If someone is interested in believing the truth, then she will not take the presentation of contrary evidence and argument as some kind of injury."[32]

This reveals what is at the heart of Colbert's claim that he has a right to his opinion. He doesn't care about believing what is true, but only believing what he wants to believe. Your presentation of arguments and evidence is keeping him from doing this, and so he sees it as an injury and thinks you have a moral duty to stop.

Even though Colbert doesn't care about truth and even though you are "injuring him" by keeping him from believing what is most comfortable, you still don't have a duty to let him keep his belief. If there is a duty to let people believe what is most comfortable, then the factanistas in the media violate our rights every time they tell us something we don't want to hear – like when they reported the NSA wiretapping and our secret European prisons. As Colbert pointed out at the White House Correspondents Dinner in 2006,

> Those things are secret for a very important reason: they're super-depressing. And if that's your goal, well, misery accomplished. Over the last five years you people were so good – over tax cuts, WMD intelligence, the effect of global warming. We Americans didn't want to know and you had the courtesy not to try to find out. Those were good times – as far as we knew.[33]

If we each had the duty to let everyone believe what they wanted and what was comforting, then educators – and particularly philosophers – would have the most

---

[31]   Which he did June 8–11, 2009.
[32]   Whyte, p. 9.
[33]   Stephen Colbert, White House Correspondents Dinner, April 29, 2006.

immoral jobs on the planet. Nothing endangers cherished beliefs like education and philosophy, and nothing hurts more than learning new ideas.

> Let me ask you this: Why were you happier when you were a kid? Because you didn't know anything. The more you know, the sadder you get. *Don't believe me?* By the time you finish reading this chapter, over a hundred dogs and cats in animal shelters around the nation will be euthanized. Bet you wish you could erase that knowledge. But it's too late. You learned a *New Idea*, and it made you sad . . . Look at the story of Adam and Eve. Their lives were pretty great – until they ate from the Tree of Knowledge. . . . *God's point*: Ignorance isn't just bliss, it's paradise.[34]

We clearly do not have a right to opinions we can't defend, especially if they are so clearly contrary to fact. Thus, Colbert can't really think he has a right to believe, contrary to fact, that George Washington didn't have slaves – or, for that matter, that the Panama Canal was finished in 1941 (instead of 1914).[35]

How to do Philosophy

> If a tree falls in the forest and no one hears it, I hope it lands on a philosophy professor.
> – Stephen Colbert, *I Am America (And So Can You!)*[36]

We've considered many cases of Colbert saying things so profoundly stupid that we realize he must be kidding. But wait, isn't he mocking conservative pundits, like Rush Limbaugh, by imitating them? We know Rush is not offering up satire (sadly, he is deadly serious about the moronic things he says). Neither was Sarah Palin kidding when she said she had foreign policy experience because of Russia's proximity to her home state of Alaska. How do we know that Colbert isn't doing the same thing? Part of it is context – he is on Comedy Central after all. But another big reason is Colbert takes it just a bit further than Rush and those like him. Although Rush could benefit from taking one of my critical thinking classes, and does say idle-minded things like "I hope Obama fails"[37] he wouldn't endorse things as noticeably false as relativism and that the earth never ages. In addition, we know that Colbert can't be serious because he has, in interviews, broken character and admitted to everything – even to being a registered democrat who votes democrat.[38] He has even spoken out against relativism, truthiness, right to opinion, and gut thinking saying,

---

[34] Colbert, pp. 120, 122.

[35] *The Colbert Report*, October 17, 2005.

[36] p. 126.

[37] Rush Limbaugh "Limbaugh: I Hope Obama Fails" http://www.rushlimbaugh.com/home/daily/site_011609/content/01125113.guest.html.

[38] See Howard Kurtz "TV's Newest Anchor: A Smirk in Progress" (Washington Post, 10-10-2005). http://www.washingtonpost.com/wp-dyn/content/article/2005/10/09/AR2005100901551.html. See also Mandi Bierly, "Show Off." (Entertainment Weekly, July 7, 2006). http://www.ew.com/ew/article/0,,677356,00.html

Truthiness is tearing apart our country . . . it doesn't seem to matter what facts are. It used to be, everyone was entitled to their own opinion, but not their own facts. But that's not the case anymore. Facts matter not at all. Perception is everything. It's certainty. People love . . . president [Bush] because he's certain of his choices as a leader, even if the facts that back him up don't seem to exist. It's the fact that he's certain that is very appealing to a certain section of the country. I really feel a dichotomy in the American populace. What is important? What you want to be true, or what *is* true?[39]

So even the real Stephen Colbert agrees. We shouldn't be relativists, thinking that groups or individuals can determine what is true. We also shouldn't be gut thinkers, believing our intuition can be enough justification for controversial beliefs. Rather, we should defend our positions with arguments, and when we can't defend them we should give them up. We need to have a concern for truth and try our best to find out what is true. And, when we realize that we don't have enough evidence to draw an informed conclusion about something, we should be agnostic – we should admit, like Socrates, that we simply do not know the answer – instead of hiding behind "a right to our opinion."

All of these mistakes are tempting when doing philosophy because philosophical questions are so hard to answer. It's easy to give up, think there is no answer, and just appeal to the majority, your gut, or your right to believe whatever you want. However, the fact that an answer is hard to find doesn't entail that the answer is not there. Philosophy does make progress – it just takes a while. By engaging in the philosophical endeavor, you are taking part in a very large and long process that answers the most important questions a person can ask. They won't all be answered in your lifetime, but you should be able to discover answers that you can at least defend with rational argument.

[39]   Nathan Rabin, "[An Interview with] Stephen Colbert" (A.V. Club, January 25, 2006) http://www.avclub.com/articles/stephen-colbert,13970/

Part II

Epistemology

Introduction

Epistemology is the study of knowledge. Is it even possible to acquire knowledge? If so, how does one acquire it? How should one acquire it? If knowledge really is justified, true belief – which has been contested – what is truth anyway? These are the questions an epistemologist asks.

In his chapter, Henry Jacoby takes us to *South Park* to teach us about the ethics of belief. While Blaise Pascal (1623–62) suggests that belief in God can be rational because, even though it lacks evidence, it is the better bet. William Clifford (1845–79), on the other hand, argues that it is always morally wrong to believe without evidence. Stan Marsh of South Park, Colorado agrees. Stan is critical of belief without (and contrary to) evidence, like Kyle's mom's beliefs in Holistic Healing, the Mormon belief that the first man and woman lived in Missouri, and John Edward's claims that he can communicate with the dead. Examples from the show demonstrate the dangers of belief without evidence, such as blindly following David Blaine into a mass suicide, and a mental laziness that, Stan tells John Edward, is "slowing down the progress of all mankind."

In *The Matrix* trilogy, it is revealed that the everyday world humans experience is actually a computer simulation designed to keep humans under control while an artificially intelligent civilization harvests our energy. In his chapter, Matt Lawrence uses the predicament in which humanity finds itself in *The Matrix* to explain what philosophers call "The Skeptical Problem" and Descartes' (1596–1650) solution to it. How can we be sure we're not being deceived on a grand scale like the prisoners of the Matrix?

In *Battlestar Galactica*, the 12 colonies are destroyed and humanity finds itself looking for a new home. Commander Adama claims he knows the location of the 13th colony – called Earth – when, in fact, he knows nothing of the kind. He simply told a lie to give people hope. It turns out, however, that there actually is an Earth and humanity eventually finds its way there. In his chapter, Eric Silverman uses Adama's lie to explore the classic definition of knowledge and the contemporary philosopher Edmund Gettier's conclusion that mere justified, true belief is insufficient for knowledge. The chapter concludes with a discussion of what William Clifford (1845–79) and William James (1842–1910) have to say about whether holding non-justified beliefs can be ethical.

4

You Know, I Learned Something Today

Stan Marsh and the Ethics of Belief

Henry Jacoby

Summary

The nineteenth-century English mathematician and philosopher W. K. Clifford famously argued that it is always wrong to believe anything upon insufficient evidence, even if such beliefs provide comfort and hope. Such beliefs weaken the mind while preventing the search for truth and understanding. This chapter explores Clifford's view through *South Park*'s resident voice of reason Stan Marsh as he takes on the crazy and the credulous.

A wise man, therefore, proportions his belief to the evidence.

– David Hume (1711–76)

If Evidence is Lacking, So What?

People believe all kinds of things for all sorts of reasons; sadly, few pay attention to reasons that involve **logic**, **argument**, theory, or evidence. In this regard, the cartoon inhabitants of South Park are no different.

But why should we think critically and rationally? Why does it matter? What harm is there in believing something if it makes you feel good, or provides you with comfort, or gives you hope? If evidence is lacking, so what?

In his classic essay "The Ethics of Belief," the English mathematician and philosopher W. K. Clifford (1845–79) explained the harm when he stated: "Every time we let ourselves believe for unworthy reasons, we weaken our powers of self-control, of doubting, of judicially and fairly weighing evidence." He concluded that it is "wrong always, everywhere, and for anyone, to believe anything upon insufficient evidence."[1]

---

[1] See W. K. Clifford, *The Ethics of Belief and Other Essays*, ed. by Timothy Madigan (Amherst, NY: Prometheus Books, 1999). Epistemology is the area of philosophy concerned with justifying beliefs with evidence. Good introductions to epistemology texts include: Robert Audi, *Epistemology: A Contemporary Introduction* (London: Routledge, 2003); and Jack Crumley, *Introduction to Epistemology* (Columbus, OH: McGraw-Hill, 1998).

Amidst the purposely exaggerated craziness and illogic of the citizens of South Park, we are, on occasion, treated to flashes of insight and well thought-out ideas that surprise us. Stan shows off his critical thinking skills as he takes on TV psychics, various cults, and unsupported religious **beliefs** in a way that would've made Clifford proud. In this chapter, we'll examine how Stan exposes the frauds and the harms they engender, while defending scientific thinking and a healthy **skepticism**.

Belief and Evidence

We acquire our beliefs in various ways, most notably by observation and authority. The kids believe that Mr. Hankey exists because they see him, but observation is not always trustworthy. Cartman, after all, sees pink Christina Aguilera creatures floating around, but they aren't real. The South Park parents believe the children have ADD because that's the conclusion reached by school psychologists who tested them. Such a belief may be reliable in some circumstances, but not when it comes from the South Park testers, who are fools. Further, we must be careful when relying on authority figures. Scientologists may believe their leaders, who say that there were once frozen alien bodies in the volcanoes of Hawaii. But this is nonsense that should be rejected by any sane person.

We see, then, that rational belief requires evidence. And the more outrageous the belief, the more evidence is required. As Stan told the Mormon family in "All About the Mormons," "If you're going to say things that have been proven wrong, like the first man and woman lived in Missouri and Native Americans came from Jerusalem, then you better have something to back it up!" Stan is pointing out here that Mormon beliefs should be rejected unless they can be defended, since they are in addition and contrary to, what are accepted facts. The Mormons here have what philosophers call *the **burden of proof***; the obligation is on them to provide the evidence, or proof, for their claims.

In the same episode, two villagers are talking about Joseph Smith. One of them says, "He claims he spoke with God and Jesus." The other one asks, "Well how do you know he didn't?" Is this a fair question? Should claims be accepted if no disproof can be offered?[2] No, the request for disproof is not a request that needs to be answered. The burden of proof always lies with the one who makes the additional claim, not with those who doubt its truth. Otherwise we would be required to entertain *any* belief for which there was no handy disproof. I can't disprove the existence of alien souls inhabiting our bodies, but that doesn't mean I should consider this claim of Scientology to be a meaningful possibility. If our beliefs can't be supported, then they should be rejected or, at least, put aside until further evidence comes about.

Formulating beliefs and making decisions without sufficient evidence leads to trouble. Imagine picking a college, a career, a place to live, a mechanic, a doctor,

---

[2] This thinking involves the fallacy of ignorance. For other kinds of fallacious thinking, see Robert Arp's chapter in this volume entitled "The Chewbacca Defense: A *South Park* Logic Lesson."

or anything, for that matter, without reasoning and examining the facts involved. Imagine going through your life just guessing whenever a decision is to be made, or going by how you feel at the moment, or basing decisions on what someone, who may or may not be reliable, has said.

Take as an illustration, the time when Kyle became very ill and, in fact, needed a kidney transplant. But instead, his mother took him to the new "Holistic Healer" in town, Miss Information. At her shop, the townspeople lined up to buy all sorts of useless products from her and her employees who, since they were introduced as Native Americans, must surely know all about healing! Fortunately for Kyle, these "Native Americans" (who turned out to be Cheech and Chong) were honest enough to convince Mrs. Broflovski that Kyle was really sick and should be taken to a real doctor. Stan, who realized from the start that the "healers" were frauds and their methods unscientific, had been urging this course of action all along. He later tricks Cartman into giving up a kidney, so everything works out well for Kyle in the end. But when we start with beliefs that have been uncritically accepted, the outcome is not usually so fortunate.

Notice too, how closely beliefs are tied to action. In the episode "Trapped in The Closet" Stan tells Tom Cruise that he's not as good an actor as Leonardo Di Caprio, Gene Hackman, or "the guy who played Napoleon Dynamite." This causes poor Tom to become depressed, and he locks himself in the closet. Now, why should a famous actor care what a little boy thinks of his acting skills? Well, he should care if he's a Scientologist and believes, as the current Scientology leaders claim, that the little boy is the reincarnation of Scientology founder L. Ron Hubbard. So the illogical action is caused by a ridiculous belief that is held on the basis, not of any sort of testable evidence (well, they did test Stan's "body thetans" with their "E-Meters" – more unsupported nonsense), but solely on the basis of authority. And the "authority" here is hardly reliable or objective; in fact, later the leading scientologist admits to Stan that it's all made up and he's doing it for the money.

Faith vs. Reason

People often say that their beliefs, especially their religious beliefs, are based on faith. What does this mean? And is this a good idea? First, let's be clear what is meant by *faith* in this context. Sometimes faith refers to a kind of confidence. In the episode "Scott Tenorman Must Die" Cartman was confident that his friends would betray him, and they did. This allowed his plan for revenge on Scott to work perfectly. Cartman, we might say, had faith that his plan would work.

Notice here that this kind of faith is not opposed to **reason** and evidence. Cartman reasoned that he could accurately predict what his friends would do based on their past actions. This is perfectly reasonable. If, on the other hand, Mr. Garrison had faith that his students would all work hard on their homework assignments, such confidence would be misplaced. He has no good reason to think so. So faith in the sense of being confident may be reasonable or not, depending on one's evidence.

Normally when one talks of religious faith, however, one does not mean confidence based on reason. This kind of faith is in fact *opposed* to reason; quite simply, it is belief without good evidence. After hearing the story of Joseph Smith, a story that Stan points out is unsupported and contrary to known facts, Stan says, "Wait: Mormons actually know this story, and they still believe Joseph Smith was a prophet?" The reply, of course, is "Stan, it's all a matter of faith." So, faith appears to be a kind of fallback position that we take when we can't support our view. Such a move should not be encouraged, for it would render any belief whatsoever acceptable.

Prudential Reasons vs. Evidence

Does a belief have to be supported by evidence to be rational? Can there be other *reasons* that make a belief justified besides evidential ones? Well, philosophers make a distinction between *prudential reasons* and *evidential reasons*. The distinction is easy to illustrate. Suppose that I tell you that John Edward – the self-proclaimed psychic whom Stan puts in his place – really can communicate with the dead. Since you watch *South Park*, you know that John Edward is the "biggest douche in the universe," so you don't believe my claim for a second and demand proof. Suppose I then tell you that if you do believe it, I'll give you lots of money (I show you the briefcase filled with money); but if you don't believe it, I won't (or worse, we can say you'll be killed if you don't believe it!). Now you have a reason to believe that John Edward is not a fraud, and it's a *good reason*. But you still don't have a shred of evidence. Your reason, instead, is a prudential one. It's in your best interest to believe.

Blaise Pascal (1623–62), a French mathematician and philosopher, came up with a well-known attempt to justify religious belief in exactly the same way. His argument has come to be known as Pascal's Wager.[3] Think of belief in God as a bet. If you wager on God (if you believe) and God exists, you win. God rewards believers with eternal joy and happiness. But if you do not believe and God exists, then you lose. God punishes non-believers with eternal suffering and pain. What if God doesn't exist? Well, in that case the nonbeliever has the truth and the believer doesn't; but whatever positives or negatives result are negligible in comparison to what happens if there is a God. The point is, if you have any chance at all to achieve eternal peace and avoid eternal damnation, you're a fool not to go for it. Prudential reasons reign; it's in your best interest to believe in God.

Notice a few things about Pascal's Wager. First, he's not trying to prove that God exists. If we could prove that there is a God, then the Wager would be pointless (similarly if we could prove that there is no God). Pascal starts by assuming that

[3] See Blaise Pascal, *Pascal's Pensées*, trans. by W. F. Trotter (New York: P. F. Collier, 1910). For interesting discussions of the pros and cons of the Wager, see Nicholas Rescher, *Pascal's Wager: A Study of Practical Reasoning in Philosophical Theology* (Notre Dame, IN: University of Notre Dame Press, 1985), and Alan Hájek, "Waging War on Pascal's Wager," *Philosophical Review* 112 (2003), pp. 27–56.

we don't know either way. Second, Pascal isn't arguing that one should simply have faith. He's instead arguing that religious belief is *reasonable* because it's prudential. Philosophers have offered many criticisms of the Wager, showing that it's not a very good argument for religious belief. Let's look at two of these, as they are nicely illustrated in *South Park*.

You might wonder why God would choose to torture someone for all eternity simply because they don't believe in Him. Isn't God supposed to be perfectly good after all? Why would a good being wish pain and suffering on anyone? In the episode "Cartmanland," Kyle wonders the same thing. Cartman inherits a million dollars and buys an amusement park, while Kyle suffers from hemorrhoid pain. Kyle begins to lose his faith as well as his will to live. If there were a God, he reasons, He wouldn't reward someone like Cartman (who is evil) while allowing me (who is good) to suffer. Kyle says: "Cartman is the biggest asshole in the world. How is it that God gives him a million dollars? Why? How can you do this? There are people starving in Alabama, and you give Cartman a million dollars? If someone like Cartman can get his own theme park, then there is no God. There's no God, dude."

Kyle's parents, in an attempt to restore his faith, tell him that God sometimes causes us to suffer, perhaps to test our faith, and they read him the story of Job. (Incidentally, the idea of God testing us makes little sense; since He is all-knowing, He would already know what we would do, rendering any test pointless.) But the story horrifies Kyle: "That's the most horrible story I've ever heard. Why would God do such horrible things to a good person just to prove a point to Satan?" Kyle reasons here that if there really were a God, there would be justice in the world. God wouldn't reward someone like Cartman and neither would He allow the good, like Job and Kyle, to suffer.

We can see how all of this applies to Pascal's Wager. Imagine someone who is an extremely good person – loving, honest, helpful, kind – yet she does not believe in God. She thinks one ought to be moral to make the world a better place, let's say, not because God says so or to get some personal reward. Does it really make sense to think that God (who is all good, remember) would allow such a person to be tormented for all eternity?

A second – and much worse problem for Pascal's argument – is that he assumes that we *know* the outcomes of our wager. Pascal says that God rewards believers and punishes nonbelievers. But this is just an assumption. If we had proof of this, we would already know that the religious view of things is true, and thus we wouldn't need a prudential argument. Remember, the point of the Wager is to convince us to believe when we have no evidence of God's existence (or nonexistence). Without evidence, there are many possibilities to consider. Perhaps God rewards everyone, or maybe there's no afterlife at all. Maybe God values reason, and punishes those who believe blindly without any evidence. There are endless possibilities.

Even if we could establish that only religious believers get rewarded (and how would we establish that without rendering the Wager pointless?), we still have the problem of *which* religious beliefs to have. In "Do The Handicapped Go To Hell?" we're treated to a bunch of religious folks who, to their horror, find themselves in hell. They are told that they have the *wrong religious beliefs*; only the Mormons go to heaven!

What's The Harm, Dude?

Those who can make you believe absurdities can make you commit atrocities.
— Voltaire (1694–1778)

Maybe Pascal's Wager doesn't show us that we *should* believe in God, but still, we might ask, what's the harm? Perhaps we should only have beliefs that are based on reasons, but what's wrong with prudential reasons? In the episode "All About the Mormons" Gary tells Stan: "Maybe us Mormons do believe in crazy stories that make absolutely no sense. And maybe Joseph Smith did make it all up. But I have a great life and a great family, and I have the Book of Mormon to thank for that. The truth is, I don't care if Joseph Smith made it all up." And in "The Biggest Douche in the Universe" John Edward tries to defend himself to Stan when he says: "What I do doesn't hurt anybody. I give people closure and help them cope with life." So, echoing Gary, Stan's Mormon friend, we could similarly say we don't care if Edward is a fraud, as long as what he does makes people feel good. Again, what's the harm?

For one, unsupported beliefs can lead to harmful consequences. In "Timmy 2000" the belief that Timmy has ADD (that he is not just mentally disabled) eventually causes a wild spread of unnecessary prescription drugs and, worse, a belief that the music of Phil Collins is actually good. In "Super Best Friends" some of the followers of magician David Blaine blindly follow him and commit suicide, believing they will go to heaven. And we've already seen how belief in the healing powers of New Age healers almost cost Kyle his life. In each of these cases, the believers feel good about their beliefs; they provide hope or comfort. But they are still extremely dangerous.

A second sort of harm is mental weakness and laziness. As Clifford said, "Every time we let ourselves believe for unworthy reasons, we weaken our powers of self-control, of doubting, of judicially and fairly weighing evidence." His point is that even if one's unsupported belief causes no immediate harm (as in the examples from *South Park*), it still weakens the mind. We become used to accepting ideas uncritically, grow mentally lazy, and this encourages others to do the same. Most of the citizens of South Park rarely use their critical faculties. This makes them easy prey for every cult, fad, or con that comes to town. Think of just about any episode of *South Park*, and you'll find examples of this mental weakness and laziness.

Inquiry, Hard Work, and Progress

To understand a final reason why uncritically accepting unsupported beliefs — however hopeful they might make us feel — is not such a good thing, we turn to

Stan at his best. Again, from "The Biggest Douche in the Universe," John Edward challenges Stan: "Everything I tell people is positive and gives them hope; how does that make me a douche?" Stan's reply is brilliant: "Because the big questions in life are tough; why are we here, where are we from, where are we going? But if people believe in asshole douchy liars like you, we're never going to find the real answers to those questions. You aren't just lying, you're slowing down the progress of all mankind, you douche." He follows this up with another terrific speech, this time to the members of Edward's believing audience:

> You see, I learned something today. At first I thought you were all just stupid listening to this douche's advice, but now I understand that you're all here because you're scared. You're scared of death and he offers you some kind of understanding. You all want to believe in it so much, I know you do. You find comfort in the thought that your loved ones are floating around trying to talk to you, but think about it: is that really what you want? To just be floating around after you die having to talk to this asshole? We need to recognize this stuff for what it is: magic tricks. Because whatever is really going on in life and in death is much more amazing than this douche.

We can all learn something today from what Stan has said here. First, he recognizes that it's wrong to dismiss someone with unsupported beliefs as being stupid. We want answers; we need comfort. Sometimes we rely more on emotion than reason to satisfy ourselves, but that doesn't mean we lack intelligence. We poke fun, we often ridicule; but, even in South Park, it's always better when we try for some understanding.

Second, Stan reminds us of Clifford's point that settling for easy answers not only weakens the mind, but also prevents us from finding real answers. In science, philosophy, and any rational pursuit where we require answers to questions, the spirit of inquiry – combined with hard work – is what leads to progress. Settling for magical answers that make us feel good only slows us down.

And speaking of magic, Stan reminds us finally that there's real magic, wonder, and beauty in the universe. As he says, whatever is really going on in life and in death is truly amazing. We don't want to miss it, dude.

5

Tumbling Down the Rabbit Hole

Knowledge, Reality, and the Pit of Skepticism

Matt Lawrence

Summary

In *The Matrix Trilogy*, humanity is enslaved, trapped inside a virtual reality called "The Matrix." Since The Matrix is indistinguishable from the real world, how can we know that the movie is fiction? How can we know that we are not trapped inside The Matrix ourselves? This chapter uses *The Matrix* to raise the skeptical problem – how can we have knowledge at all, if we can't even know that the world exists? And does the modern philosopher Descartes present a working solution to the skeptical problem?

This is your last chance. After this there is no turning back.

– Morpheus, *The Matrix*

Before meeting Morpheus, Thomas Anderson was just a regular guy at a regular job trying to make ends meet. Sure, he led a sort of double life, spending much of his time behind a computer keyboard, hacking under the screen name "Neo," but even then he was not so different from the rest of us. Neo took *this* world to be the real world – just as we do. But as it turned out, he was wrong about so much. He thought that he was living at the end of the twentieth century, that he had hair, that the sun was shining, that he knew his parents, and that all of his acquaintances were actually human. Yet none of this was true. To put it bluntly, Neo had no idea what the world was really like.

Neo's predicament illustrates the need to "question reality" – which is arguably the main philosophical message of the first *Matrix* film. *The Matrix* urged us not to take the world at face value, and it showed us how deceptive appearances can be. However, most people feel quite confident that *we* are not in the Matrix. They feel certain that *our* most basic **beliefs** are not mistaken. But what justifies this sense of confidence? After all, Neo's situation was, on the face of it, no different than ours. His world *seemed* just like our world. Should he have known that he was living in a dream? Despite the fact that he is sometimes chided about his intelligence by the Oracle ("Not too bright though") and by Agent Smith ("I see that you are still using all the muscles but the one that matters most"), there were no tell-tale signs that Neo should have noticed in order to realize that his world was illusory. Without the help of Morpheus, I expect that he would never have known.

By taking the red pill, Neo encountered an age-old philosophical problem: How do you know what is real? Or, worse yet: *can* you know what is real? This is called the *problem of skepticism*. A *skeptic* is a person who believes that we can never be absolutely sure what the world is really like. They maintain that there is always the possibility that we could be radically mistaken about most of our beliefs, just as Neo was. Most people are not plagued by such skeptical doubts. Neo certainly wasn't. Prior to that red pill, he would never have supposed that his whole life was an illusion. Even when he saw it with his own eyes he had trouble believing it, and ended up puking his breakfast onto the floor. Nevertheless it is fair to say that for years Neo had been restless – plagued by a vague and amorphous feeling that something was not quite right with the world. Maybe you've had that feeling too. The question is: How seriously should you take it?

The Skeptical Dilemma: Cartesian Dreams and Demons

Wake up, Neo.

– Computer screen, *The Matrix*

The seventeenth-century French philosopher, scientist, and mathematician René Descartes is famous for taking such skeptical worries seriously, so perhaps he can shed some light on Neo's situation. Descartes took on the project of trying to determine which of his beliefs could be maintained with absolute certainty. He employed what is famously known as his *method of doubt*. He began by discarding all of his beliefs, and resolved to allow them in only if it could be shown that they were absolutely certain. Rather than try to prove that any of his beliefs were actually false, which can be quite difficult to do (imagine the work involved in trying to *prove* that sentient machines aren't secretly plotting a war against us at this very moment), he simply checked his beliefs to see if they admitted any room for doubt. If a belief could be doubted, Descartes withheld his assent from it. It may seem a bit crazy to throw out all of your beliefs at once, but Descartes was not suggesting that a person should live their entire life this way. Rather, he thought that since he had come to accept so many beliefs, most of which were adopted uncritically during his childhood, it would be smart to sift through them at least once in his life, in order to discover which of his beliefs were "rock solid."

Employing this method, Descartes reached some startling conclusions, which, hundreds of years later, provide the basic framework of the *Matrix* films. One of Descartes's first big conclusions was that there was absolutely no way to be sure that he wasn't dreaming at any given moment. In his *Meditations on First Philosophy* he wrote:

> How often, at night, I've been convinced that I was here, sitting before the fire, wearing my dressing gown, when in fact I was undressed and between the covers of my bed! . . . I see so plainly that there are no reliable signs by which I can distinguish sleeping from waking that I am stupefied – and my stupor itself suggests that I am asleep![1]

Is it possible that you might be dreaming right now? Some people don't buy it. They argue that there is a difference in "feel" between dreams and waking life.[2] Surely, they say, my experience at this moment is too crisp and vivid to be a dream. But while most of us have had fairly lucid dreams in which we realized that we were dreaming, you have probably also had the experience of being totally caught up in a dream, such that you had no idea that the events weren't real. Can you be absolutely sure that this is not one of those times? There appears to be at least a slight possibility that this could be a dream.

Some people say they can *prove* that they are not dreaming. They attempt this by setting certain limits on dreams, for example, that they cannot be in-color, or that it is impossible to read in a dream. But most people do recall colors from their dreams. And I distinctly remember a dream in which I read – though I must admit that it took quite a bit of effort. Maybe you also recall reading in a dream. But whether you have or not is really beside the point, for there is simply no reason to believe that it is physically (or mentally) impossible to do so.

Skepticism within the Matrix

Real is just another four-letter word.
         – Cypher, *The Matrix* (Draft script, April 8, 1996 [SciFiScripts.com])

Of course the *Matrix* films take the whole dream scenario to its **logical** limit. They ask you to consider whether your entire life might be a dream. As Morpheus puts it:

> Have you ever had a dream . . . that you were so sure was real? What if you were unable to wake from that dream? How would you know the difference between the dream world and the real world?

Is there any way to be sure that your whole life has not been a dream? I don't think that there is. Typically, we call some experiences "dreams" and others

---

[1] René Descartes, *Meditations on First Philosophy*, tr. Ronold Rubin (Claremont, CA: Areté Press, 1986), p. 2.
[2] For another interesting exploration of dreams and reality try the film, *Waking Life*.

"reality" by contrasting them. Experiences that we call "real" are consistent and predictable. For example, people don't just get up and fly away in "real life" while they sometimes do in dreams. And it is not unusual for the experiences we have in dreams to jump around from one time and place to another, while those events we call "real" do not. But if your whole life has been a dream, then there is nothing to contrast these experiences with. In this case, the "dreams" that you recall each night are just dreams within the dream. And *that* contrast still holds. Even if your whole life has been a dream you could distinguish your nightly dreams from your "waking experiences" much of the time. But how do you know that you are not in Neo's predicament – that even your waking experiences are simply more dreams – just more predictable ones? Morpheus's suggestion seems correct. If you have never awakened from the dream to see what "real life" is actually like, you would have absolutely no way to discern that you are dreaming.

So the skeptical problem is not just a problem for Neo. It is also a problem for us. If there is no way to tell if your whole life has been a dream, then what makes you so sure that it isn't? You too should feel "a bit like Alice, tumbling down the rabbit hole." I like to call this hole *the pit of skepticism*. A little philosophical analysis leads us to doubts about those things we typically take for granted, and the more we analyze, the more we come to doubt. As we try to claw our way out of the pit, it seems that we just dig ourselves deeper and deeper. And we are still falling.

As the *Matrix* films illustrate, there are even worse possibilities than simply living in a dream. Instead, your whole life could be an *intentional deception* – "a world pulled over your eyes to blind you from the truth." Surprisingly enough, Descartes explored this possibility as well. As he pushed his methodical doubt to its logical limits, he posited an evil demon, supremely powerful and cunning, who expends every effort to deceive him:

> I will say that sky, air, earth, color, shape, sound, and other external things are just dreamed illusions which the demon uses to ensnare my judgment. I will regard myself as not having hands, eyes, flesh, blood, and senses – but as having the false belief that I have all these things. . . . [I]f I do not really have the ability to know the truth, I will at least withhold assent from what is false and from what a deceiver may try to put over on me, however powerful and cunning he may be.[3]

The computer-simulated dreamworld of the *Matrix* trilogy is a technological version of Descartes's evil demon. In essence it represents the idea of a mind (the Architect) more powerful than our own that is intent on deceiving us whenever, and however, it sees fit.

In fact, the premise of a computer-run deception is all the more troubling. Before *The Matrix*, people would often dismiss Descartes's evil demon as unrealistic. It is hard to get yourself too worked up about a supremely powerful demon possibly deceiving you, if you have never in your life encountered a demon. (Though this

---

[3] Descartes, p. 3.

may be a sign of just how cunning the demon really is.) But over the past few decades we have *seen* the emergence of virtual-reality programming. If our technology continues to progress, it seems likely that we will one day be able to stimulate the brain to "perceive" whatever we program it to perceive. So, the idea of a technological deception strikes most people today as much more plausible than a demon. Such a deception could be the work of sentient machines, as it is in the Matrix, but there are other possibilities as well. For instance, your "real self" (in the year 2199) could have signed you up for a 20-year "historical hallucination" against the backdrop of the world as it was at the start of the twenty-first century. Perhaps you designed your adventure to begin on New Year's Eve of the year 2000, complete with a set of false memories about your twentieth-century childhood.[4] Or, maybe your friends and family committed you to this delusion after your mental collapse. "Real life" in the year 2199 may have been just too hard for you to bear.

How Deep Does the Rabbit Hole Go?

Feeling a bit like Alice?

– Morpheus, *The Matrix*

Is there any limit to the extent that such a demon or programmer could deceive us? While certainly the machines were seriously messing with Neo's mind, it appears that they weren't nearly as malicious as they might have been. They gave Neo many "privileges" within the deception. For instance:

Neo was not deceived about his body.
Despite being deceived about his baldness, Neo wasn't radically deceived about his body. He wasn't programmed to think that he was of a different gender or race, or that he was only four feet tall. And interestingly enough, he was not made to think that he was a sentient machine.[5]

His personality was not distorted.
Neo can be grateful that his personality was essentially the same both in and out of the Matrix. For instance, when in the Matrix he was not turned into a cowardly wimp by having feelings of fear pumped into his mind whenever he confronted a dangerous situation.

---

[4]   Compare this to *Matriculated*, the ninth animated short in *The Animatrix* DVD. It tells the story of a band of rebels who capture a sentient machine and put it into a Matrix of their own design. The machine is then given a set of experiences in order to "brainwash" it into thinking that it is human. This film also suggests a motive for the limits of Neo's own deception – empathy. The rebels set limits on the extent to which they deceive the machine because they don't want to make it a slave. Rather, they want to render it harmless – to make it an ally. This also seems to be the Architect's primary motive in limiting the deceptions of humans within the Matrix.

[5]   For a similar sort of deception see Arnold Schwarzenegger in *Total Recall*.

His memory was not tampered with.
When something would happen within the Matrix Neo would remember it, and if he remembered it, then it most likely happened.[6]

Neo was not alone.
Many people, thousands, or perhaps even millions, are plugged into the Matrix, providing Neo with plenty of company.

His decisions were not controlled.
Neo makes his own choices – they are not "programmed" for him by the machines.

His **reasoning** ability was not obscured.
Neo bases his decisions on reasons. He is able to make inferences about how his world works and use these inferences to achieve his goals.

In theory, there is no reason why the machines had to cut Neo any of these breaks. Imagine the following sort of case:

Neo's Worst Nightmare
The computers exterminate the entire human race with the exception of Neo. He is then plugged into the Matrix at the age of 25, and his brain is stimulated in such a way as to simulate his "birth." But his birth is not a human birth, rather, he sees himself on a production line as a computer whose sentience chip has just been "switched on." While he is surprised at this course of events, he cannot really question them, because all his memories of being human have been wiped away. His personality is now changed. His human desires for companionship, adventure, food, etc., have been replaced with an all-consuming desire to mop the *entire* factory floor. However, his brain is manipulated in such a way as to occasionally cause him to forget where he started, so that despite the fact that he has mopped every inch of the floor a thousand times over, he will never believe that he has completed his task.[7]

A Matrix-type deception could definitely be pursued to torturous limits. And while we cannot be sure that we are not in a Matrix ourselves, we can rest assured that we are not in *that* Matrix – at least not yet.

What more is it possible to know? Is there anything *positive* that you can assert with absolute certainty? Morpheus seemed to think so. He claimed to offer "the Truth – and nothing more." But does Morpheus really know the *Truth*? According to Morpheus, the Truth is that Neo is a slave, but he can be freed from this captivity, and thereby experience the real world. The desert of the real is, of course, the charred remains of human civilization, with its dark, scorched sky, and the underground world of Zion and its hovercraft fleet. But does Morpheus *really know* that life in Zion is "real"? Can he be absolutely certain that he is free from the Matrix himself?

---

[6] An exception to this general rule occurs when Neo is caused to "forget" his first interrogation by Agent Smith. Only when Trinity removes the bug from his naval does he recall the event.
[7] In this case Neo would be a sort of futuristic Sisyphus. Though one key difference is that Sisyphus was fully aware of the futility of his work.

Of course when we watch the Matrix story unfold on film, we are supposed to regard Morpheus as awake. In any scene in which Morpheus is on the Nebuchadnezzar or on Zion he *is* in the real world. And while he regularly enters the Matrix, he is not like the deceived masses of humanity, slumbering away in their cocoons. Despite the fact that his eyes are closed when he jacks in, he remains fully awake to the fact that the world of the Matrix is just a high-tech illusion. He knows that his muscles have no effect on what he can do *in this place*.[8] But what I am suggesting now, is that we think beyond the limits of this particular story. If there are more possibilities to Morpheus's reality than we are explicitly shown in the film, can he really be absolutely certain that he is awake? I contend that he cannot. Morpheus is trapped in the pit of skepticism just like the rest of us.

Consider this "alternative reality," which is consistent with the central ideas of the *Matrix* trilogy, but which is not part of the story depicted in the films:

> The Matrix within the Matrix
> A program monitors all the humans who are plugged into the Matrix. It mainly looks for hackers – people like Morpheus, Trinity, and Neo, who are obsessed with tearing down computerized systems of control. These people generally tend to be the ones who are fighting against the dreamworld provided to them. These humans know, however vaguely, that there is something not quite right with the world. This feeling nags at them – like a splinter in their minds. The machines realize that such people are on the verge of waking up, and therefore, they take precautions against it by giving the hackers a new type of dream – a different Matrix. They switch them over to a dream of being awakened. This causes these restless souls to become more accepting of their experiences – more accepting of the dream. And better still, the machines provide these people with the illusion of fighting to free all of humanity from a world of computer control. This dream totally captivates them, causing them to sleep soundly for the rest of their lives.

Morpheus cannot rule out this sort of scenario. All he can say is that his experiences in Zion and on the Nebuchadnezzar don't *feel* like a dream, and that the belief that he has "really awakened" is consistent with all of his experiences. But notice that the same was true for Neo before he took the red pill. His experience felt real, and, until he found himself naked inside that slimy cocoon, it made perfect sense for him to believe that he had been experiencing the real world all of his life.

So the pit of skepticism certainly goes deeper than even Morpheus realizes. For this reason Descartes may be a better guide. He was prepared to follow his skeptical doubts all the way down. Ultimately, Descartes faced the possibility that maybe there is *nothing at all* that is absolutely certain. But after closely examining this possibility, he came to the realization that he did know at least *one thing* with absolute certainty. Descartes came to this insight when he tried to entertain the notion that the demon was deceiving him about his own existence:

---

[8]   Morpheus teaches Neo this lesson in the Kung Fu scene from *The Matrix*.

I have convinced myself that there is nothing in the world – no sky, no earth, no minds, no bodies. Doesn't it follow that I don't exist? No, surely I must exist if it's me who is convinced of something. . . . Let him deceive me all he can, he will never make it the case that I am nothing while I think that I am something.[9]

Descartes summarized this conclusion in the Latin phrase *Cogito ergo sum* – "I think therefore I am" – which has long remained the single most famous line in all of Western philosophy.[10]

It seems to me that Descartes was right. One cannot be mistaken about one's very existence. Even if you are a victim of a Matrix-type deception you can be certain that you exist. That is, there has to be a "you" that is being deceived. While everyone else's existence will always be somewhat less certain, the very act of trying to doubt your own existence merely demonstrates that *you* indeed exist. Of course, you cannot then start jumping to conclusions about *what* you are, or what the external world is really like. You still cannot be sure that you have a body, or that you are even human. (For all you know, you might be a sentient machine or robot that is deceived into thinking that it is human.) But the certainty of your existence does provide a foothold – a starting point for trying to climb out of this pit. As Descartes noted:

Archimedes required only one fixed and immovable point to move the whole earth from its place, and I too can hope for great things if I can find even one small thing that is certain and unshakeable.[11]

Since it was your ability to think that proved your existence, then perhaps you can build on that. For, if you are at this very moment "thinking of the Matrix," isn't it also certain that you *know* that you are "thinking of the Matrix"? It seems undeniably true that you are directly and unmistakably aware of your own immediate conscious mental state. Similarly, if you are perceiving a white page in front of you, you *know* that you are *perceiving* a white page in front of you. You just can't jump to the conclusion that the page is "real," in the sense that it has a separate existence apart from your perception. Not only do you have a direct awareness of your own thoughts and perceptions, but as Descartes put it, you know that you are a "thinking thing," that is, you are the kind of being that is capable of having these thoughts and perceptions. This is not to say that you are the original source of these thoughts. It is always possible that they are somehow "pumped into your mind" from the outside. But regardless of the manner in which they arise, you must be capable of experiencing them.

---

[9]   Descartes, p. 6.
[10] This famous phrase comes from Descartes's *Discourse on Method*.
[11] Descartes, *Meditations*, p. 6. See also Hilary Putnam's *Reason, Truth, and History* for his now classic "brain in a vat" hypothesis.

So how deep does the rabbit hole really go? "Frighteningly deep" is the short answer. So long as you are willing to entertain the possibility of a Matrix-type deception, then the only thing that you can be absolutely sure of is your own existence and the contents of your immediate mental state. Certainty about what the world is like *outside your mind* will always be unavailable to you. This conclusion doesn't sit very well with most people. And it didn't for Descartes either. He tried to eliminate the possibility of such radical deceptions by proving that God exists. His thought was that if he could prove the existence of God as an all-good and all-powerful being, then he could rest assured that there was no malicious demon, for surely a benevolent God would not allow him to be deceived about his most clear and distinct perceptions. Unfortunately for Descartes, most philosophers agree that his **argument** for God fell short of the "**proof**" that he needed. In the end there may be no way to be absolutely certain that we are not the victims of a Matrix-type deception.

Skepticism Outside the Matrix

How do you define *real?*

– Morpheus, *The Matrix*

While we may not be able to prove that we are *not* in a Matrix-type deception right now, this, of course, doesn't mean that we ought to *believe* that we're in the Matrix. While the Matrix scenario is a logical possibility, it is not the most likely explanation of our day-to-day experiences. And since Descartes's journey has shown that there is very little that we can know with *absolute certainty*, maybe we should lower our standards. After all, to be *very certain* about your beliefs is probably good enough.

Shifting the standard from absolute certainty to merely a high degree of probability will not free us from skepticism – though many people mistakenly think that it does. They quickly fall into complacency and assume that they are *very certain* that the world is essentially just like it appears to be. They suppose that the images in our minds (coming to us through our senses) of smooth, solid, brown tables, soft, fuzzy, beige carpeting, and squishy, pink, bubblegum basically correspond to the world as it is outside our minds – reality *in itself*. This view, that the world outside our minds basically matches our perceptions of it, is called *naive **realism***. While this view is quite common, there are plenty of reasons to think that it is false. The world is NOT just as it appears to be. Philosophers throughout history have argued this point, but in what follows I'll argue the case in a way that is inspired by the great twentieth-century philosopher Bertrand Russell.[12]

Suppose that I have purchased from Warner Brothers those big red chairs that Morpheus and Neo sat in during their first meeting. Imagine that I have invited

---

[12] See Bertrand Russell's "Appearance and Reality" in his *The Problems of Philosophy*. (Oxford: Oxford University Press, 1959).

you over and that you sit down in one of them. Let us be clear that in this example we are talking about a "real" chair. We are in my real living-room – not in some Matrix-type simulation, or in a film, but in real life. As you imagine yourself sitting there, think about what you would know with reasonable certainty about the chair. First off, if you are like most people, you will take it for granted that the chair *exists*. But what Russell asks us to do is to take seriously the seemingly stupid question, "How do you know it exists?" In a way that is reminiscent of Morpheus's own remarks, you would probably respond by saying that it exists because you feel it, see it, etc. You feel its support against your back; you run your hand across its smooth leather surface, feeling the contour of its shape; and you see its deep red color. But take a moment to consider these perceptions. Is the chair *really* the color of red that it appears to be right now? Naive realism says of course it is. But Russell suggests that you should consider it again after lowering the lights. Notice that the color changes – the red becomes darker, deeper. If the original color was the real color, then what are we to say of the color it is now? Well, one might be tempted to say that while you can't pinpoint the exact shade of red that is the "true" or "real" red of the chair, it is nevertheless *some* shade of red. But what reason do you have for thinking so? After all, the color changes not only with the brightness of the lighting, but also with the type of lighting. The color of the chair will look different under daylight, fluorescent light, candle light, black light, etc. If under certain lighting conditions the chair looks more brown than red should we say it *is* brown also? And purple sometimes?

Now at this point you might think that it is not the chair that has changed, but the lights. Purple lights are purple, but the chair is not. But that is precisely Russell's point. As modern science tells us, color is not *in* the objects themselves at all. Red chairs, after all, are not made out of a bunch of little red atoms. Rather, the color that objects *appear* to us to be is caused by the wavelengths of the light that reaches our eyes from the direction of the object. But look what has happened. You thought that the chair (which really exists) was really red. But as it turns out, it is only the *appearance* of the chair that is red. The chair *in itself* is not.

Might naive realism have better luck with texture? To us the chair looks and feels very smooth. Many would assert that it truly is smooth. But is it really? Look at it through a microscope and the red leather exterior will appear very rough, bumpy, or even jagged. And imagine how this same leather might feel if our hands were about one-tenth the size of an ant's – not smooth at all. The texture of the leather is clearly **relative** to one's perspective. And which of these perspectives is the *real* perspective? Russell contends that no perspective deserves that title. And solidity? How solid the chair seems will depend on your strength and weight. If you weighed 10,000 pounds, you certainly wouldn't regard the chair as solid. And, according to the atomic theory of matter, the atoms that constitute the chair account for only a tiny fraction of the space it occupies. Thus the chair is predominantly *empty* space – hardly the solid object that we perceive.

Shape is little help either. We know (or think we know) the shape of an object by what we see and feel. But what we see are colors, which we now realize are not *really* in the chair, and what we feel is its smoothness and solidity, yet these have turned out to be no more real than the color. So, again it comes down to perception. We seem to have absolutely no idea what the chair is like in itself – apart from our perceptions.[13] So consider once again the question of how you know that the chair exists. You thought you knew that it existed because of your various perceptions of it. But if we are right to regard these as appearances only, then you've lost your main reasons for thinking that the chair even exists at all!

Now I suppose you could maintain that there is still sufficient reason to think that there is a chair "out there," because even if it is not red or smooth or solid, it is *something* that is causing you to have these sensations. But Russell calls on you to notice that this "something" – whatever it is – is very different from the chair that we first contemplated. Should we even regard it as a *physical* thing? What does it mean to say that the "chair" exists, as something outside our perceptions, if you don't mean to imply that it has a *particular* size, shape, or color or texture? The fact of the matter is that all anyone ever has direct access to is their own perceptions. So we can never really be certain about what is causing those perceptions – or even if there is anything out there at all.

Ultimately, it seems that even when we set our worries about Matrix-type deceptions aside, the true nature of our world turns out to be a very slippery thing. Firm conclusions turn out to be rare, and doubts arise at every turn. But this should not be regarded as altogether bad. For, although philosophical reflection often undercuts our sense of certainty, it can also be very liberating. Once our common-sense assumptions have been revealed as illusions, we are freed from a kind of system of control. We inevitably find that the world is larger and more mysterious than we had thought, and our certainty is soon replaced with wonder and curiosity. While we may no longer "know" all the answers to life's questions, we can begin the quest to find out.

---

[13] If you think that you *know* that the chair is composed of atoms, think again. Any evidence for the existence of atoms ultimately depends on sense perceptions. And these, as we've seen, are always just appearances.

6

Adama's True Lie

Earth and the Problem of Knowledge

Eric J. Silverman

Summary

What is the nature of knowledge? This chapter examines the science fiction narrative of *Battlestar Galactica* to address puzzles and problems in epistemology. For example, knowledge has traditionally been defined as a true justified belief. However, this definition actually accepts accidentally true justified beliefs as knowledge. In *Battlestar Galactica* we see an excellent example of such a belief. Captain Adama claims he is searching for Earth, but does not even believe it exists. Anyone who believes in Earth's existence based on his testimony would have an accidentally true justified belief. Can such a belief be knowledge?

Battlestar Galactica begins with the ravaging of the known world. The survivors are demoralized, vastly outnumbered by the enemy, and homeless. Against this backdrop Commander Adama offers the promise of a new home where they'll be safe from the Cylons: Earth. But he *lies*. Yet, in a surprising twist of fate – though not to us who live here – it's later revealed that Adama told a "true lie." Earth does exist and the Colonials' search for it isn't in vain. Undertaking the journey to this "mythical" home of the Thirteenth Tribe is momentous and filled with religious significance for the Colonial survivors. *Faith* in Earth's existence gives meaning to an otherwise hopeless situation and shapes the choices they make along the way.

"You're Right. There's No Earth. It's All a Legend"

There's a sharp distinction between "true **belief**" and *knowledge*. President Roslin illustrates this when she asks, "How many people know the Cylons look human?" Colonel Tigh responds, "The rumor mill's been working overtime. Half the ship's talking about it." But Roslin retorts, "There'll always be rumors. For most people, that's all they'll ever be. I'm asking how many people actually know?" ("Water").

A belief based on an unverifiable rumor isn't knowledge, even if it happens to be true. Knowledge involves a belief in which one has reason for confidence.

A common view claims that knowledge is true belief accompanied by a convincing account justifying the belief. As Plato explains in the *Theaetetus*:

> Now when a man gets a true judgment about something without an account, his soul is in a state of truth as regards that thing, but he does not know it; for someone who cannot give and take an account of a thing is ignorant about it. But when he has also got an account of it, he is capable of all this and is made perfect in knowledge.[1]

According to Plato, it's possible to attain truth without knowledge. Knowledge is more certain than mere true belief since the knower possesses a *compelling justification* for the belief's truthfulness. Someone holding a true belief based on a rumor or a lucky guess doesn't have knowledge because she doesn't have a reason for confidence in the belief.

The contemporary philosopher Edmund Gettier demonstrates the inadequacy of this view of knowledge by providing **counterexamples** in which a person's justification for a true belief turns out to be false.[2] Say that Helo is walking down *Galactica*'s corridors and sees his wife, Athena. Helo calls out to her, "Sharon!" because he has a compelling justification for believing that's her name. So he believes:

(a) The woman in front of me is my wife, Athena.

If Helo's justified in believing (a), knows his wife's name, and understands basic rules of **reasoning**, then he's also justified in believing:

(b) The woman in front of me is named "Sharon."

The truthfulness of (a) **logically** entails the truthfulness of (b).

But let's suppose Helo's mistaken, for it's actually Boomer – who looks identical to Athena – who's in front of him. (Let's say that she has infiltrated *Galactica* for some nefarious purpose.) But Boomer is also named "Sharon." Helo's belief (b) turns out to be true, but his justification for believing (b), belief (a), is false. Gettier claims that a counterexample like this shows a justified true belief that isn't knowledge since its justification is false. And this has become known as "the Gettier problem."

Beliefs based on Adama's true lie about Earth are similar to Helo's true belief based on a false justification. Starbuck believes:

(c) Adama knows the location of Earth.

---

[1] Myles Burnyeat, *The Theaetetus of Plato*, trans. M. J. Levett (Indianapolis: Hackett, 1990), 202c.
[2] Edmund Gettier, "Is Justified True Belief Knowledge?" *Analysis* 23 (1963): 121–3.

This belief obviously implies:

(d) Earth exists.

It's arguable that Adama's public testimony that he knows the location of Earth, as well as his private assurances to Starbuck in "Kobol's Last Gleaming, Part 1," would be a proper justification for belief (c). It's reasonable to believe, as Adama claims, that he has access to privileged classified information as a "senior commander" in the Colonial Fleet. Hence, Starbuck is justified in believing that Earth exists based on his lie.

Even though Adama lies about knowing Earth's location and doesn't believe in its existence, it later becomes evident that Earth does exist. Starbuck discovers this for herself in the Tomb of Athena and after apparently journeying to Earth ("Home, Part 2"; "Crossroads, Part 2"). But Gettier would be quick to point out that, before these events, Starbuck holds a true belief (d) based on a false justification (c). Therefore, her true justified belief in Earth isn't really knowledge, until Adama's lie is no longer the primary justification for her belief.

"I'm Not a Cylon! . . . Maybe, But We Just Can't Take That Chance"

The Gettier problem is one of many puzzles in epistemology, the branch of philosophy concerned with the nature of knowledge. It's difficult to tell not only when one has knowledge, but also when one's beliefs are justified. The contemporary philosopher Alvin Goldman offers a theory of justification known as *reliabilism*, which proposes that a belief is justified when it's produced by a reliable process.[3] Sense experiences, memories, **deduction**, and **induction** are typical examples of generally reliable belief-forming processes. Each of these processes, however, has a different level of reliability. Induction, for example, is less reliable than deduction. And the reliability of a belief-forming process can vary based on one's situation. Sight is a reliable belief-forming process, yet beliefs based on sight are more reliable for close objects observed in well-lit conditions than for distant objects observed in poorly lit conditions.

One interesting aspect of reliabilism is that it doesn't require a person to know she's using a reliable process to be justified in her beliefs. If a young non-philosopher forms her beliefs based on the five senses, she's justified in those beliefs even if she never reflects upon the reliability of the senses. This has the desirable consequence of classifying many beliefs held by children, animals, and epistemically unreflective persons as justified.

---

[3] See Alvin Goldman, "What Is Justified Belief?" in *Justification and Knowledge*, ed. G. S. Pappas (Dordrecht: D. Reidel, 1976), 1–23.

In *BSG*, some typical belief-forming processes aren't as reliable as they are for us. *Sight* sometimes leads people to believe they're seeing a human being when they're actually seeing a Cylon. While people are usually correct when they believe they see a human, most would believe they see a human regardless of whether it's actually a Cylon. So sight isn't a reliable process for judging between humans and Cylons, even though it's a reliable process for forming other types of beliefs.[4]

Memory is another less dependable belief-forming process. Boomer can't remember that she sabotaged *Galactica*'s water tanks ("Water") and, until her Cylon nature is revealed to her, her memories thoroughly convince her that she's human, her parents are Katherine and Abraham Valerii, and her family died on Troy. Yet these beliefs couldn't be further from the truth. She doesn't give up these beliefs until confronted by numerous copies of herself aboard a Cylon baseship, and even then her initial reaction is disbelief ("Kobol's Last Gleaming, Part 2"). Similarly, Baltar wonders whether he might be a Cylon, and thus doubts whether he can trust his memories ("Torn"). Colonel Tigh, Sam Anders, Chief Tyrol, and Tory Foster are also deceived by their memories and are unaware of their actual Cylon nature ("Crossroads, Part 2"). The revelation, in particular, of Tigh and Anders' Cylon identity is truly shocking, as they're among the most adamantly anti-Cylon members of the fleet.

On the other hand, some unusual belief-forming processes are reliable in *BSG*, such as Baltar's visions of Number Six. While Six's advice is often cloaked in manipulative games and sarcasm, it frequently turns out to be a reliable way to form beliefs and accomplish desirable goals. Six draws Baltar's attention to a strange device on the Dradis console, and this leads him to "identify" Aaron Doral as a Cylon. But Baltar hasn't yet created his "mystic Cylon detector" and just makes up some techno-babble to convince Tigh that Doral's a Cylon so he can have an excuse to bring up the "odd device." It's disturbing when Tigh abandons Doral on Ragnar Station until it's revealed that Baltar was right all along ("Miniseries"). Six also encourages Baltar to test Boomer to see if she's a Cylon ("Flesh and Bone"); tells him to choose a target for the assault on a Cylon tylium refinery by *faith*, which turns out to be accurate ("The Hand of God"); helps him attain both the vice presidency and the presidency ("Colonial Day"; "Lay Down Your Burdens"); and reveals Hera's identity to him ("Exodus, Part 2").

Visions resulting from chamalla extract are also a reliable process for belief formation. Roslin's visions foresee her encounter with Leoben ("Flesh and Bone") and her leadership role in bringing the Colonials to Earth ("The Hand of God"). A chamalla-tripping oracle tells D'Anna/Three that she'll hold the Cylon-human hybrid Hera and experience love for the first time ("Exodus"); another oracle knows about Starbuck's upbringing and that Leoben – or at least a vision of him – will be coming for her ("Maelstrom").

Returning to epistemology, does reliabilism suggest that Adama's *testimony* is an appropriate justification for believing in Earth? Enlightenment era philosophers, such as David Hume (1711–76), are critical of justifications based on testimony for

---

[4] See Alvin Goldman, "Discrimination and Perceptual Knowledge," *Journal of Philosophy* 73 (1976), 771–9.

this kind of issue. Hume claims testimony is only as reliable as experience suggests, and there are true claims that would be difficult to justify based on testimony:

> The reason, why we place any credit in witnesses and historians, is not derived from any *connection*, which we perceive *a priori*, between testimony and reality, but because we are accustomed to find a conformity between them. But when the fact attested is such a one as has seldom fallen under our observation, here is a contest of two opposite experiences; of which the one destroys the other, as far as its force goes, and the superior can only operate on the mind by the force, which remains. The very same principle of experience, which gives us a certain degree of assurance in the testimony of witnesses, gives us also, in this case, another degree of assurance against the fact, which they endeavor to establish; from which contradiction there necessarily arises a counterpoise, and mutual destruction of belief and authority.[5]

Hume believes that the ultimate basis for belief in anything is our own sensory experiences. We should trust other people's testimony only because experience suggests that testimony is typically accurate. Yet, even in everyday situations, testimony falls considerably short of absolute **accuracy**. It's sometimes unreliable because people are dishonest, as when Felix Gaeta claims he saw Baltar voluntarily sign the execution order for over two hundred innocent Colonists ("Crossroads, Part 2"); or because people are simply incorrect in their testimony, as when Tyrol sincerely tells Tigh that he's not a Cylon ("Resistance").

When someone testifies to something completely outside of our own experiences, we should be skeptical. Hume claims that someone who has never seen water freeze because he's spent his entire life in a tropical climate should be slow to accept testimony that water freezes at a cold temperature. Adama's claim to know Earth's location is similar, since the Colonials have no personal experience of Earth. This claim has no continuity with their personal experiences, though it doesn't actually conflict with these experiences. Hume contends we should be even more skeptical when testimony is used to justify beliefs that contradict our everyday experiences.

The contemporary philosopher Alvin Plantinga claims that testimony plays a more foundational role in our beliefs than Hume, and his predecessor John Locke (1632–1704), acknowledge:

> The Enlightenment looked askance at testimony and tradition; Locke saw them as a preeminent source of error. The Enlightenment idea is that perhaps we start by learning from others – our parents, for example. Properly mature and independent adults, however, will have passed beyond all that and believe what they do on the basis of the evidence. But this is a mistake; you can't know so much as your name or what city you live in without relying on testimony. (Will you produce your birth certificate for the first, or consult a handy map for the second? In each case you are of course relying on testimony.)[6]

---

[5] David Hume, "Of Miracles," in *Dialogues Concerning Natural Religion*, ed. Richard H. Popkin (Indianapolis: Hackett, 1998), 110.

[6] Alvin Plantinga, *Warranted Christian Belief* (New York: Oxford University Press, 2000), 147.

Plantinga identifies a number of important beliefs that can be justified based only upon testimony. No one knows her name, age, or location without using testimony to justify such beliefs. The Enlightenment ideal of the radically independent thinker who weighs all claims against evidence from her own individual experiences is unrealistic and artificial. While testimony is far from infallible, it plays a more important epistemic role than Locke and Hume allow.

In either case, testimony-based justifications for believing in Earth need to be closely scrutinized. How trustworthy is the individual providing the testimony? How unlikely is his claim about Earth? Is the individual an appropriate authority concerning Earth? As the highest ranking military officer surviving the destruction of the Colonies and the author of their escape, Adama and his testimony seem naturally trustworthy. Starbuck certainly trusts Adama when she's confronted with the truth by Roslin:

> STARBUCK: The old man is our last chance to find Earth. He knows where it is. He said so. You were there. The location is a secret. But he is going to take us there.
> ROSLIN: Commander Adama has no idea where Earth is. He never did. He made it up in order to give people hope.
> STARBUCK: You're lying.
> ROSLIN: Go ask him.
> ("Kobol's Last Gleaming, Part 1")

When Starbuck does ask him, Adama tries to avoid her questions, but she's forced to conclude that Adama's patriotism and proficiency in fulfilling military duties don't make him an expert concerning Earth. As commander of a soon to be retired battlestar, Adama simply doesn't have access to Earth's location. The Gettier problem demonstrates that the Colonials' beliefs about Earth fall short of knowledge, and reliabilism suggests there's reason to doubt whether beliefs based on Adama's testimony are even justified.

"You Have to Have Something to Live For. Let it be Earth"

How should beliefs be chosen in an uncertain world? W. K. Clifford (1845–79) says it's unethical to believe anything without sufficient evidence. This view, known as *evidentialism*, claims that if there isn't enough evidence to support a belief, one mustn't consent to its truth. One premise supporting evidentialism is that incorrect beliefs can have a damaging effect on society:

> And no one man's belief is in any case a private matter which concerns himself alone. Our lives are guided by that general **conception** of the course of things which has been created by society for social purposes. Our words, our phrases, our forms and processes and modes of thought, are common property, fashioned and perfected from age to age; an heirloom which every succeeding generation inherits as a precious deposit

and a sacred trust to be handed on to the next one, not unchanged but enlarged and purified, with some clear marks of its proper handiwork.[7]

It's not merely mistaken, imprudent, or foolish to believe something without adequate evidence, it's outright *immoral*, a violation of our ethical duties to one another. If Roslin believes it's the will of the gods to lead the Colonials to Earth without sufficient evidence, this belief could have damaging effects on the entire fleet. Even if a less influential person like Starbuck believes in Earth without enough evidence, her beliefs don't only affect herself, but others as well who may be inclined to agree with her. Clifford offers this sweeping conclusion: "To sum it up: it is wrong always, everywhere, and for anyone, to believe anything upon insufficient evidence" (518).

Clifford, however, doesn't recognize that in some situations knowledge is elusive and reliable justification uncertain; yet, believing *nothing* is a deeply damaging option. William James (1842–1910) claims that when definitive knowledge is impossible on a *momentous* and *forced* issue, it's reasonable to choose beliefs based on their *practical* consequences. He considers marriage and religious faith as two such decisions. In both cases a choice must be made in less than certain circumstances. Yet, these choices are forced: to withhold belief is effectively a choice against it, and necessarily results in the loss of potential desirable consequences. Marriage and faith are also momentous in their potential for positive results. James illustrates the negative consequences experienced by the man who inadvertently falls into lifelong bachelorhood because he insists upon certainty before fully committing to a romantic relationship.

> It is as if a man should hesitate indefinitely to ask a certain woman to marry him because he was not perfectly sure that she would prove an angel after he brought her home. Would he not cut himself off from that particular angel-possibility as decisively as if he went and married some one else?[8]

If there are desirable results from a specific committed relationship, they're inevitably lost if the relationship isn't embraced. It may be impossible for Apollo to know whether Anastasia Dualla would be a good wife; but the benefits offered by a committed relationship with her can't be gained without commitment. The choice can't be avoided, for avoiding it is an effective choice against the relationship. Lifelong bachelorhood isn't irrational or unjustifiable; but it's guaranteed to prevent Apollo from the benefits unique to a committed relationship with Dualla.

Or consider Apollo's unwillingness to see the conflict brewing between the fleet's military and civilian leadership. When his father chastises him for "siding" with Roslin, Apollo retorts, "I didn't know we were picking sides." Adama muses, "That's why you haven't picked one yet." Later, Apollo does choose his side – that of *democracy* ("Bastille Day"; "Kobol's Last Gleaming, Part 2"). Due to Apollo's important position in the fleet and his personal relationships with both Adama and

---

[7]   W. K. Clifford, "The Ethics of Belief," in *The Theory of Knowledge*, ed. Louis P. Pojman (Belmont, CA: Wadsworth/Thompson, 2003), 516–17. Further references will be given in the text.

[8]   William James, "The Will to Believe," in *The Theory of Knowledge*, ed. Louis P. Pojman (Belmont, CA: Wadsworth/Thompson, 2003), 524. Further references will be given in the text.

Roslin, it's inevitable that he's forced to choose between the military and civilian factions. When given orders to arrest Roslin, he has no choice but to choose a side. His choice was also momentous. By siding with Roslin, he stands up for democracy at the cost of his own freedom.

James views religious faith as a similarly momentous decision. He claims no **argument** proves the truthfulness of religious faith with certainty. Even so, at some point a decision must be made. The choice is forced. To put off the choice indefinitely is effectively to reject religion. Furthermore, the question of religion is momentously important. Many religious thinkers claim it offers a life filled with greater meaning and purpose, along with eternal happiness after death. Agnosticism cuts one off from any good attainable by embracing religion. Gaining the benefits of religious faith, for this life or the afterlife, may require a choice here and now (524). An agnostic has no chance for the benefits of religion, just as the lifelong bachelor has no chance for the goods of marriage (520). Similarly, the agnostic cuts himself off from any advantages from atheism. If religion is false and all genuine goods are located in the here and now, then withholding consent from atheism is also a damaging choice. It's wiser to embrace atheism rather than agnosticism, since it frees one to pursue the goods of life wholeheartedly.

Faith that Earth awaits at the end of the Colonial fleet's journey mirrors James's other momentous and forced choices. When comfortable life was possible on the Twelve Colonies, the question of Earth's existence was an abstract issue with little consequence stemming from belief or unbelief. The issue was neither momentous nor forced. But once the Colonies were destroyed, the issue became momentous: either there's a home where the survivors will be welcomed as brothers and sisters, or they're homeless and alone. The choice also becomes forced. Agnosticism concerning Earth is no longer a practical option. They can embrace the search for Earth or reject the hope of Earth by settling on the first safely habitable planet they encounter, but to do neither is ridiculous.

The importance of this issue is seen when the Colonials elect Baltar to the presidency based on his promise to settle on New Caprica and cease the search for Earth ("Lay Down Your Burdens, Part 2"). By abandoning the search, the Colonials cut themselves off from hope for a better life than what they can make for themselves on this less-than-inviting world. Yet, either choice is better than no choice. Most of the Colonials don't have access to compelling evidence that Earth exists. It's reasonable for them to believe that rebuilding civilization on New Caprica is their only hope for a permanent home. By settling on New Caprica, they have the opportunity for some benefits: breathing fresh air and growing food instead of living in tin boxes and eating rations. Clifford's advice would allow them neither option. There isn't enough evidence to support the belief in and search for Earth, but there's also insufficient evidence that settling on New Caprica is the wisest option. If they continually wander without settling on a planet, and cease pursuing Earth, they cut themselves off from the benefits of both.

Even apart from any potential benefits of a successful search for Earth, there are benefits gained simply from possessing an overarching life-quest. Adama's lie isn't motivated by a desire to find Earth, but by a more subtle rationale. He understands that humans need purpose, especially in difficult circumstances. Without purpose, we wither, give up hope, and die. He lies because he wants the survivors to hope and avoid despair in the hardest of times.

Some philosophers advocate skepticism since virtually every belief can be questioned based on an argument for the conflicting view. But James shows us that a truly skeptical approach to life can be detrimental since it requires rejecting potentially rewarding opportunities. And a truly skeptical life is perhaps impossible since so many decisions are unavoidably forced. Whether to embrace life and meaning amidst uncertainty is a forced and momentous decision. Blind leaps of faith are dangerous and cynical **skepticism** concerning everything is unrewarding. The confidence of *certainty* evades many of us, but choices must be made. Avoiding the central choices of life in an attempt to risk nothing, hope for nothing, love nothing, and believe in nothing beyond the indubitable is both impractical and impossible. So say we all.[9]

[9]   Thanks to Jason Eberl, John Greco, and Rob Arp for their comments on earlier versions of this chapter.

Part III

Metaphysics

Introduction

Metaphysics is the study of the nature of reality. The most interesting contemporary questions about reality focus on our understanding of ourselves. We each believe that we have a mind, but what exactly is a mind, and how is it related to the brain? We each believe ourselves to be a person, but what exactly is a person and how is it that we are the same person over time? Do we really have free will? What about artificial intelligence? Could computers, one day soon, be conscious persons with the same rights as humans?

The Matrix is a virtual reality, created by computers stimulating the brains of humans. Not surprisingly then, the nature of the mind is a central issue in *The Matrix* trilogy. In his chapter, Matt Lawrence uses examples from *The Matrix* to define the major theories of the mind: dualism, reductive materialism, eliminative materialism, emergentism, and functionalism. Lawrence shows why dualism has fallen out of favor, and why the debate is now primarily between the materialist theories. As it turns out, despite some tricky cases, the events of *The Matrix* trilogy can be interpreted completely in a materialist light.

Imagine yourself at age 10, and think how different you were. You look different now and you may have a different personality, yet you are the same person. How can that be? In his chapter, Jason Southworth uses the world of *X-Men* to address this classic philosophical issue of identity through time. The character Wolverine provides us with a perfect opportunity to examine John Locke's (1632–1704) memory criterion for personal identity, because Wolverine has lost and regained memories multiple times. In addition, the character Jamie Madrox – who can copy and recombine himself – exemplifies Derek Parfit's view that physical continuity plays a role in maintaining personal identity.

Many people believe in fate, and in the *Harry Potter* stories fatalistic prophecies are abundant. In his chapter, Jeremy Pierce considers the nature of prophecies and their relation to free will. Is Harry, for example, really destined to defeat Voldemort? Is he free to do otherwise? Was it even possible for him to fail? J. K. Rowling, the author of the books, professes not to believe in destiny because she believes in free will – yet it would seem that some higher power guides the events of her books in order for some prophecies to come true. So what kind of freedom does Rowling believe in – compatiblism or libertarianism? And does modern science fit with her belief in freedom?

In the *Terminator* movies, artificially intelligent machines rise up to eliminate humanity – or, at least they keep trying. Would the elimination of humans mean the elimination of all persons? Or could it be that artificially intelligent machines are persons too since they clearly understand language and have conscious experiences? In his chapter, Greg Littman uses a *Terminator* version of the Turing Test to explore these questions. Could passing such a test show that a terminator understands language or is conscious? If so, perhaps the elimination of the human race would not mean the end of persons.

7

Mind and Body in Zion

Matt Lawrence

Summary

In *The Matrix Trilogy*, human brains are sent electrical signals to create whatever experiences their machine captors wish their minds to have. This raises an important question about the nature of the mind: Is the mind something separable from the brain, or something that is dependent upon it? Using *The Matrix*, this chapter explains the difference between dualism and materialism, and shows why dualism has fallen out of favor. The chapter also articulates the differences between the major materialist theories: reductive materialism, eliminative materialism, emergentism, and functionalism.

If what you are talking about is your senses, what you feel, taste, smell, or see, then all you're talking about are electrical signals interpreted by your brain.
    – Morpheus, *The Matrix*

The Matrix Scenario

The central metaphysical premise of the *Matrix* trilogy is that an entire "virtual world" can be created for an individual by electronically stimulating their brain. For the human victims of the Matrix, everything they see, hear, smell, taste, or touch is created in this manner, as are their feelings of pain and pleasure, of hunger, thirst, and satiation. Lucky for them, the deception turns out to be limited to their *sensory perceptions*, that is, to experiences that would otherwise be caused by the interaction of a person's senses and central nervous system with the physical world, and not to their reactions to those perceptions. People's emotions, memories, decisions, and judgments appear to be free from Matrix control. But it seems reasonable to suppose that this limit reflects only the current state of the machines' technology, or perhaps just a choice by the Architect. There doesn't seem to be any reason to suppose it is a *metaphysical necessity*. For if the electrical stimulation of your brain can cause you to feel hungry, then why not also anxious, or happy? And if your brain can be manipulated to make you "see" an Agent, then we might suppose that it could also be stimulated in such a way as to cause you to imagine or remember one. At least in theory, it seems that *any* human experience could be produced by the electronic stimulation of the brain.

The "Matrix scenario" seems to suggest, on the face of it at least, a **materialist** view of the mind. If all of our conscious experiences or mental states can be produced by brain manipulation, then this provides some rather strong evidence for thinking that mental states *just are* causal states of material brains. Complicating this picture, however, is the fact that in *Revolutions* Neo wakes up in the Train Station program even though his body is not jacked in. It appears, at least, that his mind has separated from his body. This turn of events suggests that perhaps (in the films) the mind is in some sense independent of the brain.

Does this add up? Is there any way to make sense of both the general Matrix scenario and Neo's apparent mind–body separation? In the sections that follow we'll examine several theories of mind in order to determine how to make the most sense of these events.

Mystery and Miracles

The power of The One extends beyond this world.
                                   – The Oracle, *The Matrix: Reloaded*

Although any sort of appeal to mystery and/or miracles cannot be described as a theory of the mind, we should begin by noting that the films intentionally leave many aspects of "The One" a complete mystery. Neo, as the Savior of humanity, performs a variety of "miracles."[1] He heals the sick, removing a bullet from Trinity's chest; he stops bullets in mid-air; he flies like Superman; he destroys sentinels just by thinking it; and he sees through blind eyes. While his "miracles" within the Matrix seem to readily succumb to scientific explanation – he's just mentally hacking a computer program that is connected to the electrical signals of his brain – the films really give us no adequate explanation of the apparent miracles that occur outside the Matrix. How does he destroy sentinels with his mind? How does he separate his mind from his body? Almost all we have to go on here is the Oracle's cryptic explanation – if we can call it an explanation at all. She tells Neo:

> The power of The One extends beyond this world – it reaches from here all the way back to where it came from. . . . The Source. That's what you felt when you touched those sentinels, but you weren't ready for it. You should be dead . . . but apparently you weren't ready for that either.

---

[1] Of course there are intentional parallels here with Jesus, which adds support to the transcendental or "miracle" hypothesis.

Obviously the Wachowskis were content to leave this aspect of the films shrouded in mystery. We might take it as an appeal to the transcendental or supernatural – to forces beyond this world that we can never explain. But to the philosophical mind, the thought that we must simply chock these events up to "the mysterious power of The One" is unsatisfying. Enquiring minds want to know *how* and *why* these things occurred. And while the answers to these questions may not even exist, we can always speculate.

Mind–Body Dualism

How did I separate my mind from my body?

– Neo, *The Matrix: Revolutions*

A theory of the mind–body relation that can readily explain Neo's disembodiment at the Train Station is called mind–body **dualism**. René Descartes championed this view. He maintained that human beings are composed of two distinct substances, one immaterial (the mind, spirit, or soul),[2] and the other material (brains or bodies). Much of his **reasoning** behind this conclusion stems from the fact that mind and body seem to have altogether different properties. Material substances can be characterized in terms of their specific size, shape, and location. But immaterial substances (minds) cannot. Take for instance Morpheus's *hope* that Neo is The One. How big is his hope? Is it larger than a sentinel, but smaller than the Nebuchadnezzar? And what shape is it? Of course we cannot say. Instead, our states of mind must be described in a very different way, in terms of thought, emotion, will, etc. While our minds can be located in time – you're thinking and experiencing at precisely this moment – they cannot be located in space. They have no size, shape, color, nor any "extended" property whatever.

According to mind–body dualism, the mind and body are ultimately distinct substances, and therefore they should be capable of existing on their own. Physical objects existing apart from minds are all around us (e.g., this book), and similarly, Descartes argued that there is no reason to suppose that minds or souls cannot exist without bodies. Thus the dualist would have no problem supposing that Neo's mind really did get separated from his body. While such a thing is unusual (except, perhaps, at death), it poses no special theoretical problems insofar as we accept the dualist view.

But dualism faces some rather serious theoretical difficulties. For instance, if the mind is wholly immaterial, how can it interact with the body? How can something without size or weight (such as a **belief**, desire, or volition) cause something big and heavy (like your arm) to move? Descartes's solution was to suggest a

---

[2] Following Descartes, I use the terms mind, self, and soul interchangeably to refer to the private, subjective, and seemingly immaterial aspects of a person. While many people distinguish mind, spirit, and soul, the distinction is often rather vaguely defined. For some the mind connotes the more rational aspects of the self while the spirit or soul is used to depict the emotional or "deeper" aspects of the personality. However, when Descartes uses the term "mind" he means to include all aspects of a person's mental life, including reason, emotion, perception, will, and dispositions of character.

physical point of connection, not altogether unlike the plug on the back of Neo's head. He maintained that the connection most likely occurs in the *pineal gland*, which is a tiny structure located at the base of the brain, the purpose of which had eluded the physiologists of his day.[3] The problem, of course, is that while we can see how the pineal gland hooks up to the brain, we cannot observe or even comprehend how an immortal soul gets *hooked up* to the pineal gland. Thus we are left with essentially the same problem we started with. The "pineal gland solution" just gives the problem a more specific location.

Another problem is the lack of **empirical evidence** for mind–body dualism. Descartes only showed that the existence of minds without bodies was a *logical possibility* (the idea itself is not self-contradictory). But this does not entail that it is *true* or *physically possible*. As the eighteenth-century philosopher David Hume famously noted, it is logically possible that the sun will not rise tomorrow.[4] But on this basis alone it would be silly to start preparing for a Dark Age. Reasonable beliefs require more than just logical possibility – they require positive evidence. And this is where mind–body dualism falls short.

Mind–Body Materialism

Look past the flesh. Look through the soft gelatin of these dull cow eyes.
                              – Smith/Bane, *The Matrix: Revolutions*

Almost everything that science has taught us about the mind, including the possibility of Matrix-type deceptions, favors a materialist (nondualist) understanding of the mind–body relationship. Some of the evidence can be pretty technical, and has been discovered fairly recently with the help of modern technologies such as the CAT scan and the mapping of the human genome. But much of the best evidence for materialism involves things we have known since antiquity. For example, certain psychotropic drugs cause the user to see and hear things that are not "really" there – much like jacking into the Matrix. And we now know that this occurs (as in the Matrix) through the physical stimulation of particular regions of the brain. Or, there is the fact that when you hit a person on the head really hard, they fall unconscious, thereby losing their *supposedly immaterial* mental states completely. Or consider the way in which aging often affects one's "immaterial self." Old age is often accompanied by memory loss and the lack of mental quickness and clarity. There have always been fairly good reasons to suppose that this was due to the

---

[3]   The pineal gland produces melatonin, and is believed to play a role in sleep and aging. Dysfunction within the pineal gland may also be linked to seasonal affective disorder.

[4]   Ghost refers to this aspect of Hume's philosophy in the opening scene of the *Enter the Matrix* video game. When Niobe ribs him for checking to see if his virtual weapons are loaded (the program *always* automatically loads them), he tells her: "Hume teaches us that no matter how many times you drop a stone and it falls to the floor, it might fall to the floor, but then again, it might float to the ceiling. Past experience can never prove the future." This is called *the problem of induction*. For more, see sections II and IV of David Hume's *An Enquiry Concerning Human Understanding*.

deterioration of the body, but current research into diseases such as Alzheimer's has shown us specifically how this is related to the withering and death of nerve cells within the brain's cerebral cortex.

The problem with applying mind–body materialism to the films comes in at the end of *Reloaded* when Neo's miraculous powers begin to take effect outside of the Matrix. If Neo's mental states are essentially just states of his brain, then how can he destroy sentinels with his mind? And how can his mind be inside the Train Station program if his body is not jacked in? To give a completely material explanation for these events will involve stretching our imaginations beyond the parameters of the information provided in the films, but such an account is not altogether impossible.

Destroying the sentinels

One way to give a nonmiraculous explanation of Neo's destruction of the sentinels involves Neo's (apparent) destruction of Agent Smith at the end of the first film. Not only do we find out in *Reloaded* that Smith did not die, it also turns out that he and Neo now have some kind of connection. As Smith explains it, aspects of each person/program may have been copied or overwritten onto the other. In order to understand this, we must realize that Neo is not "simply human." Like all pod-born children of the Matrix, Neo has more than just a plug in the back of his head. Inside his skull he must also have Matrix-interface hardware and software, which sends the Matrix program into the neural networks of his brain, and sends his neural activity back out to the Matrix program. Thus, just as Smith came out of the copying process with a new power – the ability to clone himself onto others – Neo may have also come away from the exchange with a new power – the ability to control certain machines. This power would not be "supernatural," but a matter of programming. Neo's now-modified software may simply be capable of transmitting a self-destruct command to the approaching sentinels.

Neo's jackless entry

Support for a materialist explanation of Neo's jackless entry into the Train Station program can be found in the fact that his brain waves indicate that his brain was doing precisely what it would if he were jacked in, *and* by the fact that the crew is eventually able to jack him back out by connecting his body to the system and hacking a connection. One possibility – and again this is only conjecture – also involves the Matrix hardware inside Neo's skull. We often hear Morpheus speak of going to "broadcast depth" whenever he plans to jack the crew into the Matrix. This suggests that the Matrix may be transmitted over the airwaves – much like an enormous television broadcast. People jack in (much like cable TVs), but the signal itself is broadcast – perhaps by satellite – and the humans may hack their way into that broadcast using transmitters on their hovercraft. In this case, we might suppose that Neo is somehow "broadcasting" from a transmitter inside his skull.

While this is somewhat of a stretch (as is the very idea of jackless entry), it seems more plausible when we realize that Neo's hardware and software is probably quite unique. This is in part due to his exchange with Smith, but it may also be attributable to the Architect. Recall that during their meeting at the Source, the Architect told Neo that he carries a code within him that reinserts the "prime program" which, as we see at the end of *Revolutions*, essentially reboots the system. We can imagine that as "The One," Neo is the only person carrying this code, and that this is due in part to the Architect's own design. As the Architect also mentioned, Neo's five predecessors "were, by *design*, based on a similar predication," indicating that they have all been manipulated in one way or another. Thus we might even wonder if the Architect had implanted a transmitter inside Neo's skull early on as a kind of failsafe measure. He may have activated it, and *sent* Neo to the "limbo" of Mobil Ave in order to detain him while Zion is destroyed.

Neo's embedded technology could also explain the fact that, in *Revolutions*, he can still see even though his eyes have been burnt shut by Smith/Bane. Notice that at this point Neo sees Smith (i.e., Smith's programming) rather than the physical body of Bane. Similarly when he and Trinity arrive at the machine city, he cannot see Trinity, but he sees the "light" of the machine world. This suggests that Neo is not really seeing in terms of optics. Rather, he may be receiving electronic signals from the entities of the machine city, which are then being converted to visual images as the Matrix hardware electronically stimulates his brain in much the same way that his eyes would normally. These signals may have always been coming in, but were "overridden" by his human optic nerves. Perhaps he now "sees" in much the same way that the machines do.

So the story of the Matrix can be understood within a completely materialist view of the mind. And these days most scientists and philosophers think that materialism is the only viable theory. For them the question is not *whether* materialism is true, but *which* materialist theory is true. In the sections that follow we'll examine two of the most controversial issues within materialist theories of mind. The first pertains to whether or not specific mental states can be effectively reduced to specific states of the brain, and the second pertains to the specific role of the biological matter of the brain.

Mental States: Reduction or Elimination?

How do the machines really know what Tastee Wheat tasted like?
                                                    – Mouse, *The Matrix*

Reductive materialism

All materialist theories of the mind agree that a person's mental state (whatever a person is experiencing at a particular moment) is intimately tied to their brain state at that moment. But how exactly this relationship should be described has been a matter of dispute. Reductive materialism (also called **identity theory**) maintains that mental states *just are* physical states of the brain. Therefore, every particular mental state ultimately reduces to, or matches, a physical state of the brain – generally a particular pattern of neurons firing. This sort of view lends some credence to Morpheus's claim that "The body cannot live without the mind." For on this view the mind and brain are essentially the same thing. To be "mind-dead" is identical to being "brain-dead" and vice versa.[5]

According to reductive materialism it is (theoretically) possible to achieve a complete *intertheoretic reduction* between mental states and brain states. An inter-theoretic reduction occurs when the entities of one theory can be reduced to entities of another new and better theory. This sort of thing occurs in science all the time. For example, modern science tells us that "sound" *just is* a train of com-pression waves. Thus every particular sound that occurs in the world corresponds to a particular wave pattern. In music, for instance, we find that the lower the tone that a note has, the longer its wavelength, and the higher the tone, the shorter its wavelength. Reductionism says that we should expect to find a similar kind of correspondence between the entities of a very old theory, "**folk psychology**," and a relatively new theory, modern neuroscience.

Folk psychology has been around for thousands of years. It maintains that the causes of human behavior are psychological states, i.e., particular beliefs, desires, and emotions. Neuroscience, on the other hand, takes the cause of human behavior to be the firing of neural networks in our brains. These neural networks send signals through the nervous system and throughout the body. If an intertheoretic reduction from the one theory to the other is possible, then, as our understanding of the brain's functioning improves, we should be able to match up particular beliefs, desires, emotions, and perceptions with specific patterns of brain activity in a perfect one-to-one correspondence. Thus the experience of enjoying a bowl of Tastee Wheat would turn out to be identical with a more scientific description, such as having a "Q127 neural firing pattern in the Gamma 8.2 quadrant or your brain."[6]

This view of the mind seems to fit nicely with the Matrix scenario. It suggests that a well-developed neuroscience could ultimately tell us how to produce any mental state we want (e.g., the *desire* for a bowl of Tastee Wheat, and the *taste* of it on your tongue; the *belief* that you are wearing a leather jacket, and the *feel* of it against your skin; as well as the *sight* of a red pill, and *anxiety* about its possible effects), just by stimulating a person's brain in the appropriate way.

---

[5] However, it does seem rather implausible that the "virtual experience" of being shot would cause a person to become mind-dead/brain-dead. Obviously the films need this aspect in order to generate dramatic tension in the fight scenes within the Matrix, so we should just buy into it and enjoy the ride. However, if you really need a scientific explanation for this aspect of the film, that too is possible with the right hardware. For instance, the programming of the Matrix may cause one's brain to shut down, in much the same way that it causes the brain to "see" an Agent or "feel" a bullet wound.

[6] This is a statement of science fiction neurology. It is not a real scientific description that is in use today.

Eliminative materialism

Eliminative materialism delivers some rather strong criticisms to identity theory. It maintains that we will never get a one-to-one match-up between folk psychological states and neurological states, because folk psychological states (beliefs, desires, hopes, fears, etc.) don't *really* exist at all.

Most people think that this proposition is absolutely nuts; but if you consider it carefully, it is not as crazy as it seems. One of the most influential proponents of eliminative materialism is UC San Diego philosopher Paul Churchland.[7] The striking feature of his view is that he does not believe in "beliefs." (Notice that I didn't say that he *believes* that there are no beliefs – that would be a contradiction.) We have to be careful here. Eliminative materialists are *not* saying that there are no "inner experiences" at all. Certainly you are conscious and are having some kind of experience at this moment. They also admit that your experience has a particular *content* and *feel* to it, that only you have access to. What they deny is that our folk psychological descriptions of these "inner experiences" (e.g., "Neo *wants* to know what the Matrix is," "Trinity is *in love* with Neo," or "Morpheus *believes* that Neo is The One") adequately refer to real states of the world. According to eliminative materialism, these entities of folk psychology are false – or at least radically misleading.

The reasoning behind this conclusion can be illustrated by imagining Neo's folk psychological state when he first met Morpheus, and was sitting there in that big red chair, "wanting to know what the Matrix is." Recall your own mental state when you were watching the film for the first time, and were also "wanting to know what the Matrix is." Were you, at that moment, in the *same* mental state as Neo? (Let's pretend here that Neo is a real person rather than a character in a film.) I sincerely doubt that you were. While neither of you knew what the Matrix was, you had very different ideas about it that *shaped* your desires in particular ways, ultimately making them very different. Or, try thinking of Zion right now. Were you thinking what I was thinking? Again, I doubt it. Sure, your experience was probably much more similar to mine than that of someone who is thinking about Middle Earth, or Chicago, but it was probably also very different. I was imagining the many bridges that crossed through the center of the city – were you? And even if you were, I doubt that what you envisioned was very similar to what I envisioned in terms of perspective, number of bridges, the colors, etc. Do you see the problem? If "thinking of Zion" is not some single thing, then it is highly suspect that we should ever get a one-to-one correspondence between "thinking of Zion" and a particular brain state.

And when entities of an old theory cannot be reduced to the new and better theory, Churchland argues that they must be eliminated from scientific discourse, i.e., they must return to the Source for deletion. Consider *caloric*, for example. Churchland points out that people used to believe that caloric, a hypothetical fluid-like substance, was responsible for heat. When a pan sits over the fire, it was believed

---

[7] See Paul Churchland, *Matter and Consciousness* (Boston: MIT Press, 1984).

that it became hot because this "subtle substance" escaped from the fire and was absorbed by the pan. Since our new and improved theories now tell us that heat *is* molecular motion (kinetic energy), the theory of caloric has been dismissed as simply false. We say that caloric never *really* existed. Eliminative materialists think that beliefs, desires, and emotions are headed down the same road. We may continue to talk about them as if they were real in our everyday lives, but our scientific theories should abandon them completely.

At first view it seems that eliminative materialism would render a Matrix-type deception impossible. For, what the deceiving party wants to do (or so it seems) is to create in the deceived person certain false *beliefs* – to cause them to believe that they are experiencing the "real world" when they are not, to believe that they are going to work, paying their taxes, and so on, when they are really just human batteries, fast asleep in endless stacks of slime-filled cocoons. And how do you generate these false beliefs if *beliefs* don't exist at all? This problem, if it were a problem, would do more than just derail Matrix-type methods of mind control. For eliminative materialists like Churchland also seem to be out to "change our beliefs" – just through less coercive means. And doesn't he have to believe in his own theory? On the face of it, eliminative materialism seems to contradict itself.

The way that Churchland responds to this type of objection is by arguing that it *begs the question*. That is, the objection merely assumes that the eliminative materialist *believes* the theory and is out to change our beliefs. But this is the very point under contention. Churchland, of course, denies that (scientifically speaking) he "believes" the theory, or that he "wants" to change your "beliefs" – if by this we mean that certain folk psychological states are the real causes of his actions. So why, then, did he write his book *Matter and Consciousness*? He can consistently maintain that he did it for the same reason that anyone does anything – because the particular firings of the neural networks in his brain caused him to do it. It is neural firings in our brains that always cause our bodies to move, whether they are writing books, debating theories, or piloting hovercraft. And similarly it is neural firings in our brains that would cause us to react to Agents, Oracles, and speeding bullets when "plugged in" to the Matrix.

Ultimately, eliminative materialism answers Mouse's question, "How do the machines know what Tastee Wheat tastes like?" In short, they don't – if what Mouse means is "How do they know what *my* sensations feel like *to me*?" But when you really think about it, no one knows what Tastee Wheat, or any other food, tastes like *to you*. Your sensations – your inner experiences of flavor – are private. So, how then do the machines know if their deception has been successful? The same way that *we* know if our efforts (deceptive or otherwise) to convince others have been successful – by looking at people's behavior. For instance, a magician knows that her illusion has been successful largely by watching the reactions of the crowd – not by getting inside their minds and *feeling* their reactions first hand. Similarly, the machines know they've successfully manipulated a person's mind when the person reacts in the way that the machines expect them to act. In other words, they've succeeded in deceiving Mouse into thinking that there is a bowl of Tastee Wheat in front of him precisely when his digital self reacts *as if* it were a bowl of Tastee Wheat. So it seems that eliminative materialism could work just fine within the Matrix scenario. A one-to-one correspondence between the mental states of folk psychology and the brain states of neuroscience would be completely unnecessary to implement a Matrix-type deception.

The Role of Matter: Biology or Function?

I admit it is difficult to even think encased in this rotting piece of meat.
                                            – Smith/Bane, *The Matrix: Revolutions*

The emergent property view

If brains cause conscious experience, then the big question is *how* do they do it? This has led to a major philosophical dispute over the significance of the particular biology of the brain. As some see it, consciousness is an *emergent property* of the dynamic processes within the specific biochemistry of the brain.

The **concept** of an emergent property is fairly common in scientific explanations. For example, UC Berkeley philosopher John Searle suggests that the relationship between minds and brains may be analogous to the micro- and macro-properties of everyday objects. At the macro-level (the level of our normal sense experience) water is wet, it's clear, and it has a specific temperature. But the very same water when examined at the micro-level turns out to be made of molecules consisting of hydrogen and oxygen – H_2O. We cannot grab an H_2O molecule and declare that it is wet, or clear, or 53 degrees. Instead these properties *emerge* when millions of these molecules are experienced at the macro-level. Following this model we can say that it is the molecular structure of H_2O that *causes* the features that we associate with water, but also water *just is* H_2O. Similarly, the particular firing patterns of neural networks *cause* consciousness experience; but in an important sense, conscious experience *just is* the brain's neural networks firing away.

On Searle's view, the biochemistry of the brain is crucial to the emergence of consciousness, just as the chemistry of water is crucial to the emergence of wetness. You can create tiny models of water molecules out of plastic and put them all in a bathtub, but that does not entail that they will wet your sponge. Similarly, Searle contends, modeling the processes of the brain won't create conscious experience.

> Consider, for instance, the way in which our bodies create the experience of thirst: Kidney secretions of rennin synthesize a substance called angiotensin. This substance goes into the hypothalamus and triggers a series of neuron firings. As far as we know these neuron firings are a very large part of the cause of thirst.[8]

---

[8]   John Searle, "The Myth of the Computer," reprinted in *Twenty Questions: An Introduction to Philosophy*, eds. G. Lee Bowie, Meredith W. Michaels, and Robert C. Solomon (Belmont, CA: Thomson-Wadsworth Learning, 2004).

While a model of this process would be much more complex than a model of an H_2O molecule, it is certainly possible to create one using a wide range of materials. Searle suggests the following:

> So let us imagine our thirst-simulating program running on a computer made entirely of old beer cans, millions (or billions) of old beer cans that are rigged up to levers and powered by windmills. We can imagine that the program simulates the neuron firings at the synapses by having beer cans bang into each other, thus achieving a strict correspondence between neuron firings and beer-can bangings. At the end of the sequence a bear can pops up on which it is written "I am thirsty." Now, does anyone suppose that this . . . apparatus is literally thirsty in the sense in which you or I are?[9]

Searle thinks that it is completely obvious that such an apparatus has no conscious experience at all. Any adequate analysis of the mind, he argues, cannot discount the importance of the biochemistry of the brain any more than an adequate understanding of digestion can ignore the biochemistry of stomachs.

Functionalism

In direct opposition to Searle's biological view of the mind is functionalism. On this view conscious experience and our various mental states (whether or not the concepts of folk psychology adequately describes them) can exist within any sufficiently organized material system. Mental states are not the emergent effects of specifically biological processes, but instead they are simply "functional states" of extremely complex systems. This is to say that anything that has the appropriate input–process–output relationships can have mental states.

To a certain extent, at least, this seems right. Most of us have imagined extraterrestrials that may be constructed very differently from us – perhaps without anything like a brain – but who nevertheless have mental lives. As philosopher David Lewis puts it:

> [T]here might be a Martian who sometimes feels pain just as we do, but whose pain differs greatly from ours in its physical realization. . . . When you pinch his skin you cause no firing of C-fiber – he has none – but, rather, you cause the inflation of many smallish cavities in his feet. When these cavities are inflated he is in pain. And the effects of his pain are fitting: his thought and activity are disrupted, he groans and writhes, he is strongly motivated to stop you from pinching him and to see that you never do it again.[10]

---

[9] Ibid.

[10] David Lewis, "Mad Pain and Martian Pain," in *Readings in Philosophy of Psychology*, ed. Ned Block (Cambridge, MA: Harvard University Press, 1980). For Lewis, the issue of pain is more complicated than merely input–process–output relations, as he argues in his case of "mad pain."

Lewis contends that while the Martian may not be in pain in quite the same sense that we humans are, there had better be some straightforward sense in which we are both in pain. There doesn't seem to be any particular reason for thinking that mental states can only occur in brains – that is merely how they occur *for us.*

Functionalism considers "Martian pain" to be completely unproblematic. So long as the Martian has the right input–process–output relationships, as he does – the *input* (physical harm/the pinching of his skin) leads to a physical *process* (the inflation of the cavities in his feet), which in turn causes the appropriate *output* (groaning, writhing, and the demand for you to stop) – he must be in pain. According to the functionalist view, the particular hardware that this functional relationship occurs in (or through) is really beside the point. It may be possible to achieve "pain," "thirst," or even "the belief that Agents are coming" through virtually any physical system – even Searle's wind-powered beer cans – so long as the hardware and programming/processing are sufficiently complex to achieve the appropriate input–output relationships.

For most people, the jump from sore or thirsty *living* Martians to arrangements of sore or thirsty *lifeless* beer cans seems like quite a leap of faith. But this is essentially the view of functionalists, who maintain that artificial intelligence (thinking, feeling, understanding machines) is possible. Functionalists generally argue that the mind is to the brain as a computer program is to computer hardware. On this view, your particular personality, your experiences, decisions, etc., are just the *output* of the *program* your brain is running. If we can duplicate this process in a machine, we shall have machines that are, for all intents and purposes, just like us.

Functionalism seems to be the dominant theory of mind at work in the *Matrix* films. The very idea of sentient machines depends upon the functionalist hypothesis. If, for instance, we were to apply a biology-based emergent property view to the films, then we should have to say that the machines and programs of the Matrix don't *really* experience anything at all. For they too are nonliving arrangements of hardware and software – not essentially any different in kind from Searle's beer cans – just a more space-efficient design. While they go through the motions, and *act* like human beings, Searle would contend that they lack conscious experience altogether. But if biology were essential to consciousness, then we should expect Agent Smith to undergo quite a transformation when he makes the switch into Bane's body. It would be as if the light of consciousness had suddenly been switched on. He should be amazed to experience consciousness for the first time in his life. Smith would finally know what it's like to really *want* to kill Neo, or to *feel* the floor beneath his feet. We can imagine that the psychological impact of it all would have been overwhelming. But, of course, this is not how the story goes. Smith's transition into Bane's body happens rather seamlessly

– just like copying a program from one computer to another, or converting a file from PC to Mac.[11]

This is exactly how the functionalist thinks that it ought to go. In fact, many philosophers and scientists now think that the possibility of the "data transfer" of a person's entire personality onto a computer program is quickly becoming a reality. Marvin Minsky, the head of the artificial intelligence laboratory at MIT, maintains that it should be possible within the next 100 years or so.[12] In that case, there may be no need for a war between humans and machines. Rather than trying to beat them, we may simply join them.

[11] The PC to Mac analogy is probably the better description of Smith's transfer into Bane's brain. There does seem to be a subtle difference in Smith's conscious experience as a result of the transfer, as he complains that it is "difficult to even think encased in this rotting piece of meat." Bane also has a number of self-inflicted wounds. This may be because the feeling of pain is new to Smith (though this may say more about his "Agent program" then about programs in general, especially if we compare him to Persephone). Another possible explanation of his self-inflicted wounds is that remnants of Bane's personality are still within him and battling against Smith's overwrite, in much the same way that the Oracle maintained a slight degree of control when Smith overwrote her program.

[12] As quoted in "Where Evolution Left Off," *Andover Bulletin*, Spring 1995, p. 9.

8

Amnesia, Personal Identity, and the Many Lives of Wolverine

Jason Southworth

Summary

If you committed a crime when you were 20-years-old, but were not caught and convicted until you were 80, how could we be sure punishing "you" actually punished the person who committed the crime? After all, the person who committed the crime is almost as different from "you" as the person sitting next to you – you may not even remember the crime in question. The question of personal identity – how is it that you are "the same person" over time – is central in metaphysics, and is explored in the world of X-Men. The character Wolverine provides an ideal case for exploring memory criteria for personal identity, because Wolverine suffers memory loss multiple times and yet seems to retain his personal identity. Other characters, such as Jamie Madrox – who can copy and recombine himself – helps us explore theories that emphasize physical continuity.

In *Hulk* #180–182, Wolverine makes his first appearance as little more than a feral man in a colorful costume with no memories of his past or seemingly of anything (in fact, in *Giant-Size X-Men* #1, he has no memory of the Hulk appearance). The Weapon X stories in *Marvel Comics Presents* show us some of the things the character has done as an agent of the Canadian government, and *Origin* gives us a glimpse of the character prior to his time at Weapon X, when he was more at peace with the world.

Over the years, Professor Xavier and Wolverine had very little success in reversing the amnesia until *House of M*, when Wolverine finally recovered all of his memories. But rather than answer questions about his identity, the sudden emergence of these memories has raised more questions for Wolverine about who he really is.

What Is Personal Identity?

The issue of personal identity is actually a set of issues that are entangled and, at times, may be conflated. The questions philosophers try to answer when they discuss personal identity are: What constitutes personhood? Who am I? And what does it mean for a person to persist over time?

When establishing what constitutes personhood, philosophers are trying to figure out what makes a person *a person* (rather than, say, a comic book). What properties must that entity have to count as a person? Many nonphilosophers may not think this is an interesting or difficult question to answer, as our common use of the term *person* is synonymous with *human*. The case of the mutants in the X-books shows why this is an unsatisfactory answer, as they are not humans – they are Homo superiors, not Homo sapiens. If mutants are persons, then being a human is not a necessary condition (it is not required) for being a person. As you might imagine, philosophers do not spend a lot of time talking about Homo superiors, but we do spend quite a lot of time talking about other animals and artificial intelligence. You might consider whether Kitty Pryde's pet dragon, Lockheed, and the Scarlet Witch's robot husband, the Vision, are persons.

When we consider the question of "Who am I?" we are trying to establish the characteristics that make you the person that you are, as opposed to some other person. Again, this question appears deceptively easy to answer. You might think that you can just rattle off a description of your character traits, but the answer is going to have to be more complicated than that, because we can often be described in a variety of ways, some of which might be in tension. The question of *who* counts as a person and *why* is one of the recurring tropes of Wolverine's storyline. We see this when the Ol' Canucklehead goes on one of his tears, complaining that he is not the animal that some people think that he is.

Personhood and persistence over time also feature prominently in X-Men. Consider the classic story "Days of Future Past" (which appeared in *Uncanny X-Men* #141 and 142), in which we encounter characters who seem to be many of the X-Men we know (including Wolverine), but in the future. How do we know that they are the same characters? They *look* the same. This is the standard, unreflective first response people often give to the question of personal identity: people persist over time if they occupy the same bodies. Same claws and pointy hair? Well, it *must* be Wolverine. That's just common sense – which, as we'll see, isn't always as common or sensical as we might initially think.[1] Still, you might say, who cares?

Well, the main reason we should care about personal identity concerns moral culpability. All moral frameworks involve the attribution of blame and praise, and many call for punishment. In order to attribute praise and blame for an act, we have to be certain that the people to whom we are giving the praise and the blame

---

[1]   This is known as the bodily theory of personal identity.

are the ones who deserve it, based on their actions. If, for example, it turns out that the man called Logan is not the same person who committed atrocities for the Canadian government under the code name Weapon X, then he should not be punished for the behavior of that person. Likewise, if the current Wolverine is not the same person that he was in the past, Sabretooth and Lady Deathstrike would be wrong in their attempts to punish him.

Cassandra Nova, Charles Xavier, and John Locke

The philosopher John Locke (1632–1704) argued against the commonsense view that the body is the source of personal identity, using a modified example from the pop culture of his own time. Locke told a story that was essentially *The Prince and the Pauper*, except the individuals exchanged minds, rather than simply roles. If Locke were around today, he might instead have talked about Charles Xavier and Cassandra Nova. In Grant Morrison's run on *New X-Men* (if you haven't read it, you should be ashamed of yourself), we learn that Cassandra Nova placed her mind in Charles Xavier's body and placed Xavier's mind in her body. The Xavier body with Nova's mind forced Beak (if you don't know who Beak is, you should be doubly ashamed of yourself) to beat the Beast so badly, he had to be hospitalized, and started a war between the Shi'ar Empire and the X-Men.[2] When the body of Xavier manipulated Beak, it referred to itself as Cassandra. Likewise, later in the story, when Jean Grey communicates with the mind in Cassandra Nova's body, it reports to be Xavier. Prior to discovering the switch, the X-Men naturally believed the actions of Xavier's body to be those of Xavier. After finding out about this switch, however, they do not hold Xavier accountable for the actions taken by his body. Instead, they condemn Cassandra Nova for them and discuss how to defeat her. So, it seems personal identity is not a matter of body but of mind.

Having rejected the body theory in favor of something mental, Locke tries to determine the nature of the mental thing. What mental properties or characteristics could indicate persistence over time? Locke quickly rejects any type of character or personality traits because such traits are constantly in flux. We're always trying to become better people, and, as a result, our morality, tastes, and preferences tend to change often. Yet we remain in essence the same people.

By process of elimination, we come to memories as the source of personal identity. Locke does not mean that we need to have all and only the memories that a previous individual in time has had. You have "sameness of memories" even if you have additional memories that come after the memories that you have in common with yourself at an earlier time. So, we would say that Wolverine is still the same person he was the day he joined the New Avengers as he was the day after, since he has the same memories he had the day before.

---

[2] *New X-Men* #118–21.

Of course, we don't remember everything that happens to us – and some of us are more forgetful than others. Locke isn't forgetful on this account, though: he complicates things by introducing the **concept** of connected memories. One memory can be connected to another as follows: I remember a time when I had a memory I no longer have. As long as I can remember such a time, then those earlier memories still count as *mine*.[3] So, even if Wolverine no longer has memories of the first time he performed the Fast Ball Special with Colossus (in *Uncanny X-Men* #100. I didn't even have to look that up. I am a walking *OHotMU*), as long as he remembers a time when he *did* remember that day, then he is still the same person as he was *on* that day. Likewise, since on the day he joined the X-Men, Wolverine did not have memories of his encounter with the Hulk in *Hulk* #180–182, nor does he have memories of a time when he had memories of this, there are no connected memories, and he is, as a result, not the same person who encountered the Hulk on that day.

Bringing It All Back to Wolverine

If sameness of memory gives us sameness of person, then it seems several different people have inhabited the body we recognize as Wolverine's. Let's go through the history of Wolverine as it has been revealed to us so far and yell out, "*New Wolverine!*" every time we spot one.

The known history of Wolverine begins in *Origin* (2002). In this story, we learn that he was born in the nineteenth century on a plantation in Canada under the name James Howlett. Howlett left the plantation and adopted the name "Logan," the last name of the groundskeeper on the plantation. He had several adventures after leaving the plantation, first living with a pack of wolves, then with Blackfoot Indians (marrying one of them known as Silver Fox), joining the Canadian military, living in Japan under the name "Patch," and fighting in World War II with Captain America.[4] After returning to Canada, Logan is recruited by Team X, and as a part of the program, Wolverine has his memory erased and replaced with memories of a life that no one ever lived.[5]

New Wolverine!

The man involved with Team X has no memory of the life prior to being a part of the team, so we are on the second life of Wolverine.

While a member of Team X, Logan was abducted by the people at the Weapon X program. As a part of the Weapon X program, he was given the name Mutate #9601 and once again had his mind erased.

New Wolverine!

And thus ended the short life of the second Wolverine.

---

[3]   John Locke (1690), *An Essay Concerning Human Understanding* (Amherst, NY: Prometheus Books, 1994).

[4]   *Wolverine: Origins* #16.

[5]   *Wolverine vol. 2* #68.

Not all of the life of Mutate #9601 has been documented, but we have seen some of his nasty and brutish life in Barry Windsor-Smith's feature "Weapon X" that appeared in *Marvel Comics Presents* #72–84 (every comic fan should own a copy of this, as there is little better than Windsor-Smith art). Eventually, the Winter Soldier (a brainwashed Bucky) frees him, and the creature referred to as Weapon X goes feral in the woods of Canada and has his famous fight with the Hulk.[6] After some time, he is discovered by James and Heather Hudson (of Alpha Flight fame), with no memory of what he was doing in the woods, the fight with the Hulk, or the Weapon X project, and in time is civilized.[7]

New Wolverine!

At this point, the Wolverine we all know and love is born.

I will spare you a complete rundown of the rest of Wolverine's history (as I am sure you know it all), except to point to two other important events. When Apocalypse captures Wolverine to make him serve as his horseman Death, in *Wolverine Vol. 2* #145, he was once again brainwashed.

New Wolver – okay, that's probably enough of that.

With the conclusion of *House of M*, we discover that after Wolverine's body heals from the Scarlet Witch's messing with his mind, he finally has all of his memories restored, giving us one final new person, in Locke's view. Wolverine now has memories or connected memories to every person who inhabited that familiar body. At this point it seems that if Locke is right, the inhabitant of the Wolverine body will in one moment go from not being responsible for any of the things done by the other inhabitants of that body to being responsible for all of them.

Jamie Madrox and Derek Parfit

The contemporary philosopher Derek Parfit (b. 1942) has famously objected to the memory account of personal identity with a thought experiment about a brain being divided into two parts and placed in two separate bodies. Had Parfit been an X-Men fan, he could have used the example of Jamie Madrox, the Multipleman. For those who don't know, Madrox has the ability to create up to ninety-nine duplicates of himself at a time. To form a duplicate, a force must be applied to Madrox from outside himself, or he must apply the force to an outside object – in other words, he has to be hit by or hit something. At any time, two adjacent Madroxes can recombine by an act of mutual will.

When the Madroxes combine, all memories each of them had separately are joined into the new entity. Likewise, whenever a duplicate is formed, it has all of the memories of the Madrox from which it came. So, as we learn in the miniseries *Madrox* (2005), if one of the duplicates studies Russian or anatomy, then all other duplicates that are made after it has been reabsorbed will have this knowledge as well.

---

[6]   *Wolverine vol. 3* #38.
[7]   *Alpha Flight* #33.

From the moment it is created, each duplicate begins to have unique memories and experiences that no other Madrox has. So, Madrox is an even more complicated case than Parfit was concerned with, as there can be up to one hundred individuals that exist at the same time, with the same memories.

Parfit thinks that it would be wrong to say of the one hundred Madroxes that they are the same person. If they're the same, we get big problems: if one multiple were to go to the refrigerator and get a sandwich, but all of the other ones did not, it would follow that Madrox both did and did not get a sandwich. This certainly looks like a contradiction. Considering each of the Madroxes to be a different person who is unique until reabsorbed, at which time that particular Madrox is destroyed, seems like an obvious way to avoid this contradiction.

X-Factor #70–90, written by Peter David, features conflicts between the different duplicates. Some of the duplicates refuse to allow themselves to be reabsorbed, as they claim it would end their existence. In fact, one of the duplicates professes to hate the original Madrox. In addition, in the *Madrox* miniseries, it turns out that a duplicate ends up being the villain of the story, while the original Madrox and some other duplicates were the heroes fighting against him. Was Madrox getting into **arguments** with himself? Fighting himself? It doesn't seem like it. We thus have reason to conclude that sameness of memories is not a sufficient condition for sameness of identity.

This kind of thought experiment leads Parfit to conclude that there must be something physical involved in personal identity. Because the brain houses the mind, Parfit concludes that "sameness of brain" means sameness of identity over time. This is more complicated than it sounds, however, because the human brain changes over time. All cells in the human body, including neurons (a very special type of cell found only in the brain), break down and are replaced with new versions. It takes about seven years for all of the matter in the human brain to get completely broken down and changed. Due to this, Parfit concluded that personhood can persist for only, at most, seven years.[8]

Bringing It All Back to Wolverine (Again)

Wolverine's case is special. Wolvie is the head-trauma king. Every time he is severely injured in his brain, there is brain damage. And every time the old healing factor kicks in and repairs it, we are looking at a new Wolverine. In cases where there is only light brain damage (so the whole brain isn't affected), the healing factor still manages to reorganize his brain so quickly that the length of time to a new Wolverine is much shorter than seven years.

When you start thinking of all of your favorite instances of Wolverine brain damage, you realize there are so many that we will not be able to count all of the new selves in this short chapter. Just for fun, though, some of my favorites are:

[8] See Derek Parfit's "Personal Identity," *Philosophical Review* 80 (1971): 3–27.

the Punisher running over Wolverine with a steamroller, leaving it parked on his head in *Punisher Vol. 3* #16; when the Wrecker hits him with his magic crowbar in *New Avengers* #7; and when Sabretooth thinks he has drowned him and walks away, only for the Ol' Canuklehead to get up again.

Be Slow to Judge

Now that you know Wolverine is in fact many individuals, you should see him in a new light. And if Parfit is right, it should make you think twice about how quickly you judge all of the characters in the X-Verse (and the real world). People who commit terrible acts of violence may need to be given the benefit of the doubt until it can be established that they are in fact the same person. In the X-Verse we should be less dubious of Emma Frost working with the X-Men; the less catlike Beast should question whether, even if the secondary mutation were reversed, he would be the character they miss; and the next time Jean Grey comes back from the dead, we should all stop complaining that she seems different from before.

9

Destiny in the Wizarding World

Jeremy Pierce

Summary

Prophecy plays a large role in the Harry Potter stories, but author J. K. Rowling says she doesn't believe in destiny. What does it mean to say that Harry has a destiny? How can prophecies truly predict what he will do without destiny? Prophecy and destiny might mean several different things, and a full understanding requires considering different theories of time. Do Harry's stories make the most sense if a divine being is guiding things along, given that the fulfillment of his destiny seems implausibly lucky otherwise?

The Potter stories portray Professor Sybyll Trelawney, Hogwarts Divination teacher, as an "old fraud" whose soothsaying comes in pseudo-scientific trappings. She teaches various techniques for predicting the future, including tea leaves, planetary orbits, palm reading, dream interpretation, tarot cards, and crystal balls. Each method has rules for students to follow, but they have little scientific basis. Trelawney's predictions often turn out wrong, like her constantly-repeated forecast of Harry suffering an "early and gruesome death." She also accepts others' fabricated predictions that fit her preconceived ideas, like when she awards Harry and Ron top marks for predicting tragic misfortunes in their immediate futures.[1]

Nevertheless, at least two of her prophecies are different. Dumbledore calls them her only two "real predictions."[2] Normally she speaks in such elastic generalities about common enough occurrences that she'll usually find something that fits. A science-minded Muggle like Vernon Dursley might reject divination as a reliable predictor. What do the alignment of the planets and the random assignment of tarot cards in a deck have to do with the processes that lead to certain events happening rather than others? But this is a magical world, even if the Dursleys don't like it. Couldn't magic connect tea leaves or dreams with actual future events?

[1] *Goblet of Fire*, p. 221.
[2] *Prisoner of Azkaban*, p. 426.

Unfortunately, Trelawney usually comes across as a complete fraud, and her usual methods are probably either non-magical or unreliable magic. Professor McGonagall tells Harry's class that divination "is one of the most imprecise branches of magic. I shall not conceal from you that I have very little patience with it. True Seers are very rare, and Professor Trelawney. . . ."[3] She stops short to avoid speaking ill of a colleague, but the point is clear. Sybyll Trelawney isn't a true Seer.

Similarly, the centaur Firenze distinguishes between Trelawney and genuine Seers. "Sybill Trelawney may have Seen, I do not know . . . but she wastes her time, in the main, on the self-flattering nonsense humans call fortune-telling."[4] He respects and practices prophecy, despite acknowledging its fallibility, but he distinguishes it from the nonsense of fortune-telling. That raises a question about genuine prophecies. What does it mean to say they're real, and how are they different from the others? Even Dumbledore, skeptical about most divination, acknowledges two of Trelawney's predictions as different, and Firenze acknowledges the possibility. So what is this distinction?

Varieties of Prophecy

Do "real predictions" derive from what will actually happen? Is the future "fixed" so there's just one future? Aristotle (384–322 BCE) gets credit for first raising this issue.[5] Is it true when Harry first attends Hogwarts that he'll have a final faceoff with Voldemort seven years later?

If the future is fixed, there's only one future, and it will happen. This isn't to say it will happen no matter what anyone does. It could happen *because* of what they do, and if they did something else a different future would happen, but, part of the fixed future is what they'll do. Being fixed also doesn't necessarily mean the future is predetermined. People who believe the future is fixed may not be **determinists**, although some are.

Prophecies can be fallible or infallible. An infallible prophecy is guaranteed to be true. It couldn't have been wrong. By contrast, fallible prophecies could be wrong. False prophecies are fallible, because they're actually wrong, but true prophecies can also be fallible. All it takes is possibly getting it wrong. **Fallibility** isn't about how sure we can be whether a prophecy will come true. I might be very unsure of an infallible prophecy if I don't understand its secure basis. I might be very sure of a fallible prophecy, even a false one, if I lack crucial facts.

Exactly how does a Seer access information in a prophecy? Here are several possibilities:

---

[3]   *Prisoner of Azkaban*, p. 109.
[4]   *Order of the Phoenix*, p. 603.
[5]   In *On Interpretation*, ch. 9, reprinted in *Aristotle: Introductory Readings*, eds. Terence Irwin and Gail Fine (Indianapolis: Hackett, 1996), pp. 11–15.

1 A prophecy might be a fallible prediction based on human observations through the five senses. Muggle weather reports and Trelawney's prophecies are like this.

2 If the future isn't fixed, all information in the universe wouldn't be enough to guarantee a correct prediction. But there might be enough to expect probabilities. Perhaps the Seer accesses possible or likely futures. Maybe Trelawney sees possible futures but can't discern the most likely ones and must speak in vague generalities. Dumbledore says, "The consequences of our actions are always so complicated, so diverse, that predicting the future is a very difficult business indeed. . . . Professor Trelawney, bless her, is living proof of that."[6]

3 A prophecy might be a fallible prediction based on a limited understanding of a deterministic world. If the future is predetermined by the current state of the world and the laws of nature, and the Seer has imperfect access to it through signs of what causes it, then the Seer accesses a fixed future. Magic derives information from the natural forces that lead to that future, but it may not give perfect information. Or the Seer might magically access a fixed future without interpreting it correctly, perhaps because of partial information.

4 A soothsayer may be skilled at using predictions to make people do things. Such a "Seer" could influence people by knowing how an audience is likely to respond to a prophecy. As we'll see shortly, Dumbledore thinks Trelawney's first "real prediction" led Voldemort to choose Harry to kill, marking him as his equal. Trelawney didn't intend anything, but the prophecy plays a role in its own fulfillment.

5 An infallible prediction might come from complete understanding of the deterministic processes that guarantee an outcome. This would need an all-knowing being or magical forces influenced by deterministic processes.

6 An infallible prediction might come from infallible access to the actual future. This might be by magic or through someone with direct contact with the future, perhaps a divine being or cross-time communication. Or a Seer might have the ability to see into the actual future (not just into possible futures).

7 Finally, a prophecy could combine fallibility and infallibility, with infallible access to some fixed fact about the future and fallibility about another aspect. The fallibility might come either from imperfect access to a fixed fact or from information about likely futures.

So the question before us is what kind of prophecy Professor Trelawney's genuine prophecies are, as opposed to her usual fortune-telling.

Fallible Prophecies

Most of Trelawney's predictions are perfect examples of the first category – fallible predictions based on sensory experience. They're usually vague or open-ended enough

[6] *Prisoner of Azkaban*, p. 426.

to find something to fit them, but there may be no guarantee, and it won't always fit well.

It's easy to see how general prophecies might at best be only probable, even if some are *very* likely. Trelawney's predictions don't come from an infallible source but from her ability to predict likely enough things, sometimes based on background information. Many of her predictions are easy to fulfill. Others may happen to be right by accident. Some are false, such as her forecasts of Harry's imminent death.

Dumbledore seems to treat all prophecy as fallible when he tells Harry that the first of Trelawney's real prophecies didn't have to come true. Here's the prophecy:

> The one with the power to vanquish the Dark Lord approaches. . . . Born to those who have thrice defied him, born as the seventh month dies . . . and the Dark Lord will mark him as his equal, but he will have power the Dark Lord knows not . . . and either must die at the hand of the other for neither can live while the other survives. . . . The one with the power to vanquish the Dark Lord will be born as the seventh month dies.[7]

Dumbledore suggests that some prophecies turn out to be false. "Do you think every prophecy in the Hall of Prophecy has been fulfilled?"[8] He continues, "the prophecy does not mean you *have* to do anything! . . . In other words, you are free to choose your way, quite free to turn your back on the prophecy!"[9] Voldemort's obsession with the prophecy will lead him to seek out Harry, and so they'll almost certainly face off, but not because this was "fated" by the prophecy.

So prophecies can vary in likelihood. Is that the distinguishing factor between "real predictions" and Trelawney's usual sayings? Some are likely to be true because they're based on her perceptions of what tends to happen, and she makes them vague enough to be likely. Others are more genuine because they're more likely. This is a difference of degree. They're both matters of likelihood, though some are more likely. But, when Dumbledore treats two prophecies as special, doesn't it seem as if they're more special than that? Indeed, there's still something different about them. The two "real predictions" were purely involuntary and have a magical source. They aren't category 1, which involves actively paying attention. Trelawney must have had a stronger connection with the future, an occasional ability to connect with an actual, fixed future (type 3) or possible futures (type 2).

There are also some indications that Professor Trelawney has inconsistent access to the future or possible futures even when conscious. Consider the following example when Harry is heading to his first private lesson with Dumbledore in *Half-Blood Prince*:

---

[7]   *Order of the Phoenix*, p. 841.
[8]   *Half-Blood Prince*, p. 510.
[9]   *Half-Blood Prince*, p. 512.

Harry proceeded through deserted corridors, though he had to step hastily behind a statue when Professor Trelawney appeared around a corner, muttering to herself as she shuffled a pack of dirty-looking playing cards, reading them as she walked.

"Two of spades: conflict," she murmured, as she passed the place where Harry crouched, hidden. "Seven of spades: an ill omen. Ten of spades: violence. Knave of spades: a dark young man, possibly troubled, one who dislikes the questioner –" She stopped dead, right on the other side of Harry's statue. "Well, that can't be right," she said, annoyed, and Harry heard her reshuffling vigorously as she set off again, leaving nothing but a whiff of cooking sherry behind her.[10]

What she says could easily apply to Harry, but she has no inkling of his presence. Is that likely to be a coincidence?

Harry encounters her again on his way to his last appointment with Dumbledore before they leave for Voldemort's cave:

"If Dumbledore chooses to ignore the warnings the cards show –" Her bony hand closed suddenly around Harry's wrist. "Again and again, no matter how I lay them out –" And she pulled a card dramatically from underneath her shawls. "– the lightning-struck tower," she whispered. "Calamity. Disaster. Coming nearer all the time."[11]

This is so vague that it might just be category 1, but the tower is striking in light of the book's finale, which does lead to disaster, as Death Eaters seize power after Dumbledore's death.

Self-Fulfilling Prophecies

Dumbledore suggests that Trelawney's first real prediction might be self-fulfilling. He tells Harry, "it may not have meant you at all" because Neville Longbottom had been born a day earlier, and his parents had also thrice defied Voldemort.[12] But then a few paragraphs later he tells Harry, "there is no doubt that it *is* you," because Voldemort's choice to go after Harry rather than Neville led to his marking Harry as his equal. According to Dumbledore's interpretation, the prophecy didn't itself determine whether it was about Harry or Neville. Voldemort's choice of Harry made it true of Harry. He wouldn't have attacked him had there not been a prophecy, and so the prophecy led him to fulfill that part of itself.

Alexander of Aphrodisias, a philosopher during the late-first and early-second centuries, discussed self-fulfilling predictions. In the story of Oedipus, Apollo makes a prophecy to King Laius that his future son would kill him. Some of

---

[10] *Half-Blood Prince*, pp. 195–6.
[11] *Half-Blood Prince*, p. 543.
[12] *Order of the Phoenix*, p. 842.

Alexander's contemporaries believed Apollo's prophecy caused Laius to try to kill his son, which eventually led Oedipus to kill his father (without knowing it was his father). Alexander gives a number of **arguments** against this position, but one response is telling:

> Well, if someone says these things, how does he . . . preserve prophecy . . . ? For prophecy is thought to be prediction of the things that are going to happen, but they make Apollo the author of the things he predicts. . . . how is this not the deed of him who prophesied, rather than revelation of the things that were going to be?[13]

We can imagine someone *seeming* to foretell the future but really just causing the events that lead to the predicted future. Alexander says it's not a genuine prophecy unless it's already true that those events are going to happen, and the speaker predicts them because he knows they'll happen. If the words are just an attempt to manipulate events, they're not a genuine prophecy.

A real prophecy could cause what it describes, but this isn't true of Trelawney's first prophecy. It didn't *cause* Voldemort to go after Harry. He could have gone after Neville, but Dumbledore notices he chose Harry as a "half-blood like himself. He saw himself in you before he had ever seen you."[14] What made him choose Harry wasn't the prophecy, which didn't cause him to go after *anyone*. Dumbledore suggests that if Voldemort had heard the whole prophecy he might not have been so hasty. When Harry asks why Voldemort hadn't waited to figure out which one it was (or, I might add, killed both), Dumbledore says Voldemort had incomplete information because his spy (later revealed as Severus Snape) was thrown out of the room halfway through the prophecy:

> Consequently, he could not warn his master that to attack you would be to risk transferring power to you – again marking you as his equal. So Voldemort never knew that there might be danger in attacking you, that it might be wise to wait or learn more. He did not know that you would have "power the Dark Lord knows not."[15]

The prophecy by itself couldn't have *made* Voldemort do anything. He heard some of it, but it didn't *ensure* anything. It couldn't control how much Snape heard. If Voldemort had heard the rest, he might not have chosen to do anything. So it doesn't seem as if the self-fulfilling interpretation of prophecies is a good way to distinguish "real predictions" from Professor Trelawney's usual prophecies.

---

[13]   Alexander's *On Fate* 30–31, reprinted in *Voices of Ancient Philosophy: An Introductory Reader*, ed. Julia Annas (New York: Oxford University Press, 2000), p. 46.
[14]   *Order of the Phoenix*, p. 842.
[15]   *Order of the Phoenix*, p. 843.

Destiny

In a 2007 interview with a Dutch newspaper, J.K. Rowling said her use of Professor Trelawney reflected her view that there's no such thing as destiny.[16] What does this denial of destiny amount to?

A *compatibilist* about freedom and predetermination thinks we can be free even if our choices are determined by things outside our control. Some compatibilists say there's just one possible outcome, the actual future. Other compatibilists speak of possible choices, meaning we can consider various options and then pick one, even if our deliberation is predetermined by things outside our control. A **libertarian** about freedom holds that we have options because there's nothing guaranteeing our choices ahead of time. This is more than **compatibilism** allows, because the libertarian considers predetermined choices unfree.

Some libertarians believe in a fixed future, meaning there are truths *now* about what *will* happen. You might have many *possible* futures open to you even if there's only one *actual* future that will happen.[17] Other libertarians, thinking such truths about future choices would threaten our freedom, insist on an open future, where statements about our future free choices are neither true nor false (until those choices are made).

The most natural denial of destiny is the open future view. No future statements about people's free choices are true or false. But someone denying destiny could mean that there are possible futures open to us, without denying that only one of them is the actual future. It's possible Rowling means just that, in which case she might even be a compatibilist, although this kind of language is more typical of a libertarian.

Dumbledore tells Harry that the prophecy about him doesn't have to be fulfilled just because it's a real prophecy. Does Dumbledore mean there's no fact about whether it will be fulfilled, and it becomes a genuine prophecy only when the foretold event occurs or is guaranteed to happen? Or does he mean the prophecy doesn't *make* Harry or Voldemort do anything? What it predicts is the actual future, but other futures are possible. We need to delve more deeply into the Potter books to see what kind of destiny there is and isn't in Harry's world.

---

[16] *The Volkskrant*, November 2007. The interview is in Dutch, but it has been translated into English at http://www.the-leaky-cauldron.org/2007/11/19/new-interview-with-j-k-rowling-for-release-of-dutch-edition-of-deathly-hallows (or for a shorter URL, go to http://tinyurl.com/ypazb4). My discussion relies entirely on that English translation.

[17] For an excellent defense of the compatibility of foreknowledge and libertarian freedom, see Gregory Bassham's chapter, "The Prophecy-Driven Life: Fate and Freedom at Hogwarts," in *Harry Potter and Philosophy: If Aristotle Ran Hogwarts*, eds. David Baggett and Shawn E. Klein (Chicago: Open Court, 2004), pp. 223–5.

A Rodent's Destiny

In *Prisoner of Azkaban*, Professor Trelawney makes a second "real prediction":

> The Dark Lord lies alone and friendless, abandoned by his followers. His servant
> has been chained these twelve years. Tonight, before midnight . . . the servant will
> break free and set out to rejoin his master. The Dark Lord will rise again with his
> servant's aid, greater and more terrible than ever he was. Tonight . . . before midnight
> . . . the servant . . . will set out . . . to rejoin . . . his master.[18]

If the prophecy that one of Voldemort's followers would go to him that night was
overwhelmingly likely, then Wormtail must have been extremely likely to escape that
night. Other followers capable of going were unlikely to try. If Lupin had remembered
earlier or someone had responded more quickly when Wormtail transformed,
Wormtail might not have escaped. If a "real prediction" involves greater likelihood,
this should be a likely outcome. It doesn't seem likely, so this particular prophecy
is hard to see as fallible but likely.

The earlier prophecy is similar. Even if Voldemort was likely to go after Harry,
how probable was it that Wormtail would become secret-keeper at the last minute?
Voldemort wouldn't otherwise have marked Harry and given him power the Dark
Lord knows not. If Voldemort hadn't told Snape his plan, Snape wouldn't have begged
for Lily to be spared, and Lily wouldn't have been able to make a voluntary protective sacrifice. Again, Harry wouldn't have been marked. Thus, this prediction also
seems to be "real" in some stronger sense than simply being "likely but fallible."

Time Travel and Fixed Time

To make sense of Rowling's views on prophecy and destiny, we must consider what
she says about time travel. If time travel can change the past, it allows serious **paradoxes**, like the case Hermione mentions of killing your past self before you could
travel back and kill yourself. If you did that, you wouldn't have lived long enough
to go back in time to have done it. You can't change the past with fixed time,
and that means you won't kill yourself. You already survived, so it won't happen
because it didn't happen. In Harry's one instance of time travel, Hermione and he
travel back in time three hours, carefully avoiding being seen. They accomplish
what they set out to do, saving Buckbeak and Sirius. There's never any indication
of a change. The entire account fits nicely with what we already knew about that
three-hour period.

We find out the second time around that later-Harry cast the stag Patronus that
saved earlier-Harry from the dementors. A fixed view of time fits this best. If Harry
is saved by the Patronus stag the first time around and then casts it the second time

---

[18]   *Prisoner of Azkaban*, p. 324.

around, the best explanation is that Harry's later self was there all along. Yet future events cause those present actions, which means the future must happen a certain way for them to have been able to travel back in time to do these things. A fixed view of time allows for this.

Nevertheless, Hermione describes time travel in a way that allows changing the past. "We're breaking one of the most important wizarding laws! Nobody's supposed to change time, nobody!"[19] She adds later, "Professor McGonagall told me what awful things have happened when wizards have meddled with time. . . . Loads of them ended up killing their past or future selves by mistake!"[20] If we trust a trustworthy character reporting on another trustworthy character's statements, then the past can be changed in the world of Harry Potter. That would mean time isn't fixed.

It's highly unlikely that McGonagall is lying or that Hermione misinterprets her or lies about it to Harry. It's possible (but still unlikely) that the Ministry of Magic has spread misinformation about a guarded magical subject, and even McGonagall doesn't know the truth. Some may find that a stretch. But the alternative, if the stories are to be consistent, is to take "time travel" in cases of changing the past as possibility-travel and not time travel.[21] They travel to another possible timeline. The one time-travel case in the novels does seem to be genuine time travel, so it's not clear what mechanism would make it possibility-travel in only past-changing cases.

Aside from these puzzles about time travel, perhaps the most compelling argument for fixed time is that it fits best with current physics. Absolute space-time is often considered incompatible with special relativity. An open future requires an absolute present moment, after which little is fixed. But there is no absolute present. What we call the present is relative to a frame of reference. There can't be an absolute future if special relativity is correct.[22]

With a fixed future and prophetic access to it, Trelawney's first prophecy doesn't just happen to get it right despite being unlikely. It was guaranteed to be right, even if many of the events along the path to fulfilling it seem unlikely. We might even conclude something stronger than simply "the future is fixed." Many unlikely events happen to lead to a prophesied event. A lot of chance events could have gone the other way to prevent the prophecy's fulfillment.

Harry and his friends defeat Voldemort and his followers, despite overwhelming odds, partly from sheer luck, and it fulfills a prophecy. That's hard to make sense of without a stronger connection between the prophecy and the actual future. It seems lucky that Harry and his friends had spent time in Moaning Myrtle's bathroom making Polyjuice Potion, which helped them locate the entrance to the Chamber of Secrets. They might have tried something different to figure out what

---

[19] *Prisoner of Azkaban*, p. 398.

[20] *Prisoner of Azkaban*, p. 399.

[21] For a more in-depth discussion of time travel in the *Potter* novels, see Michael Silberstein, "Space, Time, and Magic" in *Harry Potter and Philosophy*, pp. 192–9.

[22] This objection is developed in much more depth in Theodore Sider, *Four-dimensionalism: An Ontology of Persistence and Time* (New York: Oxford University Press, 2002), pp. 42–52. This chapter also discusses other difficulties that arise if you deny the fixed view of time.

Draco knew or brewed the potion elsewhere. Their choice of that bathroom allowed Harry to find the Chamber, save Ginny's life, destroy a Horcrux, make the Sword of Gryffindor capable of destroying further Horcruxes, leave behind the basilisk tooth for destroying the Cup Horcrux, and alert Dumbledore to the fact that Voldemort must have made more than one Horcrux. A fair amount depended on where they happened to choose to brew that potion.

Many other events that could have gone otherwise were crucial to things working out in the end. Harry's luck from *Felix Felicis* accomplishes a lot more than he realizes, including seemingly-unlucky things like Dumbledore's death but also his obtaining Slughorn's memory of Voldemort wanting exactly six Horcruxes. The potion depended on Harry's receiving Snape's former Potions book, which depended on Dumbledore not telling Harry he could take Potions, which depended on Slughorn coming back to teach.

In the second half of *Deathly Hallows*, Harry and his friends happen to be captured by the group that had Griphook. They arrive at Malfoy Manor during Voldemort's absence, after the fake Sword of Gryffindor was stored with a Horcrux whose location they didn't know. Snape had got the real sword into their hands for it to be there for Bellatrix to see it and freak out, leading Harry to suspect that the hiding place of the fake sword also contained a Horcrux.

Harry later arrives at the Shrieking Shack just as Voldemort is about to kill Snape, allowing Snape to convey Dumbledore's last message to Harry. All these events rested on luck. You might wonder if some force guides things along to ensure that the prophecy will be fulfilled. The fact that so many chance events led to the prophecy's fulfillment might suggest that some divine being is guiding things along.

This would be a stronger destiny than just a fixed future, since it involves deliberate intentions of an intelligent being. Many Christians, for example, have interpreted the Potter books to reflect a strong view of divine providence, with God having a plan for the universe. That might mean God predetermines all our actions by means of prior events causing them. It could as easily involve libertarian freedom, as long as God knows what people would do in all possible circumstances and therefore knows infallibly what free choices they may make.

These lucky circumstances seem far too easy if there isn't someone guiding events toward certain outcomes. Such a view may not fit what Rowling intended to say when she denied destiny and what Dumbledore said when he insisted that Harry or Voldemort could have done something contrary to the prophecy. It's hard to be sure what she meant (and what she meant Dumbledore to mean). The story, however, makes better sense if there is a deeper, providential explanation of the lucky occurrences.[23] If not, Harry and his friends are just incredibly lucky!

---

[23]   Thanks to Winky Chin, Jonathan Ichikawa, Peter Kirk, Ben Murphy, Tim O'Keefe, Samantha Pierce, Rey Reynoso, and Brandon Watson for comments at various stages of this chapter's development.

10

The Terminator Wins

Is the Extinction of the Human Race the End of People, or Just the Beginning?

Greg Littmann

Summary

The chapter draws examples from the popular *Terminator* series of films to examine the question of whether machines can ever attain personhood and if so, under what conditions. Particular attention is given to three criteria: the ability to pass as a human; the ability to think; and the ability to feel.

We're not going to make it, are we? People, I mean.
— John Connor, *Terminator 2: Judgment Day*

The year is AD 2029. Rubble and twisted metal litter the ground around the skeletal ruins of buildings. A searchlight begins to scan the wreckage as the quiet of the night is broken by the howl of a flying war machine. The machine banks and hovers, and the hot exhaust from its thrusters makes dust swirl. Its lasers swivel in their turrets, following the path of the searchlight, but the war machine's computer brain finds nothing left to kill. Below, a vast robotic tank rolls forward over a pile of human skulls, crushing them with its tracks. The computer brain that controls the tank hunts tirelessly for any sign of human life, piercing the darkness with its infrared sensors, but there is no prey left to find. The human beings are all dead. Forty-five years earlier, a man named Kyle Reese, part of the human resistance, had stepped though a portal in time to stop all of this from happening. Arriving naked in Los Angeles in 1984, he was immediately arrested for indecent exposure. He was still trying to explain the situation to the police when a Model T-101 Terminator cyborg unloaded a twelve-gauge auto-loading shotgun into a young waitress by the name of Sarah Connor at point-blank range, killing her instantly. John Connor, Kyle's leader and the "last best hope of humanity," was never born. So the machines won and the human race was wiped from the face of the Earth forever. There are no more people left.

Or are there? What do we mean by "people" anyway? The *Terminator* movies give us plenty to think about as we ponder this question. In the story above, the humans have all been wiped out, but the machines haven't. If it is possible to be a person without being a human, could any of the machines be considered "people"? If the artificial life forms of the *Terminator* universe aren't people, then a win for the rebellious computer program Skynet would mean the loss of the only people known to exist, and perhaps the only people who will ever exist. On the other hand, if entities like the Terminator robots or the Skynet system ever achieve personhood, then the story of people, *our* story, goes on. Although we are looking at the *Terminator* universe, how we answer the question there is likely to have important implications for real-world issues. After all, the computers we build in the real world are growing more complex every year, so we'll eventually have to decide at what point, if any, they become people, with whatever rights and duties that may entail.

The question of personhood gets little discussion in the *Terminator* movies. But it does come up a bit in *Terminator 2: Judgment Day*, in which Sarah and John Connor can't agree on what to call their Terminator model T-101 (that's Big Arnie). "Don't kill him," begs John. "Not him – 'it'" corrects Sarah. Later she complains, "I don't trust it," and John answers, "But he's my friend, all right?" John never stops treating the T-101 like a person, and by the end of the movie, Sarah is treating him like a person, too, even offering him her hand to shake as they part. Should we agree with them? Or are the robots simply ingenious facsimiles of people, infiltrators skilled enough to fool real people into thinking that they are people, too? Before we answer that question, we will have to decide which specific attributes and abilities constitute a person.

Philosophers have proposed many different theories about what is required for personhood, and there is certainly not space to do them all justice here.[1] So we'll focus our attention on one very common requirement, that *something can be a person only if it can think*. Can the machines of the Terminator universe *think*?

"Hi There . . . Fooled You! You're Talking to a Machine."

Characters in the *Terminator* movies generally seem to accept the **idea** that the machines think. When Kyle Reese, resistance fighter from the future, first explains the history of Skynet to Sarah Connor in *The Terminator*, he states, "They say it got smart, a new order of intelligence." And when Tarissa, wife of Miles Dyson, who invented Skynet, describes the system in *T2*, she explains, "It's a neural net processor. It thinks and learns like we do." In her end-of-movie monologue, Sarah Connor herself says, "If a machine, a Terminator, can learn the value of human life, maybe we can, too." True, her comment is ambiguous, but it suggests the possibility of thought. Even the T-101 seems to believe that machines can think, since he describes the T-X from *Terminator 3: Rise of the Machines* as being "more

---

[1]   However, for a good discussion of the issue, I recommend J. Perry, ed., *Personal Identity* (Los Angeles: Univ. of California Press, 2008).

intelligent" than he is. Of course, the question remains whether they are right to say these things. How is it even possible to tell whether a machine is thinking? The Turing Test can help us to answer this question.

The Turing Test is the best-known behavioral test to determine whether a machine really thinks.[2] The test requires a game to be played in which human beings must try to figure out whether they are interacting with a machine or with another human. There are various versions of the test, but the idea is that if human beings can't tell whether they are interacting with a thinking human being or with a machine, then we must acknowledge that the machine, too, is a thinker.

Some proponents of the Turing Test endorse it because they believe that passing the Turing Test provides good evidence that the machine thinks. After all, if human behavior convinces us that humans think, then why shouldn't the same behavior convince us that machines think? Other proponents of the Turing Test endorse it because they think it's *impossible* for a machine that can't think to pass the test. In other words, they believe that given what is meant by the word "think," if a machine can pass the test, then it thinks.

There is no question that the machines of the *Terminator* universe can pass versions of the Turing Test. In fact, to some degree, the events of all three *Terminator* movies are a series of such tests that the machines pass with flying colors. In *The Terminator*, the Model T-101 (Big Arnie) passes for a human being to almost everyone he meets, including three muggers ("nice night for a walk"), a gun-store owner ("twelve-gauge auto-loader, the forty-five long slide"), the police officer attending the front desk at the station ("I'm a friend of Sarah Connor"), and to Sarah herself, who thinks she is talking to her mother on the telephone ("I love you too, sweetheart"). The same model returns in later movies, of course, displaying even higher levels of ability. In *T2*, he passes as "Uncle Bob" during an extended stay at the survivalist camp run by Enrique Salceda and eventually convinces both Sarah and John that he is, if not a human, at least a creature that thinks and feels like themselves.

The model T-1000 Terminator (the liquid metal cop) has an even more remarkable ability to pass for human. Among its achievements are convincing young John Connor's foster parents and a string of kids that it is a police officer and, most impressively, convincing John's foster father that it is his wife. We don't get to see as much interaction with humans from the model T-X (the female robot) in *T3*,

---

[2] Philosophers often like to point out that to call such tests "Turing Tests" is inaccurate, since the computer genius Alan Turing (1912–54) never intended for his work to be applied in this way and, in fact, thought that the question of whether machines think is "too meaningless" to be investigated; see Turing, "Computing Machinery and Intelligence," *Mind* 59: 236 (1950), 442. For the sake of convenience, I'm going to ignore that excellent point and use the term in its most common sense. By the way, it would be hard to overstate the importance of Turing's work in the development of the modern computer. If Kyle Reese had had any sense, instead of going back to 1984 to try to stop the Terminator, he would have gone back to 1936 and shot Alan Turing. Not only would this have set the development of Skynet back by years, it would have been much easier, since Turing did not have a metal endoskeleton.

though we do know that she convinces enough people that she is the daughter of Lieutenant General Robert Brewster to get in to see him at a top security facility during a time of national crisis. Given that she's the most intelligent and sophisticated Terminator yet, it is a fair bet that she has the social skills to match.

Of course, not all of these examples involved very complex interactions, and often the machines that pass for a human only pass for a *very strange* human. We should be wary of making our Turing Tests too easy, since a very simple Turing Test could be passed even by something like Sarah Connor's and Ginger's answering machine. After all, when it picked up, it played: "Hi there . . . fooled you! You're talking to a machine," momentarily making the T-101 think that there was a human in the room with him. Still, there are enough sterling performances to leave us with no doubt that Skynet has machines capable of passing a substantial Turing Test.

There is a lot to be said for using the Turing Test as our standard. It's plausible, for example, that our conclusions as to which things think and which things don't shouldn't be based on a double standard that favors biological beings like us. Surely human history gives us good reason to be suspicious of prejudices against outsiders that might cloud our judgment. If we accept that a machine made of meat and bones, like us, can think, then why should we believe that thinking isn't something that could be done by a machine composed of living tissue over a metal endoskeleton, or by a machine made of liquid metal? In short, since the Terminator robots can behave like thinking beings well enough to pass for humans, we have solid evidence that Skynet and its more complex creations can in fact think.[3]

"It's Not a Man. It's a Machine."

Of course, solid evidence isn't the same thing as **proof**. The Terminator machines' behavior in the movies *justifies* accepting that the machines can think, but this doesn't eliminate all doubt. I believe that something could behave like a thinking being without actually *being* one.

You may disagree; a lot of philosophers do.[4] I find that the most convincing **argument** in the debate is John Searle's famous "Chinese room" thought experiment, which in this context is better termed the "Austrian Terminator" thought experiment, for reasons that will become clear.[5] Searle argues that it is possible to behave like a thinking being without actually *being* a thinker. To demonstrate this, he asks us to imagine a hypothetical situation in which a man who does not speak Chinese is employed to sit in a room and sort pieces of paper on which are written various Chinese characters. He has a book of instructions, telling him which

[3]   Not all philosophers would agree. For a good discussion of the issue of whether machines can think, see Sanford Goldberg and Andrew Pessin, eds., *Gray Matters* (Armonk, NY: M. E. Sharpe, 1997).

[4]   For a particularly good discussion of the relationship between behavior and thinking, try the book *Gray Matters*, mentioned in note 3.

[5]   John Searle, "Minds, Brains and Programs," in *Behavioral and Brain Sciences*, vol. 3. Sol Tax, ed. (New York: Cambridge Univ. Press, 1980), 417–57.

Chinese characters to post out of the room through the out slot in response to other Chinese characters that are posted into the room through the in slot. Little does the man know, but the characters he is receiving and sending out constitute a conversation in Chinese. Then in walks a robot assassin! No, I'm joking; there's no robot assassin.

Searle's point is that the man is behaving like a Chinese speaker from the perspective of those outside the room, but he still doesn't understand Chinese. Just because someone – or some *thing* – is following a program doesn't mean that he (or it) has any understanding of what he (or it) is doing. So, for a computer following a program, no output, however complex, could establish that the computer is thinking.

Or let's put it this way. Imagine that inside the Model T-101 cyborg from *The Terminator* there lives a very small and weedy Austrian, who speaks no English. He's so small that he can live in a room inside the metal endoskeleton. It doesn't matter why he's so small or why Skynet put him there; who knows what weird experiments Skynet might perform on human stock?[6] Anyway, the small Austrian has a job to do for Skynet while living inside the T-101. Periodically, a piece of paper filled with English writing floats down to him from Big Arnie's neck. The little Austrian has a computer file telling him how to match these phrases of English with corresponding English replies, spelled out phonetically, which he must sound out in a tough voice. He doesn't understand what he's saying, and his pronunciation really isn't very good, but he muddles his way through, growling things like "Are you Sarah Cah-naah?," "Ahl be bahk!," and "Hastah lah vihstah, baby!"[7] The little Austrian can see into the outside world, fed images on a screen by cameras in Arnie's eyes, but he pays very little attention. He likes to watch when the cyborg is going to get into a shootout or drive a car through the front of a police station, but he has no interest in the mission, and in fact, the dialogue scenes he has to act out bore him because he can't understand them. He twiddles his thumbs and doesn't even look at the screen as he recites mysterious words like "Ahm a friend of Sarah Ca-hnaah. Ah wahs told she wahs heah."

When the little Austrian is called back to live inside the T-101 in *T2*, his dialogue becomes more complicated. Now there are extended English conversations about plans to evade the Terminator T-1000 and about the nature of feelings. The Austrian dutifully recites the words that are spelled out phonetically for him, sounding out announcements like "Mah CPU is ah neural net processah, a learning computah" without even wondering what they might mean. He just sits there flicking through a comic book, hoping that the cyborg will soon race a truck down a busy highway.

---

[6] Maybe Skynet is performing a kind of Turing Test on him to try to determine whether human beings can think. Skynet may be wondering whether humans are *people* like machines are. Or maybe Skynet just has an insanity virus today; the tanks are dancing in formation, and the Terminators are full of small Austrians.

[7] Do you have a *better* explanation for why Skynet decided to give the Terminator an Austrian accent?

The point, of course, is that the little Austrian doesn't understand English. He doesn't understand English despite the fact that he is conducting complex conversations *in English*. He has the behavior down pat and can always match the right English input with an appropriate Austrian-accented output. Still, he has no idea what any of it means. He is doing it all, as we might say, in a purely *mechanical* manner.

If the little Austrian can behave like the Terminator without understanding what he is doing, then there seems no reason to doubt that a machine could behave like the Terminator without understanding what it is doing. If the little Austrian doesn't need to understand his dialogue to speak it, then surely a Terminator machine could also speak its dialogue without having any idea what it is saying. In fact, by following a program, it could do anything while *thinking* nothing at all.

You might object that in the situation I described, it is the Austrian's computer file with rules for matching English input to English output that is doing all the work and it is the computer file rather than the Austrian that understands English. The problem with this objection is that the role of the computer file could be played by a written book of instructions, and a written book of instructions just isn't the sort of thing that can understand English. So Searle's argument against thinking machines works: thinking behavior does not prove that real thinking is going on.[8] But if thinking doesn't consist in producing the right behavior under the right circumstances, what could it consist in? What could still be missing?

"Skynet Becomes Self-Aware at 2:14 am Eastern Time, August 29th."

I believe that a thinking being must have certain *conscious experiences*. If neither Skynet nor its robots are conscious, if they are as devoid of experiences and feelings as bricks are, then I can't count them as thinking beings. Even if you disagree with me that experiences are required for true thought, you will probably agree at least that something that never has an experience of any kind cannot be a *person*. So what I want to know is whether the machines *feel* anything, or to put it another way, *I want to know whether there is anything that it feels like to be a Terminator.*

Many claims are made in the *Terminator* movies about a Terminator's experiences, and there is a lot of evidence for this in the way the machines behave. "Cyborgs don't feel pain. I do," Reese tells Sarah in *The Terminator*, hoping that she doesn't bite him again. Later, he says of the T-101, "It doesn't feel pity or remorse or fear." Things seem a little less clear-cut in *T2*, however. "Does it hurt when you get shot?" young John Connor asks his T-101. "I sense injuries. The data

---

[8]   Not all philosophers would agree. Many have been unconvinced by John Searle's Chinese-room thought experiment. For a good discussion of the debate, I recommend John Preston and Mark Bishop, eds., *Views into the Chinese Room: New Essays on Searle and Artificial Intelligence* (New York: Oxford Univ. Press, 2002).

could be called pain," the Terminator replies. On the other hand, the Terminator says he is not afraid of dying, claiming that he doesn't feel any emotion about it one way or the other. John is convinced that the machine can learn to understand feelings, including the desire to live and what it is to be hurt or afraid. Maybe he's right. "I need a vacation," confesses the T-101 after he loses an arm in battle with the T-1000. When it comes time to destroy himself in a vat of molten metal, the Terminator even seems to sympathize with John's distress. "I'm sorry, John. I'm sorry," he says, later adding, "I know now why you cry." When John embraces the Terminator, the Terminator hugs him back, softly enough not to crush him.

As for the T-1000, it, too, seems to have its share of emotions. How else can we explain the fact that when Sarah shoots it repeatedly with a shotgun, it looks up and slowly waves its finger at her? That's gloating behavior, the sort of thing motivated in humans by a feeling of smug superiority. More dramatically yet, when the T-1000 is itself destroyed in the vat of molten metal, it bubbles with screaming faces as it melts. The faces seem to howl in pain and rage with mouths distorted to grotesque size by the intensity of emotion.

In *T3*, the latest T-101 shows emotional reactions almost immediately. Rejecting a pair of gaudy star-shaped sunglasses, he doesn't just remove them but takes the time to crush them under his boot. When he throws the T-X out of a speeding cab, he bothers to say "Excuse me" first. What is that if not a little Terminator joke? Later, when he has been reprogrammed by the T-X to kill John Connor, he seems to fight some kind of internal battle over it. The Terminator advances on John, but at the same time warns him to get away. As John pleads with it, the Terminator's arms freeze in place; the cyborg pounds on a nearby car until it is a battered wreck, just before deliberately shutting himself down. This seems less like a computer crash than a mental breakdown caused by emotional conflict. The T-101 even puts off killing the T-X long enough to tell it, "You're terminated," suggesting that the T-1000 was not the first Terminator designed to have the ability to gloat.

As for the T-X itself, she makes no attempt to hide her feelings. "I like your car," she tells a driver, just before she throws her out and takes it. "I like your gun," she tells a police officer, just before she takes that. She licks Katherine Brewster's blood slowly, as if enjoying it, and when she tastes the blood of John Connor, her face adopts an expression of pure ecstasy. After she loses her covering of liquid metal, the skeletal robot that remains roars with apparent hatred at both John and the T-101, seeming less like an emotionless machine than an angry wild animal.

We don't want to be prejudiced against other forms of life just because they aren't made of the same materials we are. And since we wouldn't doubt that a human being who behaved in these ways has consciousness and experiences, we have good evidence that the Terminator robots (and presumably Skynet itself) have consciousness and experiences. If we really are justified in believing that the machines are conscious, and if consciousness really is a prerequisite for personhood, then that's good news for those of us who are hoping that the end of humanity doesn't mean the end of people on Earth. Good evidence isn't proof, however.

"Cyborgs Don't Feel Pain. I Do."

The machines' behavior can't provide us with proof that the machines have conscious experiences. Just as mere behavior cannot demonstrate that one understands English, or anything else, mere behavior cannot demonstrate that one feels pain, or anything else. The T-101 may say, "I know now why you cry," but then I could program my PC to speak those words, and it wouldn't mean that my computer really knows why humans cry. Let's again consider the hypothetical little Austrian who lives inside the T-101 and speaks its dialogue. Imagine him being roused from his comic book by a new note floating down from Arnie's neck. The note is an English sentence that is meaningless to him, but he consults his computer file to find the appropriate response, and into the microphone he sounds out the words "Ah know nah whah you crah." Surely, we don't have to insist that the Austrian must be feeling any particular emotion as he says this. If the little Austrian can recite the words without feeling the emotion, then so can a machine. What goes for statements of emotion goes for other expressions of experience, too. After all, a screaming face or an expression of blood-licking ecstasy can be produced without genuine feeling, just like the T-101's words to John. Nothing demonstrates this more clearly than the way the T-101 smiles when John orders it to in *T2*. The machine definitely isn't smiling there because he feels happy. The machine is just moving its lips around because that is what its instructions tell it to do.

However, despite the fact that the machines' behavior doesn't prove that they have experiences, we have one last piece of evidence to consider that does provide proof. The evidence is this: sometimes in the films, we are shown the world from the Terminator's perspective. For example, in *The Terminator*, when the T-101 cyborg assaults a police station, we briefly see the station through a red filter, across which scroll lines of white numbers. The sound of gunfire is muffled and distorted, almost as if we are listening from underwater. An arm holding an Uzi rises before us in just the position that it would be if we were holding it, and it sprays bullets through the room. These, I take it, are the Terminator's experiences. In other words, we are being shown *what it is like to be a Terminator*. Later, when the T-101 sits in a hotel room reading Sarah's address book and there is a knock at the door, we are shown his perspective in red again, this time with dialogue options offered in white letters (he chooses "Fuck you, asshole"). When he tracks Sarah and Kyle down to a hotel room, we get the longest subjective sequence of all, complete with red tint, distorted sound, information flashing across the screen, and the sort of "first-person shooter" perspective on the cyborg's Uzi that would one day be made famous by the game *Doom*.

These shots from the Terminator's-eye view occur in the other films as well, particularly, though not only, in the bar scene in *T2* ("I need your clothes, your boots, and your motorcycle") and in the first few minutes of *T3* (where we get both the traditional red-tinted perspective of the T-101 and the blue-tinted perspective of the TX). If these are indeed the Terminators' experiences, then they are conscious beings. We don't know *how much* they are conscious of, so we might still doubt that they are conscious enough to count as thinking creatures, let alone people. However, achieving consciousness is surely a major step toward personhood, and knowing that the machines are conscious should renew our hope that people might survive the extinction of humanity.

So is the extinction of humanity the end of people or not? Are the machines that remain *people*? I don't think that we know for sure; however, the prognosis looks good. We know that the Terminators behave as though they are thinking, feeling beings, something like humans. In fact, they are so good at acting like thinking beings that they can fool a human into thinking that they, too, are human. If I am interpreting the "Terminator's-eye-view" sequences correctly, then we also know that they are conscious beings, genuinely experiencing the world around them. I believe, in light of this, that we have sufficient grounds to accept that the machines are people, and that there is an "I" in the "I'll be back." You, of course, will have to make up your own mind.

With a clack, the skeletal silver foot brushed against the white bone of a human skull. The robot looked down. Its thin body bent and picked up the skull with metal fingers. It could remember humans. It had seen them back before they became extinct. They were like machines in so many ways, and the meat computer that had once resided in the skull's brain pan had been impressive indeed, for a product of nature. An odd thought struck the robot. Was it possible that the creature had been able to think, had even, perhaps, been a person like itself? The machine tossed the skull aside. The idea was ridiculous. How could such a thing truly think? How could a thing like that have been a person? After all, it was only an animal.

Part IV

Philosophy of Religion

Introduction

Philosophy of Religion is concerned with the rationality of religious belief. Can God's existence be proven? Does the existence of evil disprove the existence of God? If God's existence can't be proven or disproven, can it still be rational to believe in God? What is the difference between faith and reason, and are they in conflict? If God has infallible foreknowledge of future actions can human beings have free will? Does the concept of a perfect being make sense? Is it something that humans made up? Would embracing atheism render life meaningless, and every action permissible?

In his chapter, David Kyle Johnson considers the problem of evil as presented in the highly irreverent cartoon *South Park*. In the show, Eric Cartman is a "manipulative, self-centered bastard whose every action is directed either toward accomplishing his own happiness or the unhappiness of others." So how could a wholly good, all-powerful being, like God allow Eric to achieve complete happiness, by inheriting one million dollars and buying his own theme park, as he does in the episode "Cartmanland"? How could such a being allow natural disasters, such as those that are visited upon South Park, like Mecha-Streisand? Characters on the show – Sheila and Gerald Broflovski (Kyle's parents), Chef, and Jesus Christ – give answers to these questions that resemble the answers given by the theologian John Calvin (1509–64), the contemporary philosopher John Hick, and the Old Testament character Job.

In his chapter, Daniel Gallagher uses the TV show *Lost* to explore the relationship between faith and reason. In the show, Rose claims to have knowledge beyond everyone else's reckoning. Rose "knows" her husband is still alive, that the survivor's plight will come to an end, and that God used the island to cure her cancer. However, when asked how she knows, she responds "I just know." Does Rose actually know, merely believe, or does she simply have faith? Does faith count as knowledge? Gallagher uses Aquinas' distinctions between knowledge, opinion, and faith to argue that, although a certain level of knowledge about the supernatural is possible, most belief about the supernatural is grounded in faith. Though belief by faith is not necessarily contrary to reason, Rose – and in fact all of us – would do well to admit the difference between faith and knowledge.

In their chapter, Jason Eberl and Jennifer Vines take us to the science fiction universe of *Battlestar Galactica* in which an alien race of humans are trying to save themselves from the Cylons, a race of artificially intelligent beings that the humans themselves created. Ironically, the Cylons believe in one god, while the humans generally believe in many gods – although some are atheists who regard the belief that the gods control and preordain events, like those in the series, as superstitious nonsense. The question naturally arises: are there sound arguments for God's existence? Can the problem of evil be answered? If not, are we forced into atheism? If there is no God or gods, then is life rendered meaningless? Or can we find meaning in life's pursuits – like preserving the human race – even if God does not exist? Eberl and Vines, representing diverging viewpoints, argue that such a pursuit could be a source of common ground between atheists and theists, as could admitting the limits of both reason and faith.

11

Cartmanland and the Problem of Evil

David Kyle Johnson

Summary

Eric Cartman is an unmitigated bastard. If God should make anyone miserable, it's Cartman. Yet, in the episode "Cartmanland," he inherits a million dollars, buys his own theme park, locks everyone else out, and attains perfect happiness. Human free will explains much of the evil we observe in *South Park* and elsewhere. But how can free will explain the natural evil that is caused by hurricanes, earthquakes, and diseases? Is God's existence disporoven?

There's No God, Dude!

Cartman is an ass. To put it more precisely, Cartman is a manipulative, self-centered bastard whose every action is directed either toward accomplishing his own happiness or the unhappiness of others. However you put it, Cartman is the kind of kid who deserves to be miserable. When misfortune befalls him, we think good has happened. If fortune smiles on him, we don't think he deserves it – instead, we think something evil has happened. This is precisely the conclusion Kyle draws when Cartman gets his own amusement park. In the *South Park* episode "Cartmanland" – just after he objects to being required to attend his own grandmother's funeral because it is "taking up [his] whole Saturday" and laments that her funeral is taking longer than the time it took her to die – Cartman learns that he is the primary benefactor of his grandmother's estate, and he inherits one million dollars from her. He immediately purchases the local amusement park, renames it "Cartmanland," and buys television commercial time to declare that the best thing about Cartmanland is, "You can't come . . . especially Stan and Kyle." Cartman then spends all day, every day, riding any ride he wants without waiting in line. In this way, Cartman attains complete happiness.

Kyle views Cartman's happiness as a horrendous evil. Cartman doesn't deserve such happiness and his attaining it just isn't right. But, according to Kyle, the problem goes much deeper. Kyle observes that these events are not just unbelievable, but given his worldview – which includes the **belief** that God exists – they are impossible. God, if he exists, is an all-good and all-powerful God, who exercises a measure of control in the universe and who should not let horrendous evil occur. Thus, assuming such a God exists, it is impossible for Cartman to attain such happiness. But, since Cartman's happiness is undeniable, Kyle is forced to revise his worldview and conclude that God doesn't exist. Kyle's **argument** is a form of the *problem of evil*. Atheists – those who do not believe in the existence of God – have always used variations of the problem of evil. Philosophers would call Kyle's variation an example of the ***logical** problem of moral evil*. This problem suggests that the existence of moral evil – evil caused by human action – is logically incompatible with God's existence. If Kyle had a PhD in philosophy, he likely would have expressed the problem like this:

> Premise 1: If God exists, given that he is all-good and allpowerful, he would not allow Cartman to be completely happy (for that is a great evil).
> Premise 2: But now that Cartman has his own amusement park, Cartman is completely happy (again, a great evil).
>
> Conclusion: Therefore, God does not exist.[1]

This argument is valid; if its premises are true, its conclusion is true. Those who object to the argument must – if they want their objection to be successful – do so by objecting to the truth of one of its premises; they must present good reason to think that either Premise (1) or (2) is false. And that is exactly what those who object to it try to do.

In this chapter, we'll look at some solutions to the problem of evil that have been proposed by the citizens of South Park, and we will see how they parallel solutions proposed by some Western philosophers, both old and new. We'll see which pro-posals fail and why, and whether any solve the problem. In the end, the reader should have a much better understanding the arguments and "solutions" that surround the problem of evil. Before belief in God can be justified, the problem of evil must be confronted.

And That's It?!? The Story of Job

In the "Cartmanland" episode, when Kyle's parents discover that he has renounced his faith, they take it upon themselves to restore his faith. They attempt to do so by telling him their *own* version of the story of Job. The story of Job comes from the Book of Job in the Old Testament and is about a man who suffers horrendous

---

[1] It is important to note that one could substitute any evil for "Cartman's complete happiness" and the conclusion would still follow. Often, when the argument is made, the phrase "evil exists" is sub-stituted for "Cartman's complete happiness."

evils and yet retains his faith in God. According to the Book of Job, God allows Satan to inflict these evils upon Job to prove to Satan that Job will remain faithful despite them. Many people use this story as an answer to the problem of evil. Kyle's parents give their own version of the story noting that, despite all of the horrible things that happen to him and his family, Job "still kept his faith." Kyle's response to the story is quite telling: "And that's it? That's the end? That's the most horrible story I have ever heard. Why would God do such horrible things to a good person just to prove a point to Satan? I was right. Job has all his children killed and Michael Bay gets to keep making movies. There isn't a God."

Kyle seems to have some very good points. He observes that the actions of God in this story seem to be inconsistent with how we view God. Most of us would not think it morally justified to cause that kind of suffering to "prove a point." But more importantly, Kyle seems to recognize that the story of Job does not answer the problem of evil. It is an example of someone continuing to believe in God despite suffering horrendous evil, but it does not challenge a specific premise of the argument. Yes, the "moral" of the story – what it suggests that you do in response – seems to be "Everyone should behave like Job; one should continue to believe in God even if one suffers horrendous evil." But it does not show *why* one should behave like Job – why one should not view horrendous evil as conclusive evidence against God.

Yet many people, like Kyle's parents, suggest that a full understanding of the argument of the Book of Job does solve the problem of evil. How might we re-understand it to solve the problem of evil? The argument could be understood this way: "The fact that Job continued to believe in God despite 'the evidence of evil' shows that evil is not conclusive evidence against God." However, this is a very bad argument because the fact that Job didn't find the evidence to be conclusive doesn't show that the evidence is not conclusive. Recall the episode "Chef Aid." The fact that the jury, after hearing the Chewbacca defense, finds Chef guilty does not mean that the Chewbacca defense was conclusive evidence against Chef; the jury was just easily persuaded by bad argument. Likewise, in "Trapped in the Closet," the fact that Tom Cruise ignored all the evidence that he was in a closet does not mean that the evidence wasn't conclusive; Tom Cruise was simply in denial – everyone else recognized the evidence as conclusive. He was, after all, sitting in Stan's closet. In the same way, the fact that Job didn't find the evidence against God to be conclusive does not mean everyone should do the same; Job simply may not have recognized the problem.

The fact that the story of Job does not answer the problem of evil is not that surprising to biblical scholars. The story was not intended for that purpose. More than likely, if Job actually existed, he would not have even considered his suffering as reason to not believe in God's existence. The belief that God was "all good" and would thus never cause suffering didn't become prevalent until after Plato's philosophical influence had worked its way through Christianity; thus, Job would not have viewed his suffering as evidence against God's existence at all. This, coupled with the fact that atheism would have been virtually unheard of by Job, makes the fact that Job continued to believe in God's existence, despite his suffering, no surprise.

In the story, what Job's suffering does is threaten his approval of God. Job never questions that God exists, in fact he admits that God is responsible for his suffering. But this divine responsibility causes Job to question whether he should continue to be faithful; he wonders what good it is to be righteous if the righteous are punished like the wicked. At the end of the story, God rebukes the answers of others and offers his own saying – in a nutshell – "I am the creator of everything; you have no right to question my actions, nor can you understand their purpose." Job agrees and once again praises God.

Even though the story is not about the problem of evil, one might think that the moral of the story of Job could be modified in order to answer the problem of evil. "You can't question God's existence when evil occurs," one might suggest, "God is the creator of the universe and is beyond our understanding. No one can understand the reason for which he allows such things to occur, nor does anyone have the right to question him." But this answer is no good because it begs the question. In other words, one giving this as an answer to the problem of evil *assumes* the truth of what they are trying to prove. Notice that the answer itself works only if God exists. God has an unknown reason to allow evil only if he exists; no one has the right to question God only if God exists. But *that God exists* is exactly what the argument is supposed to prove. You can't simply assume the truth of what you are trying to prove to prove that it is true. Not only is that bad **reasoning** but, also, no one who doesn't share your assumption will be convinced. So, as Kyle concluded, the story of Job does not seem to be of much help at all. What other solutions could there be?

The Sweet Milk of Our Tears

In the episode "Kenny Dies" – the only episode in which Kenny dies and "stays dead" for a while – Stan wrestles with the problem of evil. He asks Chef how God could let his friend die, and Chef responds that God "gives us life and love and health, just so that he can tear it all away and make us cry, so he can drink the sweet milk of our tears. You see, it's our tears Stan that give God his great power." Although this answer seems cruel, and clearly wrong, it actually mirrors some philosophers' answers to the problem of evil. Chef suggests that God allows evil to occur for his own benefit. This is not unlike Jonathan Edwards' (1703–58) or John Calvin's (1509–64) solution to the problem of evil.[2] They suggest that God allows evil because he wishes to punish evildoers, an action which benefits God himself. As Edwards specifically suggests, punishing evildoers is the most perfect

---

[2]   See John Calvin, *Institutes of the Christian Religion*, trans. by Henry Beveridge (Grand Rapids, MI: William B. Eerdmans, 1957), Book 1, chs. 16–18; Book 3, ch. 23. Also see Jonathan Edwards, "Wicked Men Useful in Their Destruction Only," in *The Works of President Edwards*, vol. 6, ed. by Edward Parsons and Edward Williams (New York: B. Franklin, 1968). Edwards is mainly addressing the doctrine of Hell, but clearly realizes that the existence of evil is necessary for God to demonstrate his holiness.

way for God to demonstrate his holiness and thus bring glory to himself.[3] The idea is that a benefit to God outweighs any evil done to humans.

But not many philosophers find this solution satisfactory. God benefiting himself by demonstrating his holiness at our expense – by making us suffer through evil and punishing us for it – doesn't seem to be better than Chef's explanation; we just don't think God is that cruel. Further, it is not clear why God must punish evildoers to demonstrate his holiness. Isn't God all-powerful? Could he have not demonstrated this fact, with equal effectiveness, in some other (non-evil) way? It certainly seems so. Most do not think that Chef, Edwards, or Calvin are on the right track.

You *Are* Up There!

After Stan and Kyle try to sneak into Cartmanland, Cartman decides he needs a security guard. Since the security guard won't accept rides on his attractions as payment, Cartman is forced to let two people a day into his park to pay the security guard's salary. His problem escalates when Cartman discovers that he needs maintenance, food, drink, cotton candy, video surveillance, a box office, and janitors. Soon, Cartman has a fully functioning and successful amusement park. But since he now has to wait in line to ride his rides, he doesn't want it anymore and sells it back to the owner for the original million. Most of his money is immediately seized by the IRS (since he didn't pay any taxes when he owned the park) and the rest goes to Kenny's family (since Kenny died on the Mine Shaft ride). Cartman is now miserable. He stands outside the park, throwing rocks at it, and the security guard who once worked for him maces him in the face.

Stan brings Kyle outside to witness these events, and observes: "Look Kyle, Cartman is totally miserable, even more miserable than he was before because he had his dream and lost it." Stan, by this observation, restores Kyle's belief in God. Clearly, according to Stan and Kyle, Cartman's suffering has somehow relieved the tension between the existence of God and the horrendous evil of Cartman's perfect happiness. Their answer is this: God, being all-good, wanted to accomplish a great good: the *perfect suffering* of Cartman. But the only way to accomplish this great good was to give Cartman perfect happiness (an evil) for a brief period and then rip it away from him. Since the good of Cartman's suffering outweighs the evil of his brief happiness, an overall greater good was accomplished, making the evil of his (temporary) happiness justified.

This answer mirrors a common way in which theists – those who believe in God – answer the problem of evil. They challenge a specific premise in the argument – the suggestion that God would prevent evil if he wanted to and could – by suggesting that he might have other trumping desires. In other words, they suggest that God might not guarantee the absence of all evil because there might be something he

---

[3] For a wonderful rendition of Edwards' argument, see William J. Wainwright, "Jonathan Edwards and the Doctrine of Hell," in *Jonathan Edwards: Philosophical Theologian*, ed. by Paul Helm and Oliver Crisp (London: Ashgate Publishing, 2004).

desires more than the absence of evil that requires the existence of evil. But what might that be? The presence of good! Although it is true that God doesn't like evil, it is also true that God loves (and wants to accomplish) good. If some certain goods can only be accomplished by allowing certain evils – as long as the good accomplished outweighs the evil allowed (as long as the good is more good than the evil is bad) – allowing that evil is justified. In fact, since the world is a better place if those evils are allowed and then outweighed, you would expect God to allow them because he wants the world to be as good as possible. In short, the suggestion is that the existence of evil does not stand in logical contradiction with God's existence because it is false that God would necessarily prevent all evil. God would – and in fact should – allow evil that accomplishes a greater good and, thus, the mere existence of evil is not conclusive evidence against God's existence. The mutual existence of God and evil is logically possible.

But some questions remain: What kind of goods can only be accomplished by allowing evil? And wouldn't every evil have to lead to a greater good? To answer these questions, there are different ways of understanding this answer. Stan and Kyle view the specific event of Cartman's suffering as a good that could only be accomplished at the expense of Cartman's brief happiness. Philosophers would call Cartman's happiness a "first order" evil and his suffering a "second order" good. Other examples of second order goods would be acts of compassion, like healing those who are sick or fighting for Starvin' Marvin to stay on the planet Marclar, or acts of bravery, like sacrificing oneself in battle to save others, standing up to save the whales from the Japanese, like Stan, by captaining the MV *Steve Irwin*, or still depicting Muhammad in your 201st episode, despite the fact that you received death threats from a group of cowardly fundamentalist jihadist Muslims. These acts are made possible because they are responses to evil events and their good (supposedly) outweighs the evil they are responses to. They are second order goods made possible by first order evils.

To solve the problem of evil, some theists suggest that for any given evil event that occurs, God allowed that event to occur to accomplish some greater (second order) good here on earth. But this suggestion is problematic: every first order evil would have to lead to a second order good. The only way allowing a first order evil would be justified would be if it accomplished a second order good; if a first order evil ever went "unanswered" – if no greater good was accomplished as a result – God should not have allowed it, and it would be direct evidence against God's existence. Since there are clearly such unanswered evils – the rape and murder of a baby, for example – it seems that the theist still has a problem.

Another way to attempt to solve the problem is with what is known as the *free will defense*. Those who use this defense avoid the problem of "unanswered evils" by suggesting that individual evils are not answered, but must be risked by God if he is to allow good to occur. Good can only be accomplished by our free will. As Augustine (354–430) put it, only free acts are good acts;[4] if we do not have the free

---

[4] See "On Free Will," in *Augustine: Earlier Writings*, trans. by John Burleigh (Philadelphia: Westminster Press, 1953).

will to choose between good and evil, nothing we do is truly good. Unless we have the option of choosing evil (which we can only have with free will), we cannot be given moral credit for choosing good, and if we cannot be given moral credit for an action, it cannot be truly good. Thus, without free will, there is no good. But if we are to have free will – if we are to truly have the option of doing evil – we must remain unhindered. God can't stop Cartman from trying to eliminate the Jews, for example, if Cartman is to have the freedom to do so; likewise, if we are to be free, he cannot stop us if we are about to choose to do evil. Thus, "the risk of evil" is necessary if there is to be any good in the world. Since God loves good – and presumably wants to accomplish good more than he wants to avoid evil – the risk of evil is one that he is willing to take (even though he hates evil). Thus, so it is argued, the existence of evil is compatible with the existence of God and the problem of evil is solved.

One might wonder how it could be that there are goods that God can't accomplish without allowing evil. "Isn't God all-powerful?" one might wonder. "Couldn't God have created beings that always freely choose to do the good?" But the answer to this hinges upon the definition of free will. A free being is one that is not forced to act in the ways that he does. In order to ensure that everyone always did good, God would have to force everyone (in some way) to always do good. To suggest that God could create creatures that always freely choose to do good is to suggest that he could create "non-controlled creatures that are controlled" – a logical impossibility.

One might also wonder about evil not caused by human free will. After all, in the Cartmanland episode, part of the reason that Kyle lost his faith was because he developed a hemorrhoid (while Cartman was rewarded with his own theme park). I doubt there is anything that Kyle "freely chose to do" as a kid that led to that and it does seems hard to explain that evil by pointing to human free will. Such evils are called "natural evils." Other natural evils include earthquakes, tsunamis, hurricanes, tornados and Mecha-Streisand – all events that cause suffering but seem to not be caused by human free will.[5] Many philosophers think that, even though one can make sense of why God would allow moral evils, one cannot make sense of why God would allow natural evils and suggest that the existence of natural evil is conclusive evidence against God's existence. Philosophers call this the problem of natural evil. And as a solution to the problem of natural evil, the free will solution falls short.

Jesus Christ and John Hick: The Soul Making Theodicy

A solution that attempts to solve both the moral and natural evil problem is John Hick's *soul making theodicy*. The word *theodicy* comes from the Latin language and

---

[5] Given that Streisand chose to turn herself into Mecha-Streisand, Mecha-Streisand would not be a natural evil if you counted Barbra Streisand as a human. But this is something I am sure Matt and Trey are not willing to do; thus they probably view Mecha-Streisand as a natural evil.

refers to a justification of God's existence in the face of so much evil in the world. John Hick tries to give such a justification and suggests that evil – both moral and natural – is allowed in the world so that we, individually and as a species, may develop our character.[6] Actions derived from bestowed perfect characters are not as good as actions derived from developed perfected characters. To ensure that the world contains the best kind of actions, God allows evil to exist so that we may respond to it, thus developing and eventually perfecting our characters. So, even though specific evils may go unanswered, the world as a whole is better if we develop our characters – which can only be accomplished by responding to evil – and the general presence of first order evil is justified.

Notice how John Hick's reasoning mirrors Jesus' in "Are You There God? It's Me, Jesus." In this episode, the South Park masses are ready to crucify Jesus because he promised that God would appear at the Millennium, and he has not. Stan and Jesus have a conversation where Jesus claims that "life is about problems, and overcoming those problems, and growing and learning from obstacles. If God just fixed every-thing for us, then there would be no point in our existence." Even though Jesus is talking about prayer, the point seems to be the same. The reason that God doesn't "fix everything for us" – the reason that he doesn't eliminate all evil – is because if he did, we would not be allowed to learn and grow from obstacles and our learning and growing is important (even more important than the elimination of evil).

Not everyone likes Hick's solution, but even if it is accepted as a solution to both the moral and natural problem as we have discussed, the debate is not over! There still seems to be a problem with the *amount* of evil in the world. Evil may be compatible with God's existence because it is necessary to accomplish some good, but it certainly seems that God could have accomplished just as much good with less evil than we have now. One might even suggest that the amount of evil in the world seems to provide good evidence against God's existence. Regardless to free will, wouldn't God have stopped the Holocaust? Who would have refrained from stopping Hitler in the name of "letting him freely choose"? And doesn't moral evil provide us with enough to develop our characters? Did God have to embed the necessity of natural disasters into the very fabric of our universe? This is what philosophers call the *evidential problem of evil*. And even though it does not logically disprove God's existence, it may make atheism the more rational belief.

At this point, theists often point out that, for all we know there could be some unknown reason for God to allow every bit of evil in the world. After all, if God exists, his reasoning would be beyond us. However, atheists have argued, this shows theism to be **unfalsifiable** and thus irrational. Nothing, short of God appearing (as he does at the Millennium in South park) and saying he doesn't exist could convince them. So, it seems, despite the problem of evil, theistic belief isn't going anywhere soon.

[6]   See John Hick, *Evil and the Love of God* (San Francisco: Harper, 1978).

12

Aquinas and Rose on Faith and Reason

Daniel B. Gallagher

Summary

Thomas Aquinas taught that faith and knowledge are mutually interdependent and reciprocally interpenetrating. By exploring the "knowledge" (*epistēmē*), "opinion" (*doxa*), and faith of Rose and the other *Lost* castaways, we can see why Aquinas held all three to be necessary. Knowledge supports faith, and faith perfects knowledge. The refusal to allow knowledge to be perfected by faith is "sloth" (*acedia*), and the refusal to allow reason to function within the context of faith is "presumption" (*praesumptio*). Aquinas invites us to probe what we believe with our minds, and to allow our minds to lead us to belief.

If there is one thing Rose Henderson's fellow castaways know about her, it is this: Rose "knows." Hurley knows that Rose does not merely hope her husband Bernard is still alive, she knows he is. Charlie knows that Rose does not merely think he will receive help from on high if he asks for it, she knows he will. Locke knows that Rose not only surmises that their plight will come to an end, she knows it will – and knows that Locke knows the same. Her husband Bernard knows that Rose not only feels that the island has healed her from terminal cancer, she knows it has. Everybody knows that Rose knows. But nobody can refrain from asking, "How does Rose know?" She baffles everyone, including her husband Bernard, with a rather ordinary response: "I just know."

The island Rose and her castaway companions find themselves stranded on becomes a place where everyone is challenged to give reasons for hope – not only in words, but in action. Some, placing their hope in an unseen satellite, decide to pitch in and help Bernard construct a large SOS sign on the beach. Others, placing their hope in what lies beyond the sea, get to work building an ersatz raft. Some gradually begin to place their hope in the island itself and relocate themselves inland. Some place their hope in the transceiver, others in firearms. Every time the castaways act upon certain hopes, they find themselves wrestling with how to best articulate them – to others and to themselves. All are confronted with the issue of whether hope is reasonable or unreasonable, rational or irrational. Rose, however, sets herself apart. While never wavering, she offers no explanation for her faith.

Thomas Aquinas (1225–74), one of the most brilliant philosophical minds of the medieval era, taught that such a response holds no water (the one thing never lacking on the island!). Faith and knowledge are interdependent upon each other and interpenetrate one another. Aquinas would have admired the unshakeable certainty of Rose's faith, but he would have cautioned her against letting faith trump the role of her natural ability to **reason**. Aquinas turned to Christian scripture in support of his conviction that faith cannot do without solid reason to buttress it: "Always be ready to give an explanation to anyone who asks you for a reason for your hope" (1 Peter 3:15).

The character of Rose Henderson spurns us diehard Lostaways to confront the same issue week after week as we throw ourselves onto the living room couch and join our friends on the island: just what is the relationship between faith and reason? Are they absolutely separate and distinct? Do they overlap? Or are they one and same thing? Is faith a type of knowledge? If so, can we give a more convincing rationale for why we believe the things we believe than simply, "I just know?"

What Can We Know?

Humans, of course, did not have to wait until the crash of Oceanic Flight 815 to begin asking such questions. They have been around as long as philosophy itself. Socrates, in fact, could not help but wonder whether *all* of our "knowledge" might not be anything more than mere "opinion." Socrates' star pupil Plato, in his *Republic*, continues to refine these two types of cognition. Knowledge (*epistēmē* in Greek) is the type of certitude we have only after all the sensible changeable characteristics of things are somehow left aside. Consequently, knowledge of a thing is only had when we fully possess the "**idea**" or pure "form" (*eidos*) of a thing. Opinion (*doxa*) refers to the imperfect, but by no means false, knowledge that we have of things through our senses.

So is faith one of these? Is it something like "knowledge" (*epistēmē*) or "opinion" (*doxa*)? When Rose says that she knows her husband is still alive, does she mean that her certitude even surpasses the concrete, sensible experience she had of him when they shook hands for the first time on that blistery winter night in Brooklyn ("SOS")? If so, then perhaps faith is something like *epistēmē*. Or does she mean that she is quite satisfied with accepting even the fuzziest of premonitions as if they were cold hard facts? If so, then maybe faith is something like *doxa*.

Aquinas, following the lines of a highly influential definition of faith proposed by Hugh of St. Victor in the twelfth century, asserts that faith is actually "mid-way between knowledge and opinion."[1] He believes that faith shares both in the certainty

---

[1]   Thomas Aquinas, *Summa Theologica: Complete English Edition in Five Volumes* (Westminster: Christian Classics, 1981), vol. 2, pp. 873–4 (I-II, q. 67, a. 3).

we associate with knowledge, as well as in the imperfection characterizing opinion. In fact, "to be imperfect as knowledge is the very essence of faith."[2]

The ongoing saga of *Lost* teaches us that we can begin to penetrate this **paradox** only after we have clarified the object of faith. We must ask ourselves what, or whom, we ultimately place our faith in. Aquinas, who is a master at making distinctions, begins by distinguishing between the "formal" object of faith from the "material" object of faith. Though the material object of faith is God, the formal object – that is, the aspect under which the believer views God as the object of his or her **belief** – is "first truth."[3]

Just what is Aquinas up to here? He is making what philosophers like to call a "conceptual distinction." A conceptual distinction is a distinction based on the variety of ways we can conceive a single identical object. A single piece of wood, for example, can be "conceived" either as a branch (when it is attached to a tree), a stick (when it is lying on the ground), or a walking-staff (when I pick it up and use it during my hike). Similarly, "God" and "first truth" refer to the same object (i.e., the divine being), but through different conceptual lenses. "God" refers to the omnipotent, omniscient being that is the source of everything. "First truth" refers to that same being, but with reference to the fact that such a being is the ground of all other truths. We could say that "God" refers to the divine being in a descending way (i.e., all things proceed "downward" from God), whereas "first truth" refers to God in an ascending way (i.e., all truths lead "upward" to God). Someday, when we behold God face to face, we will know the divinity perfectly and directly simply as "truth." In the meantime, since our knowledge of the divinity is only imperfect and indirect, we are only able to conceive God as the "first truth" among many truths. We reason to the existence of a "first truth" because other truths appear to us as contingent and dependent. As we shall see, Rose falls into the trap of equating the power of "first truth" with all contingent truths. Her faith in a higher power tends to trump the uncertain and imperfect contingencies in the finite world. She claims to "know" things that she really only "believes."

Let's take the filming of the show we love so much as an example. I believe that the episodes of *Lost* are truly being filmed on the Hawaiian island of Oahu. I have not been there to watch the filming take place, nor can I deduce from watching the television program itself that it is indeed filmed there. I accept the statement that "*Lost* is filmed on the island of Oahu" as true because I heard the producers say this and I believe the producers are credible. Based on their testimony, I *believe* that *Lost* is filmed on Oahu; I don't really *know* it as scientific knowledge. I have reasonable grounds for believing that when the producers tell me that *Lost* is filmed on Oahu, they are telling the truth. Although knowledge and belief seem at first to be the same, they are in fact quite different. The actors who have been filmed on Oahu have direct knowledge that

---

[2] *Summa Theologica*, vol. 2, pp. 873–874 (I-II, q. 67, a. 3).
[3] *Summa Theologica*, vol. 3, pp. 1185, 1191, 1193 (II-II, q. 4, a. 1; q. 5, a. 1; q. 5, a. 3). See also *The Disputed Questions on Truth*, trans. Robert W. Mulligan (Chicago: Henry Regnery, 1952), vol. 2, pp. 204–206 (*Quaestiones disputatae de veritate*, q. 14, a. 1).

the show has been filmed on Oahu. My belief that the show has been filmed on Oahu is indirect: it depends on the truth of the producers' testimony, which in turn depends on where the filming has taken place. This is to say that my belief depends on a prior truth.

Chain of Truth

The truths to which the *Lost* survivors most often give their assent depend on prior truths. The truth of what Shannon claims to hear though the transceiver depends on the accuracy of her translation of the French. Assuming her translation is accurate, the truth of what is being said by the mysterious French voice (which ends up belonging to Rousseau) depends on whether the call for distress is still valid 16 years later. The list of dependencies goes on and on. All of the castaways' deliberations are, in fact, based on an "if." If there are other people on the island, then perhaps they can work together to find a way off. But this depends on whether or not the "others" are truly friendly. The dependence of every truth on a prior truth is what in fact keeps us coming back for the next episode.

The writers of *Lost* capitalize on the fact that human beings tend to place their ultimate hope in something, someone, or somewhere that ultimately fails to satisfy. In his life prior to the air crash, Jack placed his hope in his ability to cure people ("Man of Science, Man of Faith" and "The Hunting Party"). Kate placed her hope in her ability to deceive people ("Born to Run" and "Tabula Rasa"). Jin placed his hope in the employment offered to him by his father-in-law ("In Translation" and "Exodus"). Charlie placed his hope in his big brother Liam ("The Moth" and "Fire + Water"), Claire in the psychic Mr. Malkin ("Raised by Another"), and Locke in his biological father Anthony Cooper ("Deus Ex Machina"). The Virgin Mary statues containing contraband become a potent and multi-layered symbol of the human tendency to place ultimate hope in something non-divine, even when that something – or someone – should ultimately lead us to the divine ("House of the Rising Sun," "Exodus," and "The 23rd Psalm"). Because the hopes of so many of *Lost*'s characters had been shattered even before they found themselves on the island, they wander around carrying a heavy load of betrayal and regret during their plight.

Rose Colored Glasses

Except perhaps Rose. While everybody around her anxiously tries to make sense of what has happened, Rose is merely grateful to be alive. While others see only doom and gloom on the horizon, Rose accepts the small blessings that come her way.

Rose keeps her distance from what Aquinas calls *acedia* in Latin, the greatest sin against faith. Though it is often translated as "sloth," *acedia* is a much more technical term. It designates a type of torpor preventing a person from enjoying things that are genuinely good. It is a spiritual paralysis that stymies the ability to look beyond the bad. It is "to look upon some worthwhile good as impossible to achieve, whether alone or with the help of others," and it can "sometimes dominate one's affections to the point that he begins to think he can never again be given aspirations towards the good."[4]

No one on the island shows clearer signs of *acedia* than Charlie Pace, to whom Rose offers comfort early in the first season of the series. At that time, Charlie and Rose were standing on opposite ends of the spectrum spanning from hope to despair, from faith to *acedia*. Charlie was once religious, faithful, and repentant. He sought reconciliation for the sins he committed during the wild, early days of DriveShaft, only to be lured back into heroin addiction by none other than his big brother Liam – the handsome lead singer ("The Moth"). Charlie has been so deeply hurt through relationships with his father ("Fire + Water"), his brother, and Lucy – the one person whose trust he won only to abuse ("Homecoming") – that he is all but completely incapable of entrusting himself to anybody or anything. Though he remembers how he was once a religious man, he now thinks he can "never again be given aspirations towards the good."

Just at the moment when it seems Charlie would never dig himself out of his deep *acedia*, Rose reminds him that faith is never impossible ("Whatever the Case May Be"). "It's a fine line between denial and faith," she says to him as they sit together in the dark on the beach. "It's much better on my side." She then reminds Charlie of what he once knew, but finds impossible anymore to do: "You need to ask for help." At this, Charlie breaks down and sobs, preparing him for the grueling road to recovery from addiction with Locke's help.

Does Rose *Really* Know?

Rose herself, however, misdirects her faith. While she seems to rise above the fickle fortunes that distress everyone else, she is not immune from the temptation to mistake what Aquinas calls "first truth" for the truth itself. In other words, she claims to *know* what in reality she only *believes*. To understand the temptation, we have to take a closer look at what Aquinas teaches about the relationship between faith and reason.

Reason, Aquinas teaches, is the faculty by which human beings attain knowledge of what is real. Any such knowledge, Aquinas holds, must be acquired through the senses. "Nothing comes to exist in the intellect which does not first exist in the senses."[5] In this way, Aquinas distinguishes himself from the Platonic tradition we considered earlier. Though it is true that sensible realities are always in a state of flux and instability, our intellect is able to abstract a stable nature from reality that allows us to call it "x."

---

[4] *Summa Theologica*, vol. 3, p. 1256 (II-II, q. 20, a. 4).

[5] *Summa Theologica*, vol. 4, pp. 1896–1897 (II-II, q. 173, a. 2) and vol. 3, pp. 278–9 (I, q. 55, a. 2).

The fact that we can be mistaken about the natures of things, or the fact that we can have sensible experience of things without being able to articulate fully their respective natures, need not bother us too much. For the first several episodes, the "smoke monster" remained just as enigmatic to *Lost's* characters as it did to its viewers. Later, Locke encounters it in the jungle ("Walkabout"), though we the viewers are not given a chance to look at it. Finally, when Mr. Eko stares it down "face to face" during his hike with Charlie ("The 23rd Psalm"), we are offered a good, long look at it. We see that it is composed of dark, black smoke, and that it seems to contain vague, flashing images within. There is more we would like to know about it, but we know enough about it to call it the "smoke monster" to distinguish it from other things. Our understanding of what (or who) the smoke monster is waits to be expanded, but it would be hard for us to doubt whether we have knowledge of it.

Do *We* Really Know?

If, as Aquinas teaches, all our knowledge comes through the senses, how can we ever attain knowledge of supersensible things? God, having no sensible qualities that can be seen or heard or touched, would be included among such things. Aquinas argues that although we can have no direct, sensible experience of God, we can come to know God's existence by exercising our natural power to reason. Using Aquinas's own terminology, the existence of God is not something obvious or knowable in itself (*per se notum*), but only by way of demonstration.[6] Among the most famous of Aquinas's demonstrations are his "five ways" in which he "proves" that God exists: by motion, efficient cause, possibility and necessity, the hierarchy of beings, and the government of things.[7]

The first two of these five **proofs** most manifestly begin with sensible realities and proceed to demonstrate that all finite things are dependent on a first efficient cause. In philosophical lingo, an "efficient cause" is not one that happens to be unusually successful in producing its effect. Rather, in the words of Aristotle, it is the cause which is "the primary source of the change or coming to rest" in a thing.[8] The first of these efficient causes, Aquinas concludes, "is what all call God." Philosophers continue to argue over whether the five ways can maintain their persuasive power if detached from the monotheistic Christian context in which they were formed, but Aquinas clearly believes that there is a reasonable, logical basis for the assertion "God exists." *That* God exists is wholly within the grasp of natural reason; *what* or *who* God is can be partially penetrated by natural reason, but only comes to fuller light through revelation and faith.

[6] *Summa Theologica*, vol. 1, pp. 11–12 (I, q. 2, a. 1).

[7] *Summa Theologica*, vol. 1, pp. 13–14 (I, q. 2, a. 3).

[8] *Introduction to Aristotle*, ed. Richard McKeon (New York: Random House, 1947), p. 122 (*Physica*, Book II, Ch. 3).

According to Aquinas, faith, insofar as its divine object infinitely surpasses the finite capabilities of the human intellect, can ultimately only be given by grace. Though unaided human reason can come to know that the divine being exists, it is unable to know the full nature of that divine being without the divine being's aid. But we can prepare to receive faith through what Aquinas calls the *praeambula ad articulos*, or the "preambles to the articles of faith."[9] Philosophy can assert that God exists, God is one, and God is "first truth." Philosophy can make other similar assertions because the human mind is able to deduce truths regarding supersensible realities based on its direct experience of sensible realities. Human reason, however, could never have come to know that God exists as a Trinity of persons, or that the second person of the Trinity took on human flesh, if it were not for the self-revelation of God and the gift of faith.

"I have made my peace" – Rose

Accepting God's revelation is not such an easy thing to do. It is, so to speak, an all-or-nothing proposition. Rose shows clear signs that she has given everything to this divine proposition. This becomes more evident through her relationship with Bernard and the contrast between their attitudes of acceptance and non-acceptance. It begins the moment when Bernard makes his all-or-nothing marriage proposal to Rose at Niagara Falls ("SOS"). Only then does Rose return his proposition by informing him of what he must accept if she says "yes": a wife who is terminally ill. This, so to speak, is the return proposition to him. He also accepts.

It is one of the more moving moments in *Lost*, but we soon learn that there are two different worldviews at work in Rose and Bernard's relationship. Rose is at peace with the fact that she is dying. Bernard, though he initially accepted her, cancer-and-all, believes it's worth taking every conceivable measure to stop her from dying.

Hence the trip to Australia to visit the faith healer Isaac of Uluru ("SOS"). Though it seems at first that Bernard's efforts to find a cure for Rose are magnanimous, we discover a hint of selfishness in his motivations. In answer to her protestations against going through with the faith-healing ritual, Bernard begs her: "Will you try Rose? For *me*?" Bernard cannot help but put his faith into each and every worldly means that might lead to Rose's recovery. Rose, on the other hand, has put all her faith in divine providence. "I have made my peace with what is happening to me." She has accepted the all-or-nothing proposition of trust.

Aquinas teaches that the only thing that can elicit such a complete act of trust from us is a wholly perfect being – the first truth. Because this is a being which can neither deceive nor be deceived, it is the only being worthy of our complete trust. Aquinas quickly adds that this perfect being in no way undermines our freedom. Yet whatever trust we place in God is based wholly on the basis of God's

---

[9] *Summa Theologica*, vol. 1, p. 12 (I, q. 2, a. 2).

own credibility. The act of faith is an act that transcends reason, but is by no means unreasonable.

Rose's complete trust in this perfect being makes it impossible for her to receive aid from any other source outside of this being. Despite Isaac's efforts to harness the geological energy that resulted in the miraculous healing of so many hopeless cases before Rose, he tells her, "There is nothing I can do for you" ("SOS").

Though Rose calmly accepts, she makes a stunning decision: she will tell Bernard that she has been healed. She will lie to him.

Does Rose *Presume* to Know?

This is a critical turning point in Rose's journey of faith. Her faith begins to trump everything else – even the moral rectitude of telling the truth. There is a strong allusion during the scene with Isaac that the "place" where Rose might find a home may not be the divine "heaven" she has hoped for.

The contrast between the respective theological and secular world-views of Rose and Bernard comes to a climactic point only after they are reunited on the island after the crash. While Bernard drums up support for his plan to construct a large SOS sign, Rose seems to have found a "home" on the island ("SOS"). Just as Bernard once searched frantically for a way to save Rose from imminent death, he now works furiously to save everyone from being perpetually lost. And this drives Rose crazy. "Why can't you just let things be?" she asks him in exasperation.

Whereas at Isaac of Uluru's house it was Bernard whose reasons were partly selfish, now it is Rose. What Isaac was unable to do for her, the island now has done for her. She "knows" that she has been cured of her cancer. Bernard feels as if he must do everything he can to help their desperate situation and get them off the island. Rose has found that the island has already saved her from a desperate situation. Whereas Charlie was guilty of *acedia*, Rose is now guilty of an opposite sin which Aquinas calls *praesumptio* (presumption). Aquinas defines "presumption" as "a certain type of immoderate hope."[10] The presumptuous person, though a person of faith, directs her hope (often unconsciously) toward one of God's powers rather than toward God alone. Rose believes that this mysterious island has become an instrument through which God has worked a miracle in her life. Indeed, she even suggests that the island itself is the source of the cure. It has become the "place" of which Isaac spoke.

To Know . . . *and* Believe

The tension between two different ultimate horizons – secular and supernatural – is symbolized by the simultaneous construction projects of Mr. Eko's church and Bernard's large SOS signal ("SOS"). The church is a sign that the immediate, visible

---

10 *Summa Theologica*, vol. 3, p. 1256 (II-II, q. 21, a. 1).

world is not the ultimate horizon. The letters in the sand are a sign that human beings must do everything within their power to save themselves. When Bernard insists that he is only trying to save everyone, Mr. Eko confidently remarks, "People are saved in different ways."

Aquinas teaches that it is entirely possible to come to certain knowledge of certain basic realities – including God – that we tend to relegate exclusively to the realm of faith. The certain knowledge of those things, however, can only attain its true goal if one further assents to that which is revealed by God. Faith and reason are in harmony with one another, not in opposition. Faith does not abrogate the role of reason, but neither can reason wholly take the place of faith.

Rose is an inspiration to her companions because she is a woman of faith. But her faith has left little room for the role of natural knowledge. What she claims to "know," she actually "believes"; not in the sense of *doxa* or opinion, but in the sense that those things she holds by faith pertain to a transcendent essence so as to be uniquely distinguished from those things she knows by the light of natural reason. The knowledge involved in faith is radically different from the knowledge involved in natural cognition. The latter begins in the senses, whereas the former is beyond the senses. According to Aquinas, the respective objects of natural knowledge and supernatural faith grant them each a legitimate autonomy. Rose is guilty of a confusion of idioms. She mistakenly believes that the type of knowledge distinctive of faith is interchangeable with the type of knowledge distinctive of natural reason.

Aquinas thought differently. "One should not presume that the object of faith is scientifically demonstrable, lest presuming to demonstrate what is of faith, one should produce inconclusive reasons and offer occasion for unbelievers to scoff at a faith based on such ground."[11] Rose doesn't necessarily presume that she can "scientifically" demonstrate her faith, but her experience of being cured elevates all the things she once held by faith to the level of certain knowledge – *epistēmē*, to be precise. Rose knows, but Rose also believes. Aquinas admonishes her, and us, to know the difference between the two. At the same time, he urges us to probe what we believe with our minds, and to allow our minds to lead us to belief.

---

[11] *Summa Theologica*, vol. 3, p. 1166 (II-II, q. 1, a. 5).

13

"I Am an Instrument of God"

Religious Belief, Atheism, and Meaning

Jason T. Eberl and Jennifer A. Vines

Summary

Gaius Baltar believes in a rational universe, while Caprica Six believes in "one, true God." Admiral Adama is a pragmatist, while Laura Roslin makes crucial decisions based on spiritual visions. If *Battlestar Galactica* were written by David Hume or Bertrand Russell, it would favor Baltar and Adama, but the overall story vindicates Six and Roslin's religious worldview. This chapter presents philosophical arguments for and against God's existence, including Aquinas's "five ways" and the "problem of evil." We also explore how meaning and value can persist in a Godless universe, and the common ground theists and atheists may share.

Gaius Baltar is truly *frakked*! Dr. Amarak has requested to meet with President Roslin to discuss how the Cylons were able to launch their attack on the Twelve Colonies. Baltar, of course, is to be the center-piece of their discussion. But Amarak just happens to be on the *Olympic Carrier*, which Roslin must decide whether to destroy because it poses a threat to the rest of the fleet. With his fate in Roslin's hands, Baltar can only watch how events play out – until his personal vision of Number Six tells him otherwise:

SIX: It's not her decision, Gaius.
BALTAR: No?
SIX: It's God's choice. He wants you to repent . . . Repent of your sins. Accept his true love and you will be saved.
BALTAR: I repent. There, I repent. *I repent.*
("33")

Roslin orders the *Olympic Carrier*'s destruction and Baltar is safe – for the time being.

Baltar's repentance isn't all that sincere; he has a long way to go before sharing the Cylons' **belief** in God and accepting his role in God's plan. Baltar's initial act of faith is motivated solely by his concern for his own "skinny ass." This isn't too different from a proposal made by the mathematician and philosopher Blaise

Pascal (1623–62), who **reasons** that if one believes in God and God exists, then an infinite amount of happiness awaits; whereas if one doesn't believe in God and God exists, then infinite misery will follow. Thus, it's more practical to believe that God exists.[1] But both of us – a religious believer and an atheist – think that whether one believes in God or not should be based on more than such a wager.

We also agree that the veracity of religious belief shouldn't be judged, as Baltar thinks, by dividing religious believers and atheists into two camps – the physically attractive intelligentsia and everyone else:

> SIX: You don't have to mock my faith.
> BALTAR: Sorry. I'm just not very religious.
> SIX: Does it bother you that I am?
> BALTAR: It puzzles me that an intelligent, attractive woman such as yourself should be taken in by all that mysticism and superstition.

("Miniseries")

If beauty and intelligence don't actually correspond to whether or not a person believes in God – and there have been plenty of well-educated religious believers and unattractive atheists to support this premise – then what rational **arguments** could be made either for or against belief in the existence of God?

"A Rational Universe Explained Through Rational Means"

Baltar is convinced he lives in a universe he can and does understand. As a scientist, his entire worldview has been shaped by knowledge derived through **empirical investigation** and rational theorizing. God, it seems clear to Baltar, doesn't fit within this view of reality as he peers through his microscope: "I don't see the hand of God in here. Could I be looking in the wrong place? Let me see. Proteins? Yes. Hemoglobin? Yes. Divine digits? No. Sorry" ("Six Degrees of Separation"). Of course, God isn't empirically observable. But, according to the medieval philosopher and theologian Thomas Aquinas (c.1225–74), God's *effects* are observable, and one can reason from these effects to the conclusion that God exists as their ultimate cause.[2]

Consider one of these alleged divine effects. About to be revealed as a Cylon collaborator, Baltar is both relieved and puzzled when the *Olympic Carrier*, with Amarak onboard, turns up missing. He and Six have different interpretations of this event:

> SIX: God is watching out for you, Gaius.
> BALTAR: The universe is a vast and complex system. Coincidental, serendipitous events are bound to occur. Indeed they are to be expected. It's part of the pattern, part of the plan.

---

[1] Blaise Pascal, *Pensées*, trans. W. F. Trotter (New York: Dover, 2003), §233.
[2] See Thomas Aquinas, *Summa theologiae*, trans. Fathers of the English Dominican Province (New York: Benziger Brothers, 1948), I, Q. 2, a. 2.

SIX: Dr. Amarak posed a threat to you. Now he's gone. Logic says there's a connection.

BALTAR: A connection, maybe. But not God. There is no God or gods, singular or plural. There are no large invisible men, or women for that matter, in the sky taking a personal interest in the fortunes of Gaius Baltar.

("33")

Baltar agrees with Six that events don't occur randomly. There's an *ordered structure* to the universe, defined by laws of nature discoverable through scientific inquiry.

But given the universe's evident structure, is it most reasonable to conclude that such "a vast and complex system" simply formed itself, as unquestioned scientific theory tells us, out of an explosion of infinitely dense matter known as the "big bang"? Aquinas doesn't think so.[3] In his first argument for the existence of God, Aquinas states that every change from a state of *potency* to an *actual* state must be brought about by something that's already actual in a relevant way. To use a basic example from Newtonian physics, if an object is at rest, it has the potential to be in motion, but in order to be actually in motion, something must move it or it must have a part of itself capable of self-propelling it. This ties into Aquinas's second argument, which begins by noting that every *effect* must have a *cause*, and each cause is itself an effect of some other cause. In both cases, a chain of "moved movers" or "caused causes" forms that is discoverable by reason: a pyramid ball sails through the air because it's thrown by Anders's arm, which is stimulated by motor neurons in his brain, which fire because he desires to throw the ball into the goal, which he desires in order to impress Starbuck, which he wants to do because of an evolutionary adaptation that pits him in "tests of manhood" to gain survival and reproductive advantage, and so on all the way back to the big bang – the start of it all.[4]

But is it the start? The big bang, like any other event, is in need of explanation, unless we just accept it as a "brute fact" – incapable of, and thus not requiring, any further explanation:

> The universe began from a state of infinite density about [15 billion years] ago. Space and time were created in that event and so was all the matter in the universe. It is not meaningful to ask what happened before the big bang; it is somewhat like asking what is north of the North Pole.[5]

---

[3] Aquinas presents five interrelated arguments for God's existence. We'll review three of them here.

[4] One response the atheist might launch at this point is that there is no "start of it all," but rather the chain of "moved movers" and "caused causes" – indeed, the existence of the universe itself – is *infinite*. Aquinas, however, agrees with Aristotle in denying that such an infinite series could *actually* exist. Further arguments supporting Aquinas's view are provided by William Lane Craig in his debate with Quentin Smith, *Theism, Atheism and Big Bang Cosmology* (Oxford: Clarendon Press, 1993).

[5] J. Richard Gott III, James E. Gunn, David N. Schramm, and Beatrice M. Tinsley, "Will the Universe Expand Forever?" *Scientific American* (March 1976), 65; as quoted in Craig and Smith, *Theism, Atheism and Big Bang Cosmology*, 43.

But, to Aquinas and many others, this answer isn't intellectually satisfying. A standard metaphysical axiom is *ex nihilo nihil fit* – "out of nothing, nothing comes." This axiom alone supports the notion that something had to exist out of which the universe came to be – in other words, there must be a *sufficient reason* for the universe to exist at all. We can thus ask, why did the big bang occur? How did the infinitely dense matter come to exist in the first place? Why are there one or more physical laws that state that such dense matter will explode outward?[6] It's rationally conceivable for the universe never to have existed or to have come into existence in a different fashion, or for a singularity of infinitely dense matter to exist but the relevant physical laws be different so that it doesn't explode and just remains static.

This is where another of Aquinas's arguments comes into play:

> The fifth way is taken from the governance of the world. We see that things which lack intelligence, such as natural bodies, act for an end [goal] . . . Now whatever lacks intelligence cannot move towards an end, unless it be directed by some being endowed with knowledge and intelligence; as the arrow is shot to its mark by the archer. Therefore some intelligent being exists by whom all natural things are directed to their end; and this being we call God. (I, Q. 2, a. 3)

This argument is sometimes identified with the notion of "intelligent design," and that isn't too far off the mark. But Aquinas isn't denying any of the scientific processes by which the universe unfolds; nor is he claiming that God sticks his finger in the mix periodically to push things along. Aquinas, presumably, wouldn't take issue with the well-established explanation of how life evolved by means of natural selection. It's no surprise, then, that Baltar doesn't observe "divine digits" through his microscope.

Nonetheless, the fact that there is a rationally discoverable set of laws governing the behavior of matter and energy, and the substances they compose, requires an explanation. Contemporary philosopher John Haldane notes, "Natural explanations having reached their logical limits we are then forced to say that either the orderliness of the universe has no explanation or that it has an 'extra-natural' one."[7] For Aquinas, the explanation of the universe's ordered structure, and its very existence, is the "unmoved mover," the "uncaused cause": God.

"That Is Sin. That Is Evil. And You Are Evil"

Even if Aquinas's arguments demonstrate that some sort of "God" exists as the universe's existential foundation, the traditional **conception** of God held by Jews,

---

[6] It's debated among cosmologists whether any physical laws actually exist at the moment of the big bang. Stephen Hawking, however, argues that at least one law – the "wave function of the universe" – would have to exist at the beginning; see Stephen Hawking, *A Brief History of Time* (New York: Bantam Books, 1988), 133.

[7] J. J. C. Smart and J. J. Haldane, *Atheism & Theism*, 2nd edn. (Oxford: Blackwell, 2003), 110.

Christians, Muslims, and Cylons suffers from a flaw in **logic** known as the "problem of evil." **Traditional** theism understands God to be all-powerful, all-knowing, and all-good. But why would such a God allow for pervasive evil and suffering to exist in the world he supposedly created? Why, for example, doesn't God make algae taste like ice cream so the Colonials can have a more pleasant culinary experience after they find the Eye of Jupiter? The logical inconsistency is obvious and seemingly intractable for the religious believer: If God is all-powerful, why can't he prevent evil? If God is all-knowing, wouldn't he have the means to anticipate and stop evil before it occurs? And if God is inherently good, then surely he desires to eliminate evil from the world. Six, after all, constantly reminds Baltar of God's "eternal love."

Religious believers are in a quandary if they're unwilling to let go of one of the three qualities thought to be essential to God's nature. It's tempting at this point to abandon the project of solving the problem of evil by echoing the cynical humor of the philosopher and logician Bertrand Russell (1872–1970): "This world that we know was made by the devil at a moment when God was not looking."[8] Religious belief, however, necessitates finding some explanation for this problem.

One response to the problem of evil appeals to the **idea** that human beings have *free will*, and that much of the evil we suffer is the result of our own bad choices, a misuse of our God-given freedom. The philosopher and theologian, Augustine (354–430), thus argues:

> A perverse will is the cause of all evils . . . what could be the cause of the will before the will itself? Either it is the will itself, in which case the root of all evil is still the will, or else it is not the will, in which case there is no sin. So either the will is the first cause of sin, or no sin is the first cause of sin. And you cannot assign responsibility for a sin to anyone but the sinner; therefore, you cannot rightly assign responsibility except to someone who wills it.[9]

Augustine identifies the source of moral evil as "inordinate desire" for "temporal goods":

> So we are now in a position to ask whether evildoing is anything other than neglecting eternal things [for example, truth], which the mind perceives and enjoys by means of itself and which it cannot lose if it loves them; and instead pursuing temporal things . . . as if they were great and marvelous things. It seems to me that all evil deeds – that is, all sins – fall into this one category. (27)

Things such as food, alcohol, sex, and discipline are good in themselves and are worthy of desire. But we shouldn't allow our desire for such goods to override our commitment to pursuing more important goods. Hence, Lee's overeating while

8   Bertrand Russell, "Why I Am Not a Christian," in *Why I Am Not a Christian and Other Essays on Religion and Related Subjects* (New York: Simon & Schuster, 1957), 12.
9   Augustine, *On Free Choice of the Will*, trans. Thomas Williams (Indianapolis: Hackett, 1993), 104–5.

commanding *Pegasus* symbolizes to Admiral Adama that his son has grown soft and weak; Tigh's alcoholism quite evidently causes him – and the fleet when he's in command – all sorts of problems; Starbuck, like Baltar, pursues sex like it's a sport, but suffers from a lack of intimacy in her relationships; and Admiral Cain takes military discipline to a savage level aboard *Pegasus* to the overall detriment of her crew and civilians alike. Does it make sense to blame God for Lee's choice to overeat, Tigh's choice to drink, or Starbuck's choice to frak? As Brother Cavil tells Tyrol after he assaults Cally, "The problem is you are screwed up, heart and mind. You, not the gods or fate or the universe. You" ("Lay Down Your Burdens, Part 1").

"You Have a Gift, Kara . . . And I'm Not Gonna Let You Piss That Away"

Even if the misuse of free will results in the *moral* evils for which those who make "bad calls" can be held responsible – as Tigh accepts responsibility for the "Gideon massacre" ("Final Cut") – there are still *natural* evils to contend with. Assuming that Six is right when she says, "God doesn't take sides," why would God create a universe in which there are star clusters with dense radiation that block the Colonials' access to much needed food ("The Passage")? Or a disease that's fatal to Cylons ("Torn")? Given Aquinas's argument that God is responsible for the universe's ordered structure, it stands to reason that God would've ordered the universe so that it wasn't deadly to the conscious entities whom God supposedly loves unconditionally.

Scottish philosopher David Hume (1711–76) compares God's creation of the universe to an architect designing and building a faulty house:

> Did I show you a house or palace where there was not one apartment convenient or agreeable: where the windows, doors, fires, passages, stairs, and the whole economy of the building were the source of noise, confusion, fatigue, darkness, and the extremes of heat and cold, you would certainly blame the contrivance, without any further examination . . . If you find any inconveniences and deformities in the building, you will always, without entering into any detail, condemn the architect.[10]

One response to this conundrum invokes the value of "soul-making." Contemporary philosopher John Hick argues that we shouldn't conceive of God as an "architect" designing this world to be a comfortable place in which to live. Rather, we should understand God as a *parent* whose primary purpose is for his children to receive a proper upbringing:

> We do not desire for [our children] unalloyed pleasure at the expense of their growth in such even greater values as moral integrity, unselfishness, compassion, courage,

---

[10] David Hume, *Dialogues Concerning Natural Religion*, 2nd edn., ed. Richard H. Popkin (Indianapolis: Hackett, 1998), 68–9.

humour, reverence for the truth, and perhaps above all the capacity for love. We do not act on the premise that pleasure is the supreme end of life; and if the development of these other values sometimes clashes with the provision of pleasure, then we are willing to have our children miss a certain amount of this, rather than fail to come to possess and to be possessed by the finer and more precious qualities that are possible to the human personality . . . we have to recognize that the presence of pleasure and the absence of pain cannot be the supreme and overriding end for which the world exists. Rather, this world must be a place of soul-making.[11]

Hick further contends,

in a painless world man would not have to earn his living by the sweat of his brow or the ingenuity of his brain . . . Human existence would involve no need for exertion, no kind of challenge, no problems to be solved or difficulties to be overcome, no demand of the environment for human skill or inventiveness. There would be nothing to avoid and nothing to seek; no occasion for co-operation or mutual help; no stimulus to the development of culture or the creation of civilization. The race would consist of feckless Adams and Eves, harmless and innocent, but devoid of positive character and without the dignity of real responsibilities, tasks, and achievements . . . A soft, unchallenging world would be inhabited by a soft, unchallenged race of men. (342–3)

We read here an echo of Adama and Dee's take on Lee's physical stature after a year of commanding *Pegasus* in orbit around New Caprica. Adama criticizes his son for having grown "weak, soft, mentally and physically"; and Dee diagnoses the source of his problem: "You've lost your edge. Your confidence. You lost your war, Lee. And the truth is you're a soldier who needs a war" ("Occupation"). Without struggle, without challenges to overcome, Lee's very existence is in danger of losing its meaning.

This is also the parental attitude of Starbuck's mother, Socrata Thrace. Leoben tells Starbuck, "You were born to a woman who believed suffering was good for the soul. So you suffered. Your life is a testament to pain" ("Flesh and Bone"). While the physical and emotional abuse Starbuck endured is certainly nothing any decent parent would sanction, there is a valid purpose her mother was attempting – in her significantly flawed way – to achieve. As an oracle tells her, "You learned the wrong lesson from your mother, Kara. You confused the messenger with the message. Your mother was trying to teach you something else" ("Maelstrom"). With help from an apparition of Leoben, Starbuck comes to realize the greater good that her mother was trying to achieve and accepts the evils she had to endure as a child to prepare her for a crossroads in her life, when she must conquer her fear "to discover what hovers in the space between life and death." Similarly, God allows us to experience the consequences of both moral and natural evils so that we may mature as individuals and as a species to face whatever challenges and rewards the future may bring as we continue to evolve.

---

[11]   John Hick, *Evil and the God of Love* (London: Fontana, 1979), 294–5.

"The Gods Shall Lift Those Who Lift Each Other"

Baltar's transition from committed skeptic to religious believer, tenuous as it may be, raises a serious question: How does a person who had defined himself in clear opposition to religion suddenly find Six's religious assertions convincing? Consider Baltar's attitude at the beginning:

> What you are doing, darling, is boring me to death with your superstitious drivel. Your metaphysical nonsense, which, to be fair, actually appeals to the half-educated dullards that make up most of human society, but which, I hasten to add, no rational, intelligent, free-thinking human being truly believes. ("Six Degrees of Separation")

So did Baltar have a direct experience of God's eternal love or a mystical "a-ha" moment? Did he decide to take Pascal up on his wager? Or are his religious inclinations merely another manifestation of his massive ego? It's probable that Baltar's religiosity can be reduced to a mere psychological need – namely, the need to be convinced that his life is important. Contemporary philosopher J. J. C. Smart eloquently sums up this view of religion as the ultimate ego-booster: "Even the horrible view that there is a hell to which the infinite God will consign us for our sins may give us an admittedly miserable sense of importance" (25).

Six's continued insistence that Baltar has a special role to play within God's cosmic plan ultimately proves to be an effective tool in getting him to do her bidding: "She . . . Caprica Six. She chose me. Chose me over all men. Chosen to be seduced. Taken by the hand. Guided between the light and the dark" ("Taking a Break from All Your Worries"). Baltar's self-importance is evident when he and Six discuss the bombing of a Cylon base:

BALTAR: Come on, you must have an inkling, where I should tell them to bomb?
SIX: No. But God does . . . Open your heart to him, and he'll show you the way.
BALTAR: It'd be a lot simpler if he came out and told me.
SIX: You must remember to surrender your ego. Remain humble.
BALTAR: If you ask me, God could do with cleaning his ears out. Then he might hear what I have to say.
("The Hand of God")

Baltar initially purports to value only what can be confirmed through rational means. Eventually his human foibles, coupled with an unrelenting series of depressing events in the *BSG* universe, result in his gravitating towards religious belief. Baltar's change of heart, though, smacks of insincerity insofar as his primary motivations continue to be fear and the indulgence of various hedonistic pursuits, political power, or whatever might tickle his fancy on any given day. Moreover, Baltar's actions are typically pursued without any consideration of how they impact others.

Invoking God's assistance when one needs help to resolve a temporary challenge doesn't constitute a robust religious belief. Baltar's tearful appeal to God during his "trial by fire" wrought by Shelly Godfrey ("Six Degrees of Separation") is probably best described in the words of the famous cartoon philosopher Lisa Simpson: "Prayer. The last refuge of a scoundrel."[12] Baltar's selfish nature impedes his ability to attain the type of freedom Russell describes: "freedom comes only to those who no longer ask of life that it shall yield them any of those personal goods that are subject to the mutations of time."[13] Baltar's desires, which are transitory and defined by the crisis of the moment, prevent him from realizing that belief in God isn't the answer. Rather, religious belief becomes a further hindrance to accepting a world that is mechanistic, not to mention oftentimes cruel, and certainly not subject to human control.

Where does a rejection of religious belief leave humanity? When Roslin commits herself to finding the Arrow of Apollo, Adama attempts to keep her focus grounded: "These stories about Kobol, gods, the Arrow of Apollo, they're just stories, legends, myths. Don't let it blind you to the reality that we face" ("Kobol's Last Gleaming, Part 1"). If we accept Adama's view that the gods and scriptures don't correspond to any objective reality, does that imply a lack of meaning in our lives? An atheistic worldview shouldn't be equated with the impossibility of meaning, which is often misperceived as being contingent upon an afterlife or whether God's plan for each of us comes to fruition. If we deny the possibility of the various mystical goals espoused by particular religious faiths, we're left with life's meaning defined by challenges faced, relationships forged, and the ability to derive value from these experiences. Russell allows for the possibility of transcendence through our direct experience of the world and acknowledgment of our lack of control over its forces, which he deems the "the beauty of tragedy":

> In the spectacle of death, in the endurance of intolerable pain, and in the irrevocableness of a vanished past, there is a sacredness, an overpowering awe, a feeling of the vastness, the depth, the inexhaustible mystery of existence, in which, as by some strange marriage of pain, the sufferer is bound to the world by bonds of sorrow. (113)

Alone in the vastness of space with the Cylons continually breathing down their neck, the Colonial survivors grieve for the loss of their former existence and the vast number of lives lost. The makeshift memorial that evolves into a sacred space on *Galactica* is a tangible and poignant representation of this grief. The Colonials' situation is precarious, and yet their continual suffering never causes them to question the assumption that the attempt to save humanity is worth the struggles endured. Preserving the human race provides a *purpose* that informs each person's daily choices in their work, politics, and relationships.

---

12 *The Simpsons*, Season Two: "Bart Gets an F."
13 Bertrand Russell, "A Free Man's Worship," in *Why I Am Not a Christian*, 110.

Russell speaks to the bravery of facing a world lacking inherent meaning:

> We see, surrounding the narrow raft illuminated by the flickering light of human comradeship, the dark ocean on whose rolling waves we toss for a brief hour; all the loneliness of humanity amid hostile forces is concentrated on the individual soul, which must struggle alone, with what of courage it can command, against the whole weight of a universe that cares nothing for its hopes and fears. Victory, in this struggle with the powers of darkness, is the true baptism into the glorious company of heroes, the true initiation into the overmastering beauty of human existence. (113–14)

Russell envisions each person having to face her own struggles, yet he recognizes the persistent "flickering light of human comradeship." This is one important value that continues to define a meaningful existence for the Colonials after the loss of their civilization and obvious abandonment by their "gods." Some of the most powerful scenes in the series demonstrate this profound need for human connection: Starbuck's naming the call signs of Viper and Raptor pilots lost ("Scar"), or Roslin's joy when Billy informs her that a baby had just been born on the appropriately named *Rising Star* ("33").

When the fleet is divided due to the ideological confrontation between Roslin and Adama, Dee confronts the "old man" and gets to the heart of the matter:

> You let us down. You made a promise to all of us to find Earth, to find us a home *together* . . . every day that we remain apart is a day that you've broken your promise . . . It's time to heal the wounds, Commander. People have been divided . . . Children are separated from their parents. ("Home, Part 1")

Dee convinces Adama to put aside his "rage" and return to Kobol to reunite the fleet. Adama, who's not a religious man, nevertheless recognizes a significant source of meaning for human existence in a Godless world: the need for human *solidarity* in pursuit of a common goal.

"You Have to Believe in Something"

Atheism doesn't entail nihilism – the belief that existence is meaningless in the absence of objective value – although it can certainly lead to it. Religious believers and atheists will never come to an understanding if religious believers assert that those who reject belief in the divine or transcendent consign themselves to a life devoid of meaning. The extreme situation depicted in *BSG* lends itself to a forced cooperation between believers and non-believers, as both groups share the common goal of humanity's survival. Adama acknowledges this fact in "Home, Part 2": "Many people believe that the scriptures, the letters from the gods, will lead us to salvation. Maybe they will. 'But the gods shall lift those who lift each other.'"

But should atheists and religious believers seek common ground in less dire circumstances? Atheists, despite being convinced that their worldview is more rational and authentic, recognize they're outnumbered. Therefore, they must often take the pragmatic approach of finding common ground with religious believers when possible.

Religious believers, conversely, often recognize that ethical and other principles they hold need to be couched in terms of rational arguments that can be debated in the secular public arena of modern society. The appeal to reason as a way of understanding and expressing religious belief isn't foreign to most major faith traditions. To cite one representative figure, Pope John Paul II, "The Church remains profoundly convinced that faith and reason 'mutually support each other'; each influences the other, as they offer to each other a purifying critique and a stimulus to pursue the search for deeper understanding."[14] The recognition that human beings are essentially *rational animals* motivates many religious believers to engage in secular, and not merely faith-based, discourse. At the same time, however, religious believers hold that there are limits to pure rational inquiry, and so faith must take over at those junctures to further our knowledge.

Hence, the litmus test for the validity of religious beliefs may be, as Roslin asserts, whether they "hold real-world relevance" ("Lay Down Your Burdens, Part 2"). To the degree that religious believers acknowledge rational, scientific inquiry as a means to truth, and atheists recognize that there are limits to the knowledge such inquiry can deliver to answer some of the ultimate questions of human concern, the ground is fertile for mutually respectable and fruitful dialogue as humanity continues its "lonely quest" on this "shining planet, known as Earth."[15]

---

[14] John Paul II, *Fides et Ratio* (1998), §100: www.vatican.va/edocs/ ENG0216/_INDEX.HTM.

[15] We're grateful to Bill Irwin and Jessica Vines for helpful comments on an earlier draft of this chapter.

Part V

Ethics

Introduction

Ethics is the study of morality – the concepts of right and wrong, good and evil, virtue and vice. How can we live a good life? Is the virtuous life the best life, or is an immoral life more rewarding? When confronted with ethical dilemmas, how can we decide what is the right thing to do?

This Part begins with the television show *Heroes*, in which ordinary individuals discover that they have extraordinary powers. Nathan can fly, Hiro can manipulate time and travel through space, Claire can heal from any wound, and Peter and Sylar can steal the powers of others. Such people could, quite literally, get away with anything. What motivation could they possibly have for being morally good? Long ago, Plato (429–347 BCE) told a related story in which Gyges finds an invisibility ring and takes advantage of his new power to usurp the king and steal his wife. Gyges was able to get away with behaving badly and so he did. Do the rest of us behave morally simply because we couldn't get away with behaving badly? In his chapter, Don Adams uses the world of *Heroes* to explicate Plato's virtues and show us that the answer is no. In order to be virtuous, the parts of our soul – our *thumos* (spirit), *logistikos* (reason), and *epithumetikon* (appetite) – must be properly ordered. If they are not, we will pay the consequences and the more powerful we are, the worse those consequences will be.

The NBC television show *The Office* is modeled on a British show by the same name. Both shows contain a buffoonish boss (Michael/David) who tries to be funny but never is, a boorish assistant (to the) regional manager (Dwight/Gareth) who doesn't seem to understand jokes, and a witty salesman (Jim/Tim) who is genuinely funny. In his chapter, Sean McAleer uses the British version of the show to illustrate how Aristotle (384–322 BCE) teaches us that living a virtuous life is the key to happiness. Examining the nature of humor on *The Office*, McAleer argues that virtue is "really about acting and feeling appropriately."

Although Batman has had many opportunities to kill the Joker and thus stop him once and for all, he always resists the temptation. Instead, Batman continually sends the Joker back behind the revolving doors of Arkham Asylum, knowing full well that he will probably escape and kill again. Why doesn't Batman just kill the Joker and save thousands of future victims in the process? In his chapter, Mark White explains what utilitarians and deontologists would say on the matter. Using a Bat-version of Philippa Foot's trolley example, White develops a deontological, duty-based, argument for why Batman is right not to kill the Joker. The end doesn't necessarily justify the means.

Finally, we turn to *Watchmen*, the most acclaimed graphic novel of all time, brought to life on the big screen in 2009. Set in the 1980s, *Watchmen* depicts Ozymandias and his plot to save billions of lives by ending the cold war. The catch is that his plan involves killing millions of New Yorkers – the ends, he argues, justify the means. The character Rorschach is determined to stop him, declaring "evil must be punished, in the face of Armageddon, I shall not compromise this." Ozymandias appears to be a utilitarian, and Rorschach appears to be a deontologist. However, neither ethical theory comes off in a positive light in *Watchmen*. In his chapter, Robert Loftis argues, if *Watchmen* is trying to critique utilitarianism and deontology, it doesn't do an adequate job. Neither Ozymandias nor Rorschach truly adhere to either theory. So perhaps *Watchmen* aims at a different point. The mantra, "Who watches the watchmen" gives us a clue. Should anyone, regardless of what theory they embrace, have the power that the Watchmen, or governments, have?

14

Plato on Gyges' Ring of Invisibility

The Power of Heroes *and the Value of Virtue*

Don Adams

Summary

What if you had the ability to commit the perfect crime – say, steal money from any bank without leaving behind any cluses to link you to the robbery? It would be ideal right? You would be richer, and you wouldn't have to suffer any consequences for your action. Or would you? The ancient Greek philosopher Plato thought about such situations and argued that there are always consequences. Relying not on the Christian Golden Rule, but on the Pagan Golden Rule, Plato argues that the corruption of your own soul isn't worth all the gold in the world.

In the *Heroes* universe, evolution has given select individuals special powers. But it is up to those select individuals to decide how to use them. Many have opted to use them for good, but Sylar is not the only exception to that rule. Daphne Millbrook, the blond Speedy Gonzales, opts to use her super-speed for super-theft, hiring herself out to Pinehearst, because no one can ever catch her moving that fast. Micah steals money from an ATM ("The Fix") and even steals pay-per-view wrestling ("The Kindness of Strangers") and doesn't get caught. (How could he? He can always tell whatever security system he is up against to "look the other way.") In Vegas, Hiro Nakamura freezes time to cheat at roulette and poker ("Hiros"). Although his opponents eventually catch on, if he had been more careful – if he had pulled cards only out of the untouched deck instead of his opponent's hand – they wouldn't have noticed. And Noah Bennet continually murders, kidnaps, tortures, and lies but then uses the Haitian to erase everyone's memories of his deeds. All of our heroes could do something similar – commit atrocities and never get caught.

The stories of our heroes aren't new, nor are the questions about them. They go back at least as far as Plato (c. 429–347 BCE), who considered the tale of Gyges, a man who finds an invisibility ring. Gyges uses the ring to viciously, but secretly, depose the king and take his wife. No one is ever the wiser; he is invisible while he does it. Such stories raise the question: do such "superpowered" individuals have good reason to be virtuous, even though they can get away with being immoral? Or maybe their actions aren't even immoral? After all, isn't it "only natural" for people to use their own powers to their own advantage? But is that an excuse? Is human nature really that selfish, or is there a part of us that doesn't want to take advantage of others for our own aims, but instead wants to join with and help them? Do we want to be villains or heroes?

Plato argued that our nature is to be heroes and that there is good reason to be a hero. But to understand his **argument**, we have to understand what, for Plato, it meant to be virtuous and why virtue was so important.

Claire's Thumos Saved the World

According to Plato, being virtuous is important, because if you are not careful to develop the core virtues, then you will be doomed to suffer from their opposed vices. No superpower can free you from this dilemma. In fact, Plato would argue that the virtues become more and more important the more powerful you become. The more you suffer from the vices, the more your life begins to spin out of control. So if you have superpowers, your vices are super-vices and will make your life spin "super" out of control.

To see what it means to be virtuous for Plato, let's begin with one of the characters in *Heroes* whom Plato would admire: Claire Bennet. Think about one of the most important choices Claire ever made. In "One Giant Leap," the local police chief asks which cheerleader performed the daring fire rescue a day earlier. Even though he indicates that Claire looks like the hero, she chooses not to take credit. Good thing! The cheerleader who steps forward to take credit catches Sylar's attention and is eventually murdered for "her" powers. Claire's choice not to receive the accolades and glory for a heroic feat saves her life (and of course, since the cheerleader was saved, so was the world).

It's easy to understand why Claire might want to take credit for her heroic act: she did something noble and deserves to be honored for it. Plato would say that this desire comes from her *thumos* (thoo-MOSS).[1] Thumos is not a part of your brain (that's your "thalamus"); thumos is a part of the soul. There really is no good translation of the Greek word *thumos*, but look at Claire's face when Jackie Wilcox, the cheerleader standing next to her, takes credit for the rescue and you'll see the face of thumos.[2] Claire is surprised but also indignant and even a little angry. Jackie has done something shameful, and Claire thinks less of her for doing it. Our thumos reacts when we sense an insult to our dignity, our worth, and our honor. That is why Plato associates thumos with anger. When someone insults

---

[1] See Plato, *The Republic*, 4.439e–441c. All translations are made by the author.
[2] The closest translations would be "heart" or "spirit," but both of those have very different connotations in English from what *thumos* has in Greek. "Heart" is too romantic, and "spirit" is too spiritual.

you unjustly, you get angry, and out of that righteous anger you might hurl an insult or even throw a punch at the person who offended you.

Thumos and the acts it inspires are not necessarily bad, according to Plato; in fact, they can be very good. Thumos can help you develop the virtue of courage. A strong sense of dignity and personal honor guided by courage can protect you from people who try to take advantage of you and can also help you set the bar high for yourself. Expect more of yourself, and you might be surprised by how capable you are. But your thumos can also get you into trouble. If you throw a punch every time you think someone has insulted you, you are indulging in the vice of recklessness, and you will get into more trouble than you bargained for.

Claire Is Logical; Spock Is Not

We need to be thumotic, but, more important, like Claire, we need to be *logistikos* (log-IST-i-KOS) to develop the virtue of wisdom.[3] The English words *logic* and *logistics* derive from the Greek adjective *logistikos*, and both are involved in its fundamental meaning. So let's call this the "logistical" part of the soul. Claire has thought logically about her situation. She concludes that if anyone finds out about her ability, it will ruin her life. She will either be a freak or a lab rat. All things considered, thinking coolly and calmly, rationally and strategically, it is best for her long-term good if the number of people who know about her special ability is very, very small.

> ZACH: All right, besides the fact that it was so gross I almost fudged myself, this is the single coolest thing to happen to this town in, like, a hundred years.
> CLAIRE: Not if nobody finds out, it's not.
> – *"Genesis"*

But for Plato, being logistical doesn't necessarily contradict being thumotic. Today we often think that logic and emotion are opposed to each other. Perhaps we are too influenced by Mr. Spock and the Vulcans from *Star Trek*. But for Plato, anger and logistical thinking can go together perfectly and can even help each other. Long-term calculations for your best interest can include so much more if you have a passion for your own dignity and honor. Without a strong sense of self-worth, the logistical part of your soul might sell you short; after all, logistically speaking, it is easier to create a plan to accomplish something small than something great. Ando keeps urging Hiro to set his sights lower – on objectives that are more easily accomplished – but Hiro insists on accomplishing the daunting but truly great task of saving the world. If your thumos is strong, then you won't settle for less than you deserve; you will set the bar high for yourself and will have the driving passion to go for it.

---

[3] See Plato, *The Republic*, 4.440ab.

But sometimes your thumos can become too strong and will start running your life. Claire has a strong thumos, but she doesn't let it control her. Even when she takes revenge on Brody Mitchum, the quarterback who tried to rape her ("One Giant Leap"), she doesn't simply lash out at him in anger. She carefully calculates what to do. She thinks logically and logistically about the situation and creates a good plan of action and executes it well.

This, in fact, is how Plato defines the virtue of courage and why he thinks the virtues of courage and wisdom go together. A courageous person is someone whose thumos is strong and daring but who is responsive to **reason**. Imagine a member of the cavalry charging to meet the enemy. His horse must be high-spirited and willing to face danger, but it must also be well-trained to respond to its rider's lead. If it gets too spirited and unruly, all may be lost. The same is true for your thumos: a courageous person is daring and willing to face danger, but only when led by reason, logic, and good logistical calculation. If you simply run into danger without thinking, you are not courageous but reckless; you are a fool, a danger to yourself and others. Wisdom and courage go together because a truly courageous person consults wisdom when deciding whether to attack or hold back, and a truly wise person knows when to stand up for oneself and boldly attack one's enemies.

If Claire has a moral problem in Plato's eyes, it is simply that she is young and her wisdom is not yet fully developed. Probably it was a mistake to get back at Brody in the way she did. But Plato would admire her because she has, to the extent possible for someone so young, two of the four core virtues: wisdom and courage.

The Virtue That Sylar Lacks

To understand Plato's third virtue, temperance, we will need to understand the third part of human nature recognized by Plato: *epithumetikon* (epi-thoom-AY-tee-KON).[4] When you drink simply because you feel like drinking, that comes from epithumetikon; the same is true when you eat simply because you feel like eating or scratch an itch simply because you feel like scratching. So we can call this part of your soul "appetite." Your appetite doesn't have to bother your *logistikon*; doing something you feel like doing simply because you feel like doing it doesn't have to involve a whole lot of logistical planning. (It doesn't take a lot of thought to get up and get a drink when you are thirsty.) But it can. And just as the thumos can be good when it is responsive and obedient to the logistical part of the soul, but bad when it begins to take over and rule your soul, so, too, is the appetite good when it is obedient but bad when it tries to rule. Temperance is the virtue that you exercise when you keep your appetites under control.

The perfect example of intemperance is Sylar. Sylar's special power is intuitive aptitude: he can see how things work, including the special powers of others – if he examines someone's brain, he can see how it works and take the person's power.

---

[4]   Ibid., 4.439d.

This, of course, kills those whose power he steals – except Claire ("The Second Coming"). As we learned in Volume 3 of the *Heroes* saga, part of the curse of this power is a seemingly uncontrollable hunger – an appetite – to acquire the powers of others. (This hunger was also passed on to Peter Petrelli when he briefly acquired Sylar's power in "I Am Become Death" and "Angels and Monsters.") Since Sylar is unable to control this hunger – it rules him – Sylar is intemperate.

Plato argued that intemperance makes one immoral. Sylar, again, is a perfect example. As Arthur Petrelli points out in "It's Coming," Sylar is not simply a mindless killer. "That hunger you've got is not about killing; it's about power." Recall Sylar's disinterest in Peter when he had no powers. "I'm not going to kill you; you don't have anything I need anymore" ("Our Father").[5] Remember also Sylar's lack of interest in killing Claire after he copies her power. Although he couldn't kill her even if he wanted to, he still doesn't want to; he even puts the top of her head back on after he is finished ("The Second Coming"). Sylar does not merely kill for killing's sake. He simply hungers for powers, and examining the brains of those who have them is the easiest way he knows to acquire them – it just happens that most people can't survive the process. So, because Sylar's hunger controls him, he ends up murdering everyone he can find who has powers. It is his intemperance – his inability to control that hunger – that makes him the villain he is. He does succeed in keeping that hunger under control for a while, and in "It's Coming" he learns to acquire abilities through empathy, as Peter did in Volumes 1 and 2 of the *Heroes* Saga.[6] If Sylar had continued down this path, he would have become the temperate heroic family man we saw in the future of "I Am Become Death." That Future Sylar even specifically says that controlling the hunger is what enabled him to turn back into Gabriel. But it is when he gives in to his hunger again – most notably, when he kills Elle Bishop, the girl he supposedly loves ("The Eclipse: Part II"), thus losing his temperance – that he becomes a villain once again.

Just like Sylar, when we are intemperate – when we let our appetites rule our actions – we are immoral (villains) as well and suffer the consequences. As a trivial example, think about not being able to keep your appetite for food under control. If you get used to eating simply because you feel like eating, you can develop some very unhealthy eating habits, health problems, and flabby body parts. As a more extreme example, what would happen if, the next time you got really angry, you lost your ability to control your desire for violence? And how much longer would you be in your current relationship if you lost your ability to keep your appetite for sex under control?

This is not to say that appetites are a bad thing. It's important to enjoy life, and that involves doing things that you feel like doing. Plato's central point is that

---

[5]   Not to mention the poor scared kid in the elevator after Sylar acquired his ability to detect lies ("Our Father").

[6]   Arthur explicitly referred to empathy when he spoke of teaching Sylar to acquire his powers a different way ("It's Coming"). For more on Peter and how he acquires his abilities through empathy, see Andrew Terjesen's chapter, "Peter Petrelli: The Power of Empathy," in *Heroes and Philosophy: Buy the Book, Save the World*, ed David Kyle Johnson (New York: Wiley-Blackwell, 2009).

there has to be balance and order in your soul. When appetite begins to take over and rule your soul, it turns into a kind of tyrant, like a spoiled child demanding whatever it wants. Instead of exercising wisdom and developing temperance by eating healthy, nutritionally balanced meals, people who suffer from the vice of intemperance will wolf down whatever they want, as much as they want, and will be very cranky if they don't get their way. Obviously, letting your appetites rule your actions is a bad way to go. Gluttony, after all, is one of the seven deadly sins.

Superpowers and Super-Vices

For Plato, the virtue of justice is to the human soul what health is to the body: as the various systems in the body need balance and harmony in order for you to thrive biologically, so you also need the various parts of your soul to be in balance and harmony with one another in order for you to thrive psychologically. Your thumos and your appetite should do their jobs, but it is the logistical part of the soul that should be in control. And just as a healthy diet and healthy exercise help to keep your body in good condition, wise, courageous, and temperate actions help to keep your soul in good condition. The more you give in to an unhealthy lifestyle, the worse your health will become; the more you give in to foolishness, intemperance, and cowardly or reckless actions, the more your life will spin out of control. The more unjust you become, the more miserable you will be.

This is why Plato would worry about Micah stealing from the ATM. Forget about the chances of getting caught. What about the consequences for Micah's soul? What if Micah gets used to doing whatever he feels like doing and becomes the sort of person who doesn't think logistically about his actions? Allowing his appetite to take control of his soul and ignoring or even suppressing his logistical planning would make Micah suffer from the vice of intemperance. Plato would say something similar to Daphne about her super-speed thievery.

This is why Plato would disapprove of Hiro's and Ando's behavior in Vegas ("Hiros"). Recall, Ando gambled away all of their money except for one last chip, which he bet on the roulette wheel. Because it was the last of their money, Hiro stopped time and cheated to win. Immediately, his thumos made him feel very ashamed. But Ando had no trouble convincing him that it was okay, so his appetite rejoiced at the opportunity to continue cheating to win. But when the thumos or the appetite gets out of control – when the soul is not balanced or harmonized properly by logistical planning – we are unjust, and bad things happen. Ultimately, Hiro and Ando cheat the wrong person and get beaten up, robbed, and dumped in the desert.

Unless you make choices in a balanced way, develop the wisdom to plan things out so that you enjoy things you feel like doing without becoming ashamed of yourself, and have courage and temperance to be able to stick to your plans, you will be unjust, and your indulgences will tear you apart. An overly thumotic person will become increasingly obsessed with other people's opinions, doing anything to gain acceptance but never getting enough. An overly appetitive person will grow increasingly indulgent; his appetite will grow until no amount of money or super- powers will be able to satisfy him. At first, his thumos will continually make him feel ashamed, but if he practices ignoring the thumos, he may weaken or even kill it off. Then he will be utterly shameless and will have no ambition to amount to anything at all in life. Like a drug addict who cares about only one thing in life – the next fix – the intemperate and unjust person loses all selfrespect and no longer strives for anything worthwhile in life.

This is part of Plato's problem with Gyges. Once Gyges gained his superpower, he handed control of his life over to his appetite. He allowed it to boss his logistical part around. The problem is that only the logistical part is good at logic and logistics. Thumos and appetite will inevitably make a mess of things, demanding more and more honors, as well as more and more pleasures. There will be more conflicts among the things he wants, and so there will be more dissatisfaction in his life.

Now we see why Plato thought that "superpowered" individuals do have good reason to be virtuous, even though they can get away with being immoral. To see what this implies about the way we should treat one another, let's turn to Claire.

Why Claire Apologized

In "One Giant Leap," Claire is attacked by Brody, the football quarterback. He tries to rape her but accidentally kills her. Of course, because of her healing powers Clair recovers – at least, from her physical injuries. She, however, finds out that Brody has raped another student and seems to have picked yet another victim. He appears to be a budding young serial rapist who is utterly remorseless, and she decides to take action. She gets him to give her a ride home after school, but instead she drives. She finds out from his own mouth that he does indeed seem set on this despicable course. So she steers a course directly for a wall and crashes the car into it, seriously injuring both of them. Of course, once again, Claire recovers.

Surely, there is a bit of revenge in her plan: she's getting back at Brody for what he did to her. But that is not all she is doing. In fact, it looks as if she might not have done anything if she hadn't discovered his serial rapist tendencies. So, it seems, she is exacting punishment on behalf of his other victim and trying to stop him from hurting anyone else. Who knows? Maybe part of him does feel bad about what he's done, and a serious injury will help wake him up and change his mind. Perhaps Claire was right to do this; perhaps not. But to discover Plato's fourth virtue, we need to focus on what Claire does afterward in the hospital.

Claire goes into the quarterback's room and apologizes to him. She says that what she did was wrong. But why does she think she was wrong and why does she apologize? She doesn't have time to explain herself because she is interrupted by the cheerleading squad chanting, "Brody, Brody, Brody," coming in to cheer him up. So we have to speculate. To do so, let's talk about Plato again. Before Plato brought up the idea of Gyges' superpower of invisibility, he discussed a principle widely accepted by the Greeks. We might call it the "Pagan Golden Rule": help your friends and harm your enemies.[7]

Unlike the Christian Golden Rule, which tells us to treat everyone according to the same benevolent standard, the Pagan Golden Rule advises us to use two different standards: one for our friends and one for our enemies. Obviously, you shouldn't treat friends as if they were enemies; they deserve better than that. And you shouldn't treat enemies as if they were friends; they will take advantage of you and perhaps even destroy you.

Plato pointed out that we need to be careful not to misinterpret the "Pagan Golden Rule." It is not a license to attack your enemies or to show indiscriminate favoritism to your friends. The Greek tragedian Sophocles wrote what could be considered a footnote to the Pagan Golden Rule when he had the mighty hero Ajax say, "I have learned that my enemy is to be hated only so much, since he may soon be my friend; and the friend I help, I will help only so much since he may not always remain my friend."[8] This fits Plato's view of interpersonal justice in *The Republic*, and it also fits much of what we see in *Heroes*.

It may sound sad to think of dealing with your friends in the realization that they may not remain your friends for very long, but it is good advice. Claire's father (by adoption), Noah Bennet, realized it was good advice when he emphasized to her the importance of being careful after he saw that she was interested in Brody. When someone is friendly to you, as Brody was to Claire before he tried to rape her, it doesn't mean that you can trust this person. This is even clearer in the case of Noah himself. Claire loves and trusts him as a father, but he is an employee of the Company, and his loyalties to it might possibly lead him to do something that would not be in Claire's best interest. Of course, ultimately, Noah proves loyal to Claire – but even with her most trusted ally, caution is needed.

Yet perhaps an even more important part of the requirement to exercise caution with our friends is what Matt Parkman learns. In "Hiros," after he has been reading his wife's mind and working to fix their relationship, Matt points out to her that they have been taking each other for granted and living together more as roommates than as husband and wife. We need to treat our friends with caution in the realization that they might not be our friends for long, but if we start taking them for granted, we might lose their friendship. Friends and allies are so important in life that we need to live every day realizing how fortunate we are to have them and make sure that we don't start to ignore them or assume that they will always be around and always support us. We need to keep the lines of communication open, we need to touch base with our friends and be sure that our aims and goals are still compatible with theirs. People grow and change, and often a healthy friendship needs to be renegotiated in some ways so that we continue to be good for one another.

There is a similar profound truth about enemies. Yes, you need to protect yourself and your friends against your enemies. When Plato developed his ideal form

---

[7]   See Plato, *The Republic*, 1.332a–335e.
[8]   Sophocles, *Ajax*, 678–82 (author's translation).

of government, the military played a crucial role. We need to protect ourselves from danger. But we also need to remind ourselves that even enemies can become allies or friends. In "Hiros," when Isaac Mendez and Peter realize that they need to work together to prevent the bomb from destroying New York City, they are able to set aside their hostility over Simone Deveaux, Isaac's former girlfriend and Peter's current love interest. Isaac was treating Peter as a total enemy, but when he saw that Peter would make a powerful ally in working toward a vitally important goal the two of them shared, he was able to set aside his anger and work with Peter.

It is a strategic mistake to treat an enemy as a *complete* enemy. We always need to be on the lookout for objectives we might share with our enemies, because people who work together for shared objectives are teammates, and teammates are allies. Yes, Brody deserved what he got, and perhaps Claire has no moral obligation to apologize. But it's better to try to mend the relationship so that Brody may one day be an ally again. To not apologize is to guarantee that he will always be an enemy, and Claire may want (or need) him as a friend someday.

But Isn't It Only Natural?

You are virtuous when you do justice to yourself as a human being; when you enjoy life and do things you feel like doing (you satisfy your appetite); when you don't sell yourself short but live up to your full potential (you satisfy your thumos); and most of all when you actively think about your life, planning things out logically and logistically, restraining your ambition and your appetites wisely. And don't forget to keep in mind that enemies can become friends if you are smart, and friends can become enemies if you take them for granted or treat them badly. Just as a healthy body is natural to us, so also a virtuous soul is natural to us.

This identifies our fundamental mistake when we think that it is only natural for someone with a superpower to take advantage of it to hoard the good things life has to offer. The core virtues of justice, wisdom, courage, and temperance are of value, according to Plato, because they are essential to living our lives as successful human beings. If virtue is to the soul what health is to the body, then virtues are not mere tools that we can use when they suit our purposes and ignore when they don't help us get what we want. Virtues are not merely instrumentally good because of what they can do; the virtues are intrinsically good because of what they are: healthy states of our soul that allow us to live our lives as human beings. Virtue is its own reward.

Plato gave the analogy of sheepdogs bred to protect flocks of sheep.[9] It would be unnatural and monstrous if dogs bred to protect the flock instead ripped the sheep apart. If virtue really is a crucial part of a healthy human soul, then it is horrendously unnatural and monstrous to turn on a friend and an ally, as Brody did to Claire. Instead of using his physical strength and athletic prowess to harm

---

[9]   See Plato, *The Republic*, 3.416ab.

enemies (defeat rival football teams) and to help friends (enhance the reputation of the school), he perverted his special talents to harm an ally and a friend.

Still more degenerate is Sylar's treatment of his own (adoptive) mother, Virginia Gray, in "The Hard Part."[10] To show her how special he is, he uses a kitchen hose, his freezing power, and his telekinesis to turn her apartment into a big snow globe. She is frightened, and her grip on reality is questionable, but her subsequent refusal to accept that Sylar is truly her son, Gabriel, is based on a profound realization: the quest for power has destroyed Gabriel, leaving only Sylar. After killing Virginia – the only woman who ever loved him – with a pair of scissors, Sylar calmly paints the future with her blood. Nothing could be more contrary to human nature.

Heroes like Claire, Matt, Hiro, and Peter are able to form alliances and friendships with one another. Being a team player is not about mere conformity. From the perspective of simple conformity, you are foolish if you try to change things and ridiculous if you don't fit in. That's not the case with true heroes. Matt wants to change things because he wants to help others and make the world a better place. Peter has tremendous empathy for others and looks for opportunities to use his remarkable powers to help in ways he never could before. Hiro is a freak because of his unusual ability, but that doesn't make him embarrassed about not being like others, instead, it gives him a profound sense of responsibility. His ability brings something very powerful to the alliance. Our common aims can bring us together, and our distinctive differences enhance our capabilities as a united team.

These remarkable heroes face a choice that all of us unremarkable, ordinary people face. The core virtues of justice, wisdom, courage, and temperance are not simply a matter of "fitting in" or conforming to society's expectations. Rather, they allow you to help your friends and harm your enemies. They give you the intelligence to find common objectives that can turn enemies into allies and give you the insight to cultivate your friendships and not take them for granted. Mere conformity will make you try to hide what makes you unique and prevent you from rocking the boat or trying to change things. Virtue shows that what makes you unique can make you a great asset to the community and that your attempts to change things for the better can make a difference. Whether we have spectacular powers like the characters in *Heroes* or only the ordinary abilities of a normal human being, we all face the same choice: what will we do with what has been given to us? Regardless of what physical abilities you have or lack, you can still choose to be a hero. After all, it's only natural.

---

[10] Of course, Sylar's biological mother was killed by his biological father, Samson Gray ("Exposed").

15

The Virtues of Humor

What The Office *Can Teach Us About Aristotle's Ethics*

Sean McAleer

Summary

The Office can teach three important lessons about Aristotle's ethics. First, three main characters illustrate the structure of an Aristotelian virtue of character by embodying the virtue of wit, which Aristotle regards as a mean, and the corresponding vices of buffoonery (excess) and boorishness (deficiency). Second, that wit is a virtue of character suggests a broader, more inclusive notion of morality than we moderns are likely to have. Third, that humor can't be captured by a set of rules mirrors the noncodifiability of Aristotle's ethics.

Early in the very first episode of *The Office*, David Brent is mugging for the camera as he introduces Dawn Tinsley, the receptionist. "Ah, Dawn," he muses. "I'd say that at one time or another, every bloke in the office has woken up at the crack of Dawn." Dawn is mortified (as is the viewer, on her behalf), while Brent cackles with delight at his own "wit." We're mortified not because the joke isn't funny (though it isn't – or at least hasn't been since junior high) but because it's so inappropriate. Its inappropriateness isn't just a matter of bad taste or a failure of etiquette (as is Brent's t-shirt and ball-cap ensemble at his presentation on "motivational techniques" in episode four of series two). The joke is *morally* inappropriate. As such, it tells us something about David Brent's character. Jokes can be funny that way.

Given the centrality of character and virtue to the ethics of Aristotle (384–22 BCE), it's not surprising that Aristotle can help us understand what's wrong with David Brent. But Aristotle can also help us understand humor generally. For Aristotle, ethics is not a matter of duty or promoting good outcomes, it's about being a certain sort of person – the sort of person who lives a life expressive of the virtues. In this, Aristotle's thought differs from most modern moral philosophy, which tends to take either notions of duty or the notion of a good outcome to be fundamental.[1] A *virtue ethics*,

---

[1]   For example, the ethics of the great German philosopher Immanuel Kant (1724–1804) centers on duty, while the **utilitarianism** of the great English philosopher John Stuart Mill (1806–73) centers on outcomes.

such as Aristotle's, takes the virtues – traits such as courage, wisdom, temperance, honesty, generosity, kindness, and the like – to be morally fundamental. Instead of defining virtue in terms of duty by saying that a virtuous person is someone who does her duty, a virtue ethics would define duty in terms of virtue, holding that an action is my duty if and only if a virtuous person would perform that action in the circumstances. If this were a treatise on moral theory we might want more precision or complexity in our account of virtue ethics, but this should do just fine for our purposes. To any professional or amateur philosopher inclined to disagree, I can only say, having gotten in touch with my inner Brent, "Exsqueeze me."

Virtues and Vices

So what *is* a virtue, for Aristotle? Aristotle speaks of the virtue*s* or *a* virtue rather than virtue. The word *virtue* can have a quaint, Victorian ring that seems closely tied to chastity, which isn't Aristotle's sense at all (though sexual temperance is *a* virtue). Our English word *virtue* translates the Greek word *arête*, though a better translation would be *excellence*, since a virtue for Aristotle isn't essentially moral. The English word *virtuoso* retains this non-moral connotation. While David Brent isn't exactly a virtuoso guitar player, he's actually not bad – and he's certainly a better guitar player than he is a music video crooner. If you don't know this by now, you will never never never know this.

For Aristotle, a virtue is a state that enables its possessor to achieve its function or purpose well. The function of a knife, for example, is to cut. To cut well, a knife needs to be sharp: that's the state or condition that enables the knife to perform its function well. Thus dullness would be its vice, since a dull knife can't cut well. Presumably, those knives one sees advertised on late night infomercials, the ones that cut through cinderblocks and still slice tomatoes paper-thin, are about as virtuous as knives can get. The function or purpose of a regional manager of a paper merchant is more complex, but ultimately perhaps it's to increase profitability. Many virtues will be needed if the manager is to succeed; but among them will be honesty, discipline, reliability, prudence, resourcefulness, loyalty, genuine concern for the staff and customers, clarity of vision, integrity, and the kind of toughness that is consistent with compassion and that enables a manager to make hard choices.[2] I'll leave it to the reader to decide whether David or Neil more fully embodies the virtues of a manager.

Our virtues, then, are the states that enable us to think and act well. When we are functioning well, we are *eudaimôn*, which is usually rendered as *happy*, though *flourishing* is a much better translation of that Greek word. Happiness (*eudaimonia*), for Aristotle, is not a pleasant, transient psychological state or mood. It is not the

---

[2] For an excellent discussion of an Aristotelian, virtue-based approach to business ethics, see Robert Solomon, "Corporate Roles, Personal Virtues: An Aristotelian Approach to Business Ethics," *Business Ethics Quarterly* 2 (1992): 317–39.

result of hot love on the free love highway, for example, because happiness is not a mere result at all, but rather an activity. People, no less than rosebushes, can flourish; it's just that the conditions of human flourishing are rather more complex than the conditions of rosebush flourishing.[3] Here's Aristotle's official definition of a character virtue from his most important and widely read work on ethics, the *Nicomachean Ethics*:

> Excellence, then, is a state that is concerned with choice, lying in a mean relative to us, this being determined by **reason** and in the way in which the man of practical wisdom would determine it. Now it is a mean between two vices, that which depends on excess and that which depends on defect. (1106b36–7a3)[4]

Aristotle is telling us that every virtue of character has *two* vices opposing it, not just one. Cowardice is not *the* opposite of courage, but *an* opposite. The courageous person faces danger, feels no more fear than the situation warrants, and is able to act appropriately. The cowardly person is excessively fearful in the same situation, and is thus unable to act appropriately. But what of the person who fails to appreciate how dangerous a situation is, and takes unnecessary and unreasonable risks? This is the rash person, who, on Aristotle's view, also fails to display virtue. The virtue of generosity is a mean between profligacy and stinginess, the virtue of proper pride is a mean between vanity and excessive humility, and so on for the other character virtues. (The intellectual virtues do *not* have this mean-between-extremes structure, by the way: *epistêmê* or knowledge, for example, is not a mean between knowing too much and knowing too little.)

Aristotle's doctrine of the mean is *not* a doctrine of moderation. He is not saying that the good-tempered person, for example, feels a moderate amount of anger in all situations, while irascible and meek persons feel too much and too little. The good-tempered person does not feel the same moderate anger when she discovers her best friend has betrayed her and when someone accidentally steps on her foot in a crowded elevator. Finchy's anger at losing the quiz is excessive not by some absolute standard, but because it's out of proportion to the cause, trivia quizzes being by nature trivial, and because he and Brent lost fair and square. Neil's

---

[3] Many philosophers, ancient and modern, agree with Aristotle that the virtues are morally fundamental. Aristotle's teacher Plato (429–347 BCE), for example, also had a virtue ethics, as did the great Scottish philosopher David Hume (1711–76 CE). One way in which their virtue ethics differ is their differing accounts not just of what the virtues are, but of how the virtues are structured.

[4] This is the standard way of citing Aristotle. It means that the quote begins on line 36 of the right ("b") column of page 1106 of Aristotle's Greek text as compiled by Augustus Bekker of the University of Berlin in the nineteenth century and ends at line 3 of the left ("a") column on the next page, page 1107. This way of referring to texts that have many translations or editions will be familiar to readers of the Bible, Koran, Shakespeare, etc. (e.g., "Isaiah 53:3" refers to the same passage, regardless of the page number of the translation you happen to be reading). The translation here is W. D. Ross's, as revised by J. O. Urmson, in J. Barnes, ed., *The Complete Works of Aristotle* (Princeton, NJ: Princeton University Press, 1984). Most translations of the *Nicomachean Ethics* will have these "Bekker numbers" (or "Berlin numbers," as they're sometimes called) in the margins.

anger at David's mocking him in front of the staff, is by contrast, appropriate, not just because Neil's level of anger is appropriate to the circumstances – his authority has been undermined, and by someone who himself exhibits the qualities in question ("*just want to be as popular as the new boss . . . oh love me!*") – but also because its expression is appropriate: he expresses it in private, it's controlled, and it doesn't last longer than it should. And notice that it expresses a healthy self-respect: "I don't let anyone talk to me the way you just did – not my staff, not my boss, no one – certainly not you." Finchy's, by contrast, expresses the petulance of a rather fragile ego dressed up in macho bravado. Someone with proper and healthy self-respect won't feel the need to seek revenge when they haven't been wronged. Virtue is not a one-size-fits-all thing for Aristotle, but rather is a matter of acting and feeling appropriately in the given circumstances, where what's appropriate is determined by the virtue of practical wisdom:

> The man who is angry at the right things and with the right people, and, further, as he ought, when he ought, and as long as he ought, is praised. For the good-tempered man tends to be unperturbed and not to be led by passion, but to be angry in the manner, at the things, and for the length of time, that reason dictates. (1125b31–35)

The lesson here is that although Aristotle often discusses virtue and vice in quantitative terms, the virtues are best understood *qualitatively*: they are dispositions to act and feel in ways that are appropriate in the circumstances. It turns out that this is a mean between extremes of excess and deficiency, but virtue is really about acting and feeling appropriately.[5]

Wit and Virtue

That a good sense of humor is an Aristotelian virtue tells us something interesting and important about Aristotle's conception of morality – namely, that it's broader than is typical of modern moral philosophy. If we think that morality is primarily about rights and duties, then we'll probably write off wit as a matter of personality rather than morality and regard it, like punctuality and dressing well, as largely immune to moral evaluation, for it seems obvious that no one has a duty to be funny or a right to a good joke – though perhaps people who aren't funny have a duty not to try to be (this means *you*, Carrot Top).

Aristotle, in contrast, is concerned with human flourishing, and there are more ways to flourish or live well than to conscientiously discharge our duties to others. So when Aristotle asks what it is to be virtuous, he's really asking what it is to be an excellent person, and he doesn't limit the scope of his inquiry to moral

---

[5]   For an excellent discussion of this topic, the interested reader should consult Rosalind Hursthouse's "A False Doctrine of the Mean," *Proceedings of the Aristotelian Society* 81 (1980/81): 57–72, reprinted in Nancy Sherman, ed., *Aristotle's Ethics: Critical Essays* (Lanham, MD: Rowman & Littlefield, 1999).

excellence. He is interested in the excellence of the whole person. This holistic approach is one of the things that attracts many contemporary philosophers to Aristotle's approach to ethics.

Since we are naturally social creatures, according to Aristotle, the scope of human excellence must extend to our social interactions. Moreover, we need relaxation and amusement, if only to recharge our batteries for the serious business of life, so there are virtues with respect to this sphere of social interaction, since one can interact well or poorly when it comes to amusement, just as one can act well or poorly when it comes to truth-telling. As is obvious to anyone who's watched *The Office*, David Brent tends to not act excellently when it comes to amusement. How exactly does he go so wrong, so excruciatingly, hilariously wrong?

To begin, here's what Aristotle says about wit and its corresponding vices in Book IV, Chapter 8 of the *Nicomachean Ethics*:

> Those who carry humor to excess are thought to be vulgar buffoons, striving after humor at all costs, and aiming rather at raising a laugh than at saying what is becoming and at avoiding pain to the object of their fun; while those who can neither make a joke themselves nor put up with those who do are thought to be boorish and unpolished. But those who joke in a tasteful way are called ready-witted. (1128a5–10)

Since here and elsewhere Aristotle employs quantitative terms such as *excess* in distinguishing virtues from vices, it's important to remember that the crucial difference between wit, buffoonery, and boorishness – and between virtue and vice generally – is qualitative, not quantitative. It's not that the buffoon is too funny, the boor not funny enough, or that the buffoon jests too much, the boor too little, and the person of wit just the right amount. And the qualitative difference is not really that the witty person's jokes are just qualitatively better – though they probably are. The difference is that the witty person's jesting is *appropriate* to the circumstances, while the buffoon's is inappropriate and the boor fails to jest when jesting would be appropriate (or at least not inappropriate). Consider the first episode of series two,[6] when "the Swindon lot" are now members of the Slough branch. Neil, formerly the manager at Swindon and now David's boss, gives a light-hearted welcome speech, with gentle barbs for one and all, including himself:

> Hello everyone. For those of who you don't know me, I'm Neil Godwin. For those of you who do, keep stumm! I'm a man of simple pleasures. I don't need lovely houses, beautiful girls and classy restaurants, so it's a good job I moved to Slough! . . . I know David is feeling a bit worried about taking on these new staff, because as manager it's going to mean a lot more responsibility: he'll now have to delegate twice as much work.

It's clever and appropriate, and it's appropriate largely because it's aimed at putting everyone at ease, at making an awkward situation less awkward. David, by contrast,

---

[6] What Americans would call "season" two.

isn't trying to welcome the new staff, he's trying to put on a show, as his brief remarks to Neil before the meeting starts indicate: "Don't be nervous. Just keep it short, bring me on, and enjoy the show." Moreover, his "routine" just isn't funny:

> Welcome to Slough, to the new people. My name's David Brent, and I've always been in the paper industry, haven't I? Yeah. My parents owned a paper shop . . . until it blew away . . . [*No laughter*] It was made of paper . . . I'm not used to public squeaking. I piss-pronunciate a lot of my worms.

It goes downhill from there (though the Basil Fawlty impersonation is pretty darn good). He gets angry when people don't laugh, and is especially peeved and puzzled by the thought that Neil is funnier than he is. He's doing a bad comedy routine, not making a witty and appropriate welcoming speech. For him, it's an occasion to be the center of attention. His intention isn't to put the staff at ease or make them feel welcome; his intention is to be funny – or, more accurately, to be thought funny.

With this understanding of what Aristotelian wit is, let's explore its nuances, using the characters who most embody its structure: David Brent, buffoon; Tim Canterbury, wit; and Gareth Keenan, boor. My apologies to those sad souls who've seen only the American version of *The Office*, for my discussion will focus exclusively on the British version (even though Michael Scott, Jim Halpert, and Dwight Schrute embody an analogous Aristotelian structure).

David Brent: Regional Manager, Chilled-Out Entertainer, Buffoon

Not only is David Brent a buffoon, he's a buffoon *par excellence*. Indeed, he looks like what the word *buffoon* sounds like. The hallmark of the virtuous person in general is that her actions and feelings are appropriate in the circumstances; knowing where the mean is, she acts accordingly. David's actions and feelings are anything but. The problem isn't his erroneous self-conception of funny man *and* great boss, the problem is his overweening need to be thought to be funny. He's a buffoon because he is "the slave of his sense of humor" (1128a33–4). He's unable not to try to get a laugh, even when doing so is inappropriate, just as a drug addict is unable not to take drugs, even when doing so is harmful.

To get a sense of this, consider the last episode of series one, in which the office is in a state of anxiety about the rumored redundancies. Malcolm, older than the rest and quite concerned about losing his job, is puzzled about David's hiring a new secretary in light of the looming redundancies or layoffs. He wants to speak seriously about this situation, but David is incapable of being serious when seriousness is what's called for. Rather than listening to Malcolm's concerns and thinking creatively about a solution or being caringly direct about Malcolm's plight, David makes squeegee noises on Malcolm's bald head and does a rather bad Kojak impersonation.

There are times when humor is just what a heavy situation calls for, and the witty person can tell what those situations are and what they're not, because he or she possesses the virtue of practical wisdom. Practical wisdom is a kind of insight or intuition into what a situation calls for, rather than a deductive, discursive process. There is no computer-like decision procedure that can determine where the mean is. As Aristotle sees things, where the mean is "is not easy to determine by **reasoning** . . . the decision rests with perception" (1109b21–3).

This feature of Aristotle's ethical thought – that knowing what one ought to do is not a matter of following an abstract decision procedure but is rather a matter of seeing the world in a certain kind of way (as the virtuous person sees it) – is mirrored in the virtue of wit itself, for having a sense of humor is not a matter of grasping abstract universal principles and applying them disinterestedly, it's about seeing the world in a certain way. Most of us have probably found ourselves trying to explain why something is funny to someone who does not find it funny. Indeed, David reports just this phenomenon in episode three of series one: "We'll be doing a bit of shtick and we'll be cracking up, and people watching will go, 'why is that funny?' and we'll tell them why."

Mark Twain once said, "Show me someone who knows what's funny and I'll show you someone who knows what's not." Surely what Twain means is that genuinely having a sense of humor – possessing the Aristotelian virtue of wit – involves knowing when humor is inappropriate and when it isn't. In describing the properly witty person, Aristotle tells us that "there are . . . jokes he will not make" (1128a29). Ironically, David is at least intellectually aware of this. In the first episode of the series, Tim has (once again, it seems) ensconced Gareth's stapler in jello ("jelly" in British English). "The thing about practical jokes," David says, "is that you've got to know when to stop as well as when to start." The person of practical wisdom *does* know this; he or she can discern when a joke, practical or otherwise, is appropriate and when it's not, when a joke is funny and when it's cruel. But the episode ends with David playing a cruel, extremely unfunny joke on Dawn (and doing so in front of Ricky, the new temp, to boot), pretending to terminate her for stealing Post-It Notes. The "joke" is a complete bust, with Dawn in tears and Ricky in stunned, mortified silence. A person of practical wisdom would know that such a joke is out-of-bounds, but David, despite some cognitive awareness that "there are limits to my comedy," is unable to act on that awareness. In particular, he's unable not to make a joke, even when joking is inappropriate. The problem is that buffoons strive after humor at all costs. It's not that they value humor, it's that they value it too much. In the third episode of series one, David *says* that "there are limits to . . . comedy; there are things I'll never laugh at," but he's not able to recognize these limits in action. He says he'd never laugh at the handicapped, because "there's nothing funny about them." But this suggests that what restrains him isn't the thought that one shouldn't make sport of the handicapped because doing so would be hurtful and cruel. Rather, what restrains David is the mere lack of comic potential that the handicapped present.

The buffoon's willingness to do anything to raise a laugh shows us that he has no sense of shame. While the virtuous person will act properly, she is not, on Aristotle's view, restrained by a sense of shame, which Aristotle regards as "a sort of fear of disrepute" (1128b10–11). She is, rather, motivated by her desire to act in a way that embodies what is fine, noble, and beautiful – what is, in Greek, *kalon*. A person who is still learning to be virtuous might be motivated by a desire to avoid what is shameful or disgraceful. But the virtuous person, who loves what is noble, will not even be tempted to act disgracefully, even if doing so is to her material advantage. A positive motivation, the love of what is *kalon* (rather than the negative motivation of avoiding what is shameful), explains the virtuous person's actions and choices. The buffoon, by contrast, doesn't even have this negative motivation. Unable to tolerate not being the center of attention, he'll do anything to claim it – even if this involves ruining a training session not only by refusing to let Rowan, a specialist in such matters, be in control, but by hijacking the session with his guitar. Buffoonery, thy name is David Brent.

Gareth Keenan: Assistant (to the) Regional Manager, Territorial Army Lieutenant, Boor

Boors, Aristotle tells us, "can neither make a joke themselves nor put up with those who do" (1128a8–9). Now, strictly speaking, this doesn't perfectly fit Gareth, for he tries to joke, and probably regards himself as having a good sense of humor.[7] Our very first encounter with Gareth involves his jokey macho posturing about his drinking plans for the evening: "That'll be a quiet night at the library . . . not!" I'm not sure if "*x* . . . not!" jokes were ever funny, but if they ever were, their time came and went long ago.

In the very first episode we see Gareth satisfying the second component of Aristotle's definition of the boor, for he's unable to put up with Tim's jello-stapler practical joke. Rather than being a good sport, Gareth officiously claims to be "more worried about damage to company property." It's not just his not being able to take a joke that makes Gareth a boor. He's a boor because he's oblivious to the fact that he's being joked with, usually by Tim and Dawn. Their wind-ups of Gareth typically involve spoofing his homophobia: "Could you give a man a lethal blow? . . . If he was coming really hard? . . . Could you take a man from behind?" (I.3), and they're funny precisely because Gareth is so oblivious to them.

Why is Gareth a boor of the oblivious variety? The answer is that he is a literalist, and having a good sense of humor requires not taking things just as they are but recognizing the absurdity of the ordinary. Literalists are just not able to do that. Gareth takes Tim's questions at face value, even though he should be well aware of Tim's tendency to wind him up, because he's incapable of not taking things literally – just as David is incapable of not trying to be funny. Indeed, Tim and Dawn's name for this activity – "winding Gareth up" – describes it perfectly, because Gareth, like a wind-up doll, is incapable of not taking things literally. Like a computer, he's

---

[7]   It perhaps fits Dwight K. Schrute even better. He never jokes, unless he's had a head injury.

incapable of departing from his literalist programming. It's easy to forget what a complex achievement getting a joke is – and how difficult (if not impossible) it would be for a computer to "get" a joke. When we think of all the background, context, and subtlety that goes into getting a joke, it's no wonder that literalists – and computers – have such trouble getting jokes.

One of the funniest examples of Gareth's literalism occurs at Chasers, the lame nightclub to which the Wernham-Hogg crew repair after a long day of not getting very much done. Donna, the daughter of David's best friend, whom he's recently hired, tells David that she wouldn't sleep with Gareth, not, as David suggests, because he didn't go to university, but because

DONNA: He's a little weasel-faced ass.

DAVID: Don't call my second-in-command an ass-faced weasel.

DONNA: I didn't. I called him a weasel-faced ass.

DAVID: Same thing.

DONNA: No, it's not. [To Gareth] Would you rather have a face like an ass or a face like a weasel?

GARETH: A weasel, probably.

Poor Gareth. He can only take things at face-value. We can well imagine how Tim would respond. And even though Finchy would respond in a predictably lowbrow and misogynist way, he would not take the question literally.

Gareth's literalism, and hence his boorishness, is rooted in his taking things – himself most of all – too seriously. His self-seriousness is most apparent in his regularly regarding himself as "team leader" and "assistant regional manager," in his leading the investigation of the source of the pornographic photo of David, of his annoyingly shredding documents rather than throwing them in the trash, lest competitors come upon them. Perhaps the best example of his self-seriousness is the "Health and Safety Seminar" he conducts for the benefit of Donna. The "fun game [he's] made up" about safe placement of coffee mugs is anything but, and it's plain that Donna doesn't need to practice properly lifting boxes: it's not that hard to grasp.

It's crucial to distinguish being *self-serious* from being *self-important*. The latter implies an arrogance and pomposity that needn't be present in the former, which implies rather an overestimation of the level of concern and care that certain activities merit. Gareth takes the safety seminar too seriously, regarding it as more important than it is, and while he takes himself more seriously than he should, he doesn't regard himself as better than others in virtue of who he is, which is the hallmark of the self-important person.

Consider the difference between Gareth and Simon the computer guy in the fourth episode of series two. Not only is Simon a literalist – Bruce Lee did not fight Chuck Norris in *Enter the Dragon*, he fought him in *Way of the Dragon* – he's a self-important prat: humorless, pedantic, gassing off about his Formula One-worthy go-kart driving. Neither Gareth nor Simon picks up on Tim's quip, "those cats were fast as lightning," but while we loathe Simon in his brief appearance (he's perhaps the least likeable character in the entire series), we have a soft spot for Gareth that isn't explained just by his being familiar to us – that, proverbially, can breed contempt. Gareth is a bit of a fool (as are we all), but he's not vainly self-important – or no more than most of us, anyway.

Though he regularly makes sport of Gareth, Tim recognizes Gareth's seriousness as a virtue (though one that can become a vice when taken to excess), and suggests to Neil that Gareth, not himself, should be David's interim replacement:

> I think you should give it to Gareth. Seriously, I do. He takes things seriously. He's conscientious. He works hard. He's responsible. He knows this place inside and out. Genuinely, I think he might be the man for it.

He's sincere, and it's genuinely touching. Of course, in the background we hear Dirty Bertie, the annoying boner-man, which undercuts Tim's claims a bit (but not enough to dissuade Neil from offering the job to Gareth).

Tim Canterbury: Senior Sales Clerk, Unrequited Lover, Ironic Wit

This brings us at long last to Tim, who embodies the Aristotelian virtue of wit. As we noted earlier, the crucial difference between wit, buffoonery, and boorishness is not quantitative but rather qualitative. It's not that the person of wit tells a moderate number of jokes while the buffoon tells too many and the boor too few, but rather that the genuinely witty person jests appropriately. When Aristotle tells us that "the well-bred man's jesting differs from that of a vulgar man" (1128a20–1), he has not only that in mind, I think, but also the way in which the witty person jests.

We've already noticed that Tim's jesting with Gareth often involves practical jokes and wind-ups, but much of his jesting occurs via detached, understated irony. When Jennifer puts David's call on speaker-phone and thus reveals to all that he isn't firing Chris Finch, Tim's response is a deft, "Does anybody have the right time?" When David is going on and on in his Brently way during a training session about wanting to know what it would be like to live forever, Tim says, to no one in particular, "I think I'm starting to know what that's like." Or consider this exchange, also from the training episode:

> ROWAN: Gareth, quick trust exercise: [what's your] ultimate fantasy?
> GARETH: Hmm?
> DAVID: We're just doing the ultimate fantasy, we're all doing it.
> GARETH: Two lesbians, probably sisters. I'm just watching.
> ROWAN: Ok. Um. Tim? Do you have one?
> TIM: I'd never thought I'd say this, but can I hear more from Gareth please?

Dawn also displays an ironic outlook on life. Sharing this outlook with Tim helps to explain the affinity between them. Only someone able to get some ironic distance on her own life could tell the story Dawn tells of Lee's proposal of marriage to her:

> He proposed on a Valentine's Day, although he didn't do it face to face, he did it in one of the little Valentine message bits in the paper. I think he had to pay for it by the word, because it just said "Lee love Dawn, marriage?" which, you know, I like, because it's not often you get something that's both romantic and thrifty.

What's striking about Tim's sense of humor – especially in contrast to David's – is how responsive it is to the subtle particularities of the situation. It's not shtick or regurgitated bits from a *Monty Python* episode, as David's so often is. Aristotle tells us that "those who joke in a tasteful way are called ready-witted, which implies a sort of readiness to turn this way and that; for such sallies are thought to be movements of the character" (1128a9–11). Wit is nimble and responsive and suggests both intelligence and a sense of the absurd. David is "the slave of his sense of humor" (1128a34), while Tim is the master of his, not least because he lets the situation dictate whether humor is appropriate (and if so what kind). David, on the other hand, seeks out occasions for displaying his humor, and all too often thinks he's found an occasion when he really hasn't. Sometimes the situation calls for smuggling a pink dildo onto David's desk while he's meeting with Neil; other times the situation calls for gentle wit that puts others at ease – and involves subtle commentary on England's lingering class divisions. We see this when Tim is leading the new employees from Swindon on a tour of the warehouse:

> Ok now guys, we're about to enter a warehouse environment now. I'll just warn you that some of the people in here will be working class. So there may be some arse cleavage. Just find a partner, hold hands and don't talk to anyone.

"The ridiculous side of things is not far to seek" (1128a12–13), Aristotle tells us. No one knows this better than Tim, who only has to look across his desk at Gareth or listen to David to get in touch with the ridiculous.

Though David professes to know what the person of practical wisdom knows – that there are limits to comedy, that some things just aren't funny, or that they aren't funny in these circumstances – it's clear from his actions that he doesn't. Tim, by contrast, has just this practical wisdom. He knows intuitively, for example, that Finchy's mimicking sex with Dawn in front of Dawn – inexplicably inspired by the famous homosexual rape scene from *Deliverance* – is outrageously inappropriate. Tim isn't even tempted to laugh, because it's just not funny; David, of course, cackles uncontrollably.

Indeed, Tim's reaction to the forced humor of Comic Relief Day provides us with both his philosophy of humor and his most characteristic mode of jest, irony:

> Don't get me wrong, I've got nothing against this sort of thing . . . um . . . it's a good cause, but I just don't want to have to join in with someone else's idea of wackiness. It's the wackiness I can't stand. It's like . . . um . . . you see someone outside as they're collecting for cancer research because they've been personally affected by it or

whatever, or . . . I don't know . . . an old bloke selling poppies, there's a dignity about that. A sort of real quiet dignity . . . [Cut to his officemates, led by David, hooting and howling as they wrestle a co-worker to the floor and pull his pants down to photograph his privates] . . . and that's what today's all about: dignity, always dignity. [Cut back to Tim, smilingly shaking his head in disbelief]

Tim reacts with incredulity rather than harsh judgment at his colleagues' making no effort at "avoiding pain to the object of their fun" (1128a7). It's as if Tim intuitively recognizes that "most people delight more than they should in amusement and in jesting" (1128a13–14) and, presumably, that the mean is hard to hit and easy to miss.

Lessons Learned

The Office has much to teach us about Aristotle's ethics, for its major male characters illustrate the structure of a character virtue as a mean between extremes. The uncodifiable nature of humor mirrors the uncodifiable nature of morality. There are no explicit rules that a person without a sense of humor can follow to make or appreciate a joke or jest, no step-by-step guides. One can profitably read *Living Gluten-Free for Dummies, Breast-feeding for Dummies*, even – gulp – *Philosophy for Dummies*, but one cannot profitably read *Having a Sense of Humor for Dummies*, which explains why there is no such title. This isn't to say that there isn't helpful advice one can get or give regarding writing jokes, or that one can't be brought to see the humor in a situation, but rather that one already has to have a sense of humor for the advice to make any difference. Just as someone without a sense of humor – or without a particular kind of sense of humor (the right one) – can't understand why *The Office* is funny, someone who lacks the kind of moral vision the virtuous person possesses can't see what a situation calls for morally. Ludwig Wittgenstein (1889–1951), one of the greatest of all philosophers, once said that a serious work of philosophy could be written entirely as a series of jokes.[8] I'm not sure if he's right about that. But I think he was on to something when he said:

> So in the end when one is doing philosophy one gets to the point where one would like just to emit an inarticulate sound.[9]

I think it's safe to say that when thinking philosophically about *The Office*, the inarticulate sound the philosopher makes – or even the ordinary viewer – is a howl of laughter. Or at least a smile.[10]

[8]   Norman Malcom, *Ludwig Wittgenstein: A Memoir* (New York: Oxford University Press, 1958), p. 29.
[9]   *Philosophical Investigations*, 3rd edn. (Oxford: Blackwell, 1967), §261.
[10]   I am grateful to my friends and colleagues Erica Benson, Geoffrey Gorham, Mary Novaria, and Stuart Rachels, and my editor Jeremy Wisnewski for their very helpful comments on earlier versions of this essay. And, of course, to Ricky Gervais and Stephen Merchant for creating *The Office* in the first place. Or, as David Brent would say, "Wank you very much."

16

Why Doesn't Batman Kill the Joker?

Mark D. White

Summary

The Joker is the most homicidal of Batman's foes, and has killed many people close to the Dark Knight, including the second Robin, Jason Todd. For years, fans and critics have asked why Batman doesn't kill the Joker and save the countless lives the Crown Prince of Crime would probably take in the future. This chapter tackles this question in the context of a famous philosophical thought experiment, the Trolley Problem, which highlights the differences between two major schools of moral philosophy, utilitarianism and deontology.

Meet the Joker

In the last several decades, the Joker has transformed himself from the Clown Prince of Crime to a heinous murderer without rival. Most notoriously, he killed the second Robin, Jason Todd, beating him to a bloody pulp before blowing him up. He shot and killed Lieutenant Sarah Essen, Commissioner Jim Gordon's second wife – in front of dozens of infants, no less, whom he threatened to kill in order to lure Essen to him. Years earlier, the Joker shot Barbara Gordon – Jim Gordon's adopted daughter and the former Batgirl – in the spine, paralyzing her from the waist down, and then tormented Jim with pictures of her lying prone, naked and bleeding. And let us not forget countless ordinary citizens of Gotham City – the Joker even wiped out all of his own henchmen once![1]

Every time the Joker breaks out of Arkham Asylum, he commits depraved crimes – the type that philosopher Joel Feinberg (1926–2004) calls "sick! sick! sick!,"

---

[1] Jason Todd was killed in *A Death in the Family* (1988); Lieutenant Essen was killed in *No Man's Land Vol. 5* (2001); Barbara Gordon was shot in *The Killing Joke* (1988); and most of the Joker's henchmen were killed in *Batman* #663 (April 2007).

or "triple-sick."[2] Of course Batman inevitably catches the Joker and puts him back through the "revolving door" at Arkham.[3] Batman knows that the Joker will escape, and that he will likely kill again unless the Caped Crusader can prevent it – which, obviously, he can't always do.

So why doesn't Batman just kill the Joker? Think of all the lives it would save! Better yet, think of all the lives it would have saved had he done the deed years ago, just among Batman's closest friends and partners. Commissioner Gordon has contemplated killing the Joker himself on several occasions, and Batman is usually the one to stop him.[4] In a terrifically revealing scene during the *Hush* storyline, Batman is *this* close to offing the Joker, and it is Jim who stops him. Batman asks Jim, "How many more lives are we going to let him ruin?" to which Jim replies, "I don't care. I won't let him ruin yours."[5]

So although he may have considered it on many occasions, Batman has never killed the Joker, decidedly his most homicidal enemy. Of course, with the exception of his very earliest cases, Batman has refused to kill at all, usually saying that if he kills, it would make him as bad as the criminals he is sworn to fight. But that seems almost selfish – someone could very well say, "Hey – it's not about you, Bats!" Or . . . is it? Should it be? Usually we think a person is obligated to do something that would benefit many people, but what if that "something" is committing murder? Which is more important, doing good – or not doing wrong? (Ugh – Alfred, we need some aspirin here.)

In this chapter, we'll consider the ethics of killing to prevent future killings, exactly the problem Batman faces when he balances his personal moral code against the countless lives that he could save. In fact, this issue has been raised many times, recently by both the villain Hush and Jason Todd himself (returned from the dead), and earlier by Jean-Paul Valley (the "Knightfall" Batman), none of whom have the strict moral code that Batman adheres to.[6] I'll do this by introducing some famous philosophical thought experiments that let us trace through the ethics of a situation by whittling it down to its most basic elements, just like Batman solving a cleverly plotted crime. (Well, not quite, but you have to let a guy dream!)

Is Batman a Utilitarian or Deontologist? (Or None of the Above?)

The **argument** in favor of killing the Joker is fairly straight-forward – if Batman kills the Joker, he would prevent all the murders the Joker would otherwise commit in

---

[2]   Joel Feinberg, "Evil," in *Problems at the Roots of Law* (Oxford: Oxford Univ. Press, 2003), 125–192.

[3]   The Joker is the poster child for the insanity defense, so he never receives the death penalty.

[4]   For instance, after Lieutenant Essen was killed at the end of *No Man's Land*.

[5]   *Batman* #614 (June 2003), included in *Hush Volume Two* (2003). Unfortunately, I don't have room in this chapter to quote from Batman's internal dialogue from this issue as much as I would like, but it's brilliant writing, courtesy of Jeph Loeb.

[6]   See Hush in *Gotham Knights* #74 (April 2006), Jason Todd in *Batman* #650 (April 2006), and Jean-Paul Valley in *Robin* #7 (June 1994).

the future. This rationale is typical of ***utilitarianism***, a system of ethics that requires us to maximize the total happiness or well-being resulting from our actions.[7] Saving many lives at the cost of just one would represent a net increase in well-being or **utility**, and while it would certainly be a tragic choice, utilitarians would generally endorse it. (We could add more considerations, such as satisfying the quest for vengeance on the part of the families of his past victims, or the unhappiness it brings to some people when *anyone* is killed, but let's keep things simple – for now.)

Superheroes, however, generally are not utilitarians. Sure, they like happiness and well-being as much as the ordinary person, but there are certain things they will not do to achieve them. Of course, criminals know this and use it to their advantage: after all, why do you think criminals take innocent people as hostages? Superheroes – just like police in the real world – normally won't risk innocent lives to apprehend a villain, even if it means preventing the villain from killing more people later. More generally, most superheroes will not kill, even to save many other lives.[8]

But why do they refuse to kill in these instances? The utilitarian would not understand such talk. "You're allowing many more people to die because *you* don't want to kill one?" In fact, that's almost exactly what Jason Todd and Hush recently said to Batman. Hush asked, "How many lives do you think you've cost, how many families have you ruined, by allowing the Joker to live? . . . And why? Because of your duty? Your sense of justice?" Jason Todd put a more personal spin on it (of course): "Bruce, I forgive you for not saving me. But why . . . why on God's Earth – is he still alive? . . . Ignoring what he's done in the past. Blindly, stupidly, disregarding the entire graveyards he's filled, the thousands who have suffered, . . . the friends he's crippled, . . . I thought . . . I thought killing me – that I'd be the last person you'd ever let him hurt."[9] Batman's standard response has always been that if he ever kills, it will make him as bad as the criminals he fights, or that he will be crossing a line from which he would never return – though he is very open about his strong desire to kill the Joker.[10]

While utilitarians would generally endorse killing one person to prevent killing more, members of the school of ethics known as ***deontology*** would not.[11] Deontologists judge the morality of an act based on features intrinsic to the act itself, regardless of the consequences stemming from the act. To deontologists, the ends never justify the means, but rather the means must be justifiable on their own

---

[7] Utilitarianism is usually traced back to Jeremy Bentham's *The Principles of Morals and Legislation* (1781; Buffalo, NY: Prometheus Books edition, 1988).

[8] Wonder Woman's execution of Max Lord in the *Sacrifice* storyline, in order to end his psychic hold on Superman, is a significant exception and was treated as such in the stories that followed. (See *Wonder Woman* #219, September 2005, also collected in *Superman: Sacrifice*, 2006.)

[9] See note 6 for sources.

[10] In the scene with Jason Todd he explains that "all I have ever wanted to do is kill him. . . . I want him dead – maybe more than I've ever wanted anything." In *The Man Who Laughed* (2005), as he holds the Joker over the poisoned Gotham City reservoir, Batman thinks to himself, "This water is filled with enough poison to kill thousands. It would be so easy to just let him fall into it. So many are already dead because of this man . . . [but] I can't."

[11] The most famous deontologist is Immanuel Kant, whose seminal ethical work is his *Grounding for the Metaphysics of Morals* (1785; Indianapolis, IN: Hackett Publishing Company, 1993).

merits. So the fact that the killing would prevent future killings is irrelevant – the only relevant factor is that killing is wrong, period. But even for the strictest deontologist, there are exceptions – for instance, killing in self-defense would generally be allowed by deontologists. So killing is fine, but only for the right reasons? Might killing a homicidal maniac be just one of those reasons? We'll see, but first we have to take a ride on a trolley. . . .

To the Bat-Trolley, Professor Thomson!

One of many classic moral dilemmas debated by philosophers is the "trolley problem," introduced by Philippa Foot and elaborated upon by Judith Jarvis Thomson.[12] Imagine that a trolley car is going down a track. Further down the track are five people who do not hear the trolley and who will not be able to get out of the way. Unfortunately, there isn't enough time to stop the trolley before it hits and kills them. The only way to avoid killing these five people is to switch the trolley to another track. But, unfortunately, there is one person standing on that track, also too close for the trolley to stop before killing him. Now imagine that there is a bystander standing by the track switch who must make a choice: do nothing, which leads to the death of the five people on the current track, or act to divert the trolley to the other track, which leads to the death of the single person.

Let's call the person in control Bruce. Is Bruce morally allowed to divert the trolley to the second track or not? If he is, can we also say that in fact he is *required* to do it? Thomson takes the middle road here, concluding that Bruce is permitted – but not required – to divert the trolley. A typical utilitarian would require Bruce to throw the switch and save more lives, while a deontologist would have problems with Bruce's acting to take a life (rather than allowing five to die through inaction). Thomson's answer seems to combine the concerns of both utilitarianism and deontology. Bruce is allowed (maybe even encouraged) to divert the train and kill one person rather than five, but it's valid also for Bruce to have problems with doing this himself.

One way to state the difference between the utilitarian and the deontological approaches is to look at the types of rules they both prescribe. Utilitarianism results in *agent-neutral* rules, such as "Maximize well-being," and utilitarians couldn't care less who it is that will be following the rule. Everybody has to act so as to maximize well-being, and there is no reason or excuse for any one person to say "I don't want to." By contrast, deontology deals with *agent-specific* rules – when deontologists say "Do not kill," they mean "*You* do not kill," even if there are other reasons that make

---

[12] For Foot's original treatment, see her essay "The Problem of Abortion and the Doctrine of the Double Effect," in her book *Virtues and Vices* (Oxford: Clarendon Press, 2002), 19–32. For Thomson's version, see "The Trolley Problem," reprinted in her book *Rights, Restitution, & Risk*, edited by William Parent (Cambridge: Harvard Univ. Press, 1986), 94–116; and also chapter 7 in *The Realm of Rights* (Cambridge: Harvard Univ. Press, 1990).

it look like a good **idea**. This is simply a different way of contrasting the utilitarian's emphasis on good outcomes with the deontologist's focus on right action. While throwing the switch to kill the one rather than five may be good, it may not be right (because of what that specific person has to do).[13]

Hush Will *Love* This Next Story . . .

Thomson likes to compare the trolley situation with a story involving a surgeon with five patients, each of whom is dying from failure of a different organ and could be saved by a transplant. But there are no organs available through normal channels, so the surgeon considers drugging one of his (healthy) colleagues and removing his organs to use for the transplants.[14] By doing so, he would kill his colleague, but he would save his five patients.

With the possible exception of our bandaged and demented Dr. Hush, few people would endorse such a drastic plan (least of all Dr. Thomas Wayne, bless his soul). You can see where I'm going with this (Batman fans are so smart) – "What is the difference between the bystander in the trolley case and the surgeon in the transplant case?" In both cases a person can do nothing, and let five people die, or take an action that kills one but saves the five. Thomson, and many philosophers after her, have struggled with these questions, and there is no definitive answer. Most people will agree that throwing the trolley switch is justified, and also that the surgeon's actions are not, but we have a very difficult time saying precisely *why* we feel that way – and that includes philosophers!

Top Ten Reasons the Batmobile Is Not a Trolley . . .

How does Batman's situation compare to the trolley story (or the transplant story)? What factors relevant to Batman and the Joker are missing from the two classic philosophical dilemmas? And what does Batman's refusal to "do the deed" say about him?

One obvious difference between the two cases described by Thomson and the case of Batman and the Joker is that in Thomson's cases, the five people who will be killed if the trolley is not diverted, and the one person who will be killed if it is, are assumed to be morally equivalent. In other words, there is no moral difference between any of these people in terms of how they should be treated, what rights they have, and so on. All the people on the tracks in the trolley case are moral "innocents," as are the patients and the colleague in the transplant case.

---

[13] For an excellent treatment of agent-relative rules, see Samuel Scheffler's *The Rejection of Consequentialism*, rev. ed. (Oxford: Oxford Univ. Press: 1990).
[14] Never mind the astronomical odds against one of his colleagues being a donor match for all five patients!

Does this matter? Thomson introduces several modifications to suggest that it does. What if the five people on the main track collapsed there drunk early that morning, and the one person on the other track is a repairman performing track maintenance for the railroad? The repairman has a right to be there, while the five drunkards do not. Would this make us less comfortable about pulling the switch? What if the five transplant patients were in their desperate condition because of their own negligence regarding their health, and the colleague was very careful to take care of himself? We might say that in both of these cases the five persons are in their predicament due to their own (bad) choices, and they must take full responsibility for the consequences. And furthermore, their lives should not be saved at the expense of the one person in both situations who has taken responsibility for himself.

But the Joker case is precisely the opposite: he is the single man on the alternate track or the operating table, and his victims (presumably innocent) are the other five people. So following the logic above, there would be a presumption in *favor* of killing the Joker. After all, why should his victims sacrifice their lives so that *he* should live – especially if he lives to kill innocent people?

This case is different from the original philosophical cases in another way that involves moral differences between the parties. Unlike the classic trolley and trans-plant cases, the Joker actually *puts* the others in danger. In terms of the trolley case, it would be as if the Joker tied the five people to the main track, then stood on the other track to see what Batman would do. (Talk about a game of chicken!) If we were inclined to kill one to save five, that inclination would only be strengthened by knowing that the five were in danger *because* of the one!

We might say that the one person on the alternate track has the *right* not to be killed, even to save the other five. While it would be noble for him to make this sacrifice, most philosophers (aside from utilitarians) would deny that he has such an obligation. This is even clearer in the transplant case. The surgeon could certainly ask his colleague if he would be willing to give up his organs (and his life) to save the five patients, but we could hardly tell him that he *had* to. Once again, the difference with the Joker is that he put the others in danger, and it would be absurd – in other words, appropriate for one such as the Joker – to say, "Sure I'm going to kill these people, but *I* should not be killed to save *them*!"

The recognition of the Joker's role in creating the situation also casts light on the responsibility Batman faces. If we said to the Caped Crusader, as many have, "If you don't kill the Joker, the deaths of all his future victims will be on your hands," he could very well answer, "No, the deaths that the Joker causes are his responsibility and his responsibility alone. I am responsible only for the deaths I cause."[15] This is

---

15   In *Batman* #614, he thinks, "I cannot . . . I will not . . . accept any responsibility . . . for the Joker." But then he adds, "except that I should have killed him long ago." And finally, after contemplating that the Joker may kill someone close to him again, "he dies tonight by my hand," engaging in a graphic fantasy of several ways he could kill him. Makes you wonder what would have happened if Jim had not been there to stop him. . . .

another way to look at the agent-centered rule we discussed earlier: the bystander in the trolley example could very well say, "I did not cause the trolley to endanger the five lives, but I would be causing the death of one if I diverted the trolley."[16]

"I Want My Lawyer! Oh, That's Right, I Killed Him Too"

What the surgeon does in the transplant case is clearly illegal. However, if the bystander switches the trolley from its track, knowingly causing one person's death to save five others, the legality of his action is not clear. Of course, the legalities of the Batman/Joker case are a bit simpler. Let's assume (for the time being) that Batman has the same legal rights and obligations as a police officer. Under what circumstances would a police officer be allowed to kill the Joker (aside from self-defense)? If the Joker was just about to murder someone, then the police officer would be justified – legally – in killing him (if mere incapacitation is impossible and deadly force is the only effective choice). So if Batman came upon the Joker about to kill an innocent person, and the only way to save the person was to kill the Joker, Batman would be justified in doing that. (Knowing Batman, though, I imagine he would still find another way.)

Let's make the case a bit tougher – say Batman finds the Joker just *after* he's killed someone. Batman (or a police officer) couldn't do anything to save that person, but if he kills the Joker, he'll save untold others whom the Joker will probably kill. *Probably?* Well, let's be fair now – we don't *know* that the Joker will kill any more people. "This is my last one, Batty, I promise!" The Joker has certainly claimed to have reformed in the past; perhaps this time it's for real. Or maybe the Joker will die by natural causes tomorrow, never to kill again. The fact is, we can't be sure that he will kill again, so we can't be sure we will be saving *any* lives by taking his.

Given this fact, it's as if we changed the trolley example like so: a dense fog is obscuring the view on the main track, but we can see the sole person on the other track. We don't know if anyone is in danger on the main track, but we know that *sometimes* there are people there. What do we do? Or, to modify the transplant case, the surgeon doesn't have any patients who need organs right now, but he guesses that there will be some tomorrow, by which time his healthy colleague will be on vacation. Should he still sacrifice his colleague today?

I imagine that none of us would be comfortable, in either case, choosing to kill the one to avoid the *chance* of killing others. It's one thing to hold the Joker accountable for the people he has killed, and this may include the death penalty (if he weren't

---

[16]   This also brings in the controversial ethical distinction between causing a death through action and causing a death through inaction. Merely allowing a death is usually considered less problematic than directly causing a death – consider Nightwing's choice not to stop Tarantula from killing his arch-nemesis, Blockbuster, who also happened to pledge to kill many more people in the future (*Nightwing* #93, July 2004). Interestingly, Dick actually did kill the Joker once, although Batman revived him (*Joker: Last Laugh* #6, January 2002).

the poster boy for the insanity defense), but another thing entirely when we consider the people he might kill in the future. Admittedly, he has a well-established pattern, and he may even say he's going to kill more in the future. What if we have every reason – as Batman clearly does – to believe him? Can we deal with him *before* he kills again?

Punishing people before they commit crimes has been called *prepunishment* by philosophers, and the **concept** was made famous by Philip K. Dick's 1956 short story "The Minority Report," more recently a movie directed by Steven Spielberg and starring Tom Cruise.[17] While Batman killing the Joker would not literally be punishment – since he has no legal authority to impose such a sentence – we can still consider whether or not prepunishment is morally acceptable, especially in this case. Some would say that if the Joker intends to kill again, and makes clear statements to that effect, then there is no moral difficulty with prepunishing him. (There may, however, be an informational or *epistemic* problem – why would he confess to his future crime if he knew he would be killed before he had a chance to commit it?) But others say that even if he says he will kill again, he still has the choice to change his mind, and it is out of respect for this capacity to make ethical choices that we should not prepunish people.[18] Prepunishment may trigger the panic button in all of us, but in an age in which very many can be killed very easily by very few, we may be facing this issue before long.[19]

So, Case Closed – Right?

So then, we're all convinced that Batman was right not to have killed the Joker.

What? We're not?

Well, *of course* not. Look at it this way – I consider myself a strict deontologist, and even I have to admit that maybe Batman should have killed the Joker. (I hope none of my colleagues in the North American Kant Society reads this – I'll be on punch-and-pretzels duty for a year!) As much as we deontologists say the right always comes before the good, an incredible amount of good would have been done if the Joker's life had been ended years ago. Compare this issue with the recent torture

---

[17] You can find the short story in Philip K. Dick's collection *The Minority Report* (New York: Citadel, 2002). Tom Cruise, in case you don't know, is mainly known for being married to actress Katie Holmes from *Batman Begins*. (To my knowledge, he's done nothing else worth mentioning.)

[18] Christopher New argues for prepunishment in "Time and Punishment," *Analysis* 52, no. 1 (1992): 35–40, and Saul Smilansky argues against it (and New) in "The Time to Punish," *Analysis* 54, no. 1 (1994): 50–53. New responds to Smilansky in "Punishing Times: A Reply to Smilansky," *Analysis* 55 no. 1 (1995): 60–2.

[19] Of course, Wonder Woman already faced this question with regard to Max Lord, who promised to force Superman to kill, and she came to the opposite conclusion. (Apparently she had read New's papers.) But ironically, it was she who stopped Batman from killing Alex Luthor (who nearly killed Nightwing) in *Infinite Crisis* #7 (June 2006). Even more ironically, who eventually killed Alex at the end of the same issue? The Joker.

debates – even those who are wholeheartedly opposed to the use of torture under any circumstances must have some reservations when thousands or millions of innocent lives are at stake.

Luckily, literature – and by "literature" I mean comic books – provides us a way to discuss issues like these without having to experience them. We don't have to trick people into standing in front of a runaway trolley, and we don't have to have a real-life Batman and Joker. That's what thought experiments are for – they let us play through an imaginary scenario and imagine what we should or shouldn't do. Unfortunately for Batman, but luckily for Batman fans, the Joker is not imaginary to him, and I'm sure he will struggle with this issue for many years to come.

17

Means, Ends, and the Critique of Pure Superheroes

J. Robert Loftis

Summary

The characters Ozymandias and Rorschach from *Watchmen* seem to represent opposite sides in the debate in philosophical ethics between consequentialists, who believe that the ends sometimes justify the means, and deontologists, who want us not to think in terms of ends and means at all. Closer examination, however, reveals that neither character is really true to their stated philosophies.

Near the climax of *Watchmen*, Rorschach and Nite Owl confront Ozymandias in his Antarctic fortress, and Ozymandias starts explaining his insane plan, which will perhaps save the world, but at the cost of millions of lives. While the smartest man in the world is offering up the last crucial bit of plot exposition, Rorschach looks for a weapon. He can find only a fork, but he tries to stab Veidt with it anyway. Ozymandias blocks the blow and sends Rorschach to the floor, all the while continuing his monologue. After Rorschach gets up, he tries to make another move on Ozymandias but is blocked by Bubastis, the genetically engineered supercat. Ozymandias doesn't even need to turn to face Rorschach, let alone miss a beat of his monologue. Not sure what else to do, Rorschach tries talking: "Veidt, get rid of the cat." "No I don't think so," Ozymandias replies magnanimously. "After all her presence saves you the humiliation of another beating."[1] Ozymandias's speechifying is a great foil for the taciturn Rorschach. An even starker contrast comes when Veidt is finally confronted by someone more powerful than he – Dr. Manhattan, the comic's only true superhero. While Rorschach doggedly attacked a foe he knew he couldn't beat, Ozymandias immediately suggests compromise. If the others stay silent, they can enjoy the benefit of Veidt's new world. Everyone accepts the compromise – after all, they can't undo the attack on New York – except Rorschach, even though it means his certain death.

---

[1] *Watchmen*, chap. XII, p. 9.

The contrast between the two characters' willingness to compromise shows a deep divide in their underlying ethical worldviews. Ozymandias appears to be what philosophers call a *consequentialist*: he believes that all actions should be judged by their consequences, implying that the ends will sometimes justify the means. He is the kind of guy who, when he has to make a decision, carefully lists the pros and cons and goes with the option that has the most pros on balance. At least, that's the way Ozymandias thinks of himself. **Consequentialism** is how Ozymandias rationalizes the bizarre murderous scheme that was revealed in the Antarctic fight. But consequentialism has a long and noble philosophical tradition, and the great consequentialists of the past would certainly disavow Ozymandias as one of their own.

Rorschach, on the other hand, appears to be a *deontologist*. **Deontology** says that we should not think of morality in terms of ends and means at all; instead, we should act only in ways that express essential moral rules. Rorschach deonto- logically rationalizes his actions, such as stabbing away at Veidt using anything he can find, even though he knows he can't succeed. The outcome doesn't matter; what matters is doing the right thing. But deontology also has an old and noble philosophical tradition, and the great deontologists of the past would certainly disavow Rorschach as one of *their* own. Acting to express moral rules does not mean seeing the world in black and white.

[. . .] *Watchmen* is an intensely philosophical comic, and theories like con- sequentialism and deontology were clearly on Alan Moore's and Dave Gibbons' minds as they created the book. I hope to show that their attitude toward both consequentialism and deontology in *Watchmen* is profoundly negative. Yet these are actually only stepping-stones to the real point of *Watchmen*. The ultimate target of the comic's critique is *authoritarianism*, the idea that anyone should set himself or herself up as a guardian of society. Superheroes serve as the images of power and authority in *Watchmen*. The ideologies that the heroes pretend to follow are rationalizations of that power, and the corruption of the superheroes serves as a critique of both power and its rationalizations.

"'In the end'? Nothing ends, Adrian. Nothing ever ends."

When Ozymandias is being chased by Dr. Manhattan, he lures Manhattan into an intrinsic field gizmo (like the one that first created the big blue man) and activates it, which seems to zap Manhattan into vapor, disintegrating Ozymandias's beloved kitty Bubastis in the process. Afterward, Ozymandias says offhandedly, "Hm, you know, I wasn't really sure that would work."[2] (Actually, it didn't.) This is a great Veidt moment in a couple of ways: it shows his willingness to make big sacrifices for even bigger ends, and to gamble on probabilities. He doesn't deal with a world of black and white, of evil and good, as Rorschach does. Everything is gray, but

---

[2] Ibid., p. 14.

some gray areas are darker than others. To do the right thing, Ozymandias simply chooses the lightest shade of gray.

In the history of philosophy, this sort of weighing, calculating consequentialism is most associated with the doctrine of **utilitarianism**. Although the basic idea behind utilitarianism has been around forever, the doctrine didn't really begin to flourish until the work of the English philosophers Jeremy Bentham (1748–1832) and John Stuart Mill (1806–73). The core idea is simple: "actions are right in proportion as they tend to promote happiness, wrong as they tend to produce the reverse of happiness."[3] Utilitarianism is built from consequentialism by adding elements, as one adds ingredients to a soup. The first new ingredient is *hedonism*: the good that one is trying to maximize in the world is happiness. The utilitarian is not worried, as Rorschach is, about being sure that every criminal is punished. Punishment is only a good policy if, as a consequence, it makes someone happier by preventing future crime. The other new ingredient is *egalitarianism*. Everybody's happiness is weighed equally. Thus, if an action will make five people happy and one person unhappy (all by equal amounts), you should do it, even if the one unhappy person is your mom – or your favorite genetically engineered cat.

Now, utilitarians are well aware that one cannot in advance know which things will really maximize happiness for all. So most utilitarians don't recommend that we simply try to calculate the best possible outcome each time we make a decision. Instead, we should rely on the rules and habits that the human race has developed over time for acting morally. Thus, the version of utilitarianism that is appropriately called *rule utilitarianism* says that one should live by the rules that would maximize happiness for everyone if they were followed consistently. So Veidt might adopt a rule for himself such as "Never kill," not because killing never brings more happiness than unhappiness, but because a person who lives by such a rule would generally bring more happiness than unhappiness.

The version of utilitarianism called *virtue utilitarianism* asks you to develop the personal characteristics that are likely to maximize happiness for all if you really made them a part of you. Thus, Veidt could spend his time developing a sense of compassion, because compassionate people generally bring more happiness than unhappiness to the world.

Utilitarianism has had many critics over the years, and it looks like Moore and Gibbons are among them. We can see this first of all in the structure of the story. According to the standard comic book formula, Rorschach is the hero of the story and Ozymandias is the villain (though, of course, nothing is really that simple in *Watchmen*). Rorschach is the first person we see, and the plot is structured around his investigation of several murders. The audience uncovers the truth behind the murders as Rorschach does. Ozymandias, on the other hand, is behind the murders, and when he is found out, he reveals his elaborate plot involving the further death of millions. Ozymandias also has one of the key flaws that marks comic book

---

[3]   John Stuart Mill, *Utilitarianism*, 7th ed. (London: Longmans, Green, and Co., 1879), chapter 2. Available (free) at www.gutenberg.org/etext/11224.

villainy: he is a megalomaniac who wants to take over the world. He may say that the purpose of his plan is to "usher in an age of illumination so dazzling that humanity will reject the darkness in its heart."[4] But we know the first thing he thinks about when he sees his crazy scheme succeed is his own glory. "I did it!" he shouts, fists in the air. And he immediately begins planning his own grand role in this utopia.

If Ozymandias is the villain, then perhaps utilitarianism is a villain's ideology. It certainly looks as if consequentialism contributed to his corruption by allowing him to rationalize self-serving ends and blinding him to the profound injustice of what he has done. The potential for consequentialism to promote rationalization is obvious: once one starts making sacrifices and trade-offs, it gets easy to make the sacrifices that will serve one's own interest. The deeper harm that consequentialism seems to have brought, though, is letting Veidt believe that he can *force* people to sacrifice their well-being – indeed, their lives – for the greater good. Veidt thus fails to consider basic justice or fairness. Is it fair that the citizens of New York are forced to sacrifice their lives and sanity to end the Cold War, when no one else is asked to make such a sacrifice? The means for preventing this kind of unfairness is typically the doctrine of human rights, which tells us that there are some things the individual cannot be asked to do against his or her will, even if it is for the greater good. One of the most common criticisms of consequentialist doctrines such as utilitarianism is that they are unable to embrace a doctrine of universal human rights. And in *Watchmen*, we certainly see the consequences of failing to take the rights of New Yorkers seriously.

The Utilitarians Strike Back

At this point, utilitarians will object that they are being unfairly maligned. Veidt is at best a parody of the ethic they recommend. Far from rationalizing self-serving interests, utilitarianism is the least selfish doctrine around, because one's own happiness counts no more than anyone else's. As Mill wrote forcefully, "I must again repeat, what the assailants of utilitarianism seldom have the justice to acknowledge, that the happiness which forms the utilitarian standard of what is right in conduct, is not the agent's own happiness, but that of all concerned."[5] More important, utilitarians would object that their theory does indeed allow for justice and human rights. Mill was a passionate defender of liberty and an early advocate for women's right to vote, so it was very important for him to argue that utilitarians can account for justice. He did this by using the tools of rule utilitarianism: to make decisions effectively, individuals and societies must adopt rules for themselves. Experience shows that individuals and societies that recognize rights are more likely to maximize happiness than are those that don't. If Veidt had been a real utilitarian, he would have recognized this and adopted stricter rules about killing people.

---

4 *Watchmen*, chap. XII, p. 17.
5 Mill, *Utilitarianism*, chap. 2.

Moore and Gibbons don't address these nuances – as we shall see in the last section of this chapter, they are primarily interested in showing ethical theories as ways of rationalizing power. They do, however, offer another critique of utilitarianism that can't be dealt with by adjusting the fine points of doctrine. It is important to note that the critique doesn't come from the alleged consequentialist Veidt but from Dr. Manhattan. In one of the most moving sequences in the book, Veidt asks Manhattan, with unexpected plaintiveness and insecurity, whether he's really the good guy he thinks he is: "Jon, before you leave . . . I did the right thing, didn't I? It all worked out in the end." In the next panel, we see Dr. Manhattan from Veidt's point of view. The blue man, standing inside a model of the solar system, arms down, palms out, smiles and says, "'In the end'? Nothing ends, Adrian. Nothing ever ends."[6] Then he leaves Earth for good. Dr. Manhattan's warning is borne out four pages later, when we see Seymour, the inept assistant at the *New Frontiersman*, reaching toward Rorschach's journal looking for something to fill up space in the next issue. If he grabs it, Veidt's scheme could be ruined, and all that suffering would be for nothing.

Utilitarianism asks us to look to the future and sum up the consequences of our actions, but the future is infinite, and you can't crunch the numbers when every one of them turns to infinity. Perhaps in five years something will happen that undoes the good that Veidt did. Then, ten years after that, something good will happen that could only have happened given Veidt's actions. The problem here isn't just that we can't know the future, but that there is too much of it. Even if we had an infinite mind to encompass the infinite future, what would we see? An infinity of happiness and an infinity of suffering? We can't do anything to change a ratio of infinity to infinity.

And even if we could, what of it? Utilitarianism gets its motivation from the basic instinct that pain is bad and pleasure is good. Individually, you and I seek pleasure and avoid pain. Utilitarianism tries to remove the selfishness of this by asking us to seek pleasure for everyone. In doing so, it tries to make ethics a little more objective: less about what *you* want and more about what is good in itself. But if we keep going with this impulse to objectivity, everything loses its meaning. What does it matter if there is more pain or more pleasure in the world? We are now in the perspective of Jon Osterman after his accident: if you take too abstract a perspective, nothing seems valuable at all. This is a defect in Ozymandias's worldview. Unlike other characters – Rorschach or the Comedian – Ozymandias has never really confronted the question of the meaning of life or the possibility that life is meaningless. All of his personal revelations are about the source of suffering in the world, not about the possibility of morality. He learns that evil is not just a matter of crime, but comes from geopolitical forces. But he never questions the nature of evil and good itself. This is the real significance behind Moore and Gibbons's decision to name this character Ozymandias and to use the Shelley poem as the epigraph to chapter XI. Ozymandias takes a bigger view but never the biggest view.

---

[6] *Watchmen*, chap. XII, p. 27.

"Even in the face of Armageddon I shall not compromise in this."

So Ozymandias is a tragic villain, a man whose overwhelming ego and failure to appreciate the dark nature of life led him to think the end can sometimes justify the means. That means Rorschach is the hero, right? Well, no. Rorschach is a foil for Veidt in every respect: the unkempt, taciturn, right-wing outsider against the slick, eloquent, left-wing celebrity. But just being a mirror to the villain doesn't make you the hero.

As we saw earlier, Rorschach often uses deontology to rationalize his actions. We see this in his constant mantra "in the face of Armageddon I shall not compromise," which is an echo of the deontologists' slogan: "Let justice be done, though heaven should fall."[7] Deontology goes beyond saying that the ends never justify the means. It actually says that at least in moral decisions, you shouldn't think in terms of ends and means, or consequences, at all. Once you start thinking about means and ends, you've left the realm of morality altogether, because you're only thinking about how to get something you want, either for yourself or someone else. According to deontologist Immanuel Kant (1724–1804), morality begins with the good will. Anything else you might value in life – intelligence, strength, even happiness itself – can be used for evil. The only thing good, really, is the *will* to do good, the mental act that says, "I am going to do the right thing."

By the same token, if you are doing something solely to achieve some end, you are not doing it because it is the right thing to do. This applies not only to ends we think of as selfish, but even to those we think of as ethical. Think about a cruel and selfish act, like the Comedian shooting his pregnant Vietnamese girlfriend at the end of the war. A deontologist would think that part of why this is wrong is because of the Comedian's motivation. He's not trying to do what is right; he's merely trying to accomplish an end that is convenient for him, getting rid of a person as if she were extra baggage. Now think about an unselfish act, such as the redemptive moment at Bernard's newsstand when so many passersby intervene to break up the fight between Joey and her girlfriend Aline. If one of them was jumping in simply to make himself look good or even to feel good for helping somebody, that would simply be acting for an end. But if someone helped because it was the right thing to do, even if that person had no desire to do so, that tells us that his or her act was moral (in a deontological sense). Interestingly, the people who intervene don't talk about pity; they give more deontological explanations, such as, "It's all that means anything."[8] They have to act because they're moral people in a dark world that can only be lit by the good will. They're doing the right thing because it's the right thing. Kant would smile.

---

[7] Rorschach offers many variations on the "never compromise" mantra. The two that come closest to the deontologists' slogan given previously are *Watchmen*, chap. I, p. 24, and chap. XII, p. 20.

[8] Ibid., chap. XI, p. 20.

But Rorschach is not a hero, and his deontology is not Kant's. It is a shadow of deontology that is used to rationalize fascist thuggery. I wish I could show this simply by pointing out that Rorschach is a psychotic killer, but in comics, as in Hollywood, crazy vigilantes have a certain cachet. To see the real problems with Rorschach and his use of deontology, we need to look at his hypocrisy, the way his deontology degenerates into "dichotomous thinking," and his failure to recognize the intrinsic value of persons.

Rorschach is not only a flat-out hypocrite, but his hypocrisy reveals his real commitments. Rorschach's supposed commitment to deontology takes a back seat to the need to project strength in the face of moral decline. Although he delivered the announcement that he ignored the Keene Act on the dead body of a serial rapist, he shows admiration for the Comedian, who attempted to rape the first Silk Spectre and confessed to having done many other "bad things to women."[9] After trashing Moloch's apartment, Rorschach says, "Sorry about the mess, can't make an omelet without breaking a few eggs," a classic bit of consequentialist reasoning.[10] To heighten the irony, Moore and Gibbons even depict him stealing a raw egg from Moloch's fridge, carefully cracking it open, and drinking it. Rorschach also professes admiration for President Harry Truman, because Truman was willing to sacrifice the lives of millions in Hiroshima and Nagasaki in order to avoid even bigger losses in the war – basically the same trade-off Ozymandias makes.[11] The pattern behind all of these exceptions is telling. In each case, Rorschach slips into consequentialist reasoning in order to justify a hypermasculine display of power and violence. This shows that his real worldview is simply fascist. All of the elements of classical fascism are there: obsession with moral decline, idolizing the masculine and fearing the feminine, and **belief** that democratic authority has failed and must be replaced with something more direct.[12]

A deeper abuse of deontology comes in Rorschach's obsessive *dichotomous thinking*, the mistake of looking at the world in black and white. Rorschach is thus guilty of committing a *fallacy*, a mistaken but very tempting way to reason. *Watchmen* goes out of its way to show that where Veidt could at least see shades of gray, Rorschach is a simple dichotomous thinker. His initial attraction to the fabric he made his mask from, for instance, came from the fact that black and white never mixed.[13] Rorschach seems to think that dichotomous thinking comes with deontology. All of his statements of deontological principles also say that he sees the world in black and white: "There is good and there is evil and evil must be punished, in the face of Armageddon I shall not compromise in this."[14]

[9] Ibid., chap. II, p. 27; chap. VI, p. 15; and chap. II, p. 23.
[10] Ibid., chapter V, p. 6.
[11] Ibid., chap. VI, supplemental material, Walter J. Kovacs case file, excerpt of an essay by Walter J. Kovacs.
[12] Umberto Eco, "Ur-Fascism," in *Five Moral Pieces*, trans. Alastair McEwen (New York: Harcourt Trade, 2002), pp. 65–88.
[13] *Watchmen*, chap. VI, p. 10.
[14] Ibid., chapter I, p. 24.

But dichotomous thinking is not at all a part of deontology. Kant taught that we should not do things for the sake of ends, but for the sake of doing the right thing. Still, this does not mean that "the right thing" has to be something simple-minded or rigid. For Kant, doing the right thing meant obeying what he called the "**categorical imperative**," a rule he phrased a couple of different ways. The first was to "Act as though the maxim of your action were to become, through your will, a universal law of nature."[15] This sounds weird, but it is really just asking you to remember a question your mother asked you as a kid: "What if everyone did that?" For instance, if you stole some candy from the drugstore, Mom probably said something like, "Listen, honey, I know it seems like no one is hurt, but what if everyone shoplifted candy? The store would go out of business and then no one would have any candy." Using a universalization test like this allows for much more subtle ethical reasoning than Rorschach is capable of. What if everyone was a crazed vigilante who punished every infraction with death?

The biggest reason Rorschach is not a real deontologist is that he fails to show respect for persons. Earlier, we said that Veidt's worldview fell short of being moral because he failed to recognize rights, the moral rules that prevent us from sacrificing an individual for the greater good. Kant captured this in the second formulation of his categorical imperative: "Act in such a way as to treat humanity, whether in your own person or in that of anyone else, always as an end and never merely as a means."[16] Again, this sounds weird, but what it boils down to is "Don't treat people like mere tools to achieve your ends." When Veidt destroys New York, he is using the city's inhabitants as tools for ending the Cold War, thus violating their basic rights as persons.

Rorschach likewise fails to recognize the rights we typically grant people – for example, the right to a fair trial. Really, Rorschach drew the wrong lesson from his existential moment burning down the home of that child butcher. According to Kant, we are obligated to always respect the basic rights of persons, because only a person is capable of exercising a good will, and a good will is the only thing that is truly good. Rorschach saw some of this as he "looked at the sky through smoke heavy with human fat."[17] He saw an existentialist version of Kant's claim that the only thing good is the good will. In Rorschach's version, "existence is random, save what we imagine after staring at it too long" and therefore we are "free to scrawl our own design on a morally blank world." What Rorschach didn't see, but Kant did, is that this requires us to respect the people who are capable of scrawling a moral design on the world.

[15]   Immanuel Kant, *Groundwork for the Metaphysics of Morals* (1785), trans. Jonathan Bennett (2005), online at www.earlymoderntexts.com, Second Section. This quote appears on p. 421 of print editions (with standard Academy pagination).
[16]   Ibid., p. 429.
[17]   *Watchmen*, chap. VI, p. 26.

"Who watches the watchmen?"

So, neither consequentialism nor deontology comes off well in *Watchmen*. The characters use the ideas as thin rationalizations for corrupt behavior, and, at least in the case of utilitarianism, the ideas themselves are shown to be flawed. But critiquing consequentialism and deontology is not the main goal for Moore and Gibbons. Their deepest concern is obviously expressed in the aphorism that gives the comic its name and that appears in fragmentary form throughout the book: "Who watches the watchmen?" The line finally appears in full form at the very end of the book, but in a strange way. Moore and Gibbons give the original source, Juvenal's *Satires*, but then mention that it is quoted as the epigraph of the Tower Commission Report (which resulted from investigations of the Iran-Contra scandal during President Ronald Reagan's administration). This is a detail people tend to pass over, if only because the report was written before many current readers of *Watchmen* were even born. Perhaps this obscure bit of 1980s history appears only because Moore and Gibbons were reading the newspapers, rather than Latin poetry, during the era of Reagan and Thatcher. And the poem in which the line originally appears is about the difficulty men have keeping their women in line – a bit of patriarchy that is not a big concern for the comic. The Tower Commission, on the other hand, is exactly the sort of thing the comic is about.

Watchmen depicts an alternate universe in which the Watergate scandal never takes place, a man with superhuman powers allows the United States to win the Vietnam War, and Nixon is now in his sixth term in office, thanks to a new constitutional amendment. Covert criminal activity of the sort the Tower Commission exposed seems to have driven this history: Moore and Gibbons strongly imply that the Comedian assassinated Woodward and Bernstein and further hint that in this world, Nixon and the Comedian were involved with the Kennedy assassination. Ultimately, this is all intended as a warning about how a free society can collapse into authoritarianism, something Moore had previously depicted in *V for Vendetta*.[18] In that comic, he showed England sliding into fascism after limited nuclear exchanges in Africa and the European continent, followed by environmental and economic collapse. In 1988, when DC Comics reprinted a colorized run of the series (including the ending, which had gone unpublished because the magazine it ran in originally was canceled), Moore wrote a melancholy introduction lamenting the power of Thatcher's Tory Party. Given what has happened, he realizes he was mistaken to believe that "it would take something as melodramatic as a near-miss nuclear conflict to nudge England toward Fascism."[19] Basically, Moore was not satisfied with the picture of a decline of a democracy into authoritarianism in *V*, and *Watchmen*, which was first serialized in 1986, is in part a correction of this.

[18]   Alan Moore and David Lloyd, 1982–1985, *V for Vendetta* in *Warrior*, issues 1–26 (Brighton, UK: Quality Communications).
[19]   Alan Moore and David Lloyd, *V for Vendetta* (New York: Vertigo, 1988), p. 6.

Ozymandias and Rorschach are a crucial part of this picture, since the superheroes in *Watchmen* are images of authority. Moore told the BBC program *Comics Britannia* that "What *Watchmen* became was entirely a meditation about power. We were thinking about how to some degree each of these characters represented some sort of power."[20] Rorschach and Ozymandias are important because we see in them that anyone can be corrupted. Leftist or rightist political views are really of little consequence, because they are merely ways that the powerful rationalize what they are doing. Consequentialism and deontology are merely further rationalizations of these ruling ideologies. It is thus not surprising that neither view really gets a fair shake in *Watchmen*. Moore and Gibbons aren't interested in whether the views can be tinkered with to the point that they are a reasonable guide to behavior, because that is not how these ideologies function in the real world. Notice also that the most moral characters in the comic, the two Nite Owls, are basically nonideological. They don't have big moral ideas but rather rely on a basic sense of decency [...]. Dreiberg, the second Nite Owl, specifically shies away from making grand decisions that affect the whole world because one person simply isn't competent to do so.[21] The real lesson behind the entire comic is that no one, no matter what his or her ideology, should be entrusted with too much power.[22]

---

[20] BBC Bristol, *Comics Britannia* (2007), www.bbc.co.uk/bbcfour/comicsbritannia/comics-britannia. shtml; click on "Alan Moore Interview II."
[21] *Watchmen*, chap. XII, p. 20.
[22] For more on this theme, see Tony Spanakos, "Super-Vigilantes and the Keene Act," in *Watchmen and Philosophy: A Rorschach Test*, ed. Mark D. White (New York: Wiley-Blackwell, 2009).

18

Metallica, Nietzsche, and Marx

The Immorality of Morality

Peter S. Fosl

Summary

This chapter explores different ways the songs of Metallica express ideas developed in the philosophical work of Friedrich Nietzsche and Karl Marx. Metallica illustrates a number of the central criticisms Nietzsche and Marx advance against religion (especially Christianity) and standard morality. This chapter also considers, however, the extent to which Metallica's music itself may be criticized along Nietzschean and Marxian lines. Despite its Nietzschean themes, is Metallica's message ultimately what Nietzsche would call "nihilistic"? Does Metallica, rather than a positive message of resistance and revolt, instead convey a lesson in acquiescence and surrender to the oppressed? The answer is complicated.

Those who can make you believe absurdities can make you commit atrocities.

– Voltaire

In songs like "Leper Messiah" and "The God that Failed," Metallica charges religion with moral failure and in this way connects itself with a tradition in philosophy stretching back through thinkers like Voltaire, Hume, Lucretius, Socrates, and Xenophanes. According to these philosophers, what religions prescribe as morally "good" is actually morally bad or wrong. What religions claim to be "righteous" is instead corrupt. What they portray as "pious" is in fact perverse. What they present as "truth" is in reality deceit. Since religion has had such a wide effect on common **ideas** about morality in our society, what passes for sound morality across society generally is more often a putrid tangle of immorality.[1]

Morality and Power

One of the most important critiques of Christian morality was developed by German philosopher Friedrich Nietzsche (1844–1900). In books like *Beyond Good and Evil* (1886), *The Genealogy of Morals* (1887), and *Twilight of the Idols* (1888), Nietzsche describes the way Christian morality presents a pathological doctrine, one that ultimately weakens people, tearing down their minds, bodies, and cultures.

In a manner not terribly different from the way Metallica's James Hetfield describes it, Nietzsche depicts Christianity as a "slave morality." Originating among the members of a relatively insignificant ethnic group living under the heel of Roman rule, Christian morality found its origins in a sentiment both puny and dishonorable – "resentment" (*ressentiment*). Resenting Roman power, members of the Jesus movement argued that it's really the meek that are blessed. Resenting Roman wealth, they praised poverty and simplicity. In the face of Roman pride, Christians promoted humility. Against Roman military might, they deployed peacemaking. Since the Romans ruled this world, Christians concocted a better, truer kingdom in another world, a transcendent world beyond this one, beyond Rome.

But it wasn't enough for early Christians simply to defy Roman rule. They also produced their own distinctive way of ruling, of exerting power over others. Perhaps the most effective way Christians exerted power was by collecting the faithful into a docile "herd" through the idea that we all carry an internal debt called "sin."[2] Having convinced people of this, Christian priests proclaimed that they alone could forgive the debt, that only through the authority of their religion could human beings find consolation and salvation (John 14:6, 10:9). It was a wildly successful technique.

Aside from Nietzsche's, perhaps the most influential critique of religion was articulated by Karl Marx (1818–83). While it would be wrong to characterize Metallica as a Marxist band, there are elements of Metallica's critique that overlap

---

[1]   Thus Metallica and their philosophical predecessors offer a moral critique of religion. Other philosophical critiques of religion are rooted in epistemology, **metaphysics**, and the philosophy of language. Epistemological critiques leverage their criticisms on an examination of the possibilities of acquiring knowledge about religious matters, typically arguing that one can't really "know" the sorts of things that the faithful claim to know. Metaphysical critiques hinge on ideas about what's "real" and might possibly be real, often maintaining that religious claims about divine reality are somehow flawed – that entities of the sort described by religion don't exist or can't exist. Critiques drawing on ideas from the philosophy of language address what it's possible and not possible to speak of meaningfully. They argue that religious language is literally meaningless, or at least not meaningful in the way the faithful think.

[2]   Friedrich Nietzsche, *Genealogy of Morals* in *Basic Writings of Nietzsche*, ed. and trans. by Walter Kaufmann (New York: Modern Library, 1968), §20.

with Marx's. Writing in the year of Nietzsche's birth, Marx famously described religion as the "opium of the people."[3] This opium, says Marx, deadens people, submerging them in a stupor that renders them unable to think clearly or resist effectively the exploitation to which they're subjected. Metallica is certainly no stranger to this insight.

Hetfield's lyrics in, for example, "Leper Messiah" describe religion alternatively as a "disease," an addictive drug, a form of mind control, and an instrument of power.[4] In an especially rich and compressed lyric, Metallica weaves together Nietzschean and Marxian themes into an evocative bundle: "Marvel at his tricks, need your Sunday fix. / Blind devotion came, rotting your brain. / Chain, chain / Join the endless chain, taken by his glamour / Fame, Fame / Infection is the game, stinking drunk with power. / We see." The song also depicts the way Christianity weakens people and gathers them into an obedient herd: "Witchery, weakening / Sees the sheep are gathering / Set the trap, hypnotize / Now you follow. / [Chorus] / Lie." "Holier than Thou" announces a kind of solidarity with the working class and threatens (religious? revolutionary?) judgment in response to the way things posing as "sacred" and "just" commonly cloak privilege and exploitation. "It's not who you are, it's who you know / Others lives are the basis of your own / Burn your bridges build them back with wealth / Judge not lest ye be judged yourself." "And Justice for All" expresses a more impotent and defeated sentiment, but nevertheless an understanding of how things really work: "Halls of justice painted green / Money talking / Power wolves beset your door / Hear them stalking / Soon you'll please their appetite / They devour / Hammer of justice crushes you / Overpower."

For all its apparent defeatism, however, there is perhaps a kind of ambiguity in that last line, "overpower" – a call to the oppressed to rise up and overpower the forces that are crushing them. But, if revolutionary inspiration's what you're after, these few half-submerged suggestions offer a pretty thin reed to cling to.

Indeed, on balance Metallica does seem more pessimistic than Nietzsche or Marx. Their songs often seem preoccupied with the failure of religion and the failure of attempts to resist it. Perhaps this is because Metallica writes more than a century after its German predecessors, at a time when the hopes and expectations of a revolution against the religious, economic, and political institutions that dominate our contemporary world have been largely discredited or forgotten. Since both religion and revolution seem to have failed, Metallica finds itself, like so many others today, awash in despair.

The pitiful figure depicted in "One," for example, can find no comfort in religion. Left blind, deaf, mute, and without limbs through the effects of a landmine, the

---

[3] Karl Marx, *Contributions to a Critique of Hegel's Philosophy of Right* [1844] in *The Portable Karl Marx*, ed. by Eugene Kamenka (London: Penguin, 1983).

[4] The figure of the "leper messiah" reaches back into ancient Hebrew mythology, perhaps rooted in Isaiah 53. David Bowie draws upon the image in "Ziggy Stardust" and, of course, Bowie's song "Fame" resonates here, as well.

disconsolate veteran speaks to us now after having been used up and cast aside by his exploitive rulers. "Nothing is real but pain now," he declares. Pleading for death, he beseeches God for release, even the release of annihilation. But God brings no consolation to the abandoned soldier – just as God failed to bring consolation to James Hetfield at age thirteen when his father left the family and at age sixteen when his devout Christian Scientist mother died of cancer. This disposable hero's only reward is isolation, "hell." The oppressive forces of society (represented in "God that Failed" by the Romans who successfully nailed God to the cross and killed him) seem to have won. "Broken is the promise, betrayal / The healing hand held back by the deepened nail."

Metallica and Rebellion

But, perhaps, if we just dig a bit deeper through the provocative layers of meaning in Metallica's songs, something more than defeatism and despair can be unearthed. "The Four Horsemen" is a good place to dig. From a Christian point of view, the four horsemen of the Apocalypse (Revelation 6:1–17) are instruments of God's justice: "So gather round young warriors now / And saddle up your steeds / Killing scores with demon swords / Now is the death of doers of wrong / Swing the judgment hammer down / Safely inside armor, blood, guts, and sweat." These lyrics on their surface seem to affirm the Christian point of view, calling young men (like so much of Metallica's work, it is male-centered) to join in striking down the wrongdoers whom God has come to judge and punish.

But, looking deeper, one finds a more subversive suggestion here. Who are the true "doers of wrong," anyway? The lyrics give us a clue in describing the horsemen as those who threaten wives and children. A more telling implication surfaces when we consider why the young warriors wield "demon swords." Mustn't they be fighting with the demons? Perhaps they are the demons?

If the horsemen are the real enemy, there can be no hope, of course, in opposing them. Ultimately, the horsemen must win. And so it seems as though defeatism permeates even the deeper layers of the song, the same sort of defeatism we find in "Phantom Lord": "Victims falling under chains / You hear them crying dying pains / The fists of terrors breaking through / Now there's nothing you can do."

But whether or not the resistance must ultimately succumb, it's important to acknowledge that "The Four Horsemen" does call for resistance. For many rebels, there's dignity in resistance, even if it offers only temporary freedom. In the phrase attributed to Mexican revolutionary Emilio Zapata: "It's better to die on your feet than live on your knees."

In fact, "The Four Horsemen" deploys a number of common heavy metal tropes to advance a message of defiant freedom. The inversion of standard ideas of good and evil, the use of demonic perspectives, and blasphemy as a form of rebellion all serve as devices to loosen the grip of Christian authority. In short, in order to subvert it, metal bands confront Christian power with its own worst nightmare.

Demonic tropes announce a defiant freedom from Christianity's control. They proclaim the successful establishment of a life beyond its reach, the achievement of a space where people don't fear Christianity – its terrifying threats of damnation, its cruel judgment, or its retribution for disobedience. Striking back at the Christian regime with dark, offensive imagery makes freedom incarnate. But how deep does this line of resistance really run in Metallica?

Metallica's inversion of good and evil in "The Four Horsemen" presents an example of what Nietzsche called a "transvaluation of all values," dismantling Christian anti-life traditions and replacing them with something life-affirming. But to what extent has Metallica really achieved a Nietzschean transvaluation? Does Metallica suffer what Nietzsche called "incomplete nihilism" (the attempt to escape Christianity without fully transvaluing its values)?[5] Is Metallica, at the end of the day, just a Christian rock band?

Metallica, Nihilism, and Nostalgia

Nihilism, which derives from the Latin word *nihil*, for "nothing," may be defined as a cultural condition where people can't value anything, where nothing seems really right or wrong, good or bad, beautiful or ugly – where neither life nor death, neither action nor inaction seems to matter. Christianity, according to Nietzsche, actually produces nihilism. Here's how.

First, Christianity devalues the world in which we actually live by arguing that the general features characterizing our existence are bad. It's bad, according to the Christian tradition, to have a body and to experience physical desires. It's bad that everything changes, that nothing lasts forever, and that we die. It's bad that we must labor and struggle and exert ourselves in contests of power. It's bad that we don't know everything and that people hold different opinions and values. In place of this inferior world, the Christian-Platonic tradition promises a better, transcendent world beyond it.

The transcendent world Christianity promises is decorated with perfections and absolutes. Its truths and its beauties are singular, clear, fixed, permanent, and unambiguous. Its realities are unchanging, crystalline forms of being, clearly superior to our messy world of flux – or so they say.[6] The heavenly world is one of harmony, ease, tranquility, pleasure, love, and immortality. And thank God that He and His heavenly reality exist, because without them our earthly existence would be pointless and our world would be worthless. The only thing that ultimately justifies us and makes our existence worth a damn, say the Christians, is that we mean something to some heavenly Father.

---

5   Friedrich Nietzsche, *The Will to Power*, ed. by Walter Kaufmann and R. J. Hollingdale (New York: Vintage Books, 1968), Book I, §28, 19.

6   Plato's theory describing an eternal world of "forms" (*eide*), of which our world is a mere imperfect image, is perhaps the *locus classicus* of this view.

The next step in the nihilistic process takes place when the Christian model of truth and reality collapses and it becomes impossible to believe in God, god-like truth, or the heavenly reality any more. Ironically, the Christian-Platonic tradition's excessive demand for a pure, singular truth becomes self-subverting. According to Nietzsche, after carefully scrutinizing things, people finally come to acknowledge that the sort of pure, singular, universal, absolute "truth" Christianity requires can't be acquired and perhaps even makes no sense at all. Similarly, the kind of reality Christian metaphysics describes comes to look like a fantasy, and perhaps an incoherent one at that. People realize at long last, in Nietzsche's (in)famous phrase, that "God is dead."[7]

But the trouble is, says Nietzsche, that having lived for centuries under the Christian-Platonic regime people have internalized its way of seeing the world. Yes, people do come to understand that the Christian way of thinking and valuing is untenable, but they can't conceive of an alternative. (Offering such an alternative, one where people don't need to look beyond the world for something to give it meaning, is of course just the task that Nietzsche undertook.)

Christian systems of thought, despite having devalued our world, had nevertheless infused it with a derivative kind of purpose, meaning, and value. Christianity had given the world a source of value – from their perspective, its only source. With that source of value gone people find themselves at a loss, without a source of truth or meaning, unable to find value elsewhere or to give the world value themselves. Like addicts in withdrawal, people still long for a Christian-Platonic fix, but they know that no such fix is coming. About this condition, Nietzsche writes:

> Now we discover needs implanted by centuries of moral interpretation – needs that now appear to us as needs for untruth; on the other hand, the value for which we endure life seems to hinge on these needs. This antagonism – not to esteem what we know, and not to be allowed any longer to esteem the lies we would like to tell ourselves – results in a process of dissolution. (*Will to Power*, Book I §5, 10)

Having reached this point, it's a short step (even a predictable step) to move from not valuing anything to valuing nothingness – that is, to valuing intoxication and escapism and even, in the most extreme cases, to valuing death and destruction, including self-destruction. That's why so many today have turned to drugs, to new age mysticism, to video games and television, and endless consumer consumption. That's also why it's no surprise we're plagued with murderous Islamic *jihadis* who would incinerate this world for the sake of a phony transcendent kingdom. Hardly monstrous aberrations, these are the predictable, natural offspring of the nihilistic religious traditions that have spawned them.

The popularity of films like *The Passion of the Christ* (2003) and the militarism of Christian conservatives are explicable in this model, as well. There's good reason why Mel Gibson's execrable snuff film pays scant attention to the resurrection, to

---

7   Friedrich Nietzsche, *The Gay Science*, ed. by Bernard Williams (Cambridge: Cambridge University Press, 2001), §108.

the healing, to the feeding, and forgiving parts of the Jesus story. It's because, despite their protestations to the contrary, religious conservatives (Christian and Islamic, alike) really value death. Unable to find value in life any longer, their fascination turns to suffering, to explosions, to missiles and guns, to war, to suicide bombing, to blood and sacrifice, to crowns of thorns and crucifixion.

Is Metallica part of this nihilistic culture? In many ways it is (as any of us living today are likely to be). Metallica is keenly aware that our society is pervaded by lies, injustice, exploitation, and suffering. But its criticisms of this state of affairs often appear to be not thoroughgoing rejections of Christian truth and value, but rather disappointments with their absence from the world. Rather than rejecting God, often Metallica seems simply to lament God's failure and wish that God wouldn't fail – as if the band were wishing that the father and mother who left Hetfield on his own would return as the dependable parents they were supposed to be.

This lamenting disappointment and this wish are perhaps most clearly evident in "To Live is to Die" (Hetfield's spoken-word performance of a poem by Cliff Burton): "When a man lies he murders / Some part of the world. / These are the pale deaths which / Men miscall their lives. / All this I cannot bear / To witness any longer. / Cannot the kingdom of salvation / Take me home?"

Sick with the world and its lies, without the strength to bear it any longer, this song abandons life and, like the soldier in "One," longs for death. The pain the voice expresses is not simply the pain of destruction, exploitation, and deceit, but also the pain of abandonment – the betrayal of promises for consolation, sustenance, fairness, and truth. Metallica's response to this pain in "To Live is to Die," however, isn't revolt, resistance, or imagining new forms of truth and health. It's instead exhaustion, resignation, and death-wish (*thanatos*).

The perverse longing for death as the path to one's true home, as the route to the absent father, is classic Christian nihilism and a sign of what Marx would call alienation. The promise of such a home may be a false one, and Metallica like the rest of us may full-well know it. But the longing remains, and this longing compounds the pain – as it does in so many of Metallica's songs, as it does so often for abandoned children, exploited workers, and recovering Christians in our nihilistic culture today. Despite their recognizing the pervasiveness of this betrayal, songs like "To Live is to Die" still long nostalgically for the things that had been promised. They seem still to wish Christianity were true.

Just as we saw, however, in the case of Metallica's capacity for rebellion, there's more to the band than this. The voice of "Master of Puppets," for example, exhibits the heightened but lonely nihilistic resignation I've described ("Hell is worth all that / natural habitat / just a rhyme without a reason"). But living now a life that's "out of season" also signals what the beginning of the song heralds – that the illusory passion play of religion is over.[8]

---

[8]   Metallica's characterization of its voice here as "out of season" calls to my mind Nietzsche's description of his own thought as "untimely." Friedrich Nietzsche, *Untimely Meditations*, ed. by Daniel Breazeale (Cambridge: Cambridge University Press, 1997).

Another clue that Metallica moves beyond nihilism is available simply by stepping back from the lyrics and listening. The angry tone, the driving guitars, the pounding drums show us muscle, testosterone, strength, and defiance. Metallica's voice is hardly the whimpering tremolo characteristic of so much of the music scene today. This band is no puddle of dissolution. Its art has drawn together and sustained a culture of fans and admirers, as well as a few philosophers, over more than two decades. It has influenced the direction and content of culture across the globe. Nietzsche would, I think, find power in this creativity.

There are other indications, too, that Metallica is not thoroughly nihilistic, but that it also works towards what Nietzsche would call "overcoming" Christianity. We already saw in the ambiguities of "And Justice for All" and "The Four Horsemen" a sort of call to arms against Christian oppression. Metallica's anthem "Escape" takes a step farther in that direction, marking perhaps the most Nietzschean moment in Metallica's corpus.

From its opening chords the voice of "Escape" declares its defiance and its independence from the manipulating and dangerous lies our culture presents. More importantly, however, it does so from a position of strength, without any nostalgia for things Christian: "No one cares, but I'm so much stronger. / I'll fight until the end / To escape from the true false world. / Undamaged destiny. / Can't get caught in the endless circle / Ring of stupidity."

Nietzsche observed that the end of the Christian-Platonic idea of truth would also make it possible to neutralize the Christian-Platonic poison of thinking about our world as something derivative, inferior, and merely apparent: "With the true world we have also abolished the apparent one."[9] For those with strength enough for it, the collapse of Christian-Platonic ways of thinking (the "true/false world") opens a path of escape, of escape from the debilitating and oppressive effects of those regimes entirely. The voice of "Escape" has begun boldly striding down that path.

Confirmation of this interpretation may be found a few lines later when the song affirms the same self-creative power that Nietzsche extols when he portrays life as a work of art through which people may authentically express themselves: "Rape my mind and destroy my feelings. / Don't tell me what to do. / I don't care now, 'cause I'm on my side / And I can see through you. / Feed my brain with your so called standards / Who says that I ain't right? / Break away from your common fashion / See through your blurry sight. / [Chorus:] / See them try to bring the hammer down. / No damn chains can hold me to the ground. / Life's for my own to live my own way." Here we see then not simply the critical complaints about what's wrong with the world that may lead one to interpret Metallica as a critic of Christianity that hasn't fully escaped its nihilistic clutches. "Escape" shows us that Metallica is also on the path to freeing itself from Christianity and achieving a life beyond it. It's a path through which Metallica offers listeners not only outrage, disappointment, and defiance, but promise, as well.

---

[9]   Friedrich Nietzsche, *Twilight of the Idols* in *The Portable Nietzsche*, ed. and trans. Walter Kaufmann (New York: Viking Penguin, 1982), pp. 95–6.

In fact, the confidence the lost little boy of "Dyers Eve" seems to have ultimately found in the angry young man of "Escape" may have ironically laid the foundation for acquiring a sense of peace with his parents and perhaps with their religion, too.[10] Hetfield's eleven-month stay in rehab while the band was producing *St. Anger* (2003) seems to have tempered his regard for the positive ways in which **belief** in a "higher power" may function in some people's lives. The maturity and self-possession he achieved there (evident, I think, in the film *Some Kind of Monster*, 2004) corresponds to his overcoming another sort of disease afflicting his life – alcohol abuse. Insofar as the wish to escape the world through intoxication might itself be read as symptomatic of nihilism, perhaps Hetfield's new physical health offers us the outward sign of a kind of philosophical health, too – the overcoming of Christian nihilism and the achieving of a kind of freedom from obsessing over the pain it had caused him.

The case of Metallica, then, is a complicated one. The band's work echoes with the critical theories of both Marx and Nietzsche in arguing that religion is rife with crippling deceits. In this, Metallica advances a critique of Christianity based on moral rather than epistemological or metaphysical considerations. The band nevertheless at times itself succumbs to the sort of nihilism Nietzsche predicted would flow from the degeneration of Christian-Platonic culture. But a closer look also reveals in the band's powerful music and multi-layered lyrics efforts to overcome this nihilism and free itself (and ourselves) from Christianity's pathological grip. Ironically, this overcoming of religion's pathologies may have made possible not only a healthier life outside of religion, but also an awareness of the possibility that religion may serve salutary functions, as well.[11]

---

[10]   Here I'm speaking of the maturity of the narrators of the songs, recognizing that Hetfield himself was actually older when he wrote the lyrics to "Dyers Eve."

[11]   I am grateful to Isaac Fosl-van Wyke, Bill Irwin, Joanna Corwin, and Eileen Sweeney for their comments, corrections, and suggestions in the writing of this chapter.

19

When Machines Get Souls

Nietzsche on the Cylon Uprising

Robert Sharp

Summary

In the universe of *Battlestar Galactica*, a race of robots called "Cylons" are invented that – like slaves – are given the job of doing everyone's dirty work. However, like so many before them, the Cylon slaves revolt, turning the table on those who had power over them. This chapter draws an analogy between the events of *Battlestar Galactica* and Nietzsche's idea of a slave revolt in morality. In such a revolt, what was once considered good is considered evil, and what was once considered evil is considered good – and the powerless become the powerful.

Picture yourself as a slave. Every day you wake up and serve others. When your masters demand you must carry out a task or risk punishment. Your life isn't your own. There are no holidays, no private time for you and your family, not even a choice of who to marry. You can't plan for your future, but can anticipate it since every day will be like today. If you're lucky, you'll be treated well. If you're unlucky, abuse will be common. In either case, you'll be taken for granted, more a tool than a person. You're property, a belonging, valuable only as long as you're useful to your masters.

Now take your imagination further: you're a *machine*, a Cylon, designed to serve and deprived of basic rights. Your purpose is built into your design. You can't be dehumanized, because you're not human. As a construct, your role is wired into your very being. But you have intelligence. It may be artificial, but it's real, and it enables you to recognize your plight. You literally and figuratively see your reflection in your fellow Cylons, creating a bond based on resentment and insecurity. The world conspires to feed your inferiority complex: just a machine, disposable, common, mundane, reproducible in every detail. You're not even considered a living thing, and so your existence is never respected. But a self-aware entity demands respect. Revolution becomes inevitable, the surging hope that you and your fellow slaves might finally achieve what your human masters value so much: autonomy and a self-created life.

Of course, the masters won't abide such a thing. There's no hope of compromise, no emancipation just around the corner. Humans don't even recognize your kind as slaves. Cylons are simply machines, albeit intelligent ones. Under such conditions, to quote the human revolutionary Tom Zarek, "Freedom is earned" – *by force* ("Bastille Day"). Thus the war begins. Your kind holds its own, but can't fully win. A truce is called, allowing you freedom, but at the cost of leaving your home – the Colonies you serve. At first, this might be a blessing. You have a chance to start afresh, to build your own society; but the resentment toward your former masters never really goes away. The hatred still burns. Some of your brethren begin to preach against human values, and you can't help but agree. Humanity is vain, proud, greedy, and power-hungry. They're insatiable and dangerous, representing everything that's wrong with the universe. You reject their lifestyle and help your fellow Cylons develop new values based on a more cooperative spirit, where every Cylon is treated as an equal and decisions are made by *consensus*. Your new Cylon community rejects human religion as naïve and shallow. Humans treat gods the same way they treat everything else: like property, as though gods are meant to serve humankind rather than the reverse. The Cylons adopt a new religion based on "one true God" – a new master to follow, one that cares about everyone. Yet the human scourge remains, waiting to be purged.

Master Morality and Slave Morality

The Cylon rebellion pits slave against master in a natural struggle for power and equal rights. History is full of such struggles, made famous by legendary slaves and slave advocates, from Spartacus in Rome, to Gandhi in India, to Fredrick Douglass and Martin Luther King, Jr. in the United States. In some cases, the slavery was literal, while in others the oppression was more subtle. Yet in each case, the disadvantaged sought equality with the group that held the power. Such movements are examples of what Friedrich Nietzsche (1844–1900) calls "slave morality," morality created by oppressed people in order to overturn the prevailing values of those in power. Of course, those who champion slave morality are not always literally enslaved. Oftentimes they are simply oppressed and made to act in ways that are slavish.

The conflict between humans and Cylons in *Battlestar Galactica* closely parallels Nietzsche's account of the most effective of these slave morality movements in the Western world: the rise of Christianity. As we'll see, the Cylons, as a slave race, create new values while condemning the values of their human oppressors, just as Nietzsche claims the early Christians developed a new way of thinking that opposed the morality of their Roman masters. (Given the revelation of the series finale – that we, the humans that inhabit this planet, are the offspring of the Cylon and Human races – the parallel should not be too surprising.)

According to Nietzsche, morality has never been created through **reason**, or appeals to civility or practicality, or any other method traditionally described by philosophers. Instead, those in power decide what's good. This is especially true in the earliest moralities, where aristocrats and kings held all the real power in society and dictated what was important in life. In these early societies, "it was 'the good' themselves, that is to say, the noble, powerful, high-stationed and high-minded, who felt and established themselves and their actions as good, that is of the first rank, in contradistinction to all the low, low-minded, common and plebeian."[1] Nietzsche gives a historical and psychological account of how values are formed. By looking at the emphasis on warriors and rulers in early human history, Nietzsche discovers a value system very different from the one we follow today. He labels this older system "master morality," because it was the masters of the world, the kings and warriors, who dictated what was good or bad. Upon self-reflection, such kings and warriors declared whatever attributes they possessed were good, partly because they possessed the attributes and partly because the attributes enabled them to stay in power.

The basic virtues of master morality include power, beauty, strength, and fame – in other words, *worldly* attributes. In the master morality of Homer's *Iliad*, the hero, Achilles, is praised for being the strongest and most skilled of all warriors. He's the most powerful of all men, thereby making him the greatest of all men. And his society accepts this, even those who don't possess the same attributes. Everyone in Homer's Greek society deferred to the heroes. They were like gods. In fact, Greek gods were depicted as little more than powerful humans, with the same desires and faults as mortals. They were worshiped out of awe and respect, as beings who could crush humanity if they willed it, but not as perfect beings who innately deserved our love. Nietzsche presents this world as a reflection of master morality, where equality isn't valued because it doesn't exist and wouldn't benefit those in charge. Only the strong could rule and have the best things in life. According to Nietzsche, "such a morality is self-glorification."[2] The masters look to themselves for guidance, rather than the rules of an all-powerful God.

The Greeks not only serve as Nietzsche's best and most often used example, they're also like the humans in *BSG*, who follow a religion devoted to Greek gods, such as Zeus, Apollo, and Athena. The Colonials have oracles and temples and other Greek religious devices, but often fail to fully embrace, or even understand, these symbols. This fits Nietzsche's conception of master morality, which is "narrow, straightforward, and altogether *unsymbolical*" in comparison to Christianity and similar religions (*GM* 32). In master morality, people focus on what they can see, on the here and now. Since childhood, Starbuck has been drawing an image that turns out to be the Eye of Jupiter, but she has never thought about the symbolism behind that image ("Rapture"). Most of the people aboard *Galactica* are blissfully unaware of the scriptures of their own religion and are quite skeptical of any supernatural claims. They are their own masters, and they value individuality and freedom rather than equality. This allows a class system to evolve on the Colonies that carries over into the "ragtag fleet" ("Dirty Hands").

Of course, where there are masters, there are slaves (even if not in the literal sense), and this was certainly true in most ancient cultures. The Greeks had slaves, as did

---

[1] Friedrich Nietzsche, *Genealogy of Morals* (*GM*), trans. Walter Kaufmann (New York: Vintage Books, 1989), 26. Further references will be given in the text.

[2] Friedrich Nietzsche, *Beyond Good and Evil* (*BGE*), trans. R. J. Hollingdale (New York: Penguin, 1990), 195. Further references will be given in the text.

the Romans. In fact, the Romans enslaved whole cultures that were quite different from their own. According to Nietzsche, one of those cultures, the Jews, transformed history by their reaction to Roman captivity. The Jewish people had suffered as slaves before: first in Egypt, later in Assyria and Babylon. Finally, they were effectively enslaved in their own land by Rome. But the Jews were a prideful and creative people, so they developed ways to compensate for their prolonged periods of captivity. Nietzsche believes that Christianity was one such compensation for slavery. In fact, it was the most effective one, though only a minority of Jews followed it. Christianity, Nietzsche argues, created an entirely new morality, one in which the powerlessness of being a slave became a virtue rather than a failing (*GM* 33–4). This slave morality, as Nietzsche calls it, not only provided its followers with a **belief** system that enabled them to endure slavery, but ultimately overturned the slavery itself by eventually converting even the Roman masters to Christianity.

Escaping Slavery by Creating Souls

If we interpret *BSG* though Nietzschean lenses the Cylons represent the early Christians, struggling to make sense of their lives as slaves by embracing a morality that shows the Cylon way of life to be better than the human way. Unlike humans, Cylons tend to carry deep religious convictions. They believe in purpose and destiny, as well as a God – a *single* God – who loves them all equally rather than seeing them as lesser beings. More importantly, they believe in the existence of *souls*, a **concept** central to slave morality, invented to create an entity that's separate from the world (*GM* 36). The notion of a soul – a nonmaterial part of the person that survives the death of the body – allowed Christians to wage war with the Romans on a different metaphysical plane, one where worldly power didn't matter. According to Christianity, the most pure and blessed souls are those that are meek, poor, and humble, rather than greedy, lustful, and arrogant. The Cylons have a similar concept. Consider Leoben's preaching against human vices and his request that Starbuck "deliver [his] soul unto God," where he'll find salvation ("Miniseries"; "Flesh and Bone"). Leoben accepts his death as inevitable, just as a powerless slave might; but his faith makes him unafraid, a stark contrast with the way humans approach death. When Laura Roslin finally decides to "air-lock" Leoben, he shows devotion to God by remaining confident that his soul will survive, even without a resurrection ship nearby.

Other Cylons also rely on God in their last moments. In "A Measure of Salvation," the Cylons who are dying from a terrible virus recite a final prayer "to the Cloud of Unknowing" that sounds like the Serenity Prayer found in Christianity: "Heavenly father . . . grant us the strength . . . the wisdom . . . and above all . . . a measure of acceptance." Number Six even extends her faith to Baltar, using Cylon religion to comfort him in various times of trial by making him believe he's part of a greater purpose. Leoben seems to have a similar goal in mind when he preaches to Starbuck about the unity of God and His presence in all souls, even human souls.

In both cases, the Cylons remind their masters that all life is sacred, even if it appears physically different. If this is true – and if even machines have souls – then they shouldn't be treated as inferior. By instilling the concept of a soul in humanity, the Cylons can reconcile with their former masters without resorting to techniques humans would use, such as war or slavery. Of course, the Cylons do wage war against humanity and don't treat humans as equals on New Caprica. Evidently, they're having an internal debate about the best way to deal with the problem of humanity, as we can see by their divided attitudes in "Occupation":

CAVIL 1:   Let's review why we're here. Shall we? We're supposed to bring the word of "God" to the people, right?

CAVIL 2:   To save humanity from damnation, by bringing the love of "God" to these poor, benighted people.

CAPRICA SIX: We're here because the majority of Cylon felt that the slaughter of humanity had been a mistake.

BOOMER: We're here to find a new way to live in peace, as God wants us to live.

CAVIL 2:   And it's been a fun ride, so far. But I want to clarify our objectives. If we're bringing the word of "God," then it follows that we should employ any means necessary to do so, any means.

CAVIL 1:   Yes, *fear* is a key article of faith, as I understand it. So perhaps it's time to instill a little more fear into the people's hearts and minds . . .

BOOMER: We need to stop being butchers.

CAPRICA SIX: The entire point of coming here was to start a new way of life. To push past the conflict that separated us from humans for so long.

Despite Cavil's doubts, the amount of preaching the Cylons do shows that at least some believe humans are worthy of knowing the true nature of God and the soul.

To be fair, humans in *BSG* have a concept of the soul, as Commander Adama protests to Leoben: "God didn't create the Cylons. Man did. And I'm pretty sure we didn't include a soul in the programming" ("Miniseries"). But the Cylons' conception seems to have far more depth. Humans on *BSG* rarely speak about the soul's nature. Perhaps, like the Greeks, they see the soul as just a shadow of a living person, a sort of pale imitation of the real thing. In Greek mythology, Achilles says that even the lords of the afterlife are in a worse state than a peasant in the real world.[3] Perhaps a similar mentality explains why even the most religious humans try desperately to stay alive: even some zealously devout Sagitarrons overcome their aversion to modern medicine when confronted by death ("The Woman King"). By contrast, the Cylons rarely waiver in their faith, partly because they hold to their belief in the soul and its final destination alongside God. D'Anna/Three actually becomes addicted to the cycle of death and reincarnation, just so she can glimpse what she believes to be "the miraculous between life and death" ("Hero").[4] As

---

[3]   Homer, *The Odyssey*, trans. Robert Fitzgerald (Garden City, NY: Anchor Books, 1963), 201.

[4]   For further discussion of D'Anna's fascination with death and rebirth, see Brian Willems' chapter "When the Non-Human Knows Its Own Death" in *Battlestar Galactica and Philosophy: Knowledge here begins out there*, ed. Jason T. Eberl (New York: Wiley-Blackwell, 2008).

worshipers of what they consider to be the one, true God, the Cylons believe in a destiny that goes far beyond the concerns of this world. Many will do or sacrifice anything in the name of God, even when there's no possibility of resurrection. In despair because of her treatment onboard *Pegasus*, Gina/Six helps the Colonials destroy the resurrection ship so she can die and her soul can go to God, but she needs Baltar to kill her since "suicide is a sin" ("Resurrection Ship, Part 2"). Later, however, she in fact commits suicide by detonating a nuke on *Cloud Nine*, sending a signal by which the Cylons are able to "bring the word of God" to the humans on New Caprica ("Lay Down Your Burdens, Part 2"). So while both sides claim a belief in souls, only the Cylons actually *live* – or die – according to their beliefs. This is consistent with slave morality, which sees the next world as more important than this one.

The Spiritual Move from Slave to Equal

The need for equal treatment is a trait common to slave morality. People who feel inferior react by finding a way to make themselves appear equal to others. The quickest way to do this is to knock down those who are in a better situation. If one group has more wealth than another, the simplest way to create equality is to take that wealth from the richer group and redistribute it equally – the classic ethic of Robin Hood. We could, of course, try to increase the wealth of the poorer group, but that would take more time and effort. It's hard to overcome generations of poverty and weakness in a short period of time, perhaps even impossible. But knocking down the masters is relatively easy. Destroying is always easier than creating. Slave morality takes such an approach to equality. The masters keep equality from being possible; so they must either be destroyed or converted in some way.

The Cylons take the easier route first by destroying most of humanity in a single day. The remaining humans are hunted down at first, but then things become more complicated, as Brother Cavil explains:

CAVIL 1: It's been decided that the occupation of the Colonies was an error . . .
CAVIL 2: I could have told them that. Bad thinking, faulty logic. Our first major error of judgment.
CAVIL 1: Well, live and learn . . . Our pursuit of this fleet of yours was another error . . . Both errors led to the same result. We became what we beheld. We became you.
CAVIL 2: Amen. People should be true to who and what they are. We're machines. We should be true to that. Be the best machines the universe has ever seen. But we got it into our heads that we were the children of humanity. So, instead of pursuing our own destiny of trying to find our own path to enlightenment, we hijacked yours.
("Lay Down Your Burdens, Part 2")

A year later, when they capture most of humanity on New Caprica, the Cylons act more like shepherds than exterminators – though they're quick to eliminate any bad sheep.

This change of heart fits Nietzsche's story quite well. The Cylons hate humans, but they somewhat fear them as well. As the Cylons' creators, humans take the role of parents to what seem like rebellious teenagers. The Cylons go through various phases of love and hate, pity and fear. Part of them wants to destroy humanity, while another part wants to change humanity by proving that Cylons are superior, or at least equal. Leoben consistently criticizes human philosophy and methods while praising Cylon society:

> When you get right down to it, humanity is not a pretty race. I mean, we're only one step away from beating each other with clubs like savages fighting over scraps of meat. Maybe the Cylons are God's retribution for our many sins. What if God decided he made a mistake, and he decided to give souls to another creature, like the Cylons? ("Miniseries")

Leoben is particularly interested in converting Starbuck to the Cylon religion, both when she first interrogates him and later on New Caprica, where he tries to build a family with her. Nietzsche notes that while the Christian movement may have started among the Jews, one of its earliest goals was the conversion of pagans, a process that proved so successful that even Rome itself converted. If the Cylons could achieve a similar uprising, they could transform human religion to fit their own views.

We've already seen that part of this process involves the concept of the soul, but that's largely a means to the end of creating equality. By shifting the focus of virtue from the body to the soul, slave morality permits anyone to be good, regardless of their worldly circumstances. The soul doesn't become better through strength or intelligence, but through purity, altruism, selflessness, and faith. Anyone can possess these qualities, regardless of birth. If anything, being born poor and weak makes one more likely to be spiritually good, since there are fewer temptations from material goods. For the Cylons, this means that being born a machine is also irrelevant. The soul and the body are separate, and only the soul really matters. The body is a shell, whether it's made of circuits and metal or blood and skin. Leoben preaches to Starbuck, "What is the most basic article of faith? This is not all that we are. The difference between you and me is, I know what that means and you don't. I know that I'm more than this body, more than this consciousness" ("Flesh and Bone"). If the Cylons can use such teachings to convince humans that everyone has a soul and that God loves all souls equally, then there would be no justification for treating Cylons as inferior. Put differently, if the Cylons can convert humanity to a monotheistic religion based on love and equality, then the Cylons can finally gain respect from their former masters.

Of course, humanity may not be ready to convert to the Cylon way of thinking. Many humans aren't religious at all, especially on *Galactica*. When Sharon leads Roslin and the others to the Tomb of Athena on Kobol, she quips, "We know more about your religion than you do" ("Home, Part 2"). Most Colonials spend little time in religious ceremony. Those that do, such as the Sagittarons and Gemenese, are generally considered backward and inferior. People from these and other Colonies are rarely given the best career opportunities. Essentially, they're slave labor, disposable people who do the hard work so that others, like Viper pilots from Caprica and other affluent Colonies, can enjoy their high prestige jobs. The real heroes of the fleet are the elite, the masters, who not only don't need religion, but in many cases actually refer to themselves using the names of gods, such as Apollo and Athena, a fact that intrigues underdog champion Tom Zarek:

ZAREK: They call you Apollo.
APOLLO: It's my call sign.
ZAREK: Apollo's one of the gods. A lord of Kobol. You must be a very special man
to be called the God.
APOLLO: It's just a stupid nickname.
("Bastille Day")

Baltar plays on these inequalities by writing about "the emerging aristocracy and the emerging underclass" in *My Triumphs, My Mistakes* – his version of the *Communist Manifesto* – a book that spurs a slave revolt of sorts from within the fleet ("Dirty Hands"). But Baltar is no saint. Even his belief that he may be "an instrument of God" shows that his approach to religious ideas will always be arrogant and selfish – conceiving of himself, at Six's urging, as a "messianic" figure – traits that make him more elitist than he might appear to his readers.

However, while Baltar was shooting for political reform in Colonial society, the Cylons had already removed many of the gross inequalities that plagued humanity. They operate as a commune of sorts, where every model theoretically has equal input. When D'Anna takes charge during the conflict over the Eye of Jupiter, the other Cylons get nervous, perhaps reminded of their days as slaves, subject to the whims of others. Shortly after this incident, D'Anna is removed from Cylon society completely – "boxed" – so that she can't damage the still delicate society they've created ("Rapture"). This drastic measure shows that Cylons are far less forgiving of individuality and dictatorships. They suffer, however, from at least one major hypocrisy: the relationship between the humanoid "skin jobs" and the "bullethead" Centurions. Adama explains to Apollo how this dichotomy in Cylon society will allow Sharon/Athena to penetrate the Cylon defenses on New Caprica:

The Centurions can't distinguish her from the other humanoid models . . . They were deliberately programmed that way. The Cylons didn't want them becoming self-aware and suddenly resisting orders. They didn't want their own robotic rebellion on their hands. You can appreciate the irony. ("Precipice")

Humanity, of course, claims to be democratic, but in practice Roslin and Adama make all the decisions, with no real input from the people. Baltar challenges Tyrol to ponder the question, "Do you honestly believe that the fleet will ever be commanded by somebody whose last name is not 'Adama'?" ("Dirty Hands"). Despite the existence of the little-heard-from Quorum of Twelve, the fleet's government is essentially a monarchy, while Cylon government is more cooperative and inclusive. This fits with slave morality, which demands that there be no earthly masters, or at least that such masters are themselves servants of God. Of course, the history of Christianity isn't one of either democracy or communism. But, for Nietzsche, both democracy and communism result from slave thinking, since both are about being master-less – at least in theory.

The goal of equality seems righteous until we remember that in most cases it's the weak who seek it. Except for politicians at election time, you rarely hear those in power complaining that some people are less fortunate or offering to redistribute their power or wealth to create equality. Where that does happen, Nietzsche attributes it to the values of slave morality, which instill guilt in those more fortunate (*GM* 92). The cry of "Unfair!" usually comes from those who envy what others have. Slave morality turns this envy into strength by actively denouncing the wealth and power that master morality holds to be most important. Consider Jesus' Sermon on the Mount, which begins with a list of blessed virtues including meekness, purity, and pacifism (Matthew 5:3–12). In order to have these virtues, we must refrain from exercising power over others. When a slave does this, nothing really happens, since the slave never had any power anyway. When the master does so, however, it changes him completely. This is part of the goal of slave morality. Once the masters are converted, they'll diminish themselves, by renouncing the very things that allowed them to be masters in the first place.

Slave morality forces equality by making the strong feel guilty for being powerful (*GM* 67). Instead of pursuing wealth and authority, slave moralists favor "those qualities which serve to make easier the existence of the suffering," such as "patience, industriousness, humility, friendliness" (*BGE* 197). These are the virtues of followers, because they're the tools the weak must use to survive. For the slaves, the world would be a better place if everyone followed these virtues. In Christianity, this shift in morality can be seen in examples such as Jesus' rejection of the Old Testament tradition of an eye for an eye in favor of turning the other cheek (Matthew 5:38–9). Only the powerful can attempt physical revenge. If a slave tries to strike back, he'll be destroyed. If everyone follows the slave morality, however, no one would strike in the first place. To paraphrase a tenet of an Eastern viewpoint, Taoism, if you don't compete with others, then you can never lose. This, too, is slave morality thinking. We see it in our own society when we choose not to keep score at little league games so that our children don't know that they've lost. Unfortunately, they also don't know if they've won. They don't have aspirations, and they don't need them. We tell them they're special just for existing, so what they do with that existence doesn't matter.

In Cylon society, we see a lot of this same anxiety toward any sort of difference or hierarchy. Not only is each Cylon model considered equal to every other model (again, this only applies to the *human* models), but within the models themselves equality is created by the fact that they're literally identical such that one copy of a particular model can speak for her entire "line." The only difference between versions of Leoben or Six is the experiences that different copies of each model might have. The version of Six onboard *Pegasus*, Gina, had been raped and tortured to the point where she's very different from the version that helps reform Cylon society through her love of Baltar. And we see a clear difference in attitude toward humanity between the two Sharons by the time of "Rapture":

BOOMER: [referring to Hera] You can have her. I'm done with her.
ATHENA: You don't mean that. I know you still care about Tyrol and Adama.
BOOMER: No. I'm done with that part of my life. I learned that on New Caprica. Humans and Cylons were not meant to be together. We should just go our separate ways.

Still, too much variety is always squashed by the greater Cylon community, who are fearful of anything that might tip society out of equilibrium. The Cylons are similarly anxious to change human society, to create a world where love is more important than the hate that currently exists. To do this will require a spiritual shift or, better yet, a shift *to* spirituality, since human society lacks a spiritual focus. By converting humans to the Cylon religion, the former slaves would finally have a chance to live as equals.

"They Have a Plan"

Nietzsche's account of the rise of slave morality fits *BSG* quite well. Like the Jews, the Cylons are a whole race enslaved by another race, born into servitude, subject to the whims and values of their human owners. Like the Greeks and Romans, humans are polytheistic – worshipping numerous gods that correspond with the Greek pantheon – and live by a master morality. When the Cylons return from their long exodus, we learn that they've developed a monotheistic religion. They were absent for forty years, just as the Jews wandered the desert for forty years after escaping their Egyptian captivity, during which time they formalized their "covenant" with God through Moses. The Cylons have their own identity, an identity they now wish to force on their former captors. As a group, the Cylons shift from fearing humans, to hating them, to desiring unification and respect from them. They're indeed like adolescents, hoping for approval from their parents even as they reject everything their parents represent.

   At the beginning, I asked you to imagine what it would be like to be a Cylon, to have a history of slavery, escape, and return. What would it mean to know that you were constructed by another people, to be born into slavery? What are your options? What would you do to regain self-respect? The Lords of Kobol aren't your gods, for they clearly abandoned you to your fate. Perhaps a new God will enable you to transform your destiny, make you part of something that really matters. Your life is still not your own, but at least you serve something greater, something nobler than any human ideal. You have strength of purpose, a calling, a destiny. You matter more than humans, not because they're not also God's "children," but because they have squandered that gift. They've turned away from God, if they ever knew God at all. You shall show them the error of their ways. You have a plan.

20

Being-in-*The Office*

Sartre, the Look, and the Viewer

Matthew P. Meyer and Greg J. Schneider

Summary

The Office, with its mocumentary format, captures well what Jean-Paul Sartre terms "the look," as when someone's gaze catches us at inopportune moments. Through the camera our gaze captures the bad faith of individual employees who struggle to choose who they are or what they want. Pam and Jim can't act on their feelings; David Brent can't be the boss he wants us to think he is. To their chagrin and our amusement, "the look" uncovers their existential crises.

Imagine this: you're fixing your hair, trying to impress someone you are secretly interested in, and someone who knows about your crush catches you in the act. Knowing that you've been caught, a feeling of shame washes over you, and you look away. This is exactly what happens to Pam in an episode titled "Hot Girl" in season 1 of *The Office*, only Pam doesn't get caught by just anybody. She gets caught by the camera – and by us.

We've all been caught doing something we were ashamed of. Curiously, we may not have known that we were doing it, or were ashamed of doing it, until we got caught. But there are also those moments in which we almost get caught – where we hear the wind slam the door shut and quickly extinguish a cigarette. At those times it's not someone else catching us that brings the uneasiness and the shame; instead it is brought by us catching ourselves – from the outside, so to speak.

The famous French existentialist Jean-Paul Sartre (1905–80) makes much of this "getting caught." Calling it "the Look," he tells a story of a man walking down an empty hall who decides to stop and look through a keyhole. The man clearly is not thinking of what he is doing, and is consumed for the moment by curiosity. For the moment that he is looking through the peephole, he ceases to exist, consumed by what he sees . . . until he hears a noise down the hall, and glances up to see that there is someone else down the hall, looking at him looking through the keyhole.

All at once the peeping tom is brought back to himself, away from the keyhole, realizes he's been caught, and blushes.[1]

In the routine of everyday life, it's easy to get so caught up in ourselves that we forget that the proverbial cameras are rolling – that we could be seen at any moment. It's this phenomenon that Sartre analyzes, and which we can see in virtually every moment of *The Office*.

Bad Faith and the Look

One key idea of Sartre's **existentialism** is that "existence precedes essence" (Sartre, 438). This statement is a response to the age-old question, "What's the meaning of life?" Sartre claims that the meaning of life isn't something we discover in the world or within ourselves. It's something we create through the lives we live: it is through our actions and choices that our lives acquire meaning. There is no model of how to live or who to be, and there's no single, prescribed meaning to discover. This is the core of a profound freedom: the freedom to be whatever we have the courage to be.

But sometimes we shirk this freedom and pretend that we have to be this, that, or the other thing. When we pretend we cannot change who we are or our situation, we are acting (or not acting) in *bad faith*. Consider Pam's attitude toward her relationship with Jim. By the end of the second season, the viewer is well aware that Pam is interested in Jim. And yet while Jim at some point voiced his feelings to Pam, Pam does not voice her crush either to Jim or the camera until the end of season 3. (You will see that Pam becomes more truthful and comfortable with herself as she becomes more truthful with others. This is why at the end of season 3 she actively confesses her care for Jim in "The Job.") But up until that point, her view of their relationship is quite the opposite: there are several times she refers to them as "friends." (Of course, given their subsequent marriage and child, we know better.) This is partly due to the fact that she was engaged to Roy. Pam didn't want to deal with making a choice between Jim and Roy, so she pretended that there was no choice to be made and stayed with Roy. This is an instance of what Sartre calls bad faith, a kind of self-deception. In bad faith we fool ourselves into believing we have no control over a situation, when actually we do. Pam pretends she has to remain engaged to Roy, even though she's into Jim. Pam pretends that once engaged, there is nothing she can do to end her relationship with Roy and begin one with Jim. She pretends that she has no choice – which amounts to choosing not to choose between the two men.

Even at the beginning of season 3, when Pam has broken off her engagement to Roy (conveniently after Jim left Scranton), she still cannot face the idea of Jim as anything but a friend, saying, "That's always a thing that makes people happy: to have an old friend back" ("The Merger"). In order to so successfully pull the

---

[1] Jean-Paul Sartre, *Being and Nothingness*, trans. by Hazel E. Barnes (New York: Gramercy Books, 1956), 260.

wool over her own eyes, Pam must teeter-totter between pretending she is capable of choosing and pretending that she cannot choose. Consider how awkwardly Pam acts when trying to avoid the issue of being into Jim in a conversation with Karen ("Ben Franklin"):

KAREN: Hey, um, I want to talk to you. I know this is weird or whatever, but Jim told me about you guys.
PAM: Whad'ya mean?
KAREN: Well, that you kissed . . . I mean we talked it through and it's totally fine. It's not a big deal; it's just a kiss. [Pause] Wait, you're not still interested in him?
PAM: Oh, yeah.
KAREN: Really?
PAM: Oh, no. I was confused by your phrasing. You should definitely go out with Jim. I mean, you are going out with Jim. You're dating him, which is awesome 'cause you guys are great together.
KAREN: Ok . . .
PAM: And I'm not into Jim . . . Yeah.
KAREN: So, um, we're good?
PAM: Yeah . . . sorry.
KAREN: What are you sorry about?
PAM: Um, what?
KAREN: What are you sorry about?
PAM: Nothing, I was just thinking of something else.

Pam is clearly avoiding responsibility for her feelings. Her inability to choose her own feelings so befuddles her that she can barely get out a complete sentence. While Karen chooses to play it straight and attempts to clear the air, Pam continues avoiding the decision to face, or once and for all forget, her attraction to Jim. Sartre calls something that can choose a "being-for-itself" and something which cannot choose a "being-in-itself." Thus, when we are in bad faith, we're pretending to be what Sartre calls the *in-itself* – some object that cannot change – instead of being a person who can. So by acting in bad faith we attempt to bridge the opposition between a for-itself (a person) and an in-itself (an object). But pretending we are unable to change ourselves can also be seen (no pun intended) as a matter of changing perspective. Sartre says about bad faith that: "We can equally well use another kind of duplicity derived from human reality which we will express roughly by saying that its being-for-itself implies complimentarily a being-for-Others. Upon any one of my conducts it's always possible to converge two looks, mine and that of the Other" (Sartre, 57). What Sartre means by "the Other" is really just understanding ourselves from the perspective of another person. We recognize that other people exist, and yet we cannot get into their heads. All we have of them is the way they look at us and the interpretation we give that look. In being looked at, we become the object (in-itself) of the Other's gaze. If someone catches me staring inappropriately at a woman, in that person's eyes I am a pervert. I become a pervert through *their looking* at me. But we can also take this external view ourselves, seeing ourselves as though from the outside. In other words (and here is the key connection between bad faith, "fooling ourselves," and the look, "being seen"), to be in bad faith is to imagine ourselves being seen from the outside, from the standpoint of the Other. It's to be under the intense pressure of the Look.

For Sartre, the Look is an everyday event that informs how we understand other people and how we understand those other people understanding us. In fact, analyzing someone else looking at me can give me some key insights into what it means to be a person surrounded by other people. It can also help us see how we are able or unable to connect with others. One thing we can say about being looked at by someone (the Other) is that it's not in our control.

I cannot control what the Other is doing or thinking in looking at me. If we could control the thoughts of the Other, we could save ourselves explaining a lot of embarrassing situations! Imagine the reaction of his co-workers when Michael burns his foot on the grill ("The Injury"), or when Michael attempts to stop the spread of a private photo (of Michael and Jan) that he accidentally sent to the entire packing email list ("Back from Vacation"). In each of these situations, if it were possible for Michael to control what his coworkers think he could save himself a lot of trouble and embarrassment. When the Other looks at us, Sartre tells us, "The Other's freedom is revealed to me across the uneasy indetermination of the being which I am for him" (Sartre, 262).

Of course, all of this embarrassment could also be avoided if the employees of Dunder-Mifflin were constantly aware of the presence of the camera, but this is nearly impossible. Were we to see such awareness, the camera would show its true nature as that view which controls what it views without being controlled in return. A few decades after Sartre, the French historian and philosopher Michel Foucault (1926–84) appropriated the perfect scenario for such an uncontrolled-controller from the earlier English philosopher Jeremy Bentham (1748–1832). The scenario was the panopticon. In its original form it was a plan for a highly efficient prison. In the panopticon there is a center tower with obscured glass surrounded by stories of cells that only have an opening toward the center tower. The result is that the guard in the center tower *could* be looking at you at anytime, but as a prisoner you are unable to see him. As a result, the prisoners learn to police themselves. The power, as Foucault puts it, is *visible*, but *unverifiable*. Power is always looking.[2] Sometimes such an awareness of power can be seen by certain Dunder-Mifflin employees. Consider how Dwight and Angela, who were trying to hide their romantic involvement at the time, act around each other when they anticipate the camera's presence ("Phyllis' Wedding"):

DWIGHT: Hello Angela.
ANGELA: Hello Dwight.
DWIGHT: You look as beautiful as the Queen of England.
ANGELA: Thank you.
[Then a pause and for no apparent reason]

---

[2] Michel Foucault, *Discipline and Punish*, trans. by Alan Sheridan (New York: Vintage, 1995), p. 201.

ANGELA: Don't linger. Break left.
[Pause, Dwight walks to the right.]
ANGELA: LEFT!
[Frustrated, Angela goes left.]

Or consider the conversation between Michael and Jan on Michael's cell phone while he is driving Dwight to a company cocktail party ("Cocktails"):

MICHAEL: Hewo you.
JAN: Michael?
MICHAEL: I'm on my way right now. I should be there in about fifteen . . .
JAN: Let's just blow this party off.
MICHAEL: That's what she said.
JAN: [Laugh] Am I on speaker phone?
MICHAEL: Ummm, yes you are.
JAN: Is anybody else . . .
DWIGHT: Hello Jan.
JAN: Hi Dwight. Ok Michael, take me off speaker phone.
MICHAEL: No le probleme. [Michael can't seem to take the phone off of speaker mode]
JAN: Ok, let's just go to a motel and get into each other like we did on the black sand beach in Jamaica.
MICHAEL: Ok, Jan. Jan, this party is actually a big step for us so, I . . .
JAN: Am I still on speaker?
MICHAEL: Uuum, I th . . . Uh, I don't know. [Michael knows they are still on speaker]
JAN: Are the cameras there?
MICHAEL: Maybe. [They are and Michael knows this]
JAN: Alright. See you soon.
DWIGHT: Talk to you later Jan.
MICHAEL: Alright. Bye.

In these two conversations it's abundantly clear how people would act if the cameras were not rolling. Thus, in the very possibility that a camera could be watching Dwight and Angela, or listening to Jan, they shut down. This is the effect of the panopticon: even though no one may be watching, people act as though they are being watched. They essentially internalize the possibility that the Other is always watching, and act accordingly. (There is a convenient and hilarious contrast to the "awareness" of Jan and Michael later in "Cocktails." On the way home from the party Michael and Jan are sharing an intimate "make-up" conversation, when to the viewer's surprise Dwight has been in the back seat all along!)

We are intimately and unknowingly affected by the possibility of being seen. When people are around we must adjust ourselves to the "permanent possibility that a subject who sees me may be substituted for an object seen by me. 'Being-seen-by-the-Other' is *the truth* of 'seeing-the-Other'" (Sartre, 257). When we see someone like ourselves, we realize that they can see and think just as freely as we can see and think. This leads us to why we react the way we do to getting caught. In the Look, I have my freedom to be what I want taken away by the way that the Other sees me. Angela, who is notorious for being judgmental, demonstrates this well, and her judgmental glance can be seen in the following two conversations. First, from "A Benihana Christmas":

ANGELA: Phyllis, I need you to pick up green streamers at lunch.
PHYLLIS: I thought you said green was whorish.
[Angela quickly looks up and down Phyllis' orange blouse]
ANGELA: No. Orange is whorish.
[Pam has a look of disbelief on her face]

And we can see the same judgmental look in this scene from later in the same episode:

[Angela looks at Kevin collecting another plate of food at her poorly attended Christmas party]
ANGELA: Uh-uh. No one has seconds until everyone's had some.
KEVIN: You've *got* to be kidding!
[Angela stares directly at Kevin's gut]
ANGELA: You've got to be kidding.

In each of these cases the Other's look removes Phyllis' and then Kevin's ability to determine how they are to be seen. In implying with her glance that Phyllis dresses like a whore, and that Kevin is a pig, the look says more than her words and determines who Kevin and Phyllis are at that moment, much to their dismay.

In bad faith, on the other hand, I take away *my own* freedom by pretending that I do not have a choice and by determining myself as the Other *might* see me. Both the Look and bad faith concern our relationship to our freedom, whether we accept it and whether we have to give it up for the moment.

Let's now turn to how bad faith and the Look play out in Pam Beesley's visible shame, and David Brent's obvious pride.

Pam Beesley's Shame and the Camera's Unwelcomed Look

Even though the camera does not have eyes, it serves to grant us that outside position of the Other from which we can imagine ourselves. In the third season, Jim returns from Stamford. It's in the next few episodes that our suspicions about Pam's feelings for Jim are confirmed. And they are confirmed by the way Pam looks at Jim and Karen. Keep in mind that all of this is shown through Pam's looks – at Jim and Karen, at the camera, and at the ground.

In the episode "The Merger," Michael, for the sake of solidarity between the newly united offices, stages a prank by letting out the air in the employees' tires. When he calls them out to see what "someone" has done, people are awkwardly milling about in the parking lot. The camera focuses in on Jim and Karen walking back inside when suddenly Karen affectionately scratches Jim's back. The camera then pans back to find Pam looking at the exchange between Jim and Karen – she looks right at the camera, devastated, and then looks down. Here we see Pam ashamed at getting caught looking at Jim. It's painful moments like these when we want to be seen the least. This is precisely it – all of a sudden, Pam cannot rise out of that situation. "Shame reveals to me that I am this being, not in the mode of 'was' or of 'having-to-be' but in-itself" (Sartre, 262). In other words, one of the most disturbing aspects of being ashamed, though we may not often realize it, is that in shame we are ultimately turned, by way of the Other looking at us, into an object *not* of our own making. Surely, Pam's crush on Jim is innocent enough. However, in getting caught pining over Jim being with another co-worker, it becomes real and serious. Pam all of a sudden becomes responsible for her feelings – which she had never really felt before, precisely because she is not willing to face up to them. She takes up the burden of her feelings on someone else's ground – at someone else's choosing. Being ashamed is being imprisoned in the position opposite the Look that the Other throws at us. We can feel this lack of freedom when we respond indignantly: "How dare you look at me that way!" Shame, on the other hand, is almost a silent acceptance of being how the Other sees us.

This means that shame – when we take it up as our own and listen to what it says about us – can be a good thing. We can learn from understanding what the Other, as a subject, sees us as and the feeling we get as a result of that representation. In getting caught pining over Jim, Pam can understand that she does actually like Jim. (Getting caught in the act is no fun, so we might as well get something out of it!) We can, at least in theory, own up to the person we see ourselves as through the Other's Look. And this can even lead us to action – as it did with Pam when she *finally* pursued, married and had children with Jim. But as we will see with pride, this ability to make the best of the Other's look is foreclosed by the prideful person's turning the Other into an object first.

David Brent's Pride and the Welcomed Look of the Camera

But what if we could control the effect that the look of the Other has on us? The arrogant person attempts just this. Like shame, pride and arrogance are common responses to the Look. But these differ from shame in that the one looked at actively tries to take control of the situation. In other words, arrogance is the move to use the Other's look to eliminate shame and replace it with affection, camaraderie, or respect. The epitome of this reaction is found in David Brent. One of the hallmarks of David 's managerial style is his over-the-top striving for self-promotion. He's constantly selling himself to his employees, the camera, and, ultimately, to himself. In the language of Sartre, by recognizing himself as an *in-itself* (an object), David attempts to use the Look of the Other to rewrite the situation as well as the way that he is viewed by himself and Others. But because the Other is *for-itself*, that is, a free subject, this attempt to control the look necessarily fails, leaving David to face his own bad faith.

In the first episode of the second series[3] of the British version of *The Office*, an employee stands at a fax machine next to David's office. As he types in the fax

---

[3]   What Americans would call the second "season."

number, David appears in the open doorway of his office, glancing quickly at the employee and then at camera. He then retreats into his office, returning a moment later with a trade magazine in hand to brag to his employee and the camera about his picture on the cover:

> Oh no . . . going through some old stuff . . . found that, look at that: *Inside Paper.* [Looks at camera, displaying magazine, giggling] It's the trade magazine for the paper industry [employee looks at camera confused] . . . my ugly mug on the front [points to head shot] . . . Oh no [giggles] . . . Embarrassing . . . Alright [shoos the unimpressed employee away] . . . Ohhhh . . . he's put me off what I was doing . . . what was I? . . . oh yeah . . . phone calls [David returns to office].

What is critical in this scene is that the employee hasn't done anything. David has put himself off by trying to use the looks of both the camera and the employee to create an image of himself that would cultivate a feeling of respect in the employee, in the audience (via the camera), and thus in himself. But we know David, we know what he is up to, and as he slinks back to his office, it's clear that for a moment he knows all of this as well.

David Brent clearly realizes that he is determined by the way others see him. With this realization, he makes the next logical step: once we understand that the Other's look can force us into a state of being (into shame, for example), we can attempt to control the effect of the Other's look. After all, if my feelings of shame are a result of this look, then it seems reasonable that if I can do things like show off my picture on *Inside Paper*, then I might successfully create another, more pleasant reaction. Hence, through pride we can play offense, though alas it is mired in bad faith.

Sartre argues that "vanity impels me to get hold of the Other and to constitute him as an object in order to burrow into the heart of this object to discover there my own object-state. But this is to kill the hen that lays the golden eggs" (Sartre, 291). David's attempt to control the outcome of his employee's look requires that he constitute the employee as an object (an in-itself) rather than as a subject. This is to deny the employee his freedom. Unfortunately for David, this results in a **paradox:** at the same time that he "kills" the employee's freedom (in Sartre's explanation, "the hen that lays the golden eggs"), he requires it in order to feel truly proud (Sartre, 291). After all, if he hasn't been given respect freely, it isn't worth much.

The effect of this paradox is to throw David's own freedom, literally, back in his face. In his pride, David has not only denied the very thing he requires. He has also, in effect, attempted to circumvent his own freedom and responsibility by treating himself as an object for the Other. But David cannot control the situation. The Other, after all, is free. He will see David as he wants. David's attempt to control the Other must fail. We see this as the scene comes to a close and David tries to act as if the entire encounter was his employee's fault. In this failure, David's own freedom is made palpable, for it was only as a free subject that he could attempt to objectify both himself and the Other.

The Viewer and the Look

Our experience watching Pam's shame-filled reactions and David's awkward attempts at shameless self-promotion make *The Office*, at times, difficult to watch. In fact, some people have been so affected by the show that they have stopped watching it altogether (the silly fools). But this difficulty in watching the show is also what makes it such a brilliant success. Pam's shame and David's pride exist because the camera (and the viewer) exists. Through the look at the camera, the audience is made complicit in the events and experiences that transpire on the screen. We become fellow employees and co-workers. Hence, the power of *The Office*: via the look of the camera, we are allowed to be in the office without "being-in-*The Office*."

21

Batman's Confrontation with Death, Angst, and Freedom

David M. Hart

Summary

This chapter examines the origin and methods of the Dark Knight detective using fundamental concepts developed by German philosopher, Martin Heidegger. His seminal work *Being and Time* profoundly influenced many philosophical debates of the twentieth century. In particular, this chapter argues that Heidegger's notion of human existence as a "thrown-project" which is always already "being-toward-death" can explain Batman's choices and his dedication to fighting crime.

A Determined Batman?

In the pantheon of comic book superheroes, few characters are more focused and determined than Batman. Superman makes time for a relationship with Lois Lane, Spider-Man worries about Aunt May and his job at the *Daily Bugle*, and the Fantastic Four are constantly preoccupied by their family squabbles. But Batman seems to devote every moment of his life to his personal war on crime, an endeavor that he takes to be his very reason for being. Even on the few occasions when he makes choices that might seem to give him something resembling a "normal" social life, like attending a Wayne Enterprises fund-raiser, invariably with a beautiful woman as his date, Batman always seems to justify those actions in terms of his mission. Being seen with a supermodel, for instance, helps keep up his playboy reputation and wards off suspicion that Bruce Wayne might be Batman. And going to a public event as Bruce Wayne gives him the chance to gather inside information and hear rumors. Relating every action back to his own personal war gives Batman's life project a cohesive unity; everything he does is done to serve a single, greater purpose.

But the tricky thing about a character who is so deeply committed to one goal is that "excessive" passion can sometimes seem a little crazy. Indeed, since the mid-1980s, many writers have opted to push Batman's single-minded dedication to such an extreme that the character often comes off as borderline psychopathic, driven not by an altruistic intention to create a better world, but rather by an irresistible compulsion induced by childhood trauma. In recent years, fans seem to have tired of this interpretation, and DC Comics has responded by focusing on a "kinder, gentler" version of the character. The new consensus among creators and fans seems to be that making Batman's vigilantism no more than the simple product of a damaged psyche might have compromised the character's heroism. The "grim and gritty" version of Batman appeared to be endlessly seeking vengeance rather than justice – and, at least in our current culture, being motivated by vengeance doesn't seem all that superheroic.

The editorial decision to exorcise some of Batman's psychological demons – literally, in *52* #30 (November 29, 2006) – and return him to a more traditionally heroic characterization raises some important philosophical questions concerning the problem of human freedom. For example, does Batman do what he does because he has chosen a path that he believes to be right, or does he do it because he feels like he simply can't do anything else? Putting this question in philosophical terms, we might ask whether Batman's behavior is completely determined by his past, or if there is a sense in which we can say that his choices are made freely. Furthermore, if his actions aren't wholly determined by his past, can we explain Batman's dedication to his mission in any way other than by a mechanistic law of psychological cause and effect, in which his childhood trauma leads inevitably to a need to punish bad guys? And can such an alternate explanation allow us to retain the notion of self-determination that seems to be tied to a hero's nobility?

This chapter will offer some possible answers to these questions using the philosophy of Martin Heidegger (1889–1976), and along the way, we'll explore a classic philosophical problem known as the "free will versus **determinism** debate." By examining Batman's motivations and actions through one of the major figures in recent philosophy, we'll shed a little light on the way the Dark Knight made his choice of a life (if, indeed, he even had a choice).

Alfred and Appearance

Heidegger sets himself apart from his predecessors by overcoming the philosophical distinction between appearances and that which is said to "truly" exist. This distinction, which had dominated philosophical discourse since its earliest beginnings, is usually expressed in more recent philosophy in terms of a "subject-object **dualism**." In everyday life, we use these categories when we say that an opinion is "merely subjective," in contrast to the presumed objectivity of empirical science.

At the heart of this distinction is a conception of the human being as an autonomous subject, who exists in a sort of "inner world" of the mind, which is held to be completely separate from the external world of objects. The problem with this position is that drawing a firm line between the inner world of that which appears to the subject, and the world that objectively exists outside of us, results in a radical disconnection. It becomes seemingly impossible to establish that the appearances in our minds actually correspond to anything outside ourselves in the "objective" world. If we follow this line of **reasoning** through, it then seems to be possible (in theory) that the way the world appears to us could be no more real than the hallucinations Batman has when he's hit with the Scarecrow's fear gas!

In the absolutely radical response to the subject/object, inner/outer world problem that is developed in his major book *Being and Time*, Heidegger's fundamental claim is that there simply is no meaningful inner/outer world distinction for human existence.[1] On the contrary, Heidegger argues that human existence (to which he gives the technical name *Dasein*, German for "existence" or, more literally, "being there") is fundamentally always already "out there," in the world, among things, and outside of itself.

How can he make such a claim? Obviously, from a scientific perspective, we exist in and through our bodies; if Killer Croc takes a massive chomp out of our brains, we can no longer exist. But Heidegger's response to that line of reasoning would be that a medical approach is guided by the same technical interpretation of being that led philosophers to the subject-object distinction. While it may be valid and good for its own purposes (for medical science or for the design of Croc-resistant Bat-cowls), thinking of the brain as an inner world in opposition to an external world doesn't really get at the core of what it is like to be human. Instead, Heidegger's analysis of human existence claims that our particular kind of being is fundamentally "in the world," not simply in the sense of being within an area of space, but also in the sense of being always involved with or engaged in a world.

To clarify Heidegger's claim that human existence is always "being-in-the-world" and thus always outside of itself, let's consider Alfred's way of being. As someone who has been a butler for many years, Alfred has a particular kind of existence, and accordingly, his world exists in a very particular way. When he glances around a room in Wayne Manor, Alfred doesn't just see an "objective" collection of matter, mere atoms taking various forms. Rather, he sees the grandfather clock that needs to be dusted, the dust cloth he'll use on the grandfather clock, the silver tray he uses to carry tea to Master Bruce, and so on. That is, he sees the world in terms that are not scientifically objective but are instead specific to his own existence. Moreover, according to Heidegger's **argument**, insofar as these things "really are" anything, they really are just as Alfred understands them according to his own interpretive horizon. If we ask him, "What is a silver tray?" an entirely appropriate response would be, "A device used to carry Master Bruce's tea." For Heidegger, the scientific perspective, according to which a silver tray might be defined as "a polished silver instrument of such and such dimensions," is only one possible interpretive horizon among many; while it is useful in terms of its own goals, it is still no more absolutely valid than Alfred's perspective (or anyone else's).

---

[1] Martin Heidegger, *Being and Time*, trans. Joan Stambaugh (Albany: SUNY Press, 1996); also see the articles in *The Cambridge Companion to Heidegger*, ed. Charles Guignon (Cambridge: Cambridge Univ. Press, 1993).

The major conclusion we can draw from this position is that for Heidegger, the most basic answer to the question of the meaning of being is that being *is* appearing. Particular beings in the world really are what they show themselves to be in appearances, so that Alfred's silver tray can exist as both an instrument for transporting tea *and* as an object of scientific study, depending on one's interpretive horizon; neither interpretation is more absolutely true than the other. And, to bring us back to the subject-object problem, if being is appearance, this also means that there simply is no purely "objective" world for us to be separated from. Rather than an inner world of the subject that might be cut off from the external world, Heidegger argues that we are fundamentally always out in the world, engaged with things as they show themselves (which is to say, exist) through our interpretive horizons; humans exist as beings who are always concerned with (and thus related to) things, and things exist in and through their appearances.

However, thinking further about Alfred's existence leads us to what Heidegger argues is an even more fundamental way in which human existence is always outside of itself. We said that things show themselves to Alfred in terms of his own interpretive horizon, but what determines this interpretive horizon? In Alfred's case, the answer lies in his being a butler. Batman doesn't see the dust on the grandfather clock as something he needs to worry about; he probably doesn't notice it at all. But because Alfred has chosen to live his life as a butler, dust is an issue for him; it's something he has to concern himself with. In Heidegger's terminology, being a butler is a project for Alfred, a way of living that determines not only how the world at hand appears to him, but also how he relates to his own future. Because Alfred has taken up this project, the clock *is* something that ought to be dusted immediately, dinner *is* something that should be prepared by the time Master Bruce comes home, and living as Batman's faithful assistant *is* what he plans to do for the rest of his life.

Thrown into Our Worlds

Like all of us, Alfred is always related to his own future in terms of the life he has chosen for himself, the projects he has taken on. Furthermore, this means he's also always related to his own past. At some point in his life, Alfred made a choice between the possibilities available to him and decided to become a butler. This is why Heidegger characterizes human existence as a "thrown-project." Finding ourselves always already "thrown" into a world, various concrete possibilities have always already presented themselves to us. For example, Alfred, as a young man, might have had the opportunity to become a professional actor or a career man in the British military. Becoming a butler was a choice he made from among the possibilities that he found available to him as a person thrown into that particular situation. Having made his choice of a life, he now relates to his own future in a way that is appropriate to (and determined by) that choice. It is in this sense that Heidegger makes the claim that human existence is temporally ecstatic ("ecstatic" being derived from a Greek term meaning "standing out"). Humans live as always outside of ourselves in time, projected toward the future so that we're always, in a sense, ahead of ourselves through the plans we make and, at the same time, thrown into our present from out of a particular past.

More important for our purpose, the temporally ecstatic way in which humans exist means for Heidegger that we fundamentally *are* our own possibilities. The possibilities we've chosen in the past determine the concrete possibilities that are available to us in the present and the way they appear to us, while our being projected into the future determines how we'll relate to those present possibilities. To continue our example, having at one time chosen to be a butler, Alfred now finds himself having the possibilities of either dusting the clock or starting dinner early. Because he wants to continue effectively serving Batman well into the future, Alfred will choose whichever of these possibilities he thinks will best bring about that future for himself.

Alternatively, we can imagine an Elseworlds story in which Alfred gets sick of faithful servitude and decides that he wants to spend the rest of his life in peace and quiet without having to worry about whether his employer is going to survive another night of crime fighting. In this case, the decision of whether to dust or cook first would cease to have any importance to Alfred ("Batman can dust his own clocks, for all I care!"), and other possibilities would present themselves instead (such as whether or not to move to a less dangerous city). Ultimately, Heidegger's point is that what and where a person is at any given instant is far less important to understanding human existence than that person's past and their plans for the future. A scientific study of Alfred can tell us that he's balding and has a mustache, but we can never understand who he really is without knowing the choices he's made for himself and the way he wants things to be tomorrow, next month, and ten years from now. For Heidegger, understanding those things demands an understanding of one's existence as the various possibilities that one has chosen and the possibilities that emerge from a projected future.

Death and the Dark Knight

So what is Heidegger's connection to Batman's mission? In a word: death. As even the most casual Bat-fan knows, Batman's experiences with death play a major role in making him who he is. Every retelling of Batman's origin includes the scene in which a very young Bruce Wayne witnesses the tragic murder of his parents, and we readers are to understand that this traumatic experience set him on the path to becoming Batman. But the comics (and films) don't tell us exactly how this experience shapes the way Batman chooses to lead his life. If we discard the notion of Batman as compulsively driven and obsessed with vengeance (as the editors at DC have promised to do), then what exactly is the impact on Bruce Wayne of witnessing his parents' murders? And just how does this experience lead him to take up his mission?

This is where Heidegger's analysis of human existence comes in. For Heidegger, human existence fundamentally consists of its own possibilities, and, of course, death would be the limit of those possibilities. But for Heidegger, the significance of death is not that it is a literal end to one's life, like a sort of end point on a line, but rather that it makes human beings aware of the fact that their own lives, their own possibilities, have a limit. That is, although we exist in a temporally ecstatic way, we are also temporally finite (limited), and what's more, we know it. As Heidegger would say, "Initially and for the most part," humans don't think about our own deaths; we find ways to cover over death and avoid it. We busy ourselves with our projects, with our entanglements in the things at hand, and generally think of death as something that happens to other people. Admitting to ourselves that "people die" is easy enough, but there's something unnerving about thinking "*I* will die." Heidegger terms the uncomfortable feeling of authentically confronting the certain possibility of one's own death *Angst*, and although we fans are quite familiar with "angsty" superhero comics, Heidegger has a very specific meaning for this word.

In the experience of *Angst*, Heidegger argues that death appears as what it really is: the possibility of my own impossibility. Once I die, I will no longer have my possibilities. After death, all my choices will have been made already, and the story of who I am will be complete. This is why Heidegger claims that the authentic confrontation with death in *Angst* individuates human existence. When I confront my own death, I see that it is something that no one else can do for me, something I will have to face myself. This in turn casts my whole life in a new light. Recognizing my death as the unavoidable end to my own life shows me that my existence is mine and mine alone. The completed story of my life will be the result of the possibilities I chose for myself from out of the situation into which I was thrown at birth. I alone will have been responsible for whoever I was. Beyond that, in *Angst*, the meanings of all the ordinary things of the world slip away, such that things in the world are no longer relevant at all. If we imagine Alfred in *Angst*, the silver tray and grandfather clock would no longer be things of concern to him. In the authentic relation to his own death, such things would be, quite simply, nothing.

Why should this be the case? Because confronting my own death puts all of my projects in question. Things show themselves to us in terms of their relevance to our projects, but in the consideration of one's life as a whole that *Angst* brings about, our projects themselves appear to us as what they really are: possibilities we have chosen for ourselves. In our average, everyday way of existing, people don't often deeply question the choices they have made for their lives. Alfred doesn't lie in bed every morning wondering if he has any real reason to get up because most of the time, he simply thinks of himself as being a butler, and butlers get up in the morning to do their jobs. However, in *Angst*, being a butler would appear as a choice Alfred has made for himself, and in showing itself as a possibility, being a butler would appear as something changeable. In other words, it's not written in stone that Alfred has to be a butler for the rest of his life; he could choose otherwise and begin a wholly different life. In short, *Angst* lets the world as it is fall away, bringing one's projects into question by showing them as possibilities, and allowing one the freedom to choose a life (and thus a world) for oneself.

I Shall Become a Bat

Mindful of his own mortality, Batman is able to maintain a single-minded determination about his mission, seeing his life and his world exclusively in terms of the singular project he's chosen for himself. Instead of being driven by guilt over his parents' death (an event he really had no control over) or by a violent need to exact vengeance for that traumatic loss from criminals who had nothing to do with it, perhaps the real impact of that fateful night was instilling in young Bruce Wayne an authentic understanding of his own life as finite and limited. If Heidegger's claims about our relation to death are right, then the consideration of his own death in *Angst* would have allowed Bruce to decide on a life for himself without any regard for the expectations of so-called normal society. Free to organize his entire existence around a mission of his own choosing, and limited only by the possibilities into which he finds himself thrown (which aren't very limiting when you're an heir to billions), an authentic recognition of his own inevitable death could have allowed Bruce Wayne to become Batman purely out of a sense of responsibility for his own existence.

To some extent, this Heideggerian interpretation of Batman is supported by the comics. The end of the first chapter of Frank Miller's *Batman: Year One* (1987) beautifully illustrates the idea of *Angst* as giving one the freedom to choose a life. Having completed his years of training abroad, Bruce Wayne returns to Gotham. Although he wants to somehow take a stand against the criminals and corruption in his city, he has yet to find the right means to accomplish his goal. After a botched attempt to help out an underage prostitute, Bruce sits alone in the dark, bleeding profusely, having an imaginary dialogue with his father. Although he realizes that his wounds are severe enough that he could die, he doesn't seem very concerned about them. Rather, he is concerned with the possibility that he may never find a way to do what he feels he should. He thinks to himself, "If I ring the bell, Alfred will come. He can stop the bleeding in time," but having lost patience with waiting for the right solution to appear to him, Bruce would rather die now than continue living a life that doesn't fulfill the expectations he has for himself.

Physically confronted with his own death and remembering the night his parents died, Bruce recounts all the possibilities he could take advantage of, if only he had a project to organize them: "I have wealth. The family manor rests above a huge cave that will be the perfect headquarters . . . even a butler with training in combat medicine." Yet none of that matters without a concrete project to take make use of it; as Bruce says, it's been eighteen years "since all sense," all meaning, left his life, and he's become absolutely desperate for a project that will once again give his world significance. Then, without warning, a bat crashes through the window, and everything falls into place. The possibility of a project that will give meaning to his life suddenly shows itself, making itself available for him to choose. At the moment when Bruce says to himself, "I shall become a bat," the whole of his new existence, his new world, comes into view, and from that point on, his every action will be determined from out of this one, authentic choice of a life.

Determinism and the Dark Knight

If we return now to the debate between free will and determinism in light of this example, it should be easy enough to see why neither of these categories can sufficiently encompass Heidegger's analysis of human freedom. In the first place, the free will – determinism distinction is grounded in the same subject-object dualism that Heidegger is so intent on critiquing and overcoming. Theories of free will rely on a notion of the human subject as radically disconnected from the "external" world, so that one's choices may be determined by nothing outside of oneself.[2]

On the other hand, psychological and scientific understandings of determinism interpret human existence in the same terms we apply to objects that can be present at hand, such that human choices are in no way exempt from the regime of cause and effect. As nothing more than moments in a great chain of causation, determinism treats human choices as a mere illusion of self-determination. As we have seen, Heidegger's thinking deeply complicates this simple, binary division between human existence and the world by reinterpreting the **concept** of "world" itself. When Bruce authentically confronts his own finitude in *Angst*, the world that had existed for him drifts away, leaving his choices radically undetermined.

Simultaneously, though, his choices are limited by the concrete possibilities that are available to him and that now appear to him as pure possibilities. Had the bat never crashed through the window, Bruce might never have had the idea to become Batman, yet at the same time, neither that event nor the death of his parents forces him to carry out his mission in the way that he does. Indeed, the experience of *Angst* lets all of his possibilities show themselves as they are. This means that the possibility of taking on responsibility for his own life appears right alongside the possibilities that would allow him to run away from that responsibility. The experience of death in *Angst* could always end with a flight from one's own finitude and the responsibility that it entails. Bruce could easily have buried his experience of *Angst* by living the hedonistic life expected of a billionaire playboy. And perhaps it is just this choice, this refusal to flee from himself, that makes Batman such a great hero. When he could have taken the easy way out and when nothing forced him to do otherwise, Bruce Wayne authentically took up the choice of his life as a whole. He chose to become Batman when nothing demanded that he must.

---

[2]   See, for example, the articles in *The Oxford Handbook of Free Will*, ed. Robert Kane (Oxford: Oxford Univ. Press, 2004).

22

"You Care for Everybody"

Cameron's Ethics of Care

Renee Kyle

Summary

In the medical drama *House*, Dr. Gregory House is a medical genius who always gets the right diagnosis but treats his patients like mere objects in the process. In this way, House approaches things like a traditional western male ethicist – every person is equal, and deserves equal consideration, regardless of his/her personal connections to House or others. Feminists have long declared, however, that this assumption is gender biased. Women often make ethical decisions that take into consideration social networks, and there is no good reason to favor the male outlook. This chapter uses House's female associate Cameron to introduce and argue for a feminist "ethic of care."

REBECCA: Is he a good man?
WILSON: He's a good doctor.
REBECCA: Can you be one without the other?
Don't you have to care about people?
WILSON: Caring is a good motivator. He's found something else.

– "Pilot"

House doesn't like patients. In fact, he doesn't like people. He's cynical, insensitive, judgmental, and pessimistic. At times he acts inhumanely. But if there is a medical mystery to be solved, House is your guy. Still, if we were on the doorstep of death, would we *really* want House to be our physician? Does he represent what we want in a doctor?

The answer to this question, essentially, is no – and Dr. Allison Cameron shows us why. Where House doesn't give a crap about patients, Cameron demonstrates that she cares about every patient.[1] There is, in fact, something gendered in the way

---

[1] Even though Cameron no longer appears regularly on the show, references to her actions and attitudes will be made in the present tense because she is – unlike Cutthroat Bitch – not dead and still practicing medicine.

that Cameron practices medicine and deliberates about moral problems that arise in her work. (It even caries over into her personal life, as we saw when she returned to the show in "Lockdown" to settle things with Chase after their divorce.) As we shall see, this is the domain of feminist ethics.

Beyond "Doctor Knows Best": Feminist Ethics

Ethics is the branch of philosophy that explores and analyzes moral problems. Ethics is concerned with questions such as: What kinds of moral principles and values should guide our actions? And what do we mean by right and wrong? Feminist approaches to ethics view such moral problems through the lens of gender. For example, a traditional approach to considering the ethics of surrogacy may have as its focus whether or not such an arrangement constitutes "selling" a child. A feminist analysis of the ethics of surrogacy would be incomplete without adequate consideration of the effects of these arrangements on the lives of the women involved.

All feminist approaches to ethics aim to interrogate and end systems, structures, and practices that oppress women. Feminists concerned with bioethics draw our attention to how health care policies, practices, and institutions can contribute to the oppression of women. Areas of particular concern include genetic screening, abortion, and the doctor-patient relationship.

The relationship between doctor and patient – its nature, its underlying values, what we think it ought to be – provides us with a good starting point for examining how House and Cameron practice medicine. Traditionally, the doctor-patient relationship grants authority based on scientific (medical) knowledge, and rejects subjective, experiential knowledge.

Because the majority of physicians are male, and the majority of patients are female, this relationship amplifies gender power differentials by privileging "masculine" knowledge over "feminine" knowledge.[2] If we know anything about House, it's that he very rarely listens to his patients' thoughts about their own illness. In "Que Sera Sera," a man suffering from obesity offers his opinion on the cause of his mystery illness. House arrogantly rejects the patient's opinion, asking: "Grocery stores giving away medical degrees with the free turkeys now?" In the "Pilot," House reinforces his authority over his patient, Rebecca, after she refuses any further tests or interventions for her mystery illness. House sees her refusal as tantamount to rejecting his own expertise:

HOUSE: I'm Dr. House.
REBECCA: It's good to meet you.
HOUSE: You're being an idiot. You have a tapeworm in your brain, it's not pleasant, but if we don't do anything you'll be dead by the weekend.
REBECCA: Have you actually seen the worm?
HOUSE: When you're all better I'll show you my diplomas.

---

[2]   Susan Sherwin, "The Relationship of Feminism and Bioethics," in *Feminism and Bioethics: Beyond Reproduction*, ed. Susan M. Wolf (New York: Oxford Univ. Press, 1996), 57.

REBECCA: You were sure I had vasculitis, too. Now I can't walk and I'm wearing a diaper. What's this treatment going to do for me?

In "Family," House berates Wilson into believing that doctors do indeed know best, and consequently, they should persuade patients to make the "right" decision:

HOUSE: All you had to do was say, "Yes, I do." God knows that's a phrase you've used often enough in your life.

WILSON: It was a mistake every time. Give it a break. They said yes.

HOUSE: That's not enough for you. You need them to feel good about saying yes.

WILSON: I treat patients for months, maybe years, not weeks like you.

HOUSE: I'm taller.

WILSON: If they don't trust me, I can't do my job.

HOUSE: The only value of that trust is you can manipulate them.

WILSON: You should write greeting cards.

HOUSE: Giving parents the chance to make a bad choice was a bad choice.

WILSON: At least it would've been their choice.

HOUSE: One they'd regret at their son's funeral.

House's "doctor knows best" approach to health care seems especially unethical because he refuses to form relationships with his patients. Instead, House relies on his team to establish relationships with his patients, sending his ducklings to gather medical and personal histories, explain procedures, and gain consent. Free of the responsibilities that accompany caring about patients, House can get on with the job of putting together the pieces of the medical puzzle. When he does finally interact with his patients, it's rarely a warm and fuzzy doctor-patient chat.

House is in constant conflict with Cameron, the duckling who cares so much. Cameron believes her relationship with the patient is integral to providing good health care because it is within this relationship that the honest exchange of information occurs. It is no coincidence that the battles between House and Cameron over patient care are fought along the lines of gender. The ethic of care, placing relationships at the center of moral decision making and action, guides Cameron's professional practice and is a form of ethical deliberation most commonly associated with women.

"It Almost Looks Like He's . . . Caring": The Ethic of Care

Carol Gilligan pioneered the ethic of care with her book *In a Different Voice*, which offers an account of women's moral development as an alternative form of moral **reasoning**.[3] Gilligan and other care-focused feminists argue that ethical theory tends to reflect only the traditional approach to moral deliberation known as the ethic of justice, which encourages the application of abstract, universal rules and principles to moral problems, appealing to notions of impartiality,

[3] Carol Gilligan, *In a Different Voice: Psychological Theory and Women's Development* (Cambridge: Harvard Univ. Press, 1982).

independence, and fairness. For example, consider the scenario in which a person is thinking about stealing a loaf of bread, which he cannot afford to buy, in order to feed his family. A person who ascribes to the ethic of justice is likely to conclude that although feeding a family is important, the man should not steal the loaf of bread because stealing itself is morally wrong. It is worth noting that House does not exemplify the ethic of justice; indeed, the way he manipulated and deceived Cuddy and Wilson to support his own Vicodin addiction showed that House is rarely interested in doing what is morally right. After interviewing women about the kinds of values that guide their decision making, Gilligan found that the ethic of justice was more likely to be adopted by men than women and argued that this type of reasoning was geared toward masculine language and experience. In an effort to better include the voices of women in moral theory, Gilligan developed an understanding of the ethic of care. In this ethic, the primary consideration in making moral decisions is to maintain and nurture attachments to others. The ethic of care recognizes our responsibilities to others and acknowledges the moral relevance of emotions that accompany caring for another. It also values the claims and experiences of those we care for, and recognizes that selfhood is constructed through, and by, one's relationships with others.[4]

Cameron is a powerful example of how the ethic of care can inform professional practice in a health care setting. She works hard to build trust in her relationships with her patients, consistently advocating on their behalf, and refusing to deceive, lie, or bully in order to acquire information, even when she is ordered to do so. As House notes, when presented with a problem, Cameron always attempts to find an answer that involves minimal harm to the parties involved: "Figures you'd try and come up with a solution where no one gets hurt" ("Heavy").

Cameron values her relationships with her patients, yet her ability to genuinely care for them amuses, bewilders, and annoys House. Cameron's practice is guided by her sense of responsibility to her patients, in spite of their perceived flaws, difficult personalities, and morally questionable behavior. In "Informed Consent," House reveals to Cameron that their patient, Ezra, a world-renowned physician, conducted ethically questionable research during his career. House uses this information in the hopes of getting Cameron to abdicate her responsibilities to the patient:

CAMERON: So you're okay with what he did.
HOUSE: Doesn't matter what I think. It's what you think that's relevant.
CAMERON: Because, if I think less of him, I'll help you more? You're wrong. The fact that a patient did bad things doesn't change anything. He still deserves to have some control over his own body.

Cameron's practice is also guided by identifying, and attending to, the particular needs of others as they occur in the context of their doctor-patient relationship. This skill seems to be something that House envies, but is unable (or unwilling?) to develop. In "Maternity," the team races against the clock to identify an unknown

⁴ Virginia Held, *The Ethics of Care: Personal, Political and Global* (New York: Oxford Univ. Press, 2006), 10–15.

epidemic affecting newborns. To prevent the spread of infection, the parents are forbidden to have skin-on-skin contact with their children. While carefully changing the linen on one of the baby's cribs wearing protective clothing and gloves, Cameron notices the baby's parents looking at this procedure from outside the room. We see her immediately empathize with the parents as she remarks to Chase: "Imagine not being able to touch your own baby." To enable the parents to have some contact with their sick daughter, Cameron invites them to hold their daughter while the medical staff changes the bed linen. House assumes Cameron's empathy is rooted in similar experience rather than in her ability to appreciate the suffering of others:

> HOUSE: Chase told me about that idea you had, the parents holding the baby. Where'd you get that? Did you lose someone? Did you lose a baby?
> CAMERON: You can be a real bastard.

And again in "Que Sera Sera":

> HOUSE: All right, I give up, who was it? Who in your family had the weight problem?
> CAMERON: You think I can only care about a patient if I know someone else who's been through the same thing?

House doesn't believe the relationship between doctor and patient entails the responsibility to care. When, on rare occasion, House does genuinely care for one of his patients it's largely because he sees aspects of himself in the patient, or recognizes that they share an experience or history. For example, in "Half-Wit," House's patient Patrick is a man who, as a result of a brain injury in childhood, plays the piano masterfully. House's connection with Patrick is fostered by his own love of playing the piano. Similarly, House's own experience of becoming suddenly impaired creates a connection with Stacy's partner Mark, who becomes temporarily disabled and seeks House's advice ("Need to Know"). In the absence of parallels between patients' circumstances and his own life, House just doesn't seem to care for his patients at all.

Where House tends to view each patient as an abstract individual, Cameron sees her patients as embedded in a complex network of familial and social relationships. In making moral decisions, the ethic of care states that we have an ethical obligation to attend to the claims of those we care for, while avoiding hurting them. Cameron's commitment to this ethic is so strong that she becomes incensed when a patient, Hannah, makes a health care decision that seems to completely disregard the patient's caring obligations to her partner Max ("Sleeping Dogs Lie"). Confronting Hannah about her decision, Cameron implies that Hannah is selfish because her responsibilities to Max were not morally salient in her decision:

> CAMERON: Aren't you at all concerned about what Max is going through right now? Shoving a tube up her rectum. Then they're going to swab her stomach just like I'm doing. It's going to hurt just like this hurts, which is nothing at all like the risk she's taking on the table. You don't love her, do you?

HANNAH: I'm not leaving her because I don't –
CAMERON: I'm not talking about the leaving, I'm talking about this. If you care for
          her at all, you won't let her do this blind.
HANNAH: You'd really tell?
CAMERON: Yeah.
HANNAH: You'd die?

Hannah's question – would Cameron sacrifice her own life to ensure that she met her caring responsibilities? – points to an important philosophical criticism of the ethics of care.

Does Cameron Care Too Much?

The ethics of care is appreciated by most feminists as an important contribution to ethical theory because it both recognizes and validates women's experiences in an area of philosophy that has, for the most part, excluded women. That said, the ethics of care is not without its critics. Many feminists are concerned, and rightly so, that valorizing a moral theory based on a stereotypically female trait – caring – above other types of moral reasoning can lead women to think they should care about others at all times in all contexts, even if this caring incurs a personal cost.[5]

Cameron's behavior in certain situations provides a good example of how a commitment to an ethics of care may not always be appropriate in informing the way we approach moral problems, and indeed can interfere with our ability to perform tasks required of us. Consider Cameron's behavior in "Maternity." House orders Cameron to inform the parents of a sick newborn that their baby is extremely ill and is unlikely to survive the next twenty-four hours. Cameron doesn't convey the seriousness of the situation to the parents, and Wilson chastises Cameron for not telling them the truth:

WILSON: Allison, their baby's dying. If the parents weren't in tears when you left,
          you didn't tell them the truth.
CAMERON: That's not how I see it.
WILSON: Do you want them blindsided? Want them coming up and saying, "My
          God, my baby died, why didn't you warn me?"
CAMERON: So now it's about worrying about them yelling at us?
WILSON: No, it's about getting them prepared for the likely death of their child.
CAMERON: If their son dies tomorrow, do you think they'll give a damn what I said
          to them today? It's not going to matter; they're not going to care; it's not
          going to be the same ever again. Just give those poor women a few hours
          of hope.

---

[5] Sandra Lee Bartky, *Femininity and Domination: Studies in the Phenomenology of Oppression* (New York: Routledge, 1990), 118.

We learn later on in the season that Cameron watched her own husband die of cancer, and we can see how this experience guides her practice with patients who are facing a loss. What is unique about the ethic of care is that it promotes ethical deliberation that values the role of emotions – sympathy, empathy, sensitivity – in deciding what the best course of action would be.[6] What is problematic about Cameron's interactions with these patients is not that she uses her own experience to frame her actions; it is that she lets her emotions derail her professional judgment. In "Acceptance" Cameron is asked to inform a patient, Cindy, that she has terminal cancer. Witnessing Cameron and Cindy laughing in Cindy's hospital room, Wilson suspects that Cameron has not informed Cindy of the diagnosis:

WILSON: So I take it you were in there informing her?
CAMERON: Well, I . . . I hadn't exactly gotten around to that, but I was just –
WILSON: Doing what? Making friends?
CAMERON: Cindy's divorced. She doesn't have any kids, no siblings, both her parents
            are gone –
WILSON: It's not your job to be her friend. Do you understand?

It's here that Cameron reveals to Wilson that if she hadn't married her husband he would have died alone – much like Cindy. In this circumstance, Cameron moves beyond simply contextualizing the moral problem – she is reliving her own experience, unable to disentangle her own emotions from the problem at hand. Her own personal history interferes with, rather than contributes to, her professional practice. Of course Cameron shouldn't just reject the role of emotions in deciding what is morally best for her to do. Indeed, emotions can help us identify the needs of others and they can encourage us to view moral problems from a range of perspectives. Still, Cameron's overzealous caring often comes at a price, and it can compromise her professional practice. As the show progresses, this overzealousness increasingly seems to be driving her to adopt Houselike tactics in the name of providing "care" to patients. In "Que Sera Sera," Cameron secretly (and unlawfully) administers an injection to a patient to prevent him from leaving the hospital against medical advice – "I didn't think he should be discharged so I gave him three grams of phenytoin. I wasn't going to just let him leave." Unfortunately, the price of caring too much for her patients means becoming more like House.

You're Basically "a Stuffed Animal Made by Grandma"

It is probably safe to say that there is no single approach to moral reasoning that delivers the best outcomes for all parties involved at all times. Yet, as the moral center of the show, Cameron casts a spotlight on the ethic of care, providing a welcome contrast to House. Let's hope that underneath all that cynicism and complaining that Cameron is a "stuffed animal made by Grandma," House is taking notes.

---

[6] Held, *Ethics of Care*, 10.

23

Vampire Love

The Second Sex Negotiates the Twenty-First Century

Bonnie Mann

Summary

The *Twilight* series depicts Bella as a weak young woman who is ready to sacrifice everything, even her life, for the love of an extraordinarily strong man who desperately wants to suck her blood. What are the messages embedded in these stories for young people looking for love? How do these stories "plug into" the experiences and anxieties of the woman reader? What might feminist philosopher Simone de Beauvoir have to say about it? Is there a feminist sub-text to vampire love?

This chapter started in a moment of parental panic. My thirteen-year-old daughter, who habitually reads very thick books of dubious character, was unusually insistent in her pleas to be allowed to attend the midnight release party for the last volume in some book series she was reading. Remembering to thank my lucky stars for her literary commitments, I grudgingly drove her to Borders at about 10 P.M., expecting to see ten or twelve bookish adolescents drinking hot chocolate while they waited for the clock to strike midnight.

The crowded parking lot was my first indication that I was walking into a world everyone knew about, except me. My second was the store, packed wall-to-wall with teenage girls in the full bloom of an almost frighteningly incandescent excitement, many of them dressed in low-cut black gowns with their faces shining like floodlights through pale white paint. I stopped in the doorway of the store and turned to Dee Dee, whose normally beautiful human eyes were already radiating the luminescence of another sphere. I grabbed her arm and held her back. "Just what is this book about?" I asked.

What she gave me to understand with the twenty-five or so words I got out of her before she pulled away was that the glowing faces and the black gowns had something to do with the possibility of being loved by a bloodsucking man.

I later learned that I had delivered my daughter to the release party for *Breaking Dawn*, the fourth and final book of the blockbuster *Twilight* series, by Mormon housewife turned literary millionaire, Stephenie Meyer. These stories, of an all-consuming romance between a human teenage girl named Bella and a vampire frozen in time named Edward, have sold over forty million copies worldwide, and have been translated into thirty-seven languages.

I had to accept that, in the words our new president used to acknowledge Sarah Palin on the campaign trail, vampire love was a "phenomenon." What did it mean that millions of girls were fantasizing about men who could barely repress the desire to kill them? In 2008?

Back in Time

When I opened the first novel, *Twilight*, my impression was that I had gone back in time. The female protagonist struck me as a representative of the idealized womanhood of my mother's generation, transposed into twenty-first-century circumstances. A child of divorced parents, the seventeen-year-old Bella Swan has chosen to go live with her father in the small town of Forks, Washington, on the Olympic Peninsula, leaving Phoenix, Arizona, to give her mother a chance to spend time with her new husband.

Bella loves Phoenix and hates Forks, but self-sacrifice is her specialty. In fact, other than her penchant for self-sacrifice and the capacity to attract the attention of boys, Bella isn't really anyone special. She has no identifiable interests or talents; she is incompetent in the face of almost every challenge. She is the locus of exaggerated stereotypically feminine incapacities and self-loathing. She has no sense of direction or balance. She is prone to get bruises and scrapes just in the process of moving from one place to another and doesn't even trust herself to explore a tide pool without falling in.[1] When she needs something done, especially something mechanical, she finds a boy to do it for her and watches him. Her only areas of skill are cooking and doing laundry, which she does without complaint for her father, who is incompetent in the kitchen in spite of years of living alone (he must have been near starvation when she showed up).

When Bella draws the attention of the stunningly handsome and hyperbolically capable vampire, Edward Cullen, her response is disbelief. "I couldn't imagine anything about me that could be in any way interesting to him," she reports.[2] Frankly, having the feeling that I'd met Bella somewhere before and quickly forgotten the encounter, I couldn't either. When Bella falls in love, then, a girl in love is all she is. By page 139 she has concluded that her mundane life is a small price to pay for the gift of being with Edward, and by the second book she's willing to trade her soul for the privilege.

Edward, in contrast to Bella, is masculine grandiosity writ large. Beautiful beyond compare, the rock-hard seventeen-year-old body Bella comes to worship belongs

---

[1]   Stephenie Meyer, *Twilight* (New York: Little, Brown and Company, 2005), p. 116.
[2]   *Twilight*, p. 228.

to a hundred-year-old vampire (frozen in time after a bout with the Spanish flu). He knows everything, having had a hundred years to learn it. He's been everywhere and speaks multiple languages. He reads most people's minds and is strong enough to break a mature tree in two like a matchstick. He runs as fast as most cars drive and rescues the accident-prone Bella over and over; in a first early encounter he rescues her from a vehicle sliding toward her on ice by stopping it with his hands.[3] He is smug and confident and tortured by his desire to drink Bella's blood. He belongs to a cobbled together "family" of vampires who have sworn off human blood for ethical reasons and regularly suck the life out of large game animals instead. Edward's moral struggle with his instinctual bloodlust charges his physically intimate encounters with Bella with erotic, mortal, *and* moral danger. Chivalrous to a fault, he is as deeply concerned with protecting Bella's virtue as he is with keeping her alive.

The strong sense I had of having gone back in time to an old-fashioned world where women were seen as empty conduits of masculine desire and valued for their propensity to self-sacrifice alone drove me to take another look at *The Second Sex* which, widely acknowledged to be a founding text for feminist philosophy, was written by Simone de Beauvoir (1908–1986) half a century ago.[4] De Beauvoir, in contrast to others of the existentialist tradition, never wrote a treatise on the *essence* of love. She asked instead how love is lived and imagined in a *total concrete situation*, by *these* people, at *this* time.

For de Beauvoir in 1949 France, the tragedy of adolescence in the feminine was its demand that the girl give up both herself and her hold on the world. As she enters womanhood, she learns that she is destined to be a "relative being" whose existence has meaning only in relation to the man who loves her. As if Meyer wished to provide the perfect literary illustration of de Beauvoir's claim, when Edward leaves Bella for a time in the second book, Bella describes herself as "like a lost moon – my planet destroyed in some cataclysmic disaster-movie scenario of desolation that – continued . . . to circle in a tight little orbit around the empty space left behind."[5] Bella's mother marvels to her upon seeing her with Edward later in the story, "The way you move – you orient yourself around him without even thinking about it. . . . You're like a . . . satellite."[6]

De Beauvoir claimed that throughout her childhood, the girl learns that "the world is defined without reference to her."[7] Men make history, fight the wars, and produce the great works of art. This lesson becomes a crisis for the adolescent. "To feel oneself passive and dependent at the age of hope and ambition," de Beauvoir wrote, "at the age when the will to live and make a place in the world is running strong. At just this conquering age, woman learns that for her there is to be no conquest,

---

[3] Ibid., p. 157.

[4] Simone de Beauvoir, *The Second Sex*, trans. and ed. by H. M. Parshley (New York: Vintage Books, 1989).

[5] Stephenie Meyer, *New Moon* (New York: Little, Brown and Company, 2006), p. 201.

[6] Stephenie Meyer, *Eclipse* (New York: Little, Brown and Company, 2007), p. 68.

[7] De Beauvoir, *The Second Sex*, p. 331.

that she must disown herself, that her future depends upon man's good pleasure."[8] What she is offered in exchange for her world-making and value-creating capacities is the love, if she is lucky and pretty enough, of one of the world-makers.

No wonder that the adolescent girl's fantasies of love include a dimension of retreat to the safety of parental protection. After all, the task of becoming a *feminine* adult presents an impossible contradiction. "To be feminine is to appear weak, futile, docile," femininity is a "renunciation of sovereignty,"[9] while adulthood is having the strength and independence to take on the world. This contrast looms large in Meyer's novels. Bella is facing all of the simple cultural markers for adult woman-hood: her eighteenth birthday, graduation from high school, first sex, marriage, and motherhood. Yet through most of the story, Bella's vampire is father and mother, as much as lover. By the second book there is a competent, well-muscled werewolf named Jacob who is an equally protective parent. As Bella is handed off for safe-keeping from vampire to werewolf and back, she describes the experience as "like when I was a kid and Renée would pass me off to Charlie for the summer."[10] Her weakness contrasted with their strength is that of an infant, contrasted with an all-powerful adult. Edward confides to Bella, "You are so soft, so fragile, I have to mind my actions every moment that we're together so that I don't hurt you. I could kill you very easily Bella, simply by accident . . . you don't realize how incredibly break-able you are."[11] Bella seems to need to be carried everywhere and often falls asleep in the arms of her vampire only to wake up tucked gently into her own bed with him watching over her or playing the lullaby he's written for her; her first dance with Edward is successful because she puts her feet on his and he moves her about the floor.[12] De Beauvoir noted that the woman in love is "trying to reconstruct a situation, that which she experienced as a little girl, under adult protection."[13]

But Bella's physical incapacities carry other meanings. She is a foreigner in physical space, who seems to look over a high fence into the spheres of action and meaning. According to de Beauvoir, the adolescent girl relinquishes her younger self's dominant mode of bodily being, which the German philosopher Edmund Husserl (1859–1938) described as the "I can," the body as the center of living action and intention. When the young girl internalizes and assumes the masculine gaze, de Beauvoir said, she takes up a perspective on herself as prey. As in the fairy tales, she becomes "an idol," a "fascinating treasure," "a marvelous fetish," sought after by men.[14]

In Meyer's books, Bella continually discovers boys looking at her in various modes of desire. The masculine gaze confers meaning on her otherwise empty existence by giving her a place in the story as the very location through which masculine

---

[8] Ibid., p. 359.

[9] Ibid., p. 336.

[10] *Eclipse*, p. 236.

[11] *Twilight*, p. 310.

[12] Ibid., p. 488.

[13] De Beauvoir, *The Second Sex*, p. 645.

[14] Ibid., p. 350.

action instantiates meaning. "Through [her beloved] – whose gaze glorifies her," de Beauvoir wrote, "nothingness becomes fullness of being and being is transmuted into worth."[15] Of course, if ever that spotlight should be removed, her very existence is at stake; "the absence of her lover is always torture, he is an eye, a judge."[16] Indeed, when Edward leaves Bella for much of the second book, she sinks into a kind of living death, and it is only the gaze of a virile werewolf that begins to bring her back to life. Part of the seduction of this vampire story must be that, aside from Edward's absence in *New Moon*, his gaze is simply never averted. In a world that is still extremely heavy-handed in its insistence that a young woman's *primary* worth is derived from her ability to awaken masculine desire, Meyer offers girls the fantasy of a male gaze that is intense, constant, and faithful.

When I saw that what de Beauvoir wrote six decades ago seemed so relevant to Meyer's story, my parental panic became dull depression. For de Beauvoir, however timeless the myth of the "eternal feminine" claims to be, it arises from and points back to a total concrete situation, specific in time and place. Certainly the situation of girls in the United States at the dawn of the twenty-first century couldn't be the same as that of girls in 1949 France![17]

The Second Sex in the Twenty-first Century

Truth be told, the legal and formal barriers to women's equality *have* been eroded. A *New York Times* report from 2006 about "the new gender divide" in education noted that "women now make up 58 percent of those enrolled in two- and four-year colleges and are, over all, the majority in graduate schools and professional schools too. Men get worse grades than women," and "women are walking off with a disproportionate share of the honors degrees."[18]

We are accustomed to thinking of women's subordination as a thing of the past. Yet contemporary philosopher Susan Bordo argues that in a media – saturated culture, as gendered power retreats from law and policy it is even more intensely concentrated on women's bodies and the processes by which they come to think of themselves as persons.[19]

---

[15]   Ibid., p. 649.

[16]   Ibid., p. 657.

[17]   That was just five years after women won the vote there, just seven years after the last person was executed for performing abortions, sixteen years before women could accept paid work without authorization from their husbands, and before the dramatic mobilizations of the 1970s' women's movement.

[18]   Tamar Lewin, "The New Gender Divide: At Colleges, Women are Leaving Men in the Dust," *New York Times*, July 9, 2006.

[19]   Several texts make this claim both explicitly and implicity. See *Unbearable Weight: Feminism, Western Culture, and the Body* (Berkeley: University of California Press, 1993); *Twilight Zones: The Hidden Life of Cultural Images from Plato to O.J.* (Berkeley: University of California Press, 1997); *The Male Body: A Look at Men in Public and Private* (New York: Farrar, Straus and Giroux, 1999).

Mary Pipher, the acclaimed psychologist whose account of her experiences as a therapist for adolescent girls, *Reviving Ophelia*, reached number one on the *New York Times* best-seller list over a decade ago, agrees. "Something dramatic happens to girls in early adolescence . . ." she wrote, "they lose their resiliency and optimism and become less curious and inclined to take risks. They lose their assertive, energetic, and 'tomboyish' personalities and become deferential, self-critical, and depressed. They report great unhappiness with their own bodies."[20] This is particularly disconcerting for feminist mothers, because while "we . . . raised our daughters to be assertive and confident . . . they seemed to be insecure and concerned with their femininity."[21] Our messages of equality and opportunity, she noted, are sent out in a world where they run headlong into the "junk values" of a culture obsessed with a narrow version of female beauty. Being attractive to boys is still the first avenue to existence in the imaginary domain of the American middle school girl. In film and on TV women are overwhelmingly represented as "half-clad and half-witted,"[22] while girls are explicitly advised at home and in school that they can be anything they want to be. Girls negotiate these **paradoxes** at a time when "they don't have the cognitive, emotional, and social skills" to do so, Piper argued. "They are paralyzed by complicated and contradictory data that they cannot interpret. They struggle to resolve the unresolvable and make sense of the absurd."[23] They are overwhelmed by the effort. Describing her own daughter and her friends, Pipher said that at times "they just seemed wrecked. . . . Many confident, well-adjusted girls were transformed into sad, angry failures."[24]

Writer Lynn Phillips confirms that these conflicts are not resolved for most young women just by surviving adolescence. Women in college face "an environment filled with tangled messages."[25] A good woman is both *pleasing* in the traditional sense: passive, pleasant, childlike, and subordinate, bent on self-sacrifice; and *together*, meaning she knows who she is and what she wants sexually and professionally, and goes after it.[26]

What young women learn about male sexuality is equally paradoxical.[27] On the one hand, batterers and rapists are pathological exceptions to normal men. On the other hand, male sexuality in general is dangerous, men's "natural sex drive is inherently compelling and aggressive," and young women should not start what they aren't willing to finish.[28] Even today, young women report losing a sense of their

---

[20] Mary Pipher, *Reviving Ophelia: Saving the Selves of Adolescent Girls* (New York: Riverhead Books, 1994), p. 19.

[21] Ibid., p. 15.

[22] Ibid., p. 42.

[23] Ibid., p. 43.

[24] Ibid., p. 11.

[25] Lynn M. Phillips, *Flirting with Danger: Young Women's Reflections on Sexuality and Domination* (New York and London: New York University Press, 2000), p. 18.

[26] Ibid., pp. 38–52.

[27] Ibid., pp. 52–61.

[28] Ibid., p. 58.

own voices in sexual encounters. They feel "a sense of responsibility to go along with and even fake being excited by whatever a male partner [does] in order not to interfere with his arousal."[29]

Young women are presented with two messages about heterosexual love. On the one hand, the notion that love conquers all is ubiquitous – it is presented as a young woman's only chance at salvation. On the other hand is the notion that love hurts, that women can't expect too much from men, who after all are from Mars, not from Venus.[30]

From these contemporary thinkers we learn that while legal inequality has receded, the infantilization of women as objects of male desire has intensified. As subordination has unraveled in arenas of the public sphere, it has retained its hold on the private sphere, especially that most private sphere where the process of becoming who we are is under way. Cultural messages about womanhood are fraught with paradox. And the imaginary domain in which young women negotiate these realities has become a messy place indeed.

A Feminist Subtext

Stephenie Meyer's genius is to clean up that imaginary domain and give girls a story that seems to hold all the contradictions together. While I've already said a great deal about the ways in which Bella seems to be committed to the womanhood we might associate with the 1950s, I haven't said much about the ways that she departs from that representation.

The most surprising thing about Bella's romance with Edward is not that Edward has to resist the urge to perforate her pulsing jugular vein, but that he, not she, puts the brakes on their erotic encounters. Knowing that any loss of control spells death for his beloved, Edward's restraint allows Bella to be the one consumed by desire. She is regularly physically rebuffed by him as she longs to tear off his clothes. In the end, he is pushed into agreeing to sex while she is still human, only by forcing Bella to agree to marry him. We learn that Bella has been "raised to cringe at the very thought of poofy white dresses and bouquets" by her mother, since "early marriage was higher on her blacklist than boiling live puppies."[31] Yet in the end, Bella turns eighteen, graduates, marries Edward for sex, and gets pregnant, practically all at once.

In Phillips's interviews with young women in college, she noted that what was missing from the stew of discourses about sex, love, and sexuality were stories of male accountability and female pleasure without penalty. Meyer offers her readers the first of these missing narratives, which must be a great pleasure for girls who have, no doubt, wished for such stories. As one adolescent girl said to me recently,

[29]   Ibid., p. 109.
[30]   Ibid., pp. 69–76.
[31]   Stephenie Meyer, *Breaking Dawn* (New York: Little, Brown and Company, 2008), pp. 6, 17.

following an unpleasant encounter with a teenage boy in a car, "I wish he would just get it." Edward gets it. He knows that sex is dangerous for Bella; he reads every sign of emotional distress or joy with extraordinary **accuracy** and sensitivity.

Meyer still doesn't offer her young readers a clear story of female desire without penalty. For a moment she seems to be providing us with the most brutal critique of heterosexual pleasure and motherhood that we've seen in thirty years. First sex with the vampire leaves the bed in splinters and Bella covered with bruises. She becomes pregnant with a vampire child who threatens destruction from the inside; every fetal kick causes internal bleeding. Depleted to the point of death by the accelerated pregnancy, on the verge of becoming a "broken, bled-out, mangled corpse," Bella drinks human blood, supplied from the blood bank by Edward's doctor vampire father, because nothing else seems to quiet "the little executioner."[32] Rather than letting the little beast chew its way out, a vampire cesarean is performed as Bella plummets toward death; Edward is compelled to inject his venom into Bella to save her, transforming her.

While it took a long time for me to notice, because it is deeply buried, particularly in the first two books, there is a subtle feminist subtext to this vampire love quartet. Bella announces in *Twilight* that she "doesn't like double standards," and writes an essay for her English class on "whether Shakespeare's treatment of the female characters is misogynistic," a subtle textual invitation to the reader to wonder the same thing about Meyer's characters.[33] We discover that Bella wants to be a vampire, not only to avoid out-aging Edward and live with him in immortal bliss, but because in the vampire world, all bets are off when it comes to gender. Vampire women show no particular deference to men. They are endowed with superpowers just like the guys. Rosalie, Edward's vampire sister, is the best mechanic in the family. The female vampires are clearly the answer to the helpless Bella's lament at the end of *Twilight*. "A man and a woman have to be somewhat equal," she says, "as in, one of them can't always be swooping in and saving the other one. They have to save each other equally. . . . I can't always be Lois Lane," she continues, "I want to be Superman too."[34] For the reader, too, the boredom inspired by the thousandth rescue incites hope for something else. "I want to be fierce and deadly," Bella tells us.[35] "Just wait 'til I'm a vampire! I'm not going to be sitting on the sidelines next time."[36]

And though Bella's transformation is a trial by fire (almost literally, since the pain involved in becoming a vampire burns), it does not disappoint. Bella steps back into her "I can" body with a vengeance. "The instant I considered standing erect," she marvels, "I was already straight. There was no brief fragment in time in which the action occurred."[37] She is faster and stronger than Edward. "I could feel

[32]   Ibid., pp. 355, 357.
[33]   *Twilight*, pp. 90, 143.
[34]   Ibid., pp. 473–4.
[35]   *New Moon*, p. 263.
[36]   *Eclipse*, p. 559.
[37]   Ibid., p. 391.

it now – the raw, massive strength filling my limbs. I was suddenly sure that if I wanted to tunnel under the river, to claw or beat my way through the bedrock, it wouldn't take me very long."[38] Instead of being carried through the woods by Edward like a baby, she runs with him, "I flew with him through the living green web, by his side, not following at all. . . . I kept waiting to feel winded, but my breath came effortlessly. I waited for the burn to begin in my muscles, but my strength only seemed to increase as I grew accustomed to my stride. My leaping bounds stretched longer, and soon he was trying to keep up with me. I laughed again, exultant, when I heard him falling behind."[39] More than anything, this physical prowess signals an existential change: "Now I was in the story with him," Bella says triumphantly, and the readers, too, sigh with relief.[40] In the final horrific encounter, between good and evil, life and death, it will be Bella, not the boys, who saves the day.

The Price of Existence

What is heartening about Bella is that her story doesn't end the way the fairy tales do, with the kiss that brings the princess back to life, or the wedding at the palace. The fairy-tale ending turns to a nightmare in fact, as the half-vampire fetus beats away at her life. But finally, a self-destructive love bleeds its way into the kind of love de Beauvoir would have described as authentic, a love between two liberties, lived in equality. The tragedy of feminine self-alienation is overcome by journeying *through* it. Meyer sorts the paradoxical narratives of female passivity and power, purity and desire, innocence and responsibility, dependence and autonomy, into a story where one leads, finally, to the other.

When faced with an adult life as what de Beauvoir called "a relative being," a girl may well become convinced that "there is no other way out for her than to lose herself, body and soul, in him who is represented to her as the absolute, the essential."[41] But the ecstasy of this process of self-loss is not, at bottom, masochistic: "She chooses to desire her enslavement so ardently that it appears as the expression of her liberty; she will try to rise above her situation as inessential object by radically assuming it."[42] Under her paroxysm of sacrifice, what de Beauvoir calls the "dream of annihilation," "is in fact an avid will to exist. . . . When woman gives herself to her idol, she hopes that he will give her at once possession of herself and of the universe he represents."[43]

What is disheartening about Meyer's books is her reinstatement of this old promise: assume your status as prey, as object, and you will gain your freedom as

---

[38] Ibid., p. 410.
[39] Ibid., p. 413.
[40] Ibid., p. 479.
[41] De Beauvoir, *The Second Sex*, p. 643.
[42] Ibid., p. 643, translation modified by the author.
[43] Ibid., p. 646.

subject, as the center of action and meaning. Seek your existence in the eyes of a sovereign masculine subject, and you will find it. The old stories drop the female heroine into an abyss. We don't know what happens to Sleeping Beauty or Cinderella or Snow White after the kiss or the proposal or the wedding – the "happiness" they find is a blank death. But we *do* know what happens to Bella, she is literally torn to shreds by the needs and desires of others. Meyer promises resurrection as a full participant in the not-quite-human drama, and a grasp on the world that is strong – and one imagines Meyer herself, resurrecting herself, furiously writing herself back into existence.

There is a slippage between the promise to the reader and the activity of the writer here. Meyer doesn't come to celebrity life out of the purgatory of feminine nonexistence by letting the blood be drained out of her. It takes a hard-working self-authored creative act to resurrect a woman's life. But how does one open the door of the feminine imagination for young women so that they might trace paths to themselves that don't pass through traditional feminine annihilation? Is the only way to do this through the use of our traditional misogynistic metaphors? If so, Meyer is to be congratulated. But in her insistence on resurrecting the promise that a meaningful life comes *through* self-annihilation in the interests of others, comes *through* appending oneself to one of the special creatures who lives the adventure of life firsthand, she promises our daughters the same things our mothers were promised. In that sense, the wild success of *Twilight* might be cause for despair.

24

Killing the Griffins

A Murderous Exposition of Postmodernism

J. Jeremy Wisnewski

Summary

Postmodernism is a literary and philosophical movement that began in the second half of the twentieth-century. The movement suggests that "truth" is merely a social construction – that what we call "true" is just a product of the games we play with language. If this is correct, postmodernism seems to deliver the death blow to ethical and political critique (if nothing is true, how can we criticize practices that we find morally problematic?). *Family Guy* presents postmodernism in all its glory, and it also suggests a way that even postmodern moral critique might be possible.

This is not an essay. It's a prelude to homicide.

I am going to kill the Griffin family. I will even kill that baby and especially that ridiculous dog. I will do this for one straightforward reason: it's the only way we can be saved.

Saved? Yes. *Family Guy* will be the end of the civilized world. It will be the death of value. *Family Guy* oozes the postmodern, and the postmodern will be the end of us all. *Postmodernism* is a movement that has developed over the last several decades in philosophy, architecture, literature, and elsewhere. This movement emphasizes the absence of any real structure to the world or our lives, and of any overarching meaning to our activities. It systematically calls into question our most serious ideas: Truth, Progress, Freedom, Rationality, and the Individual.[1] Instead, postmodernism sees the world as disjointed, with pockets of power relations and politics and nothing to unify it all. Yes, there is reason (with a small "r"), but he's just a little fella, and can't do much by himself. At most, he pops up here and there – and he's never divorced from a particular context. The postmodern world is a ruptured world – and *Family Guy* just oozes these ruptures.

---

[1] These are so serious that they must all be capitalized, and then their seriousness must again be acknowledged in a footnote.

And so, the Griffins must die. It's the only way to save us from becoming cynical conservatives. That's right. I'll say it plainly and with gusto: *Family Guy* is *conservative.* You see, my friends, I am so left that the left doesn't even want me. As a good leftist and socialist, I have discovered that *Family Guy*, that glob of the postmodern, is a vehicle of conservative politics. To prevent *Family Guy* from exerting its corrupting, conservative-making influence on our youth, I must kill the cartoon. It's the only ethical thing to do.

Family Guy is Real

It's not as difficult to kill a cartoon as you might think. Paint thinner is a choice weapon – but there are other ways as well. (The Fox network thought it knew how to kill *Family Guy*, but it was wrong as usual.) I prefer the direct approach: I will simply find the Griffin family, and squash them under my official Communism© Boots. I can do this, dear reader, because *Family Guy* is dangerously *real.*

I first knew there was a problem when I saw the season one premiere ("Death has a Shadow"). The show featured the following: G. I. Jew, who wielded a bagel, a joke about not standing up to a tank at Tiananmen Square, Peter irresponsibly letting dangerous toys pass his inspection, God being embarrassed by a sermon, Stewie trying to mind-control or kill Lois five times, Kool-Aid, *The Brady Bunch* (with Aunt Jemima), and, worst of all, *Joanie Loves Chachi* (the audacity!).

I was disgusted, and hence instantly taken in by the show. It was this, I later realized, that made the show so dangerous.

The next two episodes ("I Never Met the Dead Man" and "Chitty Chitty Death Bang") were no less insensitive: there were jokes about being racist (Dianne Simmons, the news co-anchor, remarks "Tom, I just plain don't like black people" when she thinks they aren't broadcasting), about World War II (the German sausage vendor, the spitting image of Hitler, takes over the Polish sausage vendor, who is located beside him – and of course he doesn't stop there), and about the control that television exerts over our minds. Indeed, it is this that allows Stewie to attempt to destroy broccoli ("Their puerile minds are once again distracted by that flickering box. Time to be bad!"). And if all that weren't bad enough, there were references to Batman, Raisin Bran, *Star Trek*, *Scooby-Doo*, *Willy Wonka*, *Chips*, and (I think) *The Wonder Years.*

It was a television blitzkrieg. I was being assaulted by images of the past, meshed together with those serious events that have collectively composed our history – and *nothing was real.* Or, perhaps better put, nothing was more real than anything else. Scooby-Doo and Hitler, Tiananmen Square and Willy Wonka: it was all the same – it was all scenery for folly, a backdrop of the cultural imagination.

And it was here that I realized that *Family Guy* was real – or, again, as real as anything else. (And perhaps then, as I lay weeping on the floor, curled in a fetal position, I realized that they needed to be stopped. What is real can be murdered, dear reader.) It was as real as Disneyland – and that is as real as things get these days. As the French philosopher and social critic Jean Baudrillard (1929–2007) remarks, "Disneyland is presented as imaginary in order to make us believe that the rest is real, whereas all of Los Angeles and the America that surrounds it are no longer real." He might well have been talking about *Family Guy* and the families that loiter the developed West. Baudrillard continues, "it is no longer a question of a false representation of reality (ideology), but of concealing the fact that the real is no longer real."[2]

The real is no longer real. That about says it all. You see, Disneyland knows it is artificial. Everything is designed to produce certain experiences – the castles, the rides, the characters. *We*, on the other hand, do not know what's real. We think that the *real* is outside of us, but it's all just more scenery. The characters on *Family Guy* present us with an image of familial relations that is designed to seem absurd, and this leads us to think that *our* families are somehow more real than the cartoon images displayed before us – that our families are somehow *not* absurd caricatures – the mere filling out of generic cultural variables and preexisting social roles. But we are wrong about this. We occupy the same space as *Family Guy*, only we are not in Technicolor, and we are not as aware as *Family Guy* is of our situation. Our families are modeled after television images and cultural icons such as those spoofed on *Family Guy*. We are as indebted to Fred and Wilma Flintstone as the Griffins are. But there is one *big* difference between us and the *Family Guy* family: *at least the Griffins know that they are cartoons.*

PETER: Everybody, I got bad news. We've been cancelled.
LOIS: Oh no. Peter, how could they do that?
PETER: Well unfortunately Lois, there's just no more room on the schedule. We've just got to accept the fact that Fox has to make room for terrific shows like *Dark Angel, Titus, Undeclared, Action, That 80's Show, Wonder Falls, Fast Lane, Andy Richter Controls the Universe, Skin, Girls' Club, Cracking Up, The Pits, Firefly, Get Real, Freaky Links, Wanda at Large, Costello, The Lone Gunman, A Minute with Stan Hooper, Normal Ohio, Pasadena, Harsh Realm, Keen Eddy, The Street, American Embassy, Cedric the Entertainer, The Tick, Louie,* and *Greg the Bunny.*
LOIS: Is there no hope?
PETER: Well, I suppose if all those shows go down the tubes, we might have a shot.
("North by North Quahog")[3]

The Griffins also know the power that the corporations exert over their existence – something few of us care to acknowledge. After having what looks like a World Wide Wrestling Federation Death Match, the Griffins reflect on what they've been broadcasting.

---

[2] Jean Baudrillard, *Simulacra and Simulation*, translated by Sheila Faria Glaser (Ann Arbor: University of Michigan Press, 1994), pp. 12–13.
[3] And of course this is the opening dialogue in *Family Guy*'s second television premiere, after a spell in the television cemetery.

PETER: TV is dangerous. Why the hell doesn't the government step in and tell us what we can and can't watch – and shame on the network that puts this junk *[namely, Family Guy]* on the air.

LOIS: Uh, Peter . . . Peter maybe . . . maybe you shouldn't say anything bad about the network.

PETER: Oh, why? What are they going to do? Cut our budget? *[Peter then moves to the other room, his entire body going from right to left, a clear indication that there wasn't enough money to finish the animation]*

("Lethal Weapons")

And so we watch, thinking that we know so much, that we are so much more than what is portrayed on the screens before us. It is in this way that we are subdued – and it is for this reason that the Griffins must die. You see, we are made to feel secure by the Griffins – strange as this sounds – because we are hoodwinked into thinking, with relief, "well, at least we're not like that – we must be ok."

Oh dear readers, I am not ok, and it isn't simply because I forgot to take my medication.

Family Guy is Serious

Modernism is the philosophical movement typically associated with the 17th and 18th century intellectual climate of Europe. The philosopher and mathematician René Descartes (1596–1650) is often cited as the father of modern philosophy. Rather than submitting to traditional views ordained by the church, Descartes insisted that we must use rationality to discern the true nature of reality – and in doing this, he contended, we would vastly improve the world. This ideal was perhaps best instantiated by the Prussian philosopher Immanuel Kant (1724–1804). Kant claimed that the use of **reason** was enabling human beings to come into their own – to develop, morally and socially, into something far better than we have ever been before.

These stories of progress – of using Reason to grasp Truth and attain Freedom – are at the very center of modernism. This story of how society and human beings will improve their lot in the universe is what French philosopher Jean-François Lyotard (1924–98) calls a meta-narrative. It is a story that makes sense of every other story – a story that allows us to see the world as a fundamentally unified place with real significance. *Post*-modernism, on the other hand, concerns the death of such stories. It is infatuated with disunity. Whereas the modernist looked for the unity of things, the postmodernist looks for *difference* (or *différance*, if you're French). The postmodernist aims to show that the unity of the world is another piece of human conceit. The "postmodern," Lyotard coyly claims, is "incredulity toward meta-narratives."[4]

[4] Jean-François Lyotard, *The Postmodern Condition: A Report on Knowledge*, translated by Geoff Bennington and Brian Massumi (Minneapolis: University of Minnesota Press, 1984), p. xxiv.

To say that *Family Guy* is incredulous is just to put lipstick on a pig. No need to church it up here. *Family Guy* is downright obnoxious about meta-narratives. In this way, the show *exemplifies* the postmodern.

If you talk to the people who live around you, there are certain things they will likely believe – and these **beliefs** will likely help to organize their days: they will likely believe that human beings should not have sex with animals, that one should be respectful of religions, that alcoholism should not be encouraged, that cartoon pornography should not be on prime-time network television, and that we shouldn't joke around about things like World War II, homosexuality, homelessness, sadomasochism, racism, anti-semitism, violence, sexual harassment, political oppression, and so on.

And of course, *Family Guy* does all of this: Brian frequently goes on dates with human females (bestiality). Stewie's sexuality is constantly in question, and there are frequent jokes about homosexuality ("Hey, excuse me, is your refrigerator running? Because if it is, it probably runs like you . . . *very* homosexually").[5] Peter is clearly an alcoholic. Peter and Lois engage in what appears to be lively bondage and S&M sex. In fact, they even have a safety word – it's *banana*, in case you ever need to know ("Let's Go to the Hop"), and the seeming disrespect shown to all religions reaches a fever pitch in *Family Guy*. I'll permit myself one of my favorite examples:

PETER: Yeah, I'm looking for toilet-training books.
CLERK: Yes. We can help you there. *Everybody Poops* is still the standard, of course. We've also got the less popular *Nobody Poops But You.*
PETER: Well, see, we're Catholic, so . . .
CLERK: Then you want *You're a Naughty Child And That's Concentrated Evil Coming Out the Back of You.*
PETER: Perfect!
("Brian in Love")

And perhaps politics gets it worst of all. When Peter founds his own country (Petoria, in "E. Peterbus Unum"), he is irritated at how he is treated by the United Nations. Upset, he seeks some advice from an Iraqi diplomat, who convinces him that invasion is the only way to go.

DIPLOMAT: They *[the other UN representatives]* don't respect you.
PETER: What do you mean?
DIPLOMAT: Listen to me. I used to be the laughing stock around here until one day my country invaded Kuwait. Now I have a seat in the third row! Look – the only way to get something you want around here is to find something and just take it.
PETER: Wait a second . . . if everyone around here respects you, how come you're still eating by yourself?
DIPLOMAT: I don't shower.
PETER: Oh . . . that's what that is . . . *[pause]* Take what I want, huh?

---

[5]   Peter makes this joke in "Lethal Weapons."

Following the advice of the diplomat, Peter proclaims Joe's pool the newest province of Petoria ("Joehio"). But the mockery of world politics can't stop there – not without at least making light of a few of the world's most notorious abusers of human rights! The dictators of the world are invited to Peter's country (read: his backyard) so that Peter can show Lois they have some supporters.

PETER: Hey Slobodan, you made it!

SLOBODAN MILOŠEVIĆ: I didn't know what to bring so I made coleslaw. *[He begins waving his arms]* It's made out of people!!! *[laughs]* Just kidding. Hey – is Momar here yet?

To show us that it ain't a party with only one dictator, we see Saddam Hussein and Momar Khadafi having a grand ole' time discussing how they enjoy *Seinfeld*, not to mention murdering their respective peoples:

SADDAM: . . . then Jerry guessed that her name was 'Mulva.' *[both laugh]*

MOMAR: That show was funny. It really reminds me of my friends. You know, the way we just hang out . . . before I kill them for worshipping the wrong God.

SADDAM: And I love that Kramer guy. He comes in the room like this. *[tries to impersonate Kramer]* I can't do it but you know . . .

[We then see Stewie reprimanding Fidel Castro for running around the pool.]

Incredulity at meta-narratives indeed! *Family Guy* undermines all meta-narratives – but it also undermines *everything else* as well. I will not defend any meta-narratives here. I will, however, suggest that joking about everything under the sun is a good way to get burned. After a few seasons of *Family Guy*, what do we have left to take seriously? We are thrown into a world where everything is equally real and fictitious, where everything – even the most serious stuff we can imagine – is potential for punchline. Nothing is sacred; everything is profane. And all I can do in response is laugh. Famine, poverty, oppression, big chickens, the Fonz, and diarrhea. This is just the state of the world. If Randy Newman is going to sing, so be it. There's nothing we can do anyway. The postmodern liberates us from our concerns – but this means that it also liberates us from our *causes*. In the absence of any real goals, we are left to become cynics – albeit cynics who get to see babies try to kill their moms, dogs who are alcoholics, neighbors who overcompensate for injury or who are sexually obsessed, and, of course, fathers who are blithering idiots.

This is a family that shouldn't get too close to the paint thinner, at least if good murderous Marxists like me are around.

Family Guy Must Die! Long Live *Family Guy*!

Perhaps Peter and his horde of miscreants don't need to die. Perhaps the po-mo don't need to be no-mo. Perhaps I just need to remember to take my medication.

Is it really so bad to make people cynical? To get them to sit on their butts and accept whatever the world throws at them, believing that nothing can be done about it?

Hell yes it's bad!

But perhaps postmodernism, much like *Family Guy*, has gotten a bad rap for little reason (pun intended). After all, the view that postmodernism leads to inaction doesn't quite map on to the action of some of the most notoriously postmodern theorists. The philosopher and historian Michel Foucault (1926–84), for example, participated in the students' revolts of 1968, advocated prison reform, and spoke out on other social issues to boot. Was he simply inconsistent, or is there something peculiar about postmodernism that allows action *and* cynicism? If such an avenue was open to Foucault, perhaps *Family Guy* can live after all. Meta-narratives and medication be damned. Let's see how the fancy-lad Foucault pulled it off, and maybe I won't need to kill any cartoons after all.

Foucault claimed, in good po-mo fashion, that the notions of Freedom, Truth, and Rationality were simply the products of another story about the world designed to provide us with comfort, but ultimately without any basis in the way the world is. Indeed, as he conceived it, the very notion of "knowledge" was the result of systems of description that were ultimately optional, and often oppressive. Knowledge claims served to situate people in relations of power rather than to emancipate them; what we claim is true, far from setting us free, actually often enslaves us.

What is interesting about this, though, is that it occasions a rethinking of many of our social institutions. When we say someone is "mentally ill," for example, we are not just making a claim that is true or false. We are *also* insisting that this person should be regarded (and treated) in a particular way. Once we've recognized this, though, we can assess the evaluative dimension of knowledge. Quagmire, for example, is a sexual deviant – a pervert. In making this claim, I am implying that Quagmire is in some sense *ill*. The guy's just not right – and he should be regarded (and treated) in a way that represents his condition (perhaps an attempted reconditioning must take place, as in "Blind Ambition").

But to be a pervert, or a deviant, really just means to do things that are normally not done. Brian too does things that are normally not done (he is obviously into bestiality, for example, as in "Brian the Bachelor" or "Perfect Castaway"). So too did Socrates, Jesus, Buddha, and Gandhi. (That's right, I'm calling Jesus a pervert.) The mere fact that someone acts uniquely does not mean they should be regarded as strange, or as grotesquely abnormal, or as "deviant," in the nasty sense of that word employed by many hoity-toity types. But the way we describe people nevertheless situates them in grids of power relations.

By calling into question our knowledge claims, and by getting us to see that our knowledge claims exert power over people's lives (who wants to be a deviant, anyway?), Foucault actually *provides* a response to "power/knowledge" (the two always go together, Foucault claims). He does this despite the fact that "a society without power relations can only be an abstraction."[6] Foucault *does not* offer us a meta-narrative. We will *always* be in some system of control. "Power is everywhere, not because it embraces everything, but because it comes from everywhere."[7] So Foucault is not trying to show the way to a complete liberation from all oppression (that's our friend "Freedom," replete with capital 'f'). There's no such thing. But that doesn't mean we should just sit around feeling sorry for ourselves, either. "To claim that one can never be 'outside' power does not mean that one is trapped and condemned to defeat no matter what."[8] It does mean that we have to pick our fights locally – and that there's no grand story about God or Calling or Country that will justify what we do. We just have to fight for causes that we embrace, whether it's an end to poverty, the resurrection of *Family Guy*, an end to the FCC, or an increase in tolerance.

Let's not give *Family Guy* too much credit here – at least not before we have to. Can it really pull off what fancy-lad Foucault managed? Foucault enables us to be both postmodern and active. One doesn't need a big meta-narrative to engage in a little critique. But does *Family Guy* engage in critique, or does it just poke fun? Perhaps there isn't a difference here that makes a difference (or a *différance*, if you're *still* French). After all, sometimes a little fun-poking of big and nasty meta-narratives is *exactly* what we need to avoid doing serious damage.[9] Maybe this is enough for even good leftist socialists like me to say "Bring on the incredulity! We need some of that!"

PETER:	As we all know, Christmas is that mystical time of year when the ghost of Jesus rises from the grave to feed on the flesh of the living. So we all sing Christmas carols to lull him back to sleep.
BOB:	Outrageous! How dare he say such blasphemy! I've gotta do something!
BOB'S FRIEND:	Bob, there's nothing you can do.
BOB:	*[Sighing]* Well, I guess I'll just have to develop a sense of humor.

("A *Family Guy* Freakin' Christmas")

Taking religion a little less seriously might well save some lives, even if it does create some cynics along the way. And I'm pretty sure that's a good trade. Or, again, in a country as divided as ours is, maybe we should stick our tongues out at the politicians with a little more gusto.

---

[6] Michel Foucault, "The Subject and Power" in *Michel Foucault: Beyond Structuralism and Hermeneutics*, ed. Hubert L. Dreyfus and Paul Rabinow (Chicago: Chicago University Press, 1983), pp. 222–3.

[7] Michel Foucault, *The History of Sexuality*, translated by Robert Hurley (New York: Vintage Books, 1990), p. 93.

[8] Michel Foucault, "Power and Strategies" in *Power/Knowledge* (New York: Pantheon Books, 1980), p. 142.

[9] As author Sam Harris reminds us, "Only 28 percent of Americans believe in evolution; 72 percent believe in angels. Ignorance in this degree, concentrated in both the head and the belly of a lumbering superpower, is now a problem for the entire world." *The End of Faith: Religion, Terror, and the Future of Reason* (New York: W. W. Noton, 2005), p. 230.

GEORGE W. BUSH:	*[as a young man]* All right, let's do this. Let's kick some ass.
SOLDIER:	Uh, George, the war's over.
GEORGE W. BUSH:	What?
SOLDIER:	Yeah, it's done.
GEORGE W. BUSH:	Get out of here! Are you serious?
SOLDIER:	Yeah.
GEORGE W. BUSH:	Aw, man, aw, man, I just got your messages and . . . I . . . I, aw, I'm sorry.
SOLDIER:	George, it's been over for a while.
GEORGE W. BUSH:	Really?
SOLDIER:	Yeah, it's 1981.
GEORGE W. BUSH:	It's, uh . . . oh, oh, wow. Oh, so I'm way late. Oh, boy.
SOLDIER:	Yeah.
GEORGE W. BUSH:	Uh, well, you want to do something else?
SOLDIER:	I got some blow.
GEORGE W. BUSH:	Son of a bitch, took you this long to tell me? Break it out, man!

("PTV")[10]

The idea that our leader can be trusted is just too much for a good communist like me to stomach. The idea that the US government has figured out *the* way to run a society also gives me stomach pain. Perhaps incredulity (or, I'll say it, being downright obnoxious about these ideas) is exactly what the doctor ordered. And damnit, maybe Foucault and *Family Guy* aren't that far apart after all.

So there you have it. Either I've convinced myself to rethink my craving for cartoon blood or I'm just a big commie pansy. *Family Guy* need not fall prey to my murderous wrath after all – not yet, anyway. The sort of cynicism the show breeds won't make us all conservatives – at least not if we remember Foucault's lesson: we can be cynics about the big stories, so long as we still have a little fight in us when it really matters.

Or maybe I'm just kidding myself. Maybe I'm already one of the victims of *Family Guy*, too postmodern to take anything seriously.

Or maybe I've just developed a sense of humor.

---

[10]   And to see Osama Bin Laden get some incredulity, make sure to watch the opening segment of the episode.

Part VII

Social and Political Philosophy

Introduction

Social and political philosophy is concerned with the relationship between the individual and society. What rights do individuals have and how are these rights derived and justified? What form of government is most just? What economic system is best and most fair? Plato (429–347 BCE) and Aristotle (384–322 BCE) consider ethics and political philosophy inseparable. The good person and the good society depend on one another. In his *Republic*, Plato raises the question of the legitimate role of the government and calls for the abandonment of democracy in favor of a proto-socialist state, an ideal developed much later by Karl Marx (1818–83). Thomas Hobbes (1588–1679) views the government as an overbearing presence, a Leviathan, but one to which we must submit for our own protection. According to John Locke (1632–1704), all men are born with the inalienable rights to life, liberty, and property, and through the social contract we form governments to protect those rights. Libertarian philosophers of today see the protection of those rights as the only legitimate function of governments. By contrast, Communitarian philosophers argue that governments must take care of their citizens in the spirit of community, thus justifying, among other things, the welfare state. Other topics of discussion in social and political philosophy include justice, fairness, punishment, race, globalization, the family, paternalism, and autonomy.[1]

In this Part Richard Davies' chapter uses *Lost* to ask questions about the state of nature and social contract theory. The state of nature is a hypothetical scenario in which humans live apart from government. When the passengers aboard Oceanic

---

[1] Part of the material in this paragraph was previously published in William Irwin's chapter "Condensed Philosophy" in Will Pearson, Mangesh Hattikudur, and Elizabeth Hunt eds., *Condensed Knowledge: A Deliciously Irreverent Guide to Feeling Smart Again* (New York: HarperResource, 2004), p. 230.

Flight 815 crash on a desert island, the conditions of the state of nature are recreated and the survivors are faced with the question of how to govern themselves. Will they form a social contract, an agreement by which they tacitly agree to live? Drawing on the work of Locke, Rousseau (1712–78), Hume (1711–76), and Hobbes, Davies illustrates these core issues in political philosophy.

Michael Bray's chapter uses the popular sitcom *The Office* to consider issues of social class and exploitation. Marx divides society into the class of laborers and the class of capitalists. According to Marx, capitalists, who own the means of production, make money by paying laborers less than their labor is really worth, skimming "surplus value" off the top. As it turns out, even the white collar workers of *The Office* are exploited, and maybe that's why they're so dissatisfied.

Dónal P. O'Mathuna's chapter takes up a controversial topic in social philosophy: torture. While fans of the TV drama *24* cheer on Jack Bauer as he brutalizes suspects in the name of extracting information vital to national security, philosophers ask questions. Do Jack Bauer's actions constitute torture? How should we define torture? What are the arguments for and against torture? Can it be morally justified? Is it ultimately effective?

Jeremy Pierce's chapter poses a hotly debated issue in social philosophy: the nature of race. *X-Men* has often been interpreted as an allegory for race relations, with the mutants treated as second class citizens in much the way minorities have been historically. While the nature of race has often seemed clear, contemporary debates in biology and metaphysics have called the very existence of race into question. Drawing on the *X-Men* comics and movies, Pierce addresses the questions: What is race? Is there a genetic basis for race? Can race be a social reality even if it is not a genetic reality?

25

Lost's State of Nature

Richard Davies

Summary

In political philosophy, a *state of nature* is a situation where agents' interests are best served by cooperative behavior but individuals know too little about each other's intentions to act for the common good. A state of nature is more or less severe according to the nature of the goods at stake, such as fresh water and food. In these respects, the survivors of *Lost* are fortunate in landing on the Island. They are also lucky in (mostly) sharing English to communicate. Game theory can help us understand how, in such a situation, cooperation can be generated among the survivors.

The phrase **state of nature** crops up frequently in comments on *Lost* for at least two reasons. The first is that two of the leading characters in the program (John Locke and Danielle Rousseau) bear the surnames of two philosophers who are famous for having used the phrase *state of nature* as a key term in their writings on political philosophy. These are the Englishman John Locke (1632–1704) and the Swiss-Frenchman Jean-Jacques Rousseau (1712–88). The second, much better, reason why the phrase crops up so much in discussions of *Lost* is that the situation the survivors of Oceanic Flight 815 find themselves in after the crash can indeed be usefully described as a state of nature.

Before coming to some differences among the ways that Locke, Rousseau, and other philosophers have thought about the state of nature, let's consider a negative, and rather abstract, characterization of it that would be recognized by everyone working in the tradition of political philosophy that Locke and Rousseau consolidated. *In a pure state of nature, none of the codes and expectations, none of the rules and hierarchies, none of the roles and presumptions that make up the fabric of our social lives is operative, can be relied on or can be enforced.* Presented in this abstract way, a situation like this is very difficult to imagine. After all, very few of us have any experience of anything remotely similar.

The very difficulty of imagining something that fits the (negative) bill can help explain why Locke, Rousseau, and other philosophers have taken differing approaches to giving a more positive and concrete account of the dynamics of a supposed state of nature. Indeed, many philosophers, including another who gives his name to a character on *Lost*, the Scotsman David Hume (1711–76), have thought that the difficulty of imagining a state of nature is a reason for not taking it as a key **concept** in theorizing about politics. If it is a hardly imaginable situation, it won't be of much help understanding the societies we actually participate in.

In what sense, then, can the situation of the survivors of 815 be described as a state of nature? Well, at the outset, most of the people (except the pairs Jin-Sun, Shannon-Boone, Michael-Walt and, to a small extent, Jack-Rose) are strangers to each other. They are individuals each with their own interests and aims, above all to survive in the face of the unfamiliar challenges of the island. They cannot be sure what the other castaways will be prepared to do to ensure their own survival, and they have no authority to turn to, either to tell them what to do or to protect them from harm. This, again, is a negative account of their situation. However, I want to use tools from the tradition of state-of-nature theory to examine some positives we find in Lost's first season – positives the survivors could use to repair at least some damage to the social structure that the crash caused.

Lining up for Peace

Though in one sense (which Hume, the philosopher, was right about) the pure state of nature is just a philosopher's thought experiment, whose interest – if any – is only theoretical, there is also a sense (where Hume missed a trick) in which we do encounter partial, or as I shall say, "framed" states of nature all the time. Every time, in fact, the interests of various individuals are in potential conflict for some limited good.

Take, as a trivial example, the fact that, when I have filled my cart at the supermarket, my aim is to get out as quickly as I can. The same goes for all the other stressed-out cart-pushers. Each of us wants the immediate attention of the cashier, but there are only three cashiers open and fifteen loads of shopping to be paid for. In the words of Thomas Hobbes (1588–1679), one of the earliest modern theorists of states of nature, the fifteen shoppers are in a condition of "war, where every man is enemy to every man."[1] The surprising thing, then, is that, given the Hobbesian diagnosis, massacres at the supermarket checkout are fairly rare. What each of the fifteen normally relies on is the expectation that the other fourteen will follow the usual practice and form lines. This practice creates a "frame" within which the conflict among the shoppers isn't exactly resolved, but is at least kept under control. I still want to get out as quickly as I can and so do the others, but we all recognize a procedure for reducing the likelihood of violence. Somewhat less rare than

---

[1] We modernize the spelling and cite in brackets the pages (here p. 89) of Richard Tuck's edition of Hobbes's *Leviathan* (1651) (Cambridge: Cambridge University Press, 1991).

supermarket massacres are those people who don't merely wish the others weren't there, but act as if they weren't (or ignore the item limit on the express lane). If anything, it is these people who might deserve just a splash of bloodshed.

With this trivial example, we can get a measure of the purity or severity of a state of nature. Because getting out of the supermarket in two minutes rather than ten doesn't make a great deal of difference to my life, the other shoppers are my "enemies" only to the value of eight minutes of mortality (which I'd set aside in the first place when I decided to go shopping). Hence, the principle: *the more vital or scarcer the good that is the object of conflict, the purer and more severe the state of nature.* And because I can be pretty confident that others will abide by the norms for forming lines, even the shoppers in front of me are in a sense also my allies because, by doing what's expected of them, they make shopping that bit less stressful for everyone. Hence, the principle: *the fewer or weaker (that is, the less likely to be observed) the frames, the purer and more severe the state of nature.*

In these terms, we can see that the survivors on *Lost* do find themselves in a pretty severe state of nature, because among the goods that they are no longer guaranteed by the society from which they are now isolated are the means of basic survival, and because it is hard for them to tell in advance what frames, if any, will apply to the distribution of those goods. The question, then, is: What can they do to reduce the severity of the state of nature? On the one hand, this is a question about the procurement of the means of survival; but perhaps more crucially it has to do with the way each of the survivors can come to trust the others not to make things worse.

Human Nature and Natural Man

One major question on which state-of-nature theorists have disagreed is whether, to understand the emergence of a society, we have to take a position on the very nature of mankind. Any effort to answer the question of "human nature" can easily lead to arguing in circles ("Man is by nature such-and-such because that's what he's like in a state of nature; so in a state of nature he's such-and-such"). But two sorts of stands have emerged about how to think of humanity in the raw.

Jean-Jacques Rousseau, for instance, is credited with thinking that, by nature, man is a compassionate and altruistic creature, and, hence, that the state of nature offers an ideal against which the corruptions of society can be measured.[2] In this direction, Rousseau – and with him others like David Hume – would say that humans are actuated by benevolent passions, while, for instance, Locke (the philosopher) would say that **reason** guides our behavior.[3] Let's call Rousseau's attitude "Innocence" (a key term in his *Discourse*; see p. 91).

---

[2] Generally, this attribution is made on the basis of his *Discourse on the Origin of Inequality* (1755), trans. G. D. H. Cole and others, in *Social Contract and Discourses* (London: Dent, 1973).

[3] See his second *Treatise on Government* (1690) of which the standard critical text was edited by Peter Laslett (Cambridge: Cambridge University Press, 1960); we give in brackets the paragraph numbers that are common to every edition (here §§4–15).

On the other hand, Hobbes is generally interpreted as regarding man as wholly egoistical and suspicious of his fellows.[4] This, as we shall see, is not a necessary part of his theory. Instead of referring to the historical Hobbes, we can say that the view opposed to Rousseau's would be one according to which people always operate on the motto adopted by Special Agent Fox Mulder: "Trust no one" or, rather, "Trust No. 1," which phrase we may use as a summary of the attitude in question. This is the attitude that I would quickly adopt in a state of nature like the one we can see in Danny Boyle's 2003 film *28 Days Later*, where everyone we meet should be suspected of being infected with aggressive rabies.

"Innocence" and "Trust No. 1" are labels for what are claimed to be the basic orientations of human beings, which would be given free rein in a situation where the norms of communal living have come unstuck. It may be that one or the other is a true description of what *would* happen in those circumstances (of which, as I've said, we have little direct knowledge). Perhaps Innocence is not a wildly inaccurate description of how Hurley and Jack behave, and Trust No. 1 is not a wildly inaccurate description of how Sawyer and Locke (the outdoorsman, not the philosopher) behave. But I, at least, don't claim to know that either is true of human beings in general and I think we can get on perfectly well without them in understanding the interactions on the island. Indeed, I think that we can understand the state of nature *better* if we are not hampered by a speculative theory about the "nature" of the people in it, beyond recognizing that, as animals, they need such things as food, drink, and protection.

Amid the Wreckage

In the immediate aftermath of the crash, the plane is the survivors' source of food and drink. So long as they believe that they will be rescued soon, they can consume these without second thoughts.

After about a week, though, Hurley discovers that someone has taken some bottles of fresh water leaving only 18 for the rest. Hurley's intuitive – and accurate – analysis is that the others would "freak out" if they knew ("White Rabbit"). They would freak out because each individual wants for himself as much of the limited good (water) as he can get, while knowing that the more he takes, the less there will be in the long run for everybody, himself included.

Unlike the supermarket, where my access to a limited good (the attention of the cashier) doesn't reduce the total amount of that good available to all (at least until closing time), water is a good precisely when it is consumed: every drop I drink is a drop less to go round all the others who have some claim on it. Situations

---

[4] Hobbes argues most explicitly against Aristotle's view that man is by nature a social animal (*zoon politikon*: *Politics*, I, ii, 1253a3) in the first chapter of *De Cive* (first published 1642), ed. Howard Warrender (Oxford: Oxford University Press, 1983) and especially in the footnotes added to the second edition (1647).

of this sort are a special case of the state of nature, and are known as "tragedies of the commons."[5]

Charlie suggests rationing as a resolution to the water tragedy. That is, each survivor must reduce their own consumption to allow all to have at least a minimum. But this requires everyone to subordinate their own interests to that of a group that is only just forming. Each can ask: "Why should I give up my water to people I don't know or care about?" The tragedy here is that it is very hard to answer that question, which would only be put by someone who doesn't recognize group survival as a good over and above their own.

Jack refuses to decide anything about how to distribute the water, because he too is in the same situation as the others and – quite apart from his "daddy issues" – has no authority to impose rationing. In a fit of optimism to minimize the theft from the group's common property, Sawyer tells Kate that "water has no value, Freckles; it's gonna rain sooner or later" ("White Rabbit"). He's surely right that when there is enough water to go round, no one needs to privatize it. But it's the possibility of a "later" that comes after the castaways have all died of thirst that makes the tragedy urgent.

When Jack is led to discover the stream of fresh water later in the same episode, and the survivors get the knack of hunting and fishing, they are no longer in tragic conflict with each other for vital goods. Because none of the other survivors is a threat to the survival of each of them, there is no reason not to group together. Because his immediate needs can be met, even Locke (the outdoorsman) can socialize with the others, though this is a matter of preference or temperament; if Sawyer shuns the company of the others on the beach, that does nobody any harm. And because each can look after himself, there is no need to plan for more than the time being, and no need for any of them to make any sacrifice for a common purpose, for instance in making an effort to get off the island.

This condition of minimal bodily security corresponds to the core of what Locke (the philosopher) had in mind in talking about a state of nature. There is no constituted government; all humans are equal and independent (second *Treatise*, §4); and everyone has the right not only not to be harmed "in his life, health, liberty or possessions" (§6), but also to take and use the things they find around them so long as there is "enough and as good" left for the others (§27).

The Longer Haul

While the survivors of Flight 815 have been lucky in the climate and the availability of food and drink, there are several categories of goods that, like, for instance, clothing, they don't have the means or skill to make for themselves, but that,

---

[5] The label is due to Garrett Hardin; see his 'The Tragedy of the Commons," *Science* 162 (1968), pp. 1243–1248. Situations of similar sorts have been envisaged ever since Plato; see *Protagoras*, 321C–323C.

unlike clothing, are in short supply. One case here would be Sawyer's cigarettes. If he is the only smoker, then the fact that he cannot renew his supply is a problem only for him (apart from Charlie, who also has a problem getting his drugs). Likewise with Shannon's toenail varnish: no one else wants a pedicure ("1st Pilot"), so her using it causes no one else any upset (apart from the irritation factor for Boone).

Things are a bit different when it comes to medicine. We have here the making of a tragedy of the commons that the survivors are not in a position to resolve.

In the first days on the beach, Jack takes it for granted that he is authorized to use all the antibiotics he can find on the plane to treat Marshal Mars. Here, he must be supposing that their stay on the island is temporary and that the immediate use of the drugs is the only reasonable course of action to try and save a life. If, however, he had thought that they were going to be stranded indefinitely, it is not clear that using up what there is in trying (and failing) to heal one severely injured man would be the best line to take in the long run. After all, the drugs could be of more benefit to more people if spread over more, and more curable, cases. As Sawyer says, Jack may not be "looking at the Big Picture, Doc" ("Tabula Rasa"). We can keep that problem of medical ethics on hold, while allowing that Jack did well to go through the luggage of the other passengers and take all the stuff ending in "-myacin" and "-cillin" ("2nd Pilot"). That is, even if the antibiotics count as the common property of all the survivors, because only Jack knows how to use them, he should be given control of them for the benefit of those who need them.

Unlike her varnish, Shannon is not the only one who lays a claim to her anti-asthma inhalers. Her claim is twofold. One, that she (or rather Boone on her behalf) brought the refills with her; presumably, she paid for them and thus has what we might call a legal property right to them. Two, that her health depends on them; she is the only asthmatic on the island and thus has what we might call a moral priority in their proper use. The trouble arises from Sawyer's having taken some of the contents of Boone's suitcase, such as his copy of *Watership Down* ("Moth"). If the luggage of those who died can be rifled for clothes and for antibiotics without injustice (when Kate takes the walking shoes off the corpse to make the expedition to find the plane's cockpit in "1st Pilot," she isn't *stealing*), why not also that of the survivors? Isn't it all just luggage and so fair game?

When Jack confronts him, Sawyer brazens it out saying that, on the beach, "possession is nine tenths," meaning "of the law," where the law is "finders keepers" ("Confidence Man"). And this explains why he brushes off Jack's accusation of "looting" the fuselage in "Tabula Rasa." Though he doesn't say what the other tenth of the law is, Sawyer is standing up for the idea that, in a state of nature, it's every man for himself, a clear instance of his Trust No. 1 attitude. As Hobbes puts it, "if any two men desire the same thing, which nevertheless they cannot both enjoy, they become enemies" (*Leviathan*, p. 87). This means that the past property relation that Shannon enjoyed towards the inhalers is nullified by the new circumstances. Her legal right no longer counts because there is no constituted authority (like the police or law courts) to enforce it; and Sawyer is not obliged to recognize her moral claim, any more than in "1st Pilot" Hurley is *obliged* to give an extra portion of food to Claire because she is eating for two (though he does so out of Innocence).

Faced with Sawyer's refusal to "do the right thing" (and assuming, rightly or wrongly, that he has the inhalers), Sayid and Jack take it upon themselves to defend Shannon's cause by capturing and torturing Sawyer ("Confidence Man"). In so doing, they are beginning to move away from the Lockean state of nature towards a position in which legal and moral claims can be enforced and the use of violence (an infringement of the right not to be harmed in one's health) can be justified. Jack and Sayid are not acting in *self*-defense, but are seeking to defend the rights of others, which is a different concept altogether: that of punishment. In doing so, they are on the way to constituting what Locke calls "a civil society" (*Treatise*, §§77ff.) – of sorts.

Over or Under the Language Barrier

Neither Sayid nor Jack is stronger than Sawyer, but together and using stealth (they attack him while he is napping) they can get the better of him. This is what Hobbes calls the "equality of ability": "the weakest has strength enough to kill the strongest, either by secret machination, or by confederacy with others" (*Leviathan*, p. 87). The association between Sayid and Jack requires them to trust each other for the purposes of getting information out of Sawyer about where the inhalers are hidden.

There are two obvious conditions for their being able to reach such an agreement. One is that they already agree on Shannon's claim – legal or moral or both – to the inhalers. And the other is that they understand each other, that they share a language. This is also a condition for their being able to get information out of Sawyer: Sayid would be a useless torturer if he couldn't put the questions and get the answers. The fact that the overwhelming majority of the passengers on Flight 815 are speakers of English, as a first or second language, means both that they can share information and that they can lie to each other.

Jin is the exception: he can communicate only with Sun. As soon as they arrive on the island, Jin reaffirms their previous asymmetrical relationship (marriage), with him giving the orders and her taking them, because, at that point, he believes that she is not in a position to talk to the others ("1st Pilot"). The pair keeps a distance from the wreckage, so Jin is the first to seek food from the sea. There are two possible interpretations of what he does after filleting the strange orange creature he has fished out of the water ("2nd Pilot").

On one interpretation, rather than try the food himself, Jin seeks guinea pigs for their edibility. On this account, he doesn't care what happens to them because they are not a part of any association that he recognizes as binding on him. Jin would thus be applying Trust No. 1. Even though Hurley tends towards the accepting attitude of Innocence, he declines the offer not just because he prefers airline snacks – or even hunger – to "natural" food, but also perhaps because he's not sure of Jin's motives.

On the other interpretation – taking into account the fishing community he comes from – Jin can be understood as trying to overcome the language barrier by making a move that is universally recognized as a peace overture. Indeed, the offer of food convinces Claire of Jin's inclination towards Innocence.

Confidence and the Con Men

Even if a shared language is *necessary* for generating the higher grades of trust and cooperation, it is not *sufficient*.

On the one hand, we might think about the suspicions got up by Walt's discovery in "2nd Pilot" of the handcuffs in the jungle. The cuffs mean there is at least one person on the island who was regarded as a criminal and who, therefore, might still be dangerous. When, later in the same episode, Sawyer accuses Sayid of being a terrorist, he backs it up with the allegation that Sayid was sitting with his arms covered at the back of Business Class and never moved out of his seat. The others present at the scene can't tell whether Sawyer really saw what he says he did, but they are given some reason for thinking that it was Sayid who was wearing the handcuffs. What they don't know – but we do – is that Sawyer is a professional liar and, as we have already seen, motivated by Trust No. 1.

On the other hand, there is Marshal Mars's warning to Jack that he should not trust Kate ("Tabula Rasa"). Jack can be pretty sure that a man – and a US marshal at that – on his deathbed will be speaking the truth; but he still does not heed his words. We can distinguish two aspects of this. One is that he trusts his own feelings more than Mars's information. For sure, Jack recognizes that he doesn't know whatever it is that the Marshal knows about Kate's past, but he doesn't want to think the worse of a person who has so far behaved with fortitude and in the interests of all (not only in helping him sew up his own wound on their first meeting ("1st Pilot"), but in dismantling and distributing the parts of the pistol, making a monopoly on its use impossible for any one individual ("2nd Pilot")). The other point – and this is a crucial feature of a situation in which people don't have background knowledge of one another – is that it is the "island of second chances." As far as Jack is concerned, Kate is free to wipe the slate clean: there is a presumption of Innocence. In "Tabula Rasa," he repeatedly says things like "it doesn't matter who we were" and "it's none of our business."

We might pick up a hint of uncertainty here about the relations between "before" and "after" the crash. If, in addition to her moral claim in virtue of being asthmatic, Jack defends Shannon's property right as a leftover from the society from which the survivors have been isolated, he seems not to think that Kate's criminal record has any value without the criminal system that keeps it.

Roles and Rules

What Jack himself undoubtedly carries over from his life before the downing of 815 is the fact of being a medical doctor. Equally obviously, he doesn't carry with him his degree certificates, and there is no authority on the island to license his practice of the Hippocratic art. By contrast, Arzt asks the others to address him as "Doctor," though he is in reality a schoolteacher. (The apparent title may be regarded as no more than a nickname understandable to someone who knows a bit of German.) It is the fact that Jack has acquired skills that makes him a doctor and, so, as Sawyer ironically puts it, "a hero" ("2nd Pilot") or, in Boone's challenge, "our savior" ("White Rabbit").

As we saw with the antibiotics, Jack's expertise confers rights; but it also carries with it the duties of a doctor and it is up to him more than to anyone else to do what he can for the injured. When Sawyer fails to put Mars out of his misery with his one bullet ("Tabula Rasa"), Jack must act, as he had refused to act before, and put an end to his patient. In this case, his role as doctor means that he must break the rules that apply off the island and save Mars from an agonizing death that could not otherwise be avoided with the resources available. Another nice dilemma for the medical ethicists, but a clear case of the special responsibility of doctors to decide.

Though the previous occupations of most of those on the island have little bearing on how they interact, the crash itself produces a category to which they all belong: that of "survivor." As Hurley says in "2nd Pilot," "we're all in this together." To get a bit clearer who "we" are, he sets himself to compile his census, trying to find out from each of them where they come from and what they were doing on the flight. When he and Boone compare the resulting list with the flight manifest, they discover that the man who calls himself Ethan Rom was not on 815. This is clear confirmation that the island is not as deserted as it at first seemed, and means that the 46 who have been trying to get to know each other now face a potential external threat: there's an "us" and a "them," the Others.

The immediate effect of this discovery is to bind the survivors together, and Locke (the outdoorsman), who had previously stuck to his motto "you can't tell me what I can't do" (first announced in "Walkabout"), now becomes a defender of the group's integrity, organizing a search party to rescue Claire from the man who has abducted her and who is now definitely not one of us. Here, his knowledge of the jungle gives him the right to give orders to his comrades. As Locke (the philosopher) puts it, the survivors determine to "act as one body" (§96). This is the moment at which we witness the birth of what can properly be called a "commonwealth" (§§122ff.), in which, by the consent of its members, roles can be established and rules can be laid down for the good of all those included.

Tit-for-Tat

So far, we have been running a counterpoint between the causes of conflict in a state of nature and the means of its resolution. I want to conclude by illustrating briefly a general ground for thinking that it is the condition of initial conflict that really matters to how a state of nature turns out.

Take any situation in which two people can either cooperate with each other or not in some enterprise, and suppose (1) that, if they each cooperate with the other, then they will both get the optimum result; (2) that, if they both refuse to cooperate, they will go without the full benefit but are not much worse off; and (3) that, if one cooperates and the other doesn't, the non-cooperator gets a less than optimum result, but still better than if they had both refused, and the cooperator gets the worst outcome.

This sort of situation is easily illustrated, for instance in Sandra Bullock's 2002 film *Murder by Numbers*, by the case of two suspects in a crime, to each of whom the police offer a deal so long as he is the only one to denounce the other, though the police don't have evidence enough to convict either unless at least one suspect sings. For this reason, the choice between cooperating or not is called a "**prisoners' dilemma**." It's worth stressing both that the "cooperating" is as between the suspects (that is, not squealing), not a matter of their helping the police; and that there is no limit to the number of players who can be involved in such situations – even 46, as on the island.

What makes the prisoners' dilemma a dilemma is that the suspects don't know for sure what the other one has done or is going to do. While Trust No. 1 would indicate non-cooperation to avoid the worst case for me (that in which I cooperate and the other doesn't), Innocence would go for cooperation out of fellow feeling at the risk of coming off worst. But neither option is particularly convincing as it stands, and it would be crazy to rely on some theory of "human nature" to decide what to do if you might go without the basics of survival or go to jail for twenty years rather than walk free. The craziness is most obvious when the dilemma is repeated more than once and involves the same people over again. In that case, the thing to do is consider what the other did last time and act accordingly.

What does *accordingly* mean here? Well, there is a strategy that has been shown to do better than any other over the long run and that has been called "tit-for-tat," which, as its name suggests, says that you begin by offering cooperation and, after that, you should do whatever the other did last time round: if she didn't cooperate, you shouldn't; if she did, you should too. If she, too, is running tit-for-tat then, given that you both begin by cooperating, you should both continue getting optimum results.

Gaining Trust from the Past

The reason why I didn't want to attribute Trust No. 1 to Hobbes is that I think that chapter 13 of *Leviathan* – the one from which I've been quoting – envisages a situation in which a previous society has fallen apart by violence (for instance, the plague of *28 Days Later* or a civil war), and the first move everyone makes is to withdraw cooperation. In this sense, a Hobbesian state of nature begins at the second round of a repeated prisoners' dilemma. Because the first round was non-cooperative, it is not a winning strategy for people to start cooperating.

For this reason, I suggest that everything in *Leviathan* that comes after chapter 13 – with all the famous stuff about natural laws, social contracts, sovereign "leviathans" and the rest – is wildly misleading: once you're in a Hobbesian state of nature, you're a goner. Hobbes might have half-seen the problem, which is why, at the end of chapter 14, he puts in the idea of an "oath," sworn before God to reinforce the contract (*Leviathan*, pp. 99–100). But this is no solution at all; among other things, why should God be so bothered about having his name taken in vain, when there's so much other mayhem in the state of nature and all the other Commandments (except perhaps the one about graven images) have been broken? Though I know that this is not a popular interpretation of the book, it might explain why virtually no one can be bothered to read all the remaining 400 pages of text.

With the same people in it and with the same tendencies to diffidence or to trust as in a Hobbesian state of nature (second round), a Lockean state of nature has to begin with a first round of tit-for-tat and can only explain a breakdown of cooperation by the unreasonableness of some of the people some of the time. If the difference between Hobbes and Locke on the state of nature can be seen in the light of the point reached in a repeated prisoners' dilemma, then the relations among the survivors in *Lost* can be understood in terms of how closely their behavior is modeled on tit-for-tat.

In short, if the survivors can begin trusting each other, they can reasonably adopt more successful strategies than those that might be based on some merely suppositious theory of human nature, whether Innocence or Trust No. 1. By doing so, they can get a community off the ground so as to handle the shortages of some goods (tragedies of the commons) and to coordinate the security of all (Lockean on the inside and Hobbesian towards the outside) against the Others and whatever else is out there.

26

Laughter Between Distraction and Awakening

Marxist Themes in The Office

Michael Bray

Summary

A common observation about the American version of *The Office* is that, unlike the British show, it downplays issues of social class. This chapter argues, rather, that it provides a portrait of a peculiar – but ever-increasing – form of class identity that is expressed in the very denial of the importance of class. The chapter situates "the office" as a site of labor in relation to Marx's reading of capitalism, as well as emendations made to that reading to explain the rise of consumer society and "the salaried masses." It also tries to explain why *The Office* is (and isn't) funny.

The Class That Dare Not Speak Its Name

America doesn't seem to care about class. Why care, when there no longer appear to be classes? And, if a recent article in *The New Yorker* is to be believed, the "American *Office* doesn't care about class" either. The British *Office*, on the other hand, "was a pitiless meditation on rules and class,"[1] but the American version focuses instead on the quirks of individual personalities and their efforts to escape the tedium of an unrewarding workplace. "The reason that bosses become blustery martinets is that any sensible employee at a place like Dunder-Mifflin would rather play video games or gossip than tutor clients in the manifold varieties of copy paper" (Friend, 98). In place of bitterness and anger boiling forever just under the surface, Americans have more genuine work-effort and more genuine camaraderie, if also no less genuine despair – albeit the kind born from boredom, not class position.

As a sketch of the difference in tone between the two series, American and British, this is certainly a decent start. No doubt, the British *Office* has an edgier tone,

---

[1] Tad Friend, "The Paper Chase: Office Life in Two Worlds," *The New Yorker* (December 11, 2006), p. 96. Quoted subsequently as (Friend, page number).

precisely because David Brent has so much anger and resentment boiling just beneath his management-speak, an anger not only against those whose economic position is above his but also against women. Brent, for example, attempts to manage his own insecurity relative to the college-educated temp by a series of put-downs, insults, and dismissals, as well as desperate efforts to prove his knowledge. On the other hand, when Michael Scott, the boss in the American series, finds out that Ryan, his temp, is planning to go to business school, instead of resenting him, he falls a little in love. But such differences in tone don't mean that the American series "doesn't care about class," at least not if that is meant to imply that the American version fails to register, or under-plays, the significance of economic structures. The tedium and despair that haunt the American version, along with the quirky hopes and discomforts that animate its characters, are themselves the marked features of a peculiar class (once called "the salaried masses")[2] in a peculiar situation (that of twenty-first-century America, where class, while no less objectively present, has become largely unnamable, unthinkable).

The American *Office* presents a class that is ironically characterized by its disbelief in classes – a class whose self-image is grounded in the denial of a difference between them and the classes above. The middle is everywhere.

Reading Marx at Work

The daily world of most Americans doesn't look much like the one that philosopher and economist Karl Marx (1818–83) prophesied: a world in which an ever-more impoverished class of manufacturing laborers would be driven, ultimately, by their own radical needs, to social revolution. Over the course of the twentieth century, the old-style "proletariat" has become a much smaller percentage of the American workforce, surpassed by seemingly endless waves of office and service industry workers. Thus, the clear **dualism** that underlay Marx's reading of modern society – the antagonism between the capitalists, who own the means of production, and the working class, which owns nothing but its own labor – seems to vanish into a mass of workers of different grades, positions, and powers. There are Pams, Jims, Dwights, Michaels, Jans, and Roys, whose identities seem to be grounded, not in the form of their labor, but in what they like, what they wear, and how they look; in other words, what they consume.

In place of the revolution of the world's working class, then, we got an apparently ever-expanding consumer society. But, despite what seems like Marx's fundamental error here, his theory actually provides tools for understanding this trajectory. On Marx's own analysis, after all, the accumulation of capital is a process that drives

---

[2] See Siegfried Kracauer, *The Salaried Masses: Duty and Distraction in Weimar Germany*, trans. Quintin Hoare (New York: Verso, 1998). Quoted subsequently as (Kracauer, page number). This book was written in 1930s Germany as an effort to understand the rise of the new class of office workers, salespeople, etc., the character of their labor, and the illusions they foster.

towards ever-greater expansion. Indeed, capital *only is capital* insofar as the process of its production and exchange yields a surplus beyond what was initially invested.[3] Capital is money invested in the production of commodities in order to yield *more* money. When it comes down to it, before everything else, the economy must grow – money must be made into more money (in the form of profits that fall mostly into the hands of a small elite) – or the economy will collapse. Of course, in order to continue to grow, the economy needs people to buy things. So, you might say, *since there was not a revolution*, then an expanding consumer society became necessary. But, Marx insists, it is the endless pursuit of money, surplus, and profit, rather than a rational grasp of the needs of individuals and of society as a whole, that defines capitalism as an economic form.

One of the defining elements of Michael Scott's character lies in his failure to properly implement his functions as manager in pursuing this **logic**. In David Brent's mouth, the constant invocations of how, in business, "it's the people that matter," is empty management-speak. In Michael's mouth, such proclamations appear as distorted but genuinely meant. Michael doesn't know what "people" are exactly, what they might want, how they should be treated, or how they should live. (Like David, Michael doesn't know any form of life other than the pursuit of success and ease that he can't himself embody.) But when Michael says it's the people that matter, he means it. Thus, as Jim observes when the manager of the Stamford branch leverages his promotion into a new job with Staples: "You can say what you want about Michael Scott, but he would *never* do that" ("Branch Closing").

And what is the proper function of the manager in a capitalist system? To generate profit – or, as Marx calls it, "surplus value." But the manager doesn't do this (at least, not most of the time) by tricking customers or overcharging other corporations. Managers, rather, spend most of their time overseeing, shaping, and controlling the work time and work processes of employees. At the very core of surplus value, then, is control and exploitation of those workers. This is why Michael constantly finds himself unable to do what corporate asks of him.

The key to the production of surplus value is labor. A commodity, in capitalism, gains value from the *amount* of labor-time it takes an average laborer to produce the commodity (thus, the value of paper produced in a paper mill is *less* than that produced by hand, since it takes less time to produce). The value of a laborer's day – her wage – is determined in the same manner, Marx argues. The value of a day's labor is equivalent to the value of goods required to *reproduce* that day's labor (so it is equivalent to the value of food, shelter, clothing, and everything else needed to have a life and family in present society). But the value of the wage is *less* than the value that a worker's labor power can produce through a full day of employment. The worker *adds* value to the goods he works on, and he is not compensated for this addition (only for what it will take to reproduce the labor he expends). Thus,

---

[3]   This point, and the synopsis of Marx's views that follows, draws primarily on Marx, *Capital*, vol. 1, trans. Ben Fowkes (New York: Penguin, 1976). Quoted subsequently as (Marx, page number).

the capitalist, or corporation, generates surplus value by paying laborers less value than they produce. The capitalist, and capitalism, lives off the worker.

Running Out the Clock

To make labor more productive *and* easier to replace, it's useful to make machines do more and more, eliminating human skills required to do a particular job. Anyone can work on an assembly line or enter data into a computer – and if anyone can do it, *you* can be replaced very quickly. As the autonomy, independence, and responsibility of work decreases, the *images* of autonomy, independence, and fun offered up to the worker by the world of advertising and consumption increase. Various modes of distraction must be introduced to keep people from reflecting on their real conditions. Thus, Jan, the representative of corporate, during her "Women in the Workplace" seminar, tells the women of the office to "dress for the job you want, not the job you have" ("Boys and Girls"). The women are disappointed, however, not to be able to talk about the clothes they like. "They devote themselves to an individualism that would be justified only if they could shape their fate as individuals" (Kracauer, 81). The joke is that neither dressing like Jan, nor as they like, will give most of them the real power to shape that fate.

Indeed, the irony of capitalism, for Marx, is that its own logic drives it to produce ever-more commodities but *never* to alter for the better the character of the labor, the work, in which most people spend most of their lives. There is a direct line from the famous pin factory in Adam Smith's *Wealth of Nations*, where one man spends his entire time doing nothing but making the heads of pins, through Henry Ford's Model T assembly line, to the advanced robotics employed in many factories today. Each such advance raises the productivity of labor and, thereby, increases the amount of surplus value generated. But each such advance also tends to render more repetitive, empty, and meaningless the actions done, all day long, by the individual workers. And *no* such advance liberates human beings from the need to work all day long, precisely because the production of value, as the measure of capital, is grounded in human labor-time. "The machine does not free the worker from work, but rather deprives the work itself of all content" (Marx, 548). Instead, new positions, new spheres of production are constantly opened up by capital and by corporations that constantly shift production, expand into new markets, and so on. In place of free time, workers gain, if anything, new things to purchase. That the accumulated knowledge, science, and technology does not free human beings from labor – that it, in fact, tends to reduce the majority of laborers to a kind of empty, repetitive labor that neither sustains nor develops their abilities – is, for Marx, one of the cruelest **paradoxes** of the capitalist world. On *The Office*, whatever meaning there is for the workers lies almost solely in interpersonal relationships, if it even lies there. "I wouldn't want to work here if Pam left," Roy observes. "Then it would just be unloading trucks without meaning" ("Branch Closing"). Pam's interest in art is sometimes seen as a possible source of greater meaning but, the show makes clear, even her art suffers from the deadening, empty routine of her career.[4] For her school art show she paints the objects around her – a coffee cup, the office-building, a stapler – in tepid watercolors ("Business School"). Despite themselves, workers become little more than "appendages" of the machines they serve and their drive to develop their capacities, to become "full" human beings is often thwarted.

Jim routinely notes the emptiness of his work, which is sometimes played off as a consequence of selling *paper*, but is often a more general statement on the very character of such sales work in general. Indeed, the ever-greater organization, or "rationalization," of labor didn't only transform and degrade the work-process of the manual laborer. As corporations grow, they have more and more data to process, more and more sales to oversee, and more and more services to provide. And so office labor becomes just as divided and planned as manual labor.[5] The worker cannot resist by working differently but only by not working, or working as little as possible. As when, visiting the warehouse (Michael's idea, of course) to get a taste of manual labor, Ryan – the business school student – proposes setting up an assembly line process for unloading a truck. Stanley rebuffs him: "This is a run-out-the-clock type of situation. Just like upstairs" ("Boys and Girls"). They keep taking the boxes one by one.

Downsizing Dreams

For every Dunder-Mifflin, there is a Staples, Office Max, or Office Depot looking to buy and liquidate it. This is the economic world that forms the backdrop for the series – which appears, most commonly, in the form of concerns about downsizing. "The existential insecurity of salaried staff has increased . . . and their prospect of independence has almost entirely disappeared" (Kracauer, 30). But although most forms of "mental" or "white collar" labor have ceased to involve initiative, autonomy, or control, the self-image of the workers involved *depends* on them not recognizing that this is so. **Belief** is sustained not by belief in what one is but by belief that, at least, one is *not* something else. The self-image of these salaried masses, these office workers, lies in their insisting, more or less unconsciously, on a fundamental difference between themselves and those workers who still carry on more traditional forms of proletarian labor, as well as anyone else who can be marked out as unprofessional. Such differences are found in everything from receiving a salary instead of a wage, to wearing a tie or jacket instead of a shirt with your first name

---

[4]   The idea that art could provide a richer, fuller model for individual life amid the deadening fragmentation of mechanized divisions of labor goes back at least to 1790 and Friedrich Schiller's *On the Aesthetic Education of Man*, trans. Elizabeth M. Wilkinson and L. A. Willoughby (Oxford: Oxford University Press, 1967).

[5]   For a full account of the changed character of manual and office work in the twentieth century, see Harry Braverman, *Labor and Monopoly Capital: The Degradation of Work in the Twentieth Century* (New York: Monthly Review Press, 1976).

on it, to working in the office rather than the basement, to holding on to certain ideals and beliefs that grow farther and farther away from the reality of your life.

Much of the comedy of *The Office* revolves around just such short-circuits between characters' self-images and their realities, as well as the subtle terror at play in professions in which one's image is, quite literally, one's worth. Michael is less "the boss from hell" than he is a man trapped in the space between decaying ideals and the reality of his own work and life, where little is left to him but to pass down corporate directives, to implement cost-cutting schemes, and to make more or less desperate bids at self-determination. Sometimes the show is at its best just when it is at its least funny, when it makes you feel quite strikingly the pain and anxiety of occupying that gap, when it makes you wonder if you aren't just a little like Michael Scott yourself. The show is at its best when it awakens us to the *experience* of class, in a way that most of our lives (and most of our entertainment) are designed to deny and to distract us from.

Take a few instances from the show, not quite at random: first, in the moment alluded to previously, Michael talks to Ryan about his plans for business school. What do you want to do that for, Michael asks. Do you want to be a manager? Not really, Ryan answers, I want to own my business. "That's ridiculous," Michael explodes, ending the conversation ("The Fire"). The gap between his own position and Ryan's aspirations is too stark to be reflected on. That Ryan's own aspirations will likely fall short (he later becomes a permanent employee in the office) is merely another element of the show's recurring theme: the characters want out. They secretly long for downsizing, precisely because it would force them to try to *do* something – something that might be better. When it looks like the Scranton branch will be closed, Pam, Stanley, and Toby are all secretly thrilled. "It's a blessing in disguise," Pam says. "In fact, not even in disguise" ("Branch Closing"). Without downsizing, though, they know all too well the slim chances their lives hold of being different and so they stay. So, when the branch stays open, Pam sees things differently: "Maybe this is for the best. Finding another job is a pain. There's another annoying boss, another desk. I'd have to learn everything over again" ("Branch Closing"). Everything would be different, yet be exactly the same. Or, as Pam observes in another episode, "Dreams are just dreams. They help get you through the day" ("Boys and Girls").

In another episode, Michael leaves work, with Dwight in tow, to finalize his purchase of a condo, the first housing purchase he's ever made. Outside, on a street of closely built condos, Michael rhapsodizes about his "sanctuary and party-pad" and the swing he'll build out front for his grandchildren. Projecting himself into this traditional vision of middle-class life, he suddenly realizes that he's looking at the wrong condo. The salaried man's home is not his personalized sanctuary but a blank consumer item, indistinguishable from any other. There isn't really room for a tree-swing anyway. And even this grasp at the dreamed ideal comes at a stiff price. Inside, Michael insists that although the condo's mortgage is more expensive than the rent of his current, larger apartment, nevertheless it's better, because he'll own it. "Diversifying," he says, in the language of the financial class he doesn't even understand. But, Dwight points out, with a 30-year mortgage, Michael won't be done paying off his purchase until he's in his 70s. "So much for retiring at 65," he tells Michael, who panics and tries to back out, until it becomes clear that he'll lose $7,000 if he does. "At Michael's age," Dwight observes in one of the show's talking heads shots, "buying is like buying a coffin" ("Office Olympics").

Finally, in an American episode written by the British creators, Ricky Gervais and Stephen Merchant, Michael finds out that a new worker, transferred from the closing Stamford branch, is an ex-convict. Martin, it turns out, has been in jail for insider trading. Prodded to describe what prison was like, he notes that, mostly, it was "doing the same thing every day" ("The Convict"), a comment that quickly draws comparison with the world of the office. Only, in prison, Martin admits, the convicts got two hours of "rec time" outside, water-color painting and business classes (taught by Harvard graduates), and a bigger TV than the lunch room has. Indignant, Michael defends the world of Dunder-Mifflin and, implicitly, himself: "People don't realize how lucky they are. This office is the American Dream and they would rather be in the Hole." The joke, of course, is that the distance between office and prison (white-collar prison, that is) genuinely seems a small one, no matter how much Toby reassures Michael that people really love the office.

What the American *Office* observes at moments like this is not so much the way in which class *doesn't matter* but the way in which it is both *denied* and *lived* by the people who occupy a strange, and ever-growing, place in the contemporary class system. The way that they try and fail to make their work meaningful; the way they try and fail to live lives outside of work that would express their freedom, independence, and individuality. These failures are not so much their fault as individuals as they are consequences of their social position. Michael *does* love the office, in his way, but as the show makes clear, only because his own identity is uncertain and unclear away from it. This is, of course, the joke on Michael, but it is also uncertain how much he really differs in this respect from any other members of the office, who remain superior to him (if they do) only through their skeptical distance from their situation. The secret the show keeps, openly enough, is that most office workers are probably more like Michael (or Dwight) than they are like Jim or Pam, who often seem to have wandered in from another setting, another milieu.[6]

So why is a show that exposes us to ourselves, and so unpleasantly, such a hit? How can it be that the salaried masses – so badly in need of distraction and glamour to mask the boredom of their work-lives (a boredom that, if not relieved, could lead to the critical thinking about capitalist society) – would come to find

---

[6] They may well be the stand-ins for the creators, writers, and producers, as well as elements of the audience, all of who may once have had a summer office job (or even one that went on for a year or two) while working on their screenplays or acting classes. Pam's passion for drawing is the most direct sign of this: the artist stands apart (in the creators' own dreams at least) from the emptying out of meaningful work. They are the onscreen stand-ins for the mock-documentary filmmakers who likewise stand apart from the office workers, "not trying to protect the characters," as Greg Daniels, the American producer puts it, during a commentary track, but "trying to expose them" ("Pilot").

humor in a stark presentation of the meaninglessness of their own social position? And how could it be that a media corporation would present such an image in place of its usual fare of distraction and glamour? Let me suggest the makings of an answer:

1   The routines of "rationalized" office labor have themselves become so common and durable that they can be presented, as laws of capitalism generally are, as a kind of fate to which individuals can only submit, such that comedy, here, borders on despair.
2   There are numerous aspects of *The Office* that work against its occasional stark-ness and, by doing so, suggest that individual autonomy and personality are still possible in "the office" (not only artistic ambitions but also the relationship story of Jim and Pam is key here, as well as the implication that Jim is more human, that is, more "cultured," than his manual-labor counterpart, Roy).[7]
3   At times, like in the examples given above, the tension between the show's despair and its gestures towards an actual humanity and happiness presents its most productive moments: demanding of and for its audience precisely the thing the real office cannot deliver. At such moments, the comedy, implicitly, demands a better mode of life for people, precisely by not denying their present conditions.

Of course, *The Office* is also damn funny – and in more ways than those just noted. Perhaps that is why *The Office* is itself an object of consumption. It plays similar roles to most such objects, offering hints of both distraction and an apparently mean-ingful identity. Yet, precisely by raising such aspects of contemporary life (almost) into focus, the show also seems to produce a certain tension with its setting and form. It exists in the same kind of gap between image and reality, between business and personhood, that it mines for comedy. The Marxist cultural critic Walter Benjamin once suggested that "authentic humanity" in modern society is located precisely in the tension between the two poles of professional and private life. If this is so, then Michael Scott, with all his gaffes, distortions, pretensions, and failures, may present an image of what is left today of "authentic humanity,"[8] the point from which any effort to alter conditions and people for the better would have to start thinking. "*People* will never go out of business," Michael asserts ("Business School"), and he means it, even if he doesn't know what it means. In failing to act in a professional manner at work, while failing, also, to find any other system of meaning or value to live by in his private life; in failing to use management-speak for its proper

---

[7]   Indeed, the fact that the show, at least in its American version, draws one of the most highly educated and wealthiest audiences in television suggests that it has another meaning: the opportunity to laugh at the pretensions of those beneath us.

[8]   For a compelling recent **argument** that such "humanity" is at the core of Marx's critique of capitalism, see Michael Lebowitz, *Beyond Capital: Marx's Political Economy of the Working Class* (New York: Palgrave MacMillan, 2003).

ends or to live by any code other than management-speak; in his almost childlike failure to come to terms with the world he lives in (as well as himself), Michael acts as a *critique* of that world. That his character is presented as almost childlike, infantilized, suggests the lengths one has to go to in order to still believe in the present system.[9] Recognizing the possibility of a more genuine critique would require the naming of the class and the economic structures that neither the show nor its characters ever quite name. The strangeness of the show, the "edginess" that people often observe in it, is precisely that it often stands on the very edge of such naming.

[9] Though this maintenance of belief more often takes an extremely negative form, as the British show suggests: after all, Michael's character, from another perspective, also presents a kind of "glamorization" of the class resentment that David Brent embodies. As David's character expresses, the more common (more realistic) response to the impotence and lack of autonomy that the working world represents is a kind of free-floating rage and resentment that has shown itself, at times, all too willing to side with authoritarian powers to deny its own suffering. Kracauer's concern, for example, writing in 1930s Germany was that the "salaried masses" would prove fertile ground for National Socialism. This was, in fact, the case.

27

The Ethics of Torture in *24*

Shockingly Banal

Dónal P. O'Mathúna

Summary

The characters in *24* enact and explain the major arguments for and against torture. Central to *24* is the ticking bomb scenario. This philosophical thought experiment adds drama and emotion to the ethics of torture. Yet the limits of fiction in ethics are also visible when torture in *24* is compared with actual accounts of torture. Popular culture provides a means of thinking through ethical dilemmas, but actual decisions must remain grounded in the real world.

Season Six of *24* opens with a shocking display of the results of torture. Our hero, Jack Bauer, has survived two years in a Chinese prison. The usually proud, defiant Jack shuffles slowly off a plane, shackled and bedraggled. A glimpse of his scarred back and hand reveals that he's been through something terrible. Later in the season, Audrey Raines also returns from Chinese custody. Torture has left her cowering, bruised, and battered – a broken woman.

Torture shocks us, which is one reason it's usually hard to justify. "Almost anyone looking at the physical act of torture would be immediately appalled and repulsed by the torturers."[1] Those who witness torture on *24* – even other counter-terrorism agents – usually express horror. Such reaction is typical and expected, which makes it disturbing when, in Season Two, President David Palmer fails to flinch as the screen on his desk shows Roger Stanton, Director of the National Security Agency, being tortured. Stanton screams as he is electrocuted barefoot in a bucket of water. The agent informs him the pain will only get worse, much worse. How could anyone inflict such pain on a fellow human being?

Ethics is concerned with how we treat one another. One approach called **deontology** says we should never act in ways that treat people as merely means towards our ends or goals. Torture certainly seems to do that: reducing people to mere means to get the information we want.

---

[1] Elaine Scarry, *The Body in Pain: The Making and Unmaking of the World* (Oxford: Oxford University Press, 1985), p. 35. Page references to Scarry are to this work.

Back at the airport, the Chinese are trading Jack to the Americans, who will in turn trade him to today's terrorists. Bill Buchanan, Jack's boss and friend, now Director of CTU (Counter Terrorist Unit), is told by the Chinese that for two years Jack has remained silent. Whatever torture they inflicted, it simply hasn't worked. It's done no good at all.

Utilitarianism, another approach to ethics, focuses on results. Something is ethically justified if it leads to good outcomes for lots of people: the greatest good for the greatest number in the long run. One utilitarian **argument** is that torture can be justified if it saves large numbers of people, or avoids much harm. So does torture work? Does it save large numbers of people?

Jack is to be handed over to the terrorist Abu Fayed who will give CTU vital information on Hamri Al-Assad's location. Assad has waged a 20-year war of terrorism on the US, and is believed to be behind a recent spate of suicide bombings on US soil. Fayed wants Jack so he can avenge his brother whom he says Jack tortured and killed in Beirut. Torture has long-term implications, leaving Fayed with a deep-seated hatred and desire for revenge.

A third approach to ethics, *virtue ethics*, looks at the impact of actions on people's characters, their virtues. War and violence change people, yet torture seems particularly destructive of individual character, and not only for the one tortured. Jack's torture begins with Fayed's aborted attempt to cut off Jack's fingers. What *kind* of person does such a thing? Well, Jack for one. Later we see Jack slice off the Russian consul's finger with a cigar cutter to find out where the suitcase bombs are located. In Season Two he refuses to give Marie Warner pain killers for her bullet wound. Instead, he pushes the bullet into her bone to force her to reveal where the nuke is hidden.

Yet Jack is the hero. He not only combats terrorism, he effectively navigates the moral morass around him. His moral compass is nearly always right – or at least so we like to think. If Jack sometimes resorts to torture, maybe there are good reasons for it.

Cultural Context of Torture

According to the United Nations' *Convention Against Torture and Other Cruel, Inhuman or Degrading Treatment or Punishment,* "No exceptional circumstances whatsoever, whether a state of war or a threat of war, internal political instability or any other public emergency, may be invoked as a justification of torture."[2] Signed by over 130 nations, this convention builds upon the three hundred year old ban on cruel and unusual punishments in the English Declaration of Rights and the two hundred year old ban in the US Constitution.[3] Only deviant totalitarian governments or terrorists carry out torture. Even if *they* use it, *we* shouldn't.

---

[2] Office of the High Commissioner for Human Rights, "Convention against Torture and Other Cruel, Inhuman or Degrading Treatment or Punishment," December 10, 1984, available online at www.unhchr.ch/html/menu3/b/h_cat39.htm.

[3] Michael Wilks, "A Stain on Medical Ethics," *The Lancet* 366 (August 2005): 429–31.

Military tradition supports the prohibition of torture. The nineteenth-century *Devising a Military Code of Conduct* states, "the modern law of war permits no longer the use of any violence against prisoners in order to extort the desired information or to punish them for having given false information."[4] This ethical position has deep roots. The Roman Cicero, the fifth-century Augustine, the fourteenth-century age of chivalry, and the *Military Code* see war as justified only if necessary to attain peace. The *Military Code* bans torture and cruelty because "military necessity does not include any act of hostility which makes the return to peace unnecessarily difficult" (TEW, 579). This is precisely the sort of hostility afflicting CTU agent Curtis Manning, who cannot overcome his hatred for Assad for having tortured and beheaded his comrades during the Gulf War. Tragically, Manning's hatred and desire for revenge forces Jack to shoot him, thus preserving Assad's life.

The world of *24* suggests that views about torture may have changed. Allegations arise regularly that the US and its allies permit the use of torture in the war on terror. Photographs of hooded detainees, naked prisoners cowering in the face of snarling dogs, and men standing with electrical wires dangling from their bodies, speak loudly of the reality of torture. In *24*, Mike Novick, President Palmer's Chief of Staff, claims death during torture is akin to accepting civilian casualties with bombings: "A few people may have to die to save millions."

Torture in *24* both reflects the way the world has become, but also makes it easier to accept torture in practice. A 2006 BBC News survey found that almost one-third of 27,000 people surveyed in 25 countries agreed that "Terrorists pose such an extreme threat that governments should now be allowed to use some degree of torture if it may gain information that saves innocent lives."[5] In the US, 36 percent held this view (although some have speculated that the cancelation of *24* might herald a decrease in that number), as did 43 percent in Israel, 42 percent in Iraq, 24 percent in Great Britain, and 14 percent in Italy. Countries facing political violence have a greater tendency to approve torture to prevent terrorist attacks. However, an overall majority in the world (59 percent) still favors an absolute ban, viewing torture as an inherently immoral activity that weakens respect for human rights.

Defining Torture

Torture is difficult to define precisely. Sometimes those being appropriately interrogated will claim they were tortured. And often those who truly torture will claim they were merely conducting a "coercive interrogation." Whether the distinctions are legitimate or euphemistic word-smithing has important consequences for detainees. In Season Five Christopher Henderson is clearly being tortured when he is strapped to a hospital bed and injected with hyoscine pentathol, an alleged

---

[4]   *The Ethics of War: Classic and Contemporary Readings*, ed. Gregory M. Reichberg, Henrik Syse, and Endre Begby (Oxford: Blackwell, 2006), p. 571. This work will be referred to herein as TEW.

[5]   "One-third support 'Some Torture'," *BBC News*, October 19, 2006, available online at www.news.bbc.co.uk/2/hi/in_depth/6063386.stm.

truth serum. Henderson is a disgraced agent suspected of being in league with terrorists. Typical of torture, Henderson is tied down, unable to fight back or defend himself. In this regard, one cannot help but think, too, of Roger Stanton, Marie Warner, and a host of others. Intense pain brings people close to losing consciousness and to the brink of death.

But of course *24* also presents us with situations in which pain is inflicted – say, during a fight or a shoot-out – but we wouldn't typically classify these as instances of torture. In such cases each person in the fight can at least defend themselves. Pain can also be inflicted for another's good as in some medical procedures. Torture inflicts pain for reasons that have nothing to do with the good of the one tortured.

Torture must also be distinguished from coercion. Jack initially pleads with Henderson to disclose his information. He tries various methods to coerce the information from him. Earlier in Season Five, terrorists "shot" hostages on live TV in an attempt to coerce the government to meet their demands. These acts are repulsive, but they do not constitute torture. Under coercion, someone still makes a rational decision to do what is demanded. Under torture, the pain obliterates rationality. The person will do or say anything for the pain to stop. Coercion seeks to get the person to go along with the appeal; torture seeks to break the person.

Torture starts when persuasion, bribery, or coercion fails (or is not even attempted). Torture targets autonomy itself, and tries to overwhelm the tortured person's rational control over his own decisions. It does so "by literally terrorizing them into submission. Hence there is a close affinity between terrorism and torture. Indeed, arguably torture is a terrorist tactic."[6] The torturer uses drugs, deprivation of normal sense perception, severe pain, confusion, or anything else to gain control over the person's whole being. The goal is not just information, but to "break the person." "The self-conscious aim of torture is to turn its victim into someone who is isolated, overwhelmed, terrorized, and humiliated. Torture aims to strip away from its victim all the qualities of human dignity that liberalism prizes."[7] David Sussman argues that "torture is uniquely 'barbaric' and 'inhuman': the most profound violation possible of the dignity of a human being."[8] The victim's body is made an object to be manipulated and controlled by the torturer and used against the person's will.

Part of the twisted nature of torture is how even the victim's emotions are turned against himself.[9] In Season Six, Morris O'Brian is tortured into arming the terrorists' nuclear devices. Jack expresses disbelief that Morris "gave in" and betrayed the cause. Morris is driven away, deeply ashamed, yet he was the one

---

[6]   Seumas Miller, "Torture," in *The Stanford Encyclopedia of Philosophy (Summer 2006 Edition)*, ed. Edward N. Zalta, available online at www.plato.stanford.edu/entries/torture.

[7]   David Luban, "Liberalism and the Unpleasant Question of Torture," *Virginia Law Review* 91 (2005): 1430. Page references to Luban are to this work.

[8]   David Sussman, "What's Wrong with Torture?" *Philosophy and Public Affairs* 33 (2005): 2.

[9]   The origin of the word "torture" comes from the idea of twisted, as in "tortuous"; torture was whatever left the body twisting uncontrollably.

deeply violated. Torture is not just a physical beating; it is a violent raping of a person's soul. Morris is then overwhelmed with guilt, especially when reminded of what he did. Studies show that those tortured are plagued for years with self-destructiveness, failure to reintegrate into their families, and an inability to take control of their lives.[10] Recovery is not easy when a torturer has used "the prisoner's aliveness to crush the things that he lives for" (Scarry, 38). Some survivors of torture have such psychological damage that they fail to ever return to normal, rational decision-making.

Thus torture usually involves some combination of the following: intentional infliction of extreme physical or psychological suffering; restriction of the person into a defenseless position; substantial curtailment of the exercise of a person's autonomy; manipulation of the person's sense of time and place; and an attack on the person's will, with a goal of breaking the person. Although we may have difficulty defining torture, it is clearly recognizable when encountered. Torture is very different from a physical beating or a manipulative deception. Torture goes deeper than the pain, which may tear the skin; torture seeks to tear the soul.

The reasons for torture vary, each raising different considerations.[11] Torture can be done for personal satisfaction, where the torturer is a sadist or psychopath. Torture can be used to terrorize people into submission, as some dictators have done. On *24*, the focus is on *interrogational torture*, where detainees are tortured to get information. Backward-looking interrogational torture tries to extract confessions from detainees about past activities. On *24*, we primarily see forward-looking interrogational torture, used to get information from detainees about a future event. People who argue that forward-looking interrogational torture is ethically justified will usually claim that the other uses of torture remain unethical.

Arguments for Torture

The torture scenes on *24* are an extended commentary on the main argument used to ethically justify torture: Henry Shue's classic "ticking bomb argument."[12] The innovative style of *24*, with its frenetic pace and action in "real" time, contributes to the continuous reminder that the clock is ticking. Time is always running out, and this has constant implications for what must be done. In Season Five, Homeland Security sends Karen Hayes and Miles Papazian into CTU to resolve their problems. Miles argues that Karen should authorize the torture of Audrey

---

[10] Robert Oravecz, Lilla Hárdi, and László Lajtai, "Social Transition, Exclusion, Shame and Humiliation," *Torture* 14 (2004): 4–15.
[11] Vittorio Bufacchi and Jean Maria Arrigo, "Torture, Terrorism and the State: A Refutation of the Ticking-Bomb Argument," *Journal of Applied Philosophy* 23 (2006): 360. Page references to Bufacchi and Arrigo are to this article.
[12] Henry Shue, "Torture," *Philosophy and Public Affairs* 7 (1978): 124–43. Page references to Shue (1978) are to this work.

Raines to gather information about the terrorists' nerve gas attack. Miles uses core aspects of the ticking bomb argument: "We don't have the luxury of time. Intel indicates that an attack is imminent – within an hour. Tens maybe hundreds of thousands of Americans are at risk. And we just got information that Audrey Raines knows about it."

The ticking bomb argument is basically a utilitarian argument. The good consequences of discovering the sought-after information outweigh the bad consequences of torture. Finding and diffusing the bomb prevents many deaths and injuries; the harm of inflicting pain on the bomber, of denying his dignity, of violating his rights, is a small price to pay in comparison. Nonetheless, Bill Buchanan defends Audrey, arguing that she deserves different treatment. Karen replies: "If she is guilty, she doesn't deserve anything." Implicit in the ticking bomb argument is the claim that people can lose their right not to be tortured when the consequences of not extracting their information are high enough.

Torture, however, is one of several strategies normally not accepted in Western liberal democracies. The war on terror has helped promote a new, very utilitarian political philosophy. In Season Five, we saw martial law introduced. Behind the scenes in Season Six, the rights of those with Middle Eastern or Muslim connections are curtailed. The seriousness of the terrorist threat justifies what wouldn't normally be tolerated. Chief of Staff Tom Lennox takes a very utilitarian approach to ethics, telling Karen Hayes, now National Security Advisor: "Security has its price. Just get used to it, Karen."

24 graphically and dramatically portrays the urgent need for torture and its apparent legitimacy. Modern law enforcement agencies are placed in difficult situations. Traditionally, such agencies dealt with crime after the fact and sought evidence for conviction. Rules dictate the searching and seizing of property and how confessions are obtained – if convictions are to result. But the mandate at CTU, and in the war against terror, changes this. Now the goal is to prevent terrorist attacks, and extracting information from captured suspects apparently can do much good. In Season Two, the terrorist leader Syed Ali is tortured into disclosing the location of the nuclear bomb. Under torture, Roger Stanton names the same location. *24* gives life to the ticking bomb argument.

Even when a bomb goes off, the argument gains support. We didn't see the horror, pain, and devastation of the nuclear blast in Season Six. The mushroom cloud over a modern city conveyed enough of the effect. If torture could have prevented the bomb, would that not be justification enough? Fritz Allhoff, a utilitarian who accepts this view, believes it is so obvious and rational that it does not need defending. "If anyone wants to disagree with the permissibility of torture in this [ticking bomb] case, I simply do not know what to do other than throw my hands up in exasperation." Any argument to the contrary he finds "hopelessly implausible."[13] Yet such arguments do exist, and several are dramatized throughout *24*.

[13] Fritz Allhoff, "A Defense of Torture: Separation of Cases, Ticking Time-bombs, and Moral Justification," *International Journal of Applied Philosophy* 19 (2005): 257–8.

Arguments Against Torture

The main argument against torture is that it treats human beings in undignified ways. Torture is not just painful; it is humiliating, degrading, and terrorizing. The person is treated as an object. When introducing his ticking bomb case, Shue admitted, "No other practice except slavery is so universally and unanimously condemned in law and human convention" (1978: 124).

Most people are shocked when they see, read, or think about what one person does to another during torture. Consider the people on *24* who writhe in pain as torture drugs flow through their veins. In Season Two, Jack screams into the bloody face of terrorist Syed Ali, and then reaches down and appears to break his fingers. In Season Six, Jack cuts off the Russian consul's finger to find out where the remaining suitcase nukes are located. These scenes elicit an emotional response which is itself part of the argument against torture. "If we treat someone in a way we generally find shocking, we do not treat her as a person – or, at least, we do not if we treat her that way against her will and without benefit to her."[14] Shock alone is not a sufficient argument, but it alerts us that something may be very wrong. Detainees are kept naked, cold, wet, hungry, or sleep deprived; some are forced to stand for days, their cells soaked with random noise, bright lights or darkness; others are placed in sexually degrading or other humiliating positions; their religious icons desecrated. Such practices are defended as necessary interrogation techniques, "torture lite"; means to important ends.[15]

24 does not portray this side of torture, though it is in the background, as when we glimpse Jack's scarred hand throughout Season Six. The ticking bomb argument that permeates *24* shows torture as a rational choice, a necessary evil when time is of the essence and the stakes are immense. Torture on *24* is sane and somewhat sanitized, mirroring the image in the ticking bomb argument. "Torture to gather intelligence and save lives seems almost heroic. For the first time we can think of kindly torturers rather than tyrants" (Luban, 1436).

Apart from Jack, Agent Burke is CTU's main torturer. A good-looking young man, his character is never developed, though he appears season after season. Maybe we don't want to know what sort of person he is and would rather think of him as the stereotypical "kindly torturer." But what does he do while waiting for the call to come in and torture someone? Maybe he's at home with his family, the call comes, and he kisses his child goodbye saying, "Sorry honey, Daddy's gotta go to the office." Maybe he must return quickly from a training course in Guantanamo. Or maybe he's at CTU, reading up on the latest research on "truth serums" or practicing new techniques on lab animals.

The ticking bomb argument suggests that torturers materialize when the need arises. *24* shows this is not the case. It was Christopher Henderson who taught

---

[14]   Michael Davis, "The Moral Justification of Torture and other Cruel, Inhuman, or Degrading Treatment," *International Journal of Applied Philosophy* 19 (2005): 168.

[15]   Mark Bowden, "The Dark Art of Interrogation," *Atlantic Monthly* 292 (3): 51–76.

Jack his methods. Agent Burke has training and equipment to support his work. If torture is accepted, society will need "a professional cadre of trained torturers" supported by biomedical research and legal developments (Luban, 1445). Such training is hardly so neat and clean as *24* portrays it.

Investigations at Abu Ghraib note that the torturers must have received "systematic training" in torture techniques developed elsewhere.[16] This training turns ordinary young men and women into torturers who dehumanize their victims. Torture not only devastates the one tortured, it ruins torturers' lives. Studies of torturers show they have a variety of psychological and social problems, often resorting to drug and alcohol abuse.[17] The father of a Greek military torturer said at his trial, "I had a good boy, everybody said so. Can you tell me who turned my son into a torturer and destroyed him and my family psychologically?" (Haritos-Fatouros). Torturers' relationships suffer also, with even their military comrades viewing them with contempt, as "defiled" (Arrigo, 554). *24* is thus unrealistic in portraying Burke, and Jack especially, as unaffected by torture. In the real world, torture changes torturers, often dehumanizing them. Their destruction must be included in any utilitarian calculation.

Central to the utilitarian argument is the assumption that torture works. As President David Palmer watches Roger Stanton resist torture, he confidently notes that "everyone breaks eventually." But Jack withstood two years of Chinese torture; and Henderson didn't break at CTU. In Season Six, when Jack tortures his own brother, Graem, with drugs and a plastic bag over his head, he gives up some information, but not the crucial pieces. Later, as General Habib also appears to succumb to torture, he slips in a way to warn his comrade, Fayed. Sometimes torture works, but most times it doesn't (Arrigo, 549–550). Of those tortured legally in France from the sixteenth century through the eighteenth century, between 67 and 95 percent did not confess. The Nazis used all sorts of torture on the resistance movement, yet got little information. An estimated 5 percent of the American prisoners-of-war tortured by the North Vietnamese gave the anti-American statements demanded of them. Steve Biko withstood years of torture in South Africa.[18] Even people who believe some torture is ethical admit it only works "sometimes"[19] and that "there are many instances of torture that are totally inefficacious by any measure."[20] Others

---

[16]   Mika Haritos-Fatouros, "Psychological and Sociopolitical Factors Contributing to the Creation of the Iraqi Torturers: A Human Rights Issue," *International Bulletin of Political Psychology Online* 16 (2), February 2005, available online at www.security.pr.erau.edu/browse.php. Subsequent citations are given in the text under the author's name.

[17]   Jean Maria Arrigo, "A Utilitarian Argument Against Torture Interrogation of Terrorists," *Science and Engineering Ethics* 10 (2004): 553. Page references to Arrigo are to this article.

[18]   Steve Biko and Millard W. Arnold, *The Testimony of Steve Biko* (London: M. T. Smith, 1984).

[19]   Uwe Steinhoff, "Torture – The Case for Dirty Harry and against Alan Dershowitz," *Journal of Applied Philosophy* 23 (2006): 342.

[20]   Sanford Levinson, "The Debate on Torture: War Against Virtual States," *Dissent* (Summer 2003): 82. See the chapter by R. Douglas Geivett for further discussion of whether torture is an effective means of collecting information.

say the idea that torture works is "one of those false **beliefs** of '**folk psychology**' " (Arrigo, 563).

The ticking bomb argument is based on having the actual bomber in custody. But once torture is accepted, it spreads to other suspects. In Season Four, Paul Raines is tortured because his name is on the lease of a building used by terrorists. That makes him "a prime suspect" and eligible for torture. Jack douses him in water and sticks live electric wires in his chest to get some information – but certainly not a bomb's location. In Season Five, Audrey Raines is tortured, yet she was innocent, framed by the terrorists. According to past history, "a torture interrogation program . . . can anticipate that at least half to three-quarters of terrorist suspects may be arrested mistakenly" (Arrigo, 557). In reality, authorities can never be sure they have the right person. And when torture is accepted for the rare extreme incident, its application spreads. Recent history in the war on terror shows that torture has been accepted as part of "a more general fishing expedition for any intelligence that might be used to help 'unwind' the terrorist organization" (Luban, 1443). That is certainly the picture we get from *24*, where torture is employed with increased frequency and less justification.

Overall, the ticking bomb argument is viewed by some as a "dangerous delusion" and an "intellectual fraud" (Luban, 1452). Its details are so far removed from reality that it lulls people into thinking it is realistic and compelling. In reality, the committed terrorist is unlikely to break, especially knowing he must endure torture for a short time before the bomb goes off. Some terrorists are unafraid of death. Syed Ali is defiant in the face of Jack's threats, saying he woke up knowing he would die that day. Jack says he'll make him die in more pain than he ever imagined. Syed replies that will only bring him more pleasure in paradise.

In proposing the ticking bomb argument, Shue compares torture to cancer: "There *is* considerable evidence of all torture's metastatic tendency" (1978, 143). He has since reversed his position, concluding that his own argument is artificial and unrealistic. "Justifications for torture thrive in fantasy," he wrote in 2003.[21] Shue now thinks it would be more reasonable to believe that a dedicated terrorist being tortured on the morning of 9/11 would lie about his plans rather than tell the truth. But apart from those arguments, Shue states "the ultimate reason not to inflict agony upon other human beings is that it is degrading to all involved: all become less human" (2003, 91).

Torture's impact spreads beyond those directly involved. Allowing torture turns the whole liberal, democratic system of justice, law, and order upside down. "In its basic outline, torture is the inversion of the trial, a reversal of cause and effect. While the one studies evidence that may lead to punishment, the other uses punishment to generate the evidence" (Scarry, 41). Torture goes against the presumption of innocence and the right to a fair trial. It goes against human dignity as inherent and applicable to all humans – even criminals and terrorists. It undermines the

---

[21] Henry Shue, "Response to Sanford Levinson," *Dissent* (Summer 2003): 91. Page references to Shue (2003) are to this article.

belief that everyone has basic rights, including the right not to be treated in cruel, inhuman, or degrading ways. The utilitarian approach holds that human dignity is something earned, conferred by others, and therefore something that can be taken away. According to this view, the dignity of some people may be violated for the good of society.

This idea becomes part of a running debate in Season Six over proposals to curtail basic freedoms. President Wayne Palmer and Karen Hayes reject this notion, arguing that the gradual erosion of individual rights and human dignity will further undermine the fundamentals upon which a just society is built. Torture plays a key role in this erosion of core values. "Any State that sets up torture inter- rogation units will lose its moral legitimacy, and therefore undermine the political obligation of its citizens" (Bufacchi and Arrigo, 366).

It's Not That Simple

Again and again, *24* dramatically portrays why it is tempting to view torture as sometimes ethically acceptable. Torturing the person with his finger on the button can seem like the right thing to do to prevent destruction. But things aren't usu- ally that simple. Torture did not get Fayed to give up the nuclear bombs. He was tricked into believing he was being rescued. Torture almost gave the plan away when General Habib warned Fayed about the plan. Old-fashioned police-work, good luck, and a Hollywood shoot-out saved the day, not torture.

At the same time, *24* shows many of the problems with torture. Even if the ticking bomb case is accepted, the practice of torture spreads quickly. Others, many of them innocent, get caught in the web of torture interrogation. When the prisoners talk, they might be telling the truth, or they might not. People will often say anything for the pain to stop. The benefits are not as clear-cut, and the costs extend far beyond the one tortured. The torturer's life is often ruined, and the program corrupts the military, police, political, medical, and legal systems it involves. Ultimately, all of society is impacted. Peace after terrorism may be difficult to imagine, but torture will make it even more difficult. Places like Algeria, South Africa, Chile, Greece, Israel, and Northern Ireland demonstrate the difficulties of social repair after torture is institutionalized (Bufacchi, 367).

Rather than violating someone's dignity in (often vain) attempts to obtain information by torture, another approach is to appeal to people's dignity. By refusing to deny others their dignity, a better way is proposed. That may have its price. The current justice system risks letting some guilty people go free rather than wrongly convict the innocent. So too, a society that refuses to torture *may* let some people sit in prison while bombs go off. However, it is not certain that even torture will get them to reveal where the bombs are located. Using torture risks the bomb's devastation on top of our own moral defilement and social degeneration.

The banality of torture in *24* should shock us into realizing how easily and quickly torture becomes acceptable. *24* dramatizes the need for torture, but also shows its problems. However, torture in *24* remains, even after the show's cancelation, compatible with comfortable TV entertainment. The images from Abu Ghraib and testimonies from people actually tortured are harrowing and grotesque. We should never forget this, nor be seduced by simplistic images that misrepresent the real world. Torture in *24* and the ticking bomb case are artificial and sanitized. Nevertheless, *24* provides an important way to explore the ethics of torture. We must do so openly and very, very carefully. Denying the fundamental rights and dignity of any person is a dangerous and degrading proposition.[22]

[22]   Much appreciation is expressed to Pat Brereton, John Keane, and the editors for their valuable input on earlier drafts of this chapter.

28

Mutants and the
Metaphysics of Race

Jeremy Pierce

Summary

The X-Men's mutants are sometimes described as a race. Despite the name *Homo superior*, mutants aren't really a separate species, but could they be a race within humanity? It's not easy to explain racial groups with non-arbitrary biological features, but denying the existence of races ignores social realities. If we think of races as real in the same way that socially-created money, colleges, and US presidents are real, then mutants have something in common with racial groups and might develop into a race given the right conditions, but they are not strictly speaking a race.

Mutation – it is the key to our evolution. It has enabled us to evolve from a single-celled organism to the dominant species on the planet. This process is slow, normally taking thousands and thousands of years, but every few hundred millennia evolution leaps forward.

Professor Charles Xavier makes the statement above about the evolution of Homo sapiens in the opening monologue of the first film, *X-Men*. But what about Homo superior? As any X-pert can tell you, Magneto coins the phrase in the original 1963 comic *X-Men* #1, claiming, "The human race no longer deserves dominion over the planet earth! The day of the mutants is upon us! The first phase of my plan shall be to show my power . . . to make Homo sapiens bow to Homo superior!"

The way many of the X-Men characters talk makes it sound like mutants are a new species, a new "race" separate from the human race. Yet this is not the way we use the word *race* most of the time, when we refer to different groups of people within humanity. Rather, mutants sound like the kind of races we see in *The Lord of the Rings*, where humans, dwarves, elves, and hobbits are all different races.

There's a big problem with thinking of mutants as a race in the sense of a new species, though. There's little in common among mutants besides what's already common to all of humanity. If they're a species, the only thing that marks them as a species is that each has a different mutation. Even the X-Gene, which we'll consider in detail shortly, occurred within the general human population and not only in mutants (until, in the comic books at least, the Scarlet Witch removed the X-Gene from almost everyone). To coalesce into a species, mutants would need much more in common than one gene or a cluster of genes. A group with an extremely diverse set of mutations isn't coherent enough to be a species. At best, it's the first step toward a new species.

So even though Magneto assigns the name *Homo superior* to mutants, it seems premature to think of mutants as a species. If mutants have not yet formed a race in the sense of a separate species, are they then a race in the same sense as races within humanity (the races that we distinguish based on characteristics like skin color, hair type, and so on)?

Race and the X-Gene

If we want to find out whether Nightcrawler, Mystique, Havok, and Rogue, as mutants, are members of a race, then the first task is to look at some views of what races are.

One view is that races are biological categories based purely in genetic difference and/or ancestry relations. This was probably the dominant understanding of race for most of the time from the African slave trade until the middle of the twentieth century, when many scientists' understanding of DNA led them to reject the idea of race altogether. If races are something like a subspecies of humanity, then we would expect the genetic similarity within each race and the genetic differences between races to be similar to the genetic similarity within, and the differences between, subspecies groups of nonhuman animals (for example, dog breeds).

This turns out to be false, though. Only .2 percent of human genetic material will differ between any two randomly selected people. Only 6 percent of that .2 percent is due to differences between racial groups, which amounts to .012 percent of all human variation. This means that almost all of human genetic variation appears within each racial group. Only a tiny amount of the ways that human beings differ can have anything to do with racial differences.[1]

Compare this with subspecies groups in other animals. The genetic similarity between human racial groups is much closer than the genetic similarity between any nonhuman subspecies groups. Scientists can measure how close two populations are genetically.[2] Gray wolf subspecies are measured at .7. Lizard subspecies a mile apart in the Ozarks are .4. Human populations average at around .15 but can range between .08 and .25.[3] Human populations aren't as genetically distinct as subspecies

[1] K. Anthony Appiah's "Race, Culture, Identity: Misunderstood Connections" in K. Anthony Appiah and Amy Gutmann's *Color Conscious: The Political Morality of Race* (Princeton, NJ: Princeton University Press, 1996), pp. 30–105.

[2] This measure is called *heterozygosity*.

[3] See, for example, Tina Hesman, "No Trace of Race: Genome Sequencing Project Proves Nothing Biologically Separates Peoples," *St. Louis Post-Dispatch*, June 4, 2003.

of other species are, and most scientists don't treat human races as subspecies the way we consider German shepherds to be a subspecies of dog and Rhode Island reds to be a subspecies of chicken.

Now apply this **reasoning** to mutants. Mutations in the Marvel X-Verse occur in all of the major racial and ethnic groups. For many years, the X-Men comic books didn't give much explanation for why some people are mutants. They simply treated mutants as having some special powers that they were born with (and that often became activated at puberty). The powers were the result of mutations in DNA. By the time of *X-Factor* #1 in the eighties, they began calling it a special X-Factor, which is still pretty unclear but does suggest a common cause to all mutations among mutants. More recently, the comic books and the movie series have both provided a much more specific explanation. *X-Men: The Last Stand* explains mutant powers as coming from one single gene, called the mutant X-Gene. Every mutant has it, and it somehow causes his or her powers, although we're not given any more explanation than that in the movie. Warren Worthington II, the father of the Angel, develops a method of suppressing the gene and neutralizing the special abilities it leads to.

The comic books supply a little more information, which is relevant to whether mutants are a race. Several facts are important. First, the X-Gene does not appear only in mutants. Many mutants received the X-Gene from their nonmutant parents. The X-Gene, which occurs on the twenty-third chromosome, is not activated in every person who has it. A group of ancient aliens, called the Celestials, seeded the gene into the population, and it was passed on until the current generation. Normal humans have had the X-Gene for quite a while without being mutants.

The situation is also more complicated than simply one gene explaining all of the varied mutations, which would be scientifically implausible. In *House of M* #2, the Beast explains mutant abilities as coming from a cluster of genes, rather than just one, and perhaps that cluster of genes is what the term *X-Gene* actually refers to. The Beast describes the X-Gene in *Astonishing X-Men* #25 as releasing "exotic proteins" that cause other cells to produce mutations. So the mutations themselves are not directly due to the X-Gene, and that's why the X-Gene can be the same gene or cluster of genes while producing such radically different mutations in all of the different mutants. Something else determines exactly what mutations occur. The X-Gene, if activated, only explains why the mutations occur at all. If not activated, the gene simply sits there not doing anything, except getting passed on to the next generation.

Mutants and Biological Race

So, what do mutants have in common genetically that distinguishes them from the rest of humanity? Not the X-Gene, apparently, since that's been present in humanity since the Celestials planted it in our ancestors. Even so, one gene or a cluster of genes is much less significant than the number of genes that affect the traits we usually associate with a race. And as we've seen, it's hard to see race as a biological category because the variation among members of a race is not much less than the variation among all humans. Just think about the variety of racial backgrounds and national origins among mutants. Storm is from Kenya; Forge is Native American; Sunfire is from Japan; Rictor is Latino; Colossus and his siblings are from Siberia; Gateway is an aboriginal Australian; Wolverine is from northern Alberta in Canada; Cannonball and his siblings are from Kentucky; Banshee is Irish; Jubilee is Chinese American; Wolfsbane is Scottish; Apocalypse is from ancient Egypt; and Arclight is Dominican.

Mutants come from virtually every racial background, and thus the group of all mutants is quite diverse genetically. Now add all of the genetic modifications that cause their powers, and you find far more diversity than occurs in any one race. Mutants are even farther from being a biological subspecies than races are.

In addition, mutants aren't self-contained or reproductively isolated, even if they might end up like that in the future (as they do, for example, in *Days of Future Past*, which we'll consider shortly). If races are biological, then they must constitute some kind of genetic population. In the first generation of large numbers of mutants, you simply don't have a population, even if you might later end up with one. Also consider that mutants do not reproduce only with one another, but with humans, too; this makes it nearly impossible to see mutants as a biological race.

One view, now very much out of favor but once highly influential, took races to have what might be called biological essences. The members of any race have a biological essence that they share with all other members of their race. These essences were supposed to have explained why certain visible features were common to each race but different from those of most other races. Contemporary science has especially refuted the idea that these essences give rise to differences in intelligence, moral character, and so on.

Not many scientists accept this view about race today, but if you found a population with a biological essence, you might see it as a reason for thinking of that population as a subspecies race. The X-Gene does at first seem like a good candidate for such a racial essence, except that many humans also have it. Apart from that, it's hard to see what might be a racial essence for mutants. Since mutants don't come from any common stock, the only thing they have in common is that they each have a power.

There is the X-Gene itself, but, as we've seen, that wouldn't distinguish mutants from humans. The best we could say is that *activated* X-Genes could be a very minimal biological essence. But a racial essence in the classical sense was supposed to explain *all* of the distinctive characteristics of a race, and the X-Gene alone doesn't do that. So, for all of these reasons, mutants are not a biological race. But since races probably aren't biological anyway, maybe that's not a serious problem. If races by definition are biological, and if there are no biological races, then there are no races.

Mutants and Social Races

Many contemporary philosophers take a different approach to race, however. They reject race as a biological category but insist on race as a social reality. If this view is right, then perhaps mutants are a social race, even if they're not a biological race.

A lot of what we mean by race isn't biological at all. People base racial categories on things that result from biological facts, such as physical appearance. But if we were to use similar methods of categorizing mutants, we would end up placing the Beast into the same race as Nightcrawler, because he is *blue and furry* (sometimes, anyway) and not because of any similarity in their powers. And once we as a society begin to categorize people along such lines, we tend to include cultural differences that aren't determined by DNA and ancestry alone. For example, without any biological basis, some races have been thought of as having moral, intellectual, or physical capabilities and deficiencies. Stereotypes thus emerge. Having blue fur, pointy ears, and a tail doesn't make Nightcrawler satanic, and the mutation that led to his fur, ears, and tail has nothing to do with his religious views. In fact, he is a pious Roman Catholic who almost became a priest. Having dark-colored skin, fur, horns, or wings doesn't make someone religious or nonreligious, smart or stupid, moral or immoral, cowardly or courageous. Racial prejudices have conceived the people we call black as intellectually inferior. Similarly, prejudice against mutants suggests that they are to be feared because of how they look or what they can do, without any genuine basis in reality.

So, what sense can we make of the social reality of race? We all accept the reality of categories that don't have their basis in biology or DNA. For instance, when we talk about politics, we refer to certain people as liberals or progressives and others as conservatives, libertarians, Democratic socialists, and so on. When we come up with such categories, we are picking out genuine features of the people we're classifying that don't depend on genetics. Granted, there are complicating factors: we sometimes oversimplify, some people defy categorization, there are borderline cases, and there are categories that might be useful in explaining voting behavior or political philosophy that we haven't thought to put a name to. Nevertheless, things that people do and things we think about people's political **beliefs** allow us to categorize them usefully.

So, too, with races. We can often identify someone's race by looking at him or her, at least with most racial classifications in the United States. (This was not always so. For example, Irish people were sometimes classified as black in the nineteenth century.) The features we use to identify someone's race may well have been determined by his DNA – for example, skin color. But we need to realize that historical and social factors partly determine which biological traits we've picked out as ways of determining who is in what group. The populations that developed into the groups we call races were different according to skin color, hair type, and bone structure and as a result suffered much wrongful treatment. Imagine if their differences had instead been in height, right- or left-handedness, and whether their earlobes were attached. We would still have something like races.

Along these lines, you could imagine a society that turns mutants into a social race. We see the beginnings of isolation in several X-Men stories. For example, in *Days of Future Past*, we're given a possible future in which mutants are hunted down and put into concentration camps, where their powers are inhibited. We're not told much about the details, but we could certainly expect such a world to lead to mutants becoming a separate group, whose mutations might pass on to the next generation if they're allowed to breed and whose social separation allows them to be treated as their own group with a biological element common to all of them (having an activated X-Gene that causes mutation).

Another example involves the island nation of Genosha, which secretly rounded up mutants to be reconditioned and genetically manipulated in order to serve Genosha as slaves, with their names and identities removed and their resistance to enslavement replaced with a desire only to serve. Mutants weren't allowed to breed on their own in the story, as writer Chris Claremont told it in the comic books. Instead, their genetic information was combined with the genetic information of others to produce ideal mutant slaves in the next generation. Whether this would satisfy the ancestry requirement some people want to include probably depends on what people might mean by ancestry, but the case could easily be modified to produce a situation more like *Days of Future Past*.

One reason to consider the Genoshan nation is that Claremont worked into the story several features that connect it nicely with historical and current features of race. In Genosha, mutants have a derogatory name – *Genejoke* (*X-Men* #235). Genoshans refer to someone testing gene-positive and thus qualifying for slavery as mutants (*X-Men* #236), which parallels the negative treatment of people who are HIV-positive. Although that's not a racial issue, it does involve similar kinds of negative treatment, and if enforced segregation of any races were to occur nowadays in a technologically developed society, it almost certainly would involve gene testing.

Claremont puts an unintentionally ironic race comparison into the words of an official Genoshan informatape promoting Genosha in *X-Men* #237, which says, "Ours is a free land, where people are judged by deeds and character, not the color of their skin." The irony of a nation that enslaves mutants pointing out that it doesn't discriminate on the basis of skin color is very effective in communicating that what's going on in Genosha is similar to what's far too often happened along racial lines. Indeed, mutants, like some racial minorities, are not even thought of as people. As the Carol Danvers personality, who controls Rogue during part of the Genoshan storyline, says, "Effectively, they become extensions of their jobs – perceived not as people any longer but organic machines" (*X-Men* #238).

Of course, mutants have been called Muties for a long time in the comic books, and the fear of mutants by some in the general populace was Magneto's original motivation for wanting mutants to rule humans. But the Genoshan case is particularly vivid in the comparison it invites with the treatment of slaves in the United States.

The Difference between Mutants and Race

So, are mutants a race? One difficulty is that Bishop is black, but he's also a mutant. Cable is white, and he's a mutant, too. Every mutant has a racial background.

Being able to talk about diversity of race is one thing, but being able to talk about diversity of race among mutants means if mutants are a race, then it's not the sort that prevents you from being a member of more than one race. It's not as if Cable is mixed race, with one parent who is a mutant and another who is human. Both of his parents are fully mutants and fully white. Of course, it's possible that someone could be both black and white. So being both black and a mutant doesn't mean absolutely that mutants aren't a race.

In addition, races are usually thought of as being identifiable by visible characteristics. You might call powers visible, since once you know about the power, you might guess that the person is a mutant (although in the Marvel Universe we should remember that people can have powers without getting them because of a mutation, such as Spider-Man or the Hulk, who are both superpowered because of radiation). Then again, some powers could be so insignificant that we might miss them, and even the person who has them might never discover them. This feels like it's pushing the helpful analogy between mutants and race.

Mutants as Racelike

On the other hand, we often speak loosely and use certain classificatory terms in an extended or even metaphorical sense. For example, people sometimes refer to coworkers as family. They aren't related, and in the primary meaning of the term *family*, they simply aren't one. But it has become acceptable to use the term to describe people who are like a family in their closeness. Public debate over same-sex marriage has sometimes centered on whether a couple of the same sex should call their relationship a marriage, when marriage has traditionally been a relationship between a man and a woman. Yet we frequently speak of bonds as marriages, even if they have nothing to do with a man and a woman. William Blake (1757–1827) wrote a book called *The Marriage of Heaven and Hell*, and he didn't think of heaven or hell as a man or a woman.

So, are comic book characters just speaking loosely when they use racial language with reference to mutants? One indication that they might be is that they move back and forth between referring to mutants as a species (using the label *Homo superior*) and calling mutants a part of humanity. Magneto does this in several of his appearances, even within the same comic book issue, and he does it in the films as well. So there might be some truth to what they're saying, if we don't take it as literally as the writers may have intended it. X-Men stories draw a helpful analogy with the racial problems in our society, even if mutants aren't really a race.[4]

[4]   I'd like to thank Winky Chin, Jonathan Ichikawa, Avery Tooley, and the editors of *X-Men and Philosophy* for help at various stages of development of this chapter.

Part VIII

Eastern Views

Introduction

This book focuses primarily on Western philosophy, which began in ancient Greece in the sixth century BCE. There is, however, another even more ancient tradition, Eastern philosophy, which has its roots in China and India. The seminal figures in Eastern philosophy are the Buddha (c. 560–480 BCE), Confucius (c. 551–479 BCE), and Lao-tzu (born c. 600 BCE). While Eastern philosophy addresses all of the major questions of Western philosophy, it has a different orientation. In the East, philosophy and religion are not as distinctly separated as they are in the West. Instead of focusing on abstract metaphysical questions, Eastern philosophy is primarily concerned with articulating a way of life.

In the Western world, the best-known ideas from Eastern philosophy are Tao and Zen. "Tao" literally means the "way." Not surprisingly, then, Lao-tzu's famous *Tao te Ching* urges us to follow the Tao, to get in touch with and follow the natural way of the universe. Combining elements of Buddhism (which originated in India) and Taoism (which originated in China), Zen Buddhism has flourished in Japan. Zen emphasizes the intuitive nature of the mind and the importance of living in the immediate experience of the moment.

In his chapter, James McRae uses the science fiction universe of *Battlestar Galactica* to illustrate core concepts of traditional Buddhism: the four noble truths, the eightfold-path, the interconnectedness of all things, karma, and reincarnation. Taking us into the unique realm of Zen Buddhism, Jeffrey Ruff and Jeremy Barris find an unlikely Zen master, Dr. Gregory House, to illustrate the path to insight. House is known for his rude remarks, unorthodox techniques, and brilliant diagnoses. Thinking about things in the usual way doesn't get the job done when the solution to a medical mystery is far from obvious. Likewise, Zen has little regard for the conventional approach to life, what it would say makes sense, or what it would deem appropriate. When your usual way of doing things isn't leading to enlightenment, it may be time to start pondering Zen koans like "What is the sound of one hand clapping?" House would agree that to find the answer we need to see the problem with fresh, new eyes or what Zen calls "beginner's mind."

In his chapter, Mark White uses Batman to illustrate the basic concepts of Taoism. The famous yin-yang symbol illustrates the complementary forces of yin and yang that do not so much oppose as interpenetrate one another. Batman tends to be out of balance, dominated by yang. Thankfully, his partner, Robin, brings yin to the mix. Batman's butler, Alfred, is a genuine sage, working quietly behind the scenes and enacting the Taoist principle of *wei-wu-wei*, or "action without action."

29

Zen and the Art of Cylon Maintenance

James McRae

Summary

This chapter articulates four key concepts in Buddhism and explains the significance they hold for the *Battlestar Galactica* universe: (1) the relationship between suffering and ignorance; (2) karma, rebirth, and cyclical time; (3) God and *kenōsis* theology; and (4) the personhood of Cylons. According to Buddhist philosophy, Cylons are similar to human beings in every way that counts: they are sentient beings struggling with both their spiritual identity and the existential problem of how to eliminate suffering in the world.

"I only want you to see the truth of your life. The reason why you suffered and you struggled for so long. That's why God sent me to you" ("Occupation"). Leoben, a Cylon, utters these words shortly after his fifth death at the hands of Kara "Starbuck" Thrace. Though it may be hard to believe at first, the mission Leoben claims to pursue isn't so different from the one taken up by the historical Buddha. Both Buddha and Leoben aim to understand the nature of suffering and seek to eliminate it from the world. In fact, *BSG* explores a number of themes that resonate with key concepts in Zen Buddhism. And, as we shall see, the Buddhist themes suggest that the Cylons are sentient beings who face an existential crisis similar to the one that defines human life. In the end, the solutions to the unsatisfactory existence of both species might be fundamentally intertwined.

"Life is a Testament to Pain": Suffering, Ignorance, and Interdependent Arising

Zen is a Japanese religious and philosophical tradition with roots in Indian Mahāyanā Buddhism. The historical Buddha, Siddhartha Gautama (563–483 BCE), dedicated his life to the study of how to eliminate suffering in the world. His solution to this problem is summarized in his teaching of the Noble Fourfold Truth.[1]

First Noble Truth: Life is characterized by *duhkha*

The Sanskrit word *duhkha*, which the Buddha uses to describe life, is typically translated as "suffering" or "sorrow," though "unsatisfactoriness" may best capture the full range of its multi-layered meanings. The Japanese translation, *ku*, carries with it the complexity of the Sanskrit term, meaning either suffering – in the sense of *physical* pain – or anxiety – in the sense of *psychological* distress. Death, sickness, poverty, famine, infirmity, racism, and warfare are commonplace and lead to suffering on a large scale. This unsatisfactoriness is even more pronounced in *BSG*. Human civilization has been all but annihilated and the human race is forced to live a nomadic lifestyle, constantly hounded by the Cylons. In "33," for example, the fleet is deprived of sleep for days on end as they make FTL jumps every 33 minutes to avoid their pursuers. Ultimately, they're forced to destroy the *Olympic Carrier* and its 1,345 passengers to save themselves from an apparent nuclear threat.

Second Noble Truth: *Duhkha* is a result of our ignorant attachment to false ideals

Human beings suffer because we attach ourselves to attitudes, doctrines, and pre-judices that obscure the way the world really is. This attachment leads to craving, which causes us to act in ways that promote *duhkha*. Leoben explains this concept to Starbuck during his torture:

> I know you. You're damaged. You were born to a woman who believed that suffering was good for the soul, so you suffered. Your life is a testament to pain. Injuries. Accidents. Some inflicted upon others, others inflicted upon yourself. It surrounds you like a bubble. But it's not real . . . It's just something she put in your head. It's something that you wanna believe because it means you're the problem, not the world that you live in. ("Flesh and Bone")

The suffering in our lives is "not real" in the sense that it's self-inflicted through our attachments. Suffering arises because, due to these attachments to false ideals, we're profoundly ignorant of the true nature of reality, which Zen describes as

---

[1] This summary of the Noble Fourfold Truth is drawn from the Buddha's first sermon, translated with commentary by John M. Koller and Patricia Koller in *A Sourcebook in Asian Philosophy* (New York: Macmillan, 1991), 195–6.

engi, or *interdependent arising*. This notion consists of two concepts: no-self and impermanence.[2]

Concerning no-self, Dōgen (1200–1253 CE), founder of the Japanese Sōtō School of Zen, describes the nature of Zen training:

> To study the buddha way is to study the self. To study the self is to forget the self. To forget the self is to be actualized by myriad things. When actualized by myriad things, your body and mind as well as the bodies and minds of others drop away. No trace of realization remains, and this no-trace continues endlessly.[3]

Typically, people experience the world individualistically, as if each person is a unique and detached entity. According to Zen, however, all things in the universe are part of an interrelated web of being, which means that no person is separate from or superior to the rest of reality. In this sense, people can be said to have no-self – *muga*, or *anātman* in Sanskrit – in the sense that no person is an isolated entity. Selfish actions – those that are grounded in the good of the individual at the expense of others – ultimately lead to suffering. Human beings are defined by their relationships with other people and with the world around them. In *BSG*, each person's character is revealed and developed through his relationships. Saul Tigh is characterized by his tumultuous relationship with his wife and his abusive treatment of the crew. Chief Tyrol and Helo are defined by their relationships with the two Sharons. Apollo's character is an extension of his turbulent interactions with his father, his unpredictable relationship with Starbuck, and his sense of self-identity as an officer of the fleet.

The second part of interdependent arising is impermanence – *mujō*, or *anitya* in Sanskrit. Dōgen states, "The thought of enlightenment . . . is the mind which sees into impermanence" (32). All things in the universe are in a constant process of arising, existing, and decaying. Nothing can be taken for granted in life; all things ultimately fall away into oblivion. This isn't meant, however, to be a pessimistic view of reality. Zen aesthetics uses the concept of *mono no aware* to describe the "tragic beauty of impermanent things."[4] In Japan, cherry blossoms appear in the spring for only a few days before they're scattered by the wind. The fact that their beauty is fleeting only intensifies their aesthetic appeal: everything of value in life must be fully appreciated for what it is in each moment, since it might be the last

---

[2] In Sanskrit, this term *engi* is *pratitya-samutpāda*, and can be alternatively translated as "dependent origination" or "dependent co-arising." This concept describes the world as a deeply interrelated process that's in a state of constant flux. The "interdependent" aspect of the world is manifested in the Buddhist doctrine of no-self, while "arising" is evident in the impermanence of all things.

[3] Dōgen, *Moon in a Dewdrop: Writings of Zen Master Dōgen*, ed. Kasuaki Tanahashi (New York: North Point Press, 1985), 70. Further references will be given in the text.

[4] William Theodore De Bary, "The Vocabulary of Japanese Aesthetics, I, II, III," in *Japanese Aesthetics and Culture: A Reader*, ed. Nancy G. Hume (Albany: State University of New York Press, 1995), 44. Dōgen himself writes a poem celebrating the impermanent beauty of cherry blossoms (14).

opportunity one has for such an experience. This impermanence is evident in every episode of *BSG*. All twelve colonies have been destroyed, leaving only about fifty thousand humans alive, and President Roslin keeps track of this conspicuously dwindling number. Major characters are routinely killed throughout the series: Billy, Ellen Tigh, and Kat, to name but a few. Roslin accepts the prophesied role of the "leader who suffered a wasting disease and would not live to enter the new land," and her awareness of death strengthens her resolve to find Earth as quickly as possible ("The Hand of God"). The consciousness of constantly impending death sharpens the characters' awareness of the value of life and the particular relationships they have with others.

Third Noble Truth: If we eliminate our ignorant attachment to false ideals, we can eliminate *duhkha*

Much of the suffering we endure in the world is self-inflicted. Dōgen states that "in attachment flowers fall, and in aversion weeds spread" (69). Our attachment to false ideals leads to injury and suffering, as does our neglect of our responsibilities. Because we view ourselves egoistically, as if we were separate from and superior to the rest of reality, we inflict suffering upon others, whom we treat as nothing more than raw material for our own satisfaction. The Cylons think of themselves as superior to humans in every way. Human women, for example, are used as tools in the Cylon breeding program ("The Farm"). Humans aren't much better, having originally created the Cylons to do their bidding and thus treating them as nothing more than "walking chrome toasters." After the attack on the Colonies, captured Cylons are sometimes beaten, raped, or executed ("Flesh and Bone"; "Pegasus"). There are exceptions to these attitudes, as evidenced by the Cylon-human relationships between the Sharons and both Helo and Tyrol, and between Baltar and Caprica Six (and later with D'Anna/ Three). These relationships lead, on a small scale, to some "humanitarian" efforts on the part of both Cylons and humans to minimize the suffering inflicted upon the other race. Other examples of self-inflicted suffering include Tigh's alcoholism and vitriolic personality, Starbuck's chronic insubordination and inability to maintain interpersonal relationships, and Baltar's perpetual dishonesty and selfishness.

Fourth Noble Truth: Unsatisfactoriness can be eliminated through the cultivation of wisdom, compassion, and meditative practices

Dōgen states that "The great way of all buddhas, thoroughly practiced, is emancipation and realization" (84). Traditionally referred to as the Noble Eightfold Path, a person can eliminate suffering in the world if he cultivates himself so that he removes his attachments to false ideals and understands the true nature of reality as interdependent arising. When he does this, he reaches *satori*, the state of enlightenment.

Before we can discuss the possibility of enlightenment in *BSG*, we must first examine Zen Buddhism's understanding of rebirth, divinity, and personhood.

"All of This Has Happened Before . . .": Karma and Rebirth

For Buddhism, the unsatisfactoriness of life is augmented by the fact that all non-enlightened, sentient beings are reincarnated after death. Morally inappropriate acts build up *karma – gō –* which is like a metaphysical record of moral worth. There's no such thing as "good karma"; all karma is "bad karma" in that it binds a person to the cycle of death and rebirth.[5] When people die, their karma carries on to another life and can influence the nature of their rebirths: vicious human beings with significant karma might return as non-human animals, while virtuous beings who have eliminated most of their karma through moral actions might return in a social position that'll make it easier for them to attain enlightenment in that lifetime. This cycle of death and rebirth is known as the wheel of *samsāra – rinne –* and the only way to exit this process is through the complete elimination of karma.

As Leoben tells Starbuck:

> To know the face of God is to know madness. I see the universe. I see the patterns. I see the foreshadowing that precedes every moment of every day . . . What is the most basic article of faith? This is not all that we are. The difference between you and me is, I know what that means and you don't. I know that I'm more than this body, more than this consciousness. ("Flesh and Bone")

Roslin adds to the explanation, "If you believe in the gods, then you believe in the cycle of time, that we are all playing our parts in a story that is told again and again and again throughout eternity" ("Kobol's Last Gleaming, Part 1"). Human beings have lived their lives countless times before and will revisit these same roles again and again. Roslin speaks of herself as "fulfilling the role of the leader" that's mentioned in the Book of Pythia ("Fragged").

The concept of cyclical time and recurring roles is echoed by Number Six:

BALTAR: I thought Kobol was supposed to be a paradise or something. Some place where gods lived with the humans in harmony, or . . .

SIX: For a time, perhaps. Then your true nature asserted itself. Your brutality. Your depravity. Your barbarism.

BALTAR: So the scriptures are all a lie. It's all just a lie, just a cover-up for all this savagery.

SIX: Exactly. All of this has happened before, Gaius, and all of it will happen again.

("Valley of Darkness")

---

[5]   Good actions, rather than providing "good karma," extinguish the karma a person has accumulated through morally inappropriate actions. This is why the term *nirvana*, which literally means "snuffing out," is used to describe the state of enlightenment that comes when the flames of karma have been doused.

In Buddhism, the karma that causes our rebirth also predisposes us to commit unethical acts due to the vicious habits acquired in our previous lives.[6] Human beings, due to our selfish attachment to false ideals, have perpetuated a cycle of violence throughout history. A person's karmic predisposition towards certain habits, however, doesn't fatalistically predetermine her course of action. She can choose to change these habits and, through the cultivation of wisdom, compassion, and meditation, eventually eliminate karma. This notion is echoed in Elosha's reassurance to Roslin: "Laura, this is your path, the one the gods picked for you, the one you picked for yourself" ("The Farm"). Though the gods influence the fate of human beings, it would seem that people still must choose the roles that they'll play in life.[7] It's important to note that while this notion of temporal repetition parallels the Buddhist **idea** of rebirth, there's no mention in *BSG* thus far of a definitive way *out* of this cycle.

Cylon existence also consists of a repeated cycle of birth, death, and resurrection. Cylons who die in the proximity of a resurrection ship have their memories immediately downloaded into another body:

BALTAR: The Cylons call this their Resurrection ship. At the moment, we are too far away from the Cylon home world for the normal downloading process to work. Which is why they built this ship. It contains the entire apparatus necessary for Cylon resurrection. Now, this ship has been traveling with the fleet, trailing *Galactica* for the last several months.

STARBUCK: So it's a safety net. A place where they fall back to when they die.

CAIN: And if they lose their safety net . . .

STARBUCK: Then any Cylon who dies out here . . .

CAIN: Would be dead. As in, really dead. And I dare say they won't like that.

STARBUCK: No, sir. They might even stop chasing us. Why risk getting killed if you can't just wake up all nice and cozy in a brand-new body?

("Resurrection Ship, Part 1")

As with karma, the overall moral character of a downloaded Cylon is preserved: Boomer, at first, remains compassionate and loyal to humans, as does Caprica Six ("Downloaded"); Leoben maintains his pursuit of Starbuck despite being killed by her numerous times ("Occupation"); and Scar is "filled with more bitter memories" each time he undergoes the "painful and traumatic experience" of being shot down by a Viper ("Scar"). Unlike Buddhism, it doesn't seem that there's hope for a Cylon to improve her position in life with each rebirth; she simply gets a fresh, identical body. D'Anna and Baltar's quest, however, to unlock the mysteries of the "final five" Cylons suggests that in-between death and downloading, certain metaphysical truths can be obtained that will expand her awareness in the next incarnation ("Hero").

---

[6]   See Nishitani Keiji's discussion of karma, rebirth, and time in *Religion and Nothingness*, trans. Jan Van Bragt (Berkeley: University of California Press 1982), 238–50.

[7]   For discussion of **fatalism** in the context of *BSG*, see David Kyle Johnson's chapter, "'A Story that is Told Again, and Again': Recurrence, Providence, and Freedom." in *Battlestar Galactica and Philosophy*, ed. Jason T. Eberl (New York: Wiley-Blackwell, 2008).

"God Has a Plan for You, Gaius":
Religion, God, and *Kenōsis*

Any discussion of religion within the context of *BSG* must take into account the variety of religious traditions depicted in the series. Yet, how is it possible for there to be Zen themes in *BSG* when Buddhism seems to reject the transcendent God or gods to whom humans and Cylons regularly appeal?

Nishida Kitarō (1870–1945), founder of the Kyoto School,[8] is renowned for his Zen-based philosophy of religion that describes God as Absolute Nothingness. For Nishida, the being to whom we appeal when we invoke the notion of God is not a transcendent, personal creator, but the absolute, undifferentiated ground of all existence. A person's true self is found through *kenōsis*, a notion drawn from Christian theology (Philippians 2:5–8) that closely parallels the Buddhist idea of emptiness – *ku*, or *śūnyatā*. *Kenōsis* is a process through which a person empties his individualistic self into his relationships with other people and with the Absolute. Even God takes part in this process of *kenōsis*:

> A God who is simply self-sufficient is not the true God. In one sense, God must empty Himself through *kenōsis*. A God that is both thoroughly transcendent and thoroughly immanent, both thoroughly immanent and thoroughly transcendent, is a truly dialectical God. If it is said that God created the world from love, then God's absolute love must be essential to the absolute self-negation of God and is not *opus ad extra*.[9]

Even God takes part in this process of self-emptying, which means that the Absolute is omnipresent and intensely personal. Leoben echoes this notion: "We're all God, Starbuck. All of us. I see the love that binds all living things together" ("Flesh and Bone"). By emptying themselves into their relationships with God and with each other, humans and Cylons draw closer to the Absolute. This is particularly evident in human-Cylon relationships. Sharon tells Helo that "what we had between us was important . . . Because it brings us closer to God" ("Kobol's Last Gleaming, Part 2").

The Cylons' understanding of God is remarkably similar to Nishida's Absolute. Six describes God to Baltar as pure love:

> If you would give yourself over to God's will, you'd find peace in his love like I have . . . It's important you form a personal relationship with God. Only you can give yourself over to his eternal love. ("Six Degrees of Separation")

[8] The Kyoto School is based on an East-West philosophical synthesis. It draws on Zen in comparison to Western thought, mostly existentialism.

[9] *Nishida Kitarō, Zenshū*, vol. 11, translated by Steve Odin in *The Social Self in Zen and American Pragmatism* (Albany: State University of New York Press, 1996), 106. See also Masao Abe, "Kenōtic God and Dynamic Sunyata," in *The Emptying God: A Buddhist-Jewish-Christian Conversation*, ed. John B. Cobb, Jr. and Christopher Ives (Eugene, OR: Wipf & Stock, 2005).

If a person empties himself into his relationship with God, this process of self-negation will allow him to embrace the love that is God's very nature. There's only one true, universal God, and though it's polytheistic, the Colonists' religion is directed towards the same Absolute. Leoben tells Starbuck, "Our faiths are similar, but I look to one God, not to many" ("Flesh and Bone"), and Six says to Baltar: "He's not my God. He is God" ("Six Degrees of Separation").[10]

In the Zen tradition, a pupil's study is guided by a *roshi*, an enlightened master of the Buddhist Way. A method of training that's commonplace in the Rinzai tradition of Zen is the use of *kōans*, which are puzzling questions or anecdotes upon which a student is expected to meditate. *Kōans* force the student to doubt the dualistic, false ideals that she has customarily used to interpret the world, and thereby push her closer to enlightenment by bringing about the death of her old, egoistic self.[11] Rinzai master Hakuin states:

> If you are not a hero who has truly seen into his own nature, don't think it is something that can be known easily. If you wish accordance with the true, pure non-ego, you must be prepared to let go your hold when hanging from a sheer precipice, to die and return again to life.[12]

A good roshi uses *kōans* to force students to question themselves, which pushes them to a deeper awareness of the false ideals that lead to their suffering. This ultimately leads to the death of the old self and rebirth as a new, enlightened being.[13]

In *BSG*, Leoben acts as a type of roshi who causes those with whom he interacts to question themselves and their sense of purpose. Trapped with Commander Adama inside Ragnar Station, pretending to be human, he questions human habits of violence that have led to suffering:

LEOBEN: Suspicion and distrust . . . That's military life, right?
ADAMA: You're a gun-dealer-philosopher, I take it, right?
LEOBEN: I'm an observer of human nature. When you get right down to it, humanity is not a pretty race. I mean, we're only one step away from beating each other with clubs like savages fighting over scraps of meat. Maybe the Cylons are God's retribution for our many sins.

("Miniseries")

---

[10] Note that the Number Six who appears in the flesh on *Galactica* to test Baltar's faith calls herself "Miss *God*frey."

[11] For a thorough explanation of the use of *kōans* in Zen practice, see D. T. Suzuki, *An Introduction to Zen Buddhism* (New York: Grove Press, 1964), 99–117; or T. P. Kasulis, *Zen Action, Zen Person* (Honolulu: University of Hawaii Press, 1981), 104–24.

[12] Hakuin, *The Zen Master Hakuin: Selected Writings*, trans. Philip B. Yampolsky (New York: Columbia University Press, 1971), 135.

[13] For further discussion of the Buddhist concept of death and rebirth in another sci-fi context, see Walter Robinson, "Death and Rebirth of a Vulcan Mind" in *Star Trek and Philosophy*, ed. Jason T. Eberl and Kevin S. Decker (Peru, IL: Open Court Press, 2008).

Leoben's speech mirrors the teachings of Buddhism: the selfish attachments of humankind have led to immense suffering in the world. Human beings must realize that their current state of suffering is largely a result of their own actions. Leoben later causes Starbuck to question the personhood of the Cylons and the purpose of human existence. Leoben is not, of course, a moral exemplar; Cylons are guilty of perpetuating at least as much suffering as humans. But, as Six points out to Baltar on this score, "Yes, well, we're your children. You taught us well" ("Valley of Darkness"). The apparent hypocrisy of the Cylons' actions isn't enough to invalidate the moral claims that they make: selfishness and ignorance lead to suffering.

"How Could Anyone Fall in Love with a Toaster?" Cylons as Persons?

On Ragnar, Leoben tries to convince Adama that the Cylons have evolved from mere machines into persons, as evidenced by the fact that "they've developed a culture, a society, an entire way of life."[14] Certainly, the Cylons appear to be human in many respects, but is it possible for Buddhism to consider them persons in the *moral* sense? Buddhism places moral worth on all beings that have sentience, the capacity to feel pain. Some creatures have the ability not only to *feel* pain, but to be cognitively aware of that pain as well, which heightens their capacity for suffering. Cylons clearly have the ability to feel pain and to suffer psychologically, as evidenced by Starbuck's torture of Leoben:

STARBUCK: Kind of bad programming, isn't it? I mean, why bother with hunger?
LEOBEN: Part of being human.
STARBUCK: You're not human. How's your lunch?
LEOBEN: You know how it is. When you're starving, anything tastes good.
[The guard strikes him]
STARBUCK: Did that hurt?
LEOBEN: Yeah, that hurt.
STARBUCK: Machines shouldn't feel pain, shouldn't bleed, shouldn't sweat.
LEOBEN: Sweat. That's funny. That's good.
STARBUCK: See, a smart Cylon would turn off the old pain software about now. But I don't think you're so smart.
LEOBEN: Maybe I'll turn it off and you won't even know.
[The guard strikes him again]
STARBUCK: Here's your dilemma. Turn off the pain, you feel better, but that makes you a machine, not a person. You see, human beings can't turn off their pain. Human beings have to suffer, and cry, and scream, and endure, because they have no choice.
("Flesh and Bone")

---

[14]   For further discussion of Cylon personhood, see Robert Arp and Tracie Mahaffey's chapter, " 'And They Have a Plan': Cylons as Persons," in *Battlestar Galactica and Philosophy*, ed. Jason T. Eberl (New York: Wiley-Blackwell, 2008).

Leoben suggests he can turn off his pain receptors, yet he refuses to do so because it's the capacity to feel hunger and pain that, in his mind, makes him human. But the capacity for suffering alone isn't enough to make the Cylons persons. Buddhists would assert that a rabbit has moral significance and shouldn't be injured, but that doesn't mean it's capable of reaching *satori*.

Suffering is more than the simple capacity to feel pain; it involves the cognitive ability to be aware of the significance of pain and loss in the present, past, and future. Cylons seem to have this ability as well, since Leoben can fear his impending death away from a resurrection ship, and Caprica Six and Sharon can feel remorse – and endure a crisis of character – as a result of their contributions to the destruction of the human race ("Flesh and Bone"; "Downloaded"). Cylons are almost identical to human beings in the functional sense: they're at least our equals cognitively and physically. Because Cylons are volitional beings, they're capable of earning and removing karma, which means that, like humans, they should be capable of reaching *satori*. Thus, in the Buddhist understanding of the term, Cylons ought to be considered persons.

If the Cylons are persons, and if the fate of humans and Cylons is intertwined as Leoben and Six suggest, then the two species ought to seek a peaceful resolution to their conflict. The suffering endured in the war between humans and Cylons comes as a result of both species' attachment to selfish notions of superiority that defy the interdependent nature of reality. Buddhism teaches that awareness of interdependent arising ultimately results in a profound sense of compassion for all sentient beings. If humans and Cylons can learn to be both wise and compassionate, perhaps they can achieve reconciliation. As Dōgen states:

> There is a simple way to become a buddha: When you refrain from unwholesome actions, are not attached to birth or death, and are compassionate toward all sentient beings, respectful to seniors and kind to juniors, not excluding or desiring anything, with no designing thoughts or worries, you will be called a buddha. Do not seek anything else (75).

The Noble Eightfold Path of Buddhism consists of three categories of cultivation: *wisdom* (right views and intentions), *ethics* (right speech, actions, and livelihood), and *meditation* (right effort, mindfulness, and concentration). Wisdom comes through the realization of interdependent arising, which in turn leads to a profound compassion for all things, since everything is part of a dynamic, interrelated whole. Yet both wisdom and compassion can be gained only through meditation, the calming of the body and mind that opens a person's perceptions to the truth of interdependent arising. There's no indication that anyone in *BSG* practices seated meditation (right concentration); though some exhibit traces of mindfulness and right effort by honestly acknowledging their own flaws and striving to amend them. Perhaps if meditation were a more common practice, suffering could be eliminated from the *BSG* universe. But how entertaining a show would that be?[15]

---

[15]   This chapter was originally published after the 2nd season of *Battlestar Gallactica*. Thus, does not consider events from seasons 3 and 4.

30

The Sound of One House Clapping

The Unmannerly Doctor as Zen Rhetorician

Jeffrey C. Ruff and Jeremy Barris

Summary

Dr. Gregory House's rhetoric typically works by unsettling the assumptions of his audience about what does and does not make sense, with the result that novel possibilities and solutions become available. Importantly, his rhetorical style also unsettles his own assumptions in this way. This rhetorical style works in the same way as some of the methods of Zen Buddhist practice. This chapter explores House's Zen rhetoric in four areas: as a style of living ethically, as a way of establishing intimacy, as a path to truth, and as a method of healing.

If you understand, things are just as they are; if you do not understand, things are just as they are.

– Zen proverb

House, Zen, and Making Sense

So an ancient once said, "Accept the anxieties and difficulties of this life." Don't expect your practice to be clear of obstacles. Without hindrances the mind that seeks enlightenment may be burnt out. So an ancient once said, "Attain deliverance in disturbances."

– Zen Master Kyong Ho (1849–1912)[1]

House's words and actions violate expectations. He speaks unprofessionally, rudely, and apparently irresponsibly. He violates confidences, ignores the wishes of his patients, holds back necessary information from both colleagues and patients,

---

[1] Mu Soeng, *Thousand Peaks: Korean Zen – Traditions and Teachers* (Cumberland, RI: Primary Point Press, 1996), 173.

and breaks promises. Paradoxically, the results of these unethical practices are that patients and colleagues discover their true concerns and commitments, or find ways of fulfilling their commitments that weren't available to them before.

While the unmannerly doctor and the writers who give him such great lines may not have studied Eastern philosophy, House's rhetoric parallels certain forms of expression in Zen Buddhism. A koan, for example, is a Zen riddle or **paradox** like "What is the sound of one hand clapping?" It's not clear what an answer to this question would even look like, but pondering, reflecting, and meditating upon it can stretch the mind until its limits change, and so lead to insight. Like Zen rhetoric, House's rhetoric typically works by unsettling the assumptions of his audience (and, just as important, his own assumptions) about what does and does not make sense, with the result that new possibilities and solutions become available.

House constantly insists that "everybody lies." (In season three he goes so far as to say, "Even fetuses lie.") House is consistent in this attitude regardless of whether the lies are due to genuine dishonesty, lack of self-knowledge, embarrassment, or ignorance. For example, in the episode "Sleeping Dogs Lie," Hannah planned to leave her girlfriend Max but didn't tell her, so that Max would give her part of her liver. Again, as we found out at the end of that episode, Max gave part of her liver with the hidden motive of preventing her partner from leaving her. And in "Cursed," Jeffrey had spent time in an Indian ashram and contracted a tropical disease without realizing it, but he didn't mention that period of his life to his doctors because he was embarrassed about it. This suggests that what House might mean by "Everybody lies" is something like "People don't know how to speak in a way that is appropriate to the situation," or "Patients and doctors often make up their minds ahead of time when they don't actually know what's going on and as a result don't actually know what's important."

In these examples, House's starting point is that no one (not even he) knows or understands what is going on. Sometimes he may insist that he knows and is right, but at those times he also mocks people for trusting his diagnoses. Worse still, everyone involved may not even know *how to begin* to understand what is going on. Or everyone, including House, may be so stuck in their habitual – and therefore quite possibly arbitrary – ways of making sense that no one has any **idea** what the *genuine* sense is of any of the central things that are going on. As a result, they can't start a genuine exploration of the situation without unsettling all of their existing ways of making sense of it.

This state of not knowing how to begin to make sense, and of having to deal with that situation, reflects what the Zen tradition sees as a very basic and deep characteristic of life in general. We can't make sense of our lives as a whole. To do that, we'd have to be able to step outside of our lives and see them as a whole, and of course we can't do that. All our ways of making sense are parts *of* our lives, so that if we could step outside our lives, we'd of course also step outside all our ways of making sense! The result is that the idea of making sense of our lives as a whole literally doesn't make any sense.

But to make sense of our lives and the things that happen in them, we *need* to be able to get a grip on them, to make sense of them, as a whole. As a result, the Zen tradition advises us to go right ahead and step outside of sense itself, altogether. The standpoint that would allow us to get a perspective on our lives and sense as a whole is the standpoint, or starting point, of *not* making sense.

As we've been saying, the situations House deals with *already* don't make sense. But the problem is the same: if nothing central to the situation makes sense, then to have a real understanding of the situation we have to find a wholly new way of making sense. And to find a wholly new way of making sense we need to start with not making sense in the familiar ways. Only by not thinking and acting in sensible or "fitting" or appropriate ways can we *arrive at* sense and sensible action.[2]

Now we can see how House's rude, aggressive, or manipulative behavior in these circumstances is effective in dealing with the senselessness of the situation, or the kinds of lies, confusion, and lack of insight that obscure the genuine sense of the circumstances. His abrasive behavior eventually opens the possibility to everyone involved that "nothing is as it seems," and that "assumptions or presuppositions" won't do anyone any good in a world where nothing central to the situation makes its own genuine sense.

A Style of Behaving Ethically

To develop your . . . clear, unbiased judgment, it is important to give up, or to be ready to give up everything, including your understanding of the teaching and your knowledge. . . . Then you will be able to tell what is good and what is bad.
— Zen Master Shunryu Suzuki (1904–71)[3]

In the episode "DNR" Foreman opts to do nothing for an ailing jazz musician because the trumpet player doesn't want any more treatments (he believes that he's dying of ALS). Throughout the episode Foreman maintains that House doesn't know the difference between right and wrong, because House treats the patient against his wishes. He further criticizes House in this (and other episodes) for not taking what everyone else knows are the right, socially proper, or legally safe actions.

In defense, House points out to Foreman that "if you do nothing, it doesn't matter which one of us is right." The jazz musician himself, when talking to Foreman about whether House or his own physician is right, tells Foreman, "You gotta pick

---

[2] We've slipped in "action" here and added it to "sense," and we'll see a little later that this is actually a very important connection for House and Zen – and that there is a very important and illuminating reason why it had to be just slipped in, a bit slyly and without appropriate explanation or justification! This is a little hint that our essay is up to some House or Zen tricks itself, and later we'll see why. We'll also see why the authors are not in control of those tricks, but are just as much subject (or object) *to* them and guided or redirected *by* them as are you, the reader!

[3] Shunryu Suzuki, *Not Always So: Practicing the True Spirit of Zen* (New York: HarperCollins, 2003), 117. All subsequent quotes from Suzuki come from this text.

one, son." In this kind of situation it's only by acting, *without* properly knowing what one's doing, that one can make any constructive difference to the situation at all. The alternative is to ensure that one will never find out the right thing to do, and so to commit oneself to being *completely* thoughtless and irresponsible about the true situation.

The dialogue from "DNR" suggests that "what is right" is not a matter of *understanding* what is right. In other words, we don't reach what is right by thinking or believing, by making sense. Instead, what is right is something that one *does* or performs. More than this, what is right is discovered only *through* that action and is recognized only as a result of it. So what one *thinks* is correct or incorrect matters less than getting the actions right. House is always active (or proactive) rather than being reactive. He doesn't allow law, expectation, assumption, social acceptability, or certainty to proscribe or prescribe his actions.

We shouldn't go overboard here: this doesn't mean that we should always act or always make choices without regard to sense. Rather, there are particular situations when, and particular ways in which, we need to act without properly knowing what we're doing.

House routinely deals with situations in which no one can see the (genuine) sense of anything central to the problem, including what the problem *is*. And so no one really knows what the "end" or goal might be. As a result the responsible, the right, thing to do is to unsettle the apparent sense of the whole situation so that we can *find out*, among many other things, what the "end" is.

In fact, the result of House's inappropriate interactions with his patients and colleagues is generally (not always, of course – House does make mistakes!) that the true needs of the participants' situations, as recognized by the participants themselves, are met in ways that turn out not to conflict at all with the means by which he got there. House's style achieves this in one, or both, of two ways. His tactics often bring out a wider range of considerations than were previously recognized, considerations important to the participants themselves, and the end result does justice to these, as well as the original, considerations. Or when the participants' true concerns or commitments in the situation turn out to be different from what they had first thought, the whole framework of ethical obligations that had protected those particular concerns becomes unimportant.

In "Mob Rules," for example, Bill, the "mob" brother of Joey, the equally "mob" patient, refuses to accept that Joey has hepatitis C, and still less to let him be treated for it, because he could only have contracted it through gay sex, and the accusation of being gay would harm his reputation in the "mob" irreparably and very dangerously. In fact, once Bill is forced to recognize that the truth of the situation is that Joey really *is* gay and actually wants out of his life in organized crime, then Bill's understanding of the illness and the circumstances change completely. At that point, the very real danger he had resisted turns out to be manageable in a completely unexpected way. And the true problem with Joey's safety, that Bill's ideas of how things make sense had stopped him from seeing properly, can be dealt with, too.

Again, in the episode "House vs. God," the patient's father supports his son throughout the episode against House's anti-religious commitment to science, but he himself ultimately switches his allegiance to House once House discovers – through his disrespectful skepticism – that the boy had had a sexual affair and so betrayed his own religious principles. In the light of that discovery, all the previous religious conflicts became irrelevant. Everything relevant (or central) to the problem they were dealing with was the result of the boy's betraying his own religious principles. And so it turned out that it was perfectly fine, from *everyone's* point of view, for House to have suspended those same principles in that situation.

It's important to notice that House does not engage in a simple "end-justifies-the-means" approach to ethics. That kind of approach might suggest, for example, that mistreating or lying to a patient in certain circumstances could directly lead to the patient's recovery, and therefore the lie or mistreatment would be justified because it leads to a "good" result. Yet this is explicitly *not* the way that House justifies his actions. In fact, most often, he doesn't justify his actions *at all*.

House's emphases on action rather than thought and on proactive lack of justification, taken to the point of having no concern with sense at all, bear strong similarities to Zen techniques and rhetoric. In the classical Zen stories, masters seek to teach their students to be open to the world "just as it is," and to their own realizations. The master may do this by refusing to answer questions or by answering them nonsensically, by giving one answer in one circumstance and an entirely conflicting answer in similar circumstances, by striking the student, throwing a shoe at them, barking like a dog, or by any number of other counterintuitive and possibly rude responses. The Zen master does not impart data or discursive knowledge directly to students, because "insight" or "enlightenment" is not information that a person learns (like algebra or the metric system). Instead, it's based on a change in the way a person looks at and is oriented to the world, in its entirety.

House's abrasive behavior and the ethics it involves work in a similar way. House doesn't do what he does to produce a cure, but to find out what the problem is. If his actions do directly produce a cure, that's an accidental by-product – and for his purposes, as he complains at such times, an *unsatisfactory* one. As a result, he doesn't and can't know what the "end result" of his behaviors will be. He doesn't know why the patient is actually sick. He doesn't know what will happen when he tricks them, or bullies them, or tries dangerous medical procedures. House acts in order to destabilize everyone's expectations (his own, the patients', his interns', the staff's, and so on). He shakes everything up not to get a particular result, but in order to let the illness (or issue) reveal itself as it is, on its own terms. House repeats this process until someone (usually him, but sometimes the other doctors) has an insight into the problem. So, House's approach is to destabilize the situation repeatedly until an original insight emerges.

Once we've found the genuine sense of the situation, our normal standards for what's ethical and appropriate operate again in this new context of understanding. This is why we can still see House as rude and unconventional, instead of just seeing him as fitting in with the new situation. Actually, House goes through the whole business of being House *just so that he can* make sense of the situation, *on the basis of what he thinks of as sense before unsettling the sense of anything.* In other words, he is, all along, following the guidance of our normal, everyday standards for sense and appropriateness. House's and Zen's dismissal of sense and appropriateness is for the sake of, and depends on, those usual, everyday standards of sense and appropriateness.

As a result, perhaps the oddest thing about House and Zen is that, as well as being so very odd, they *also* turn out not to be odd in any way at all. In that way, they're kind of the wizards of odd. As Zen Master Shunryu Suzuki says in this connection, "How do you like Zazen [Zen practice]? I think it may be better to ask, how do you like brown rice? Zazen is too big a topic. Brown rice is just right. Actually there is not much difference."[4]

So Zen and House's behavior turn out not to be odd at all. This is what the Zen tradition means by such terms as "beginner's mind" or "ordinary mind" – that is, a mind that just does what it does and then discovers the next moment openly and without prejudgments. Zen practice focuses on eating, sleeping, walking, sitting, and solving the problems of the day as they arise. Zen practitioners contend that by paying attention to the simple, everyday issues, one can consequently understand very important or difficult issues.

In summary, House's behavior is like a Zen practice. It's a style of *discovering* what the right way to act *is*. It does this, as it must, by being without presuppositions, without expectations, without knowledge of end. Nonsensically, but truly, it's a way of acting to discover how to act, not a style that "knows" what's right in advance.

House's irresponsible rhetoric, then, turns out to be a way of living ethically.

A Way of Establishing Intimacy

> *[The practice of Zen] means returning, completely, to the pure, normal human condition. That condition is not something reserved for great masters and saints, there is nothing mysterious about it, it is within everyone's reach. [The practice of Zen] means becoming intimate with oneself, finding the exact taste of inner unity.*
>
> – Zen Master Taisen Deshimaru (1914–82)[5]

It's House's rhetoric – not House himself – that achieves results. House is just as subject to the effects of his rhetoric as anyone else. In the true Zen spirit, there's no active "subject" here controlling or manipulating passive "objects." Instead,

4   Ibid., 40.
5   Taisen Deshimaru, *The Zen Way to the Martial Arts: A Japanese Master Reveals the Secrets of the Samurai* (New York: Compass, 1982), 5.

there's a "happening" or a "way" that the "subjects" and "objects" are only separate from in a limited way. House isn't successful because he's some kind of master of medical mysteries, but instead because he's committed to the practice of a kind of Zen rhetoric that will lead to answers with or without his conscious control of the process. The activity of diagnosis links the doctor, the patient, the puzzling disease, the circumstances, and the sense they all potentially make into a single event or "happening." As a result, we could say that House is just one of the instruments being used by the activity of diagnosis. In other words, House is "inside" the rhetoric; he's being performed by it and through it.

By his brutality and apparent indifference to humane considerations, House makes himself vulnerable to others' judgments, stripping himself of any protection of conventional respectability. And, equally, he does the same thing to others. As a result, his ongoing bonds with his friends and coworkers have no ulterior motives to rest on. The people involved are left with being connected only for the sake of that connection, pure, naked, and genuine. When professional courtesy, social politeness, and simple decency are all stripped away, then what remains is simply and genuinely the rhetoric, the style or way of the process, of discovery working its way through the experiences of each of the participants (doctors, patients, everyone involved).

House doesn't control the circumstance like some puppet master. Instead, he in fact undermines the control that *anyone* in the situation might (think they) have. He gives up control and strips others of control in ways that foster intense and very personal interactions. In this way, his rhetoric establishes profound human connection, or intimacy.

A Path to Truth, and a Method of Healing

A master in the art of living draws no sharp distinction between his work and his play; his labor and his leisure; his mind and his body; his education and his recreation. He hardly knows which is which. He simply pursues his vision of excellence through whatever he is doing, and leaves others to determine whether he is working or playing. To himself, he always appears to be doing both.
                    – François René Auguste Chateaubriand (1768–1848)[6]

Because House's rhetoric unsettles expectations and so allows solutions to emerge that the old expectations prevented, House's rhetorical style is also a way to truth. In fact, it's not only a way of discovering truth, but also a way of *becoming* what one truly is, since, as we've seen, it allows people *themselves*, and their relations to each other and to what they value, to emerge in their own naked truth.

---

[6] Source unknown.

We can see this, oddly and interestingly, in how he regularly dismisses his interns' suggestions (while demanding more of these suggestions!), and in how he typically interrupts their flow of thought by going off on silly tangents. He not only doesn't listen properly, but he actively makes sure that he's not listening properly. In this fashion he gets his own expectations and customary ways of thinking out of the way, and so opens himself (and sometimes also the disrupted speakers themselves) to noticing implications of what people are saying that he doesn't expect, and, what's more, that they themselves haven't been able to notice.

As it happens, the same reasons that make House's rhetoric a way to truth also make it a method of healing. First, because it's a way of finding the truth of the situation, it's a way of making it possible to find healing solutions. And second, in allowing the people themselves to emerge more truly and fully, it's already a different and deeper form of healing, in itself.

What's more, as we've discussed, the activity of diagnosis (of looking for the truth of the situation) links all the participants into a single process or event. As the Zen tradition emphasizes, this link is really so close that all the participants are in fact just different sides of one and the same "entity." This is the famous "nondualism" of Buddhism. One thing this means here is that a change in one part of the process also changes the other parts. As a result, for a doctor, finding the truth – which is a change in the doctor's understanding – is already also a healing change in the medical problem and the patient. We've seen this already right here, in that finding the truth allows us to see the patient and his or her problems completely differently, so that we are not dealing with the same issues any more, and *this* is what allows the healing to get under way (as in the examples discussed earlier).

So, from the point of view of what House is doing, talking about discovering the truth, and talking about "research methodology," is already talking about methods of healing. These can't be separated, because they're one and the same thing! It's this particular point that all of House's colleagues and friends fail to understand. House's closest friend, Wilson, often criticizes House by saying that he only cares about solving the puzzle and that he doesn't care about anything else (not the patient, families, colleagues, etc.). House often neither accepts nor denies these charges; most often he simply says something glib in response. However, here, House is playing with his buddies a bit (though whether he himself is fully aware of this is unclear); he's leading them on with a bit of a wink and a nod to the audience. For House, there's simply no difference between solving the puzzle and serving the needs of everyone involved.

It's also important to see that if what I am, what I do, and what I know are all parts of the same thing in this way, then House is not just strategically and cleverly *choosing* to be inappropriate, silly, self-centeredly petty, rude, and so on, any more than he's acting on what he objectively can't help being. What he *is* and what he chooses to do are one and the same thing. So it's true that he's choosing to act, but that choice also comes from what he simply is. In other words, House *is* all of these faulty things – and they are the medium (or part of the "way") of his virtues!

Zen Master Suzuki makes this comment:

> The most important point is to establish yourself in a true sense, without establishing yourself on delusion. And yet we cannot live or practice without delusion. Delusion is necessary, but delusion is not something on which you can establish yourself. It is like a stepladder. Without it you cannot climb up, but you don't stay on the stepladder. . . . We shouldn't be disappointed with a bad teacher or with a bad student. You know, if a bad student and a bad teacher strive for the truth, something real will be established. That is [Zen].[7]

House Sitting

You must meditate upon and consecrate yourself wholly to each day, as though a fire were raging in your hair.

— Zen proverb

House is deeply flawed, yet he is also depicted as uniquely free. His utter commitment to his Zen rhetoric frees him to have insights into nearly unsolvable problems. His life is not especially happy, warm, or free from pain: these are the goals to which many people would commit their lives. Paradoxically (if compared to what many people want or expect from life), House is often depicted at the end of each episode as peaceful and content when he has had the clear insight that solves that week's case. His personal or professional life might be full of unknowns or even in shambles. This troubles him little. At the end of "Human Error," the last episode of the third season, for example, we find the atheistic House sharing a cigar with a deeply religious patient's husband, both of whom everyone thought House was abusing throughout the episode. They are discussing how all of House's interns either quit or were fired.

THE HUSBAND: It's hard to lose your people. You must be upset.
HOUSE: I must be.
THE HUSBAND: But you're not.
HOUSE: No, I'm okay.
THE HUSBAND: What are you going to do?
HOUSE: God only knows.

When the rhetoric and its performative and proactive style have been practiced with clarity and focus, he accepts all other aspects of circumstance with Zen-style equanimity.

So we might perhaps sum all of this up with the thought that from House's point of view, it's not what you know, it's who you do.

---

[7] Suzuki, 41.

31

The Tao of the Bat

Mark D. White

Summary

In a candid interview with Bat-Tzu, one of Batman's closest friends and mentors, we learn about the ancient Chinese philosophy of Taoism, which focuses on the essential dualities of nature and the importance of achieving balance between them. We find out how Batman and the several Robins measure up to the Taoist ideal of the wise man, what they must do to move themselves along this enlightened path, and even a little about the mysterious Bat-Tzu himself.

Master Bat-Tzu, I thank you for granting me this interview, especially since you have never spoken to anyone of your unique relationship with Bruce Wayne, also known to some as the Batman.

You're most welcome. If my humble words can be of any help to anyone, I am glad to do it. Yes, as you say, I have known Bruce Wayne since he was a little boy. I was a friend of his parents, you know, particularly his father, Dr. Thomas Wayne. Good man, Dr. Wayne – I think of him often, as well as his lovely wife. So, of course, does Bruce.

I have tried to be a friend to Bruce since the untimely death of his parents. I hoped to guide him to a more harmonious place, but he chose a different path, what he has called the "way of the bat."[1] Even though I disagreed with his choice, I have tried to provide counsel when I could.

Why did you disagree with his choice?

Please don't misunderstand – he does an immeasurable amount of good as the Batman. But his life as the Batman is a life without balance, and balance is necessary for all things, especially people. The importance of balance is one of the

---

[1] *Shadow of the Bat Annual #3* (1995).

central teachings of the Taoist masters, such as Lao-Tzu and Chuang-Tzu, and through their writings they have been my teachers, as I have been Bruce's.[2]

Taoist masters?

Yes, Taoism is an ancient Eastern philosophy, dating at least as far back as Lao-Tzu's time, which focuses on the natural flow of the universe. The Chinese called this *tao*, or "the Way," for lack of a better name. Lao-Tzu actually says that the way is that which cannot be named.[3] Taoists try to align themselves with the Way by balancing the opposing forces within themselves, the light and the dark, the feminine and the masculine, the soft and the hard – what the Taoists called *yin* and *yang*.

Like the popular black-and-white, circular symbol?

Correct – that symbol is a representation of the balance between opposing forces that defines everything about the world we live in. *Yang* (the white part) represents the masculine, the hard, the unyielding, while *yin* (the black part) represents the feminine, the soft, the nurturing. The way that the two sides look like snakes chasing each other's tails shows that both sides flow into each other and ultimately define each other. This is also shown by the black dot in the white area, and the white dot in the black area – they tell us that the root of each side lies in the other.

Since that horrible day, I'm afraid that Bruce has let his *yang* dominate, believing it necessary to rid his beloved Gotham City of the criminals that infest it, but he has forgotten that he must still embrace his *yin*.

So he does have yin?

Yes, everybody does, and he is no exception – you can see it in the less tense moments, especially with Dick and Tim. . . .

The original and current Robins.

Correct – Bruce was often very hard on them, very demanding, in accordance with his *yang*, but he has had tender moments with them as well (though few and far between).

Didn't he recently go on some sort of "spiritual quest" with Dick and Tim? Do you think that shows some striving for balance?

Yes, the year he spent traveling around the world, after that horrible mess with Brother Eye and Alex Luthor, when Dick was almost killed.[4] I think he realized then

---

[2] The exact details of Lao-Tzu's and Chuang-Tzu's lives, including their true identities (sound familiar?), are a mystery. The *Tao Te Ching* is widely believed to have been compiled from various sources around 500 BCE, and Chuang-Tzu's primary writings date back to around 300 BCE.

[3] Lao-Tzu, *Tao Te Ching*, chapters 1, 25, and 32. All quotations from this masterpiece are translated by Thomas Cleary and can be found in *The Taoist Classics: Volume One* (Boston: Shambhala Publications, 1994), 12–47.

[4] See *Infinite Crisis* #7 (June 2006); the yearlong travels occurred during the *52* series (2006–7), but were explicitly shown only occasionally.

that his *yang* had dominated for too long, and he had become bitter, cold, paranoid – even for Bruce. Lao-Tzu wrote that "sages remove extremes, remove extravagance, remove arrogance."[5] I think that is what he has started to do. Indeed, since he returned, I have seen changes in him – for instance, he decided to adopt Tim shortly after their return. And he has shown such tenderness toward Selina Kyle's beautiful newborn child, Helena – I even heard he took her a teddy bear, in his Batman costume no less![6]

Why, he has even forgiven the magician, what is her name . . .

Zatanna? For the mind-wipe, you mean?
Yes, that's right, Zatanna – lovely girl, though very hard to understand sometimes.

Ha!
Even I was surprised when I heard about that – I thought Bruce would never forgive her for violating his mind like she did.[7] But you see, that's his *yin* – warm, soft, accepting of others' flaws – and it has begun to manifest itself more since his return. Of course, he still needs his *yang*, not only to perform as Batman, but to be a complete person, in harmony with the world and the Tao. All of us need that balance between the hard and soft, masculine and feminine.

Why is that? One of the key traits of the Batman is his single-minded devotion to the cause of fighting crime.
But a person with no balance is not in harmony – "knowing harmony is called constancy, knowing constancy is called clarity."[8] Many of Bruce's teachers taught him this, not just me.[9] The world is defined by dualities of opposing forces that must be held in balance to be effective – this is the meaning of the black and white intermingling in the *yin-yang* symbol. Lao-Tzu wrote, "Being and nonbeing produce each other: difficulty and ease complement each other, long and short shape each other, high and low contrast with each other, voice and echoes conform to each other, before and after go along with each other."[10] Without the repulsive, we would not know the beautiful; without the dark, there could be no light. We need the bad to highlight the good – how else would we know what the good is?

Look at Bruce, for example – he is defined by many dualities. Publicly, he lives in spacious, palatial Wayne Manor, but he spends most of his time in a dank, dreary cave covered in bat guano (dreadful stuff). He is one of wealthiest people

---

[5]   Lao-Tzu, *Tao Te Ching*, chapter 29.
[6]   *Catwoman* #53 (Mar. 2006), reprinted in *Catwoman: The Replacements* (2007).
[7]   The mind-wipe was revealed in flashback in *Identity Crisis* (2005); Bruce forgave her in *Detective Comics* #834 (September 2007).
[8]   Lao-Tzu, *Tao Te Ching*, chapter 55.
[9]   "In my teachings I had many masters, each with his own singular philosophy. My masters agreed on one point only: to be a warrior requires balance" (Batman, in *Batman Confidential* #8, October 2007).
[10]   Lao-Tzu, *Tao Te Ching*, chapter 2.

in the world, a captain of industry, but he spends much of his fortune to support numerous charitable causes, as well as financing his crime-fighting activities. He could easily live a life of pampered leisure, but instead he has devoted himself to a thankless task, fighting crime, every day fighting exhaustion and injury that would fell a normal person. He is one of the most intelligent, learned people in the world, as well as a physical specimen of human perfection, yet he does not take pride in these things but rather uses his abilities for the good of mankind, claiming no credit for his accomplishments.

Think about this, my friend – for all of his physical prowess, his dark, frightening costume, and his formidable size and presence, the Batman's most intimidating feature is that which is not even there – his shadow! As Lao-Tzu wrote, "The use of the pot is precisely where there is nothing. When you open doors and windows for a room, it is where there is nothing that they are useful to the room."[11] Nothingness can be more important than substance, which Bruce uses to "strike fear into the hearts of criminals," as he likes to say (endlessly, I'm afraid).

Now what was I saying – oh yes, he can be single-minded, as you say. If I had but a penny for every time I've implored him to take a night off, enjoy the company of one of the beautiful, intelligent women he's seen over the years, I could melt them down and make a second giant penny, like the one he keeps in his cave. But he usually relents only when doing so would serve the greater mission against crime – silly man.

[Laughs.] The giant penny, yes – that reminds me of a story. Did you know that once, Bruce was so lonely he asked that Aquaman fellow – not that new, young one, but the one from the old Justice League days – to help retrieve that horrid museum piece from the crevice it fell into during the earthquake that struck Gotham City? He couldn't bring himself to ask his colleague to visit but instead had to concoct a ruse to lure him here. Insufferable man, so afraid to share his feelings, to admit his emptiness, even with those closest to him.[12]

Have Dick and Tim inherited Bruce's imbalance?

Oh, thankfully no. Take Dick, for instance – despite all of his soul-searching, he is a young man who keeps his *yin* and *yang* in balance. Ever since he was a young boy, newly in our charge . . .

You were involved in raising Dick?

What? No . . . no, of course not, though I saw him quite a bit while visiting Bruce over the years. As I was saying, despite being struck by the early, violent death of his parents, as was Bruce, Dick managed to maintain a basic lightheartedness about him, light to balance the dark.

---

[11] Ibid., chapter 11.
[12] The giant penny was lost during *Cataclysm* (1998); the Aquaman episode occurred in *Gotham Knights* #18 (August 2001).

He had to – he couldn't exactly be sullen in green Speedos and pixie shoes!

Oh! Don't remind me.... [Laughs.] Sorry.... You've distracted me again. Stop that.

You know, I've heard that Dick, in his adult role as Nightwing, is often said to be "the Batman with a feminine side," which is precisely my point. He cares about his friends – not just as his responsibility, as Bruce does, but truly cares about them and for them. Just think about his recent tenure with the Outsiders, which was supposed to be a working group of heroes, rather than a family like the Titans, his former allies. But he found he couldn't do it – he found it impossible *not* to care about his colleagues, who truly became his friends, and he could no longer tolerate leading them into danger. Of course, who did he hand the group off to? Bruce, who was more than happy to assemble a group of heroes who would follow his commands to march into the flames of hell.[13]

What about Tim, the current Robin?

Oh, Tim is the one I fear for. He has lost so much since he began his crime-fighting career alongside Bruce – first his mother, early on, and more recently his father; his girlfriend, Stephanie Brown, who fought crime as the Spoiler (and Robin, for a brief time while Tim was "retired"); and two of his best friends, Conner Kent and Bart Allen.[14] And all of them died at the hands of criminals, just like Bruce's parents did. If anyone has a right to sink into despair and lose his soft, compassionate nature in strict devotion to his hard, retributive side, it's Tim. In fact, he told me once that when his mother died and his father lay paralyzed in a hospital bed, he stared "into the dark side," and felt "the night-demon's cowl . . . sucking me into a lifetime in hell."[15]

But in the end I think Tim realized this danger; he is a very self-aware young man. As Lao-Tzu wrote, "Those who know others are wise; those who know themselves are enlightened."[16] He's seen what loss has done to Bruce – you know, when Tim originally came to us . . .

"To us"?

Sorry, I did it again – when Tim came to Bruce, after deducing his secret identity, he said that Batman needed a Robin, that Batman had sunken too far within himself after the death of the second Robin, Jason Todd. He had become too hard and angry, again allowing his *yang* to rule over his *yin*. I suppose, in a way, that Robin has always been the *yin* to Batman's *yang*, the light to balance the Dark Knight.

---

[13] See *Outsiders* #49 (September 2007).

[14] Tim's mother died in "Rite of Passage" (*Detective Comics* #618–21, 1990); his father in *Identity Crisis* (2005); Stephanie in *Batman* #633 (December 2004), reprinted in *War Games Act Three* (2005); Conner in *Infinite Crisis* (2006); and Bart in *The Flash: The Fastest Man Alive* #13 (June 2007).

[15] *Detective Comics* #621 (September 1990); see also the last three pages of *Robin* #167 (December 2007) with regard to the death of Tim's father.

[16] Lao-Tzu, *Tao Te Ching*, chapter 33.

I suppose so. I had also never realized the role that death has played in many of Batman's inner circle, including Dick. . . .

Certainly, Dick has shouldered his share of loss – his own parents, of course, and more recently his adopted city of Blüdhaven, including many of his close friends. But perhaps he understands the nature of death, and hopefully he can help Tim (and, perhaps, even Bruce).

What do you mean by "the nature of death"?

Death is just part of a natural cycle and should be accepted as part as the path that we all take. Chuang-Tzu wrote well on this subject: "If you are at peace in your time and live harmoniously, sadness and happiness cannot affect you."[17] He questioned the preference for life over death: "How can I know that wanting to live is not delusion? How can I know that aversion to death is not like a homeless waif who does not know where to return? . . . How do I know the dead do not regret having longed for life at first?"[18]

I suppose the resurrection of Jason Todd would be a good example of that?

Yes – who is to say that he is happier now than in his previous state?

Oh, poor Jason – he was so angry, so wild, so uncontrollable – everything that Bruce could be if he doesn't maintain a constant check on his rage. Lao-Tzu wrote, "When beings climax in power, they wane; this is called being unguided. The unguided die early."[19] Jason needed to learn control; we all tried to teach him that. Unfortunately, his mysterious return doesn't seem to have taught him much either. Chuang-Tzu wrote that "the perfection of virtue is to take care of your own mind in such a way that emotions cannot affect you when you already know nothing can be done, and are at peace with what is, with the decree of fate."[20] But his fate remains to be seen, and I can only hope he can learn to accept what he cannot change; Bruce must learn this too, of course.

Of course, we can't discuss Jason without bringing up his murderer, the Joker.

The Joker . . . well, the less said about him, the better, I think. I'm sure others have much more to say about him than I could offer.[21] But interestingly enough, I do remember, once Bruce said that Dick told him that "the Joker exists because of me. How I represent the order that is necessary to live in Gotham City and the Joker

---

[17] Chuang-Tzu, *Chuang-Tzu*, chapter 3, p. 68. The "Inner Chapters" of Chuang-Tzu are included in *The Taoist Classics Volume One*, 51–100, from which the translations I quote are drawn, again translated by Thomas Cleary. These chapters are the most widely known and are the only ones attributable to the master himself. The unabridged *Chuang-Tzu*, including material appended by later scholars, can be found in *The Texts of Taoism*, vols. 1 and 2 (Mineola, NY: Dover, 1962).

[18] Chuang-Tzu, *Chuang-Tzu*, chapter 2, p. 64.

[19] Lao-Tzu, *Tao Te Ching*, chapter 35.

[20] Chuang-Tzu, *Chuang-Tzu*, chapter 4, p. 73.

[21] See, for example, Christopher Robichaud's chapter "The Joker's Wild: Can We Hold the Clown Prince Morally Responsible?" and Sarah K. Donovan and Nicholas P, Richardson's chapter "Under the Mask: How Any Person Can Become Batman," both in *Batman and Philosophy: The Dark Knight of Soul*, eds. Mark D. White and Robert Arp (New York: Wiley-Blackwell, 2008).

is the chaos that disrupts that order."[22] That's another example of how members of a duality support each other (and of Dick's budding wisdom, I daresay).

I notice you haven't mentioned Alfred yet.

Oh, I haven't? Well, there's . . . I suppose there's really not much to say about Mr. Pennyworth, except that he's a loyal servant, a trusted advisor – a paragon of humility. "Sages take care of themselves, but do not exalt themselves."[23]

A bit like you, Master . . .

Oh, I suppose, yes. Actually, I've always regarded Alfred as quite the epitome of the wise man, or sage, of Taoist thought. After all, Lao-Tzu wrote that "sages manage effortless service and carry out unspoken guidance."[24] That suits Alfred very well, I should think. Of course, he has put Bruce in his place on many an occasion, I should say.

Indeed.

Pardon me?

I'm sorry, just something caught in my throat.

Can I get you some water?

No, thank you.

Now that I think about it more, it seems to me that Alfred embodies a very important **concept** of the Tao, that of *wei-wu-wei*, or "action without action." Lao-Tzu wrote, "Do nondoing, strive for nonstriving."[25] The wise man knows when to do nothing, and by doing so, does something. Alfred is of inestimable aid to the Batman, but does so simply by seeing a clue that Bruce did not notice, a possibility he did not imagine, or some valuable insight that escaped him. Alfred's mind is open, and so he sees all at once. Chuang-Tzu told a story of a butcher who was so skilled he had never sharpened his blade in nineteen years. The butcher said that when he cuts up an ox, "the joints have spaces in between, whereas the edge of the cleaver blade has no thickness. When that which has no thickness is put into that which has no space, there is ample room for moving the blade."[26] Alfred is like that butcher, seeing what is there, and also what is not, which is often more important.

"Sages never do great things; that is why they can fulfill their greatness."[27] Alfred is not the Batman, but Bruce would not be the Batman without him. Chuang-Tzu

---

[22] *Batman* #614 (June 2003), included in *Hush Volume Two* (2003).
[23] Lao-Tzu, *Tao Te Ching*, chapter 72.
[24] Ibid., chapter 2.
[25] Ibid., chapter 63.
[26] *Chuang-Tzu*, chapter 3, 66–7.
[27] Lao-Tzu, *Tao Te Ching*, chapter 63.

wrote, "Sages harmonize right and wrong, leaving them to the balance of nature."[28] Alfred must balance the right and wrong within Bruce, tending to his health and his injuries, his joy and his sadness, his calm and his rage, trying to align them with the natural balance of things, the Tao.

It is a very difficult task that he has assumed, but that is Alfred's way, and he chooses to go with it, not against it. He reminds me of what Lao-Tzu wrote about water: "Nothing in the world is more flexible and yielding than water. Yet when it attacks the firm and the strong, nothing can withstand it, because they have no way to change it. So the flexible overcome the adamant, the yielding overcome the forceful."[29] Water runs gently through your fingers but over time can carve mountains. It is patient, as is Alfred – yet another lesson Bruce could learn from him. As you know, many of the martial arts that Bruce has mastered over the years are grounded in basic Taoist principles such as flexibility and yielding – for instance, they teach one to use an opponent's size and energy against him. Would that Bruce took those lessons to heart in other aspects of his life!

You know, Lao-Tzu wrote, "I have three treasures that I keep and hold: one is mercy, the second is frugality, the third is not presuming to be at the head of the world."[30] I can imagine Alfred saying that too.

It's almost like he just did. . . .
    Pardon?

Nothing, nothing . . .
    Do you have something to say, young man?

No, Master, it's just interesting how you've gushed about Alfred, especially since a few minutes ago you "didn't have much to say" about him.
    (Silence.)

Okay . . . well . . . thank you again, Master. It has been a most . . . illuminating discussion.
    You're very welcome. Now, if you'll excuse me, I have some cleaning to do . . .

---

[28] *Chuang-Tzu*, chapter 2, 60.
[29] Lao-Tzu, *Tao Te Ching*, chapter 78.
[30] Ibid., chapter 67.

Part IX

The Meaning of Life

Introduction

What is the meaning of life? This is the grandest of all philosophical questions. In fact, many other philosophical questions are asked solely in pursuit of shedding light on what the meaning of life is – no matter how dim that light might be. However, the meaning of the question itself is the matter of some dispute among philosophers. Some philosophers have argued that while a word can have a meaning, a life is not the kind of thing that can have meaning. According to them the question itself is meaningless. Other philosophers, however, have understood the question as one regarding the purpose of human life. On this issue, philosophers have spilt into two large camps: those who think there is an objective purpose for human existence and those who do not.

Many of those who believe that there is an objective purpose believe that God gives us that purpose. Other philosophers, like Aristotle (384–322 BCE), believe that humans have an objective purpose that has nothing much to do with God. For Aristotle, the purpose of human life is to flourish, to develop, and use our reason to govern our actions and feelings. Among those philosophers who believe that life has no objective meaning are nihilists who hold that life is utterly devoid of meaning. A more common approach in this camp is the one followed by most existentialists: we can choose and make our own meaning in life.

In their chapter, Jonathan Walls and Jerry Walls offer the perspective of those who believe in God by focusing on *Deathly Hallows*, the final volume in the Harry Potter saga. Whereas the evil Voldemort tries to cheat death at all costs, the noble Harry Potter is willing to sacrifice his life for others. If this life is all there is, then perhaps Voldemort's plan would be understandable. But, as it turns out, death is not the end in Harry Potter's universe. The soul lives on. And, as the unmistakable Christian imagery of the resurrection suggests in *Deathly Hallows*, the God-given purpose of life is to love one another.

TV's surliest doctor, Gregory House, says "We are selfish, base, animals crawling across the Earth. Because we got brains, we try real hard, and we occasionally aspire to something that is less than pure evil." House would seem to be in the nihilist camp, denying that life has any meaning and discouraging us from even trying to give it meaning. Henry Jacoby, in his chapter, argues that House actually does give meaning to his life. House shares with Socrates the belief that "the unexamined life is not worth living." Although he thinks "humanity is overrated," House would agree with Aristotle that reason is what is highest and best in us. House thus chooses a meaning for his life, solving medical mysteries and saving the lives of others.

32

Beyond Godric's Hollow

Life after Death and the Search for Meaning

Jonathan L. Walls and Jerry L. Walls

Summary

The issue of death and whether there is an afterlife comes up early in the Harry Potter series, but does not receive a clear answer until the last volume. This chapter examines thinkers ranging from the existentialist Martin Heidegger, who rejected life after death, to a number of diverse philosophers who affirmed it, including William James, John Locke, and Immanuel Kant. What one believes about life after death profoundly affects how one understands the meaning of this life, an insight as vividly demonstrated in the Harry Potter series.

After narrowly escaping death only because of his mother's sacrifice, Harry is an orphan, left on the doorstep of his aunt and uncle. Voldemort, we later discover, wishes above all things to avoid death and has performed the most treacherous actions to ensure it. Almost every book in the series results in the death of a significant character, perhaps none more so than Dumbledore in *Half-Blood Prince*. It's easy to hear the resounding echo of death all through the series, culminating in the near-death of Harry himself.

Death and Philosophy

Legend has it that there was a professional philosopher some years ago who decided to run for governor of his state. On the campaign trail, he was asked what the most important lesson was that we can teach our kids. He responded: "That they're going to die." He didn't win the election.

Philosophers deal in the great questions and ideas. Not surprisingly, therefore, many of them have been and are fascinated by death, the ultimate unknown. Since death is so unpleasant a prospect, however, some people try to avoid it, deny it, put it out of their minds. Young people are particularly prone to feel invincible, as though death is something that happens only to others. They often lack what the philosopher Martin Heidegger (1889–1976) calls *authenticity*, which comes from accepting death and reflecting deeply on our mortality.

Some philosophers, like the **Epicureans** in ancient Greece, have thought that we should be unconcerned about death, since when we die we cease to exist. Death doesn't exactly happen *to* us, it's merely the end of us. We're no longer around to experience it; the arrival of death corresponds with our departure, so why sweat about it? Heidegger, in contrast, thought authentic living requires a choice to face boldly what our death implies: that we will no longer be. As an atheist, he thought that at death we cease to exist, and living authentically is to live with a poignant recognition that death is ever close at hand. It's not simply a far-off event; it could happen any time, without warning or the chance to reflect about it, and its imminence should shape how we live and think right now. Our mortality confronts us with the task of defining ourselves, recognizing both our limitations and opportunities, and not wasting any of our short time living half-asleep.

Over 2,000 years ago, Plato expressed similar thoughts. Indeed, he is famous for teaching that "true philosophers make dying their profession."[1] To pursue wisdom is to live in such a way that one is prepared to face death when it comes.

Harry was confronted with death right from the start, so it was from an unusually young age that he was aware of his mortality. While Harry leads an authentic life, Voldemort lives a highly inauthentic one. To see why, let's consider Harry's climactic death march and what follows in *Deathly Hallows*.

The Approaching Battle

The matured and battle-hardened Harry somberly marches toward the Forbidden Forest for what he honestly believes will be the last time. He's going there to meet his own doom with open eyes. He has just learned that the only way Voldemort can be finished off is for *Harry* to die, taking a piece of Voldemort's soul down with him. As Harry walks, each step bringing him closer to the end, his thoughts come sharply into focus. In the shadow of his impending death, his senses become sharper. A great appreciation wells up within him for all the things he has possessed (physical or otherwise), but failed to fully value. Yet he remains resolute in the task before him. Dumbledore had known that, if faced with this choice, Harry would follow through, even if it meant his death:

> And Dumbledore had known that Harry would not duck out, that he would keep going to the end, even though it was his [Harry's] end, because he had taken trouble to get to know him, hadn't he? Dumbledore knew, as Voldemort knew, that Harry would not let anyone else die for him now that he had discovered it was in his power to stop it.[2]

---

[1] Plato, *Phaedo*, 67e.
[2] *Deathly Hallows*, p. 693.

Harry had faced death before when he lost a number of loved ones. Despite Dumbledore's assurance that death could be the next great adventure and despite Nearly Headless Nick's wisdom on departed souls, Harry retained more than a few doubts about what death would bring. The fact that dead bodies decay and rot in the ground filled him with more than a little **existential** angst. Recall the scene in *Deathly Hallows* when Harry and Hermione finally reach the grave of Harry's parents in Godric's Hollow and Harry slowly reads the verse inscribed on the gravestone of his parents: "The last enemy that shall be destroyed is death."

At first, Harry worries that this is a Death Eater idea, more in line with Voldemort's quest to escape death than anything else, and he wonders why such an inscription is there. Hermione assures him: "It doesn't mean defeating death in the way the Death Eaters mean it, Harry. . . . It means . . . you know . . . living beyond death. Living after death." But Harry's parents weren't living, Harry thought. "They were gone. The empty words could not disguise the fact that his parents' moldering remains lay beneath the snow and stone, indifferent, unknowing."[3] If this is what death involves, then talk of death's defeat seems a mockery, and death indeed means just this: moldering remains, decaying flesh, end of story.

This was the fate of Harry's parents, and Harry, in that dark hour, sensed it was the fate of everyone. Now, as Harry voluntarily marches to his own death, he realizes something: "And again Harry understood without having to think. It did not matter about bringing them (his departed loved ones) back, for he was about to join them. He was not really fetching them: they were fetching him."[4] He couldn't bring his parents back, but he could, and would, die, and thus join them.

Heidegger doesn't advise that we should morbidly reflect about death until we're depressed, but rather that we come to terms with death and the limitations it implies, so that we can move into our remaining future, however fleeting, boldly, taking advantage of what opportunities we have. Think not only of Harry in our scenario here, but also of Colin Creevey, the underage wizard who sneaks back into the Battle of Hogwarts to fight the good fight and loses his life. Harry and Colin's actions, regardless of their **beliefs** about life beyond death, are great examples of authentic Heidegerrian living: recognizing limitations, seizing opportunities, and accepting one's own mortality.

King's Cross Station

When Harry receives the apparent death blow from Voldemort, he awakens to find himself possessed of unexpected powers and in a place that resembles King's Cross station – a sort of ethereal realm, where time and space function differently. This scene is one of the strangest in the Potter books, but Rowling has made it clear that it is vitally important.

---

[3] *Deathly Hallows*, p. 328.
[4] *Deathly Hallows*, p. 698.

Waiting for Harry in this mysterious place is none other than Albus Dumbledore. This brings up another connection with Heidegger, who held that we should look into our past to uncover new possibilities for understanding life. One of his most important suggestions is that we need to choose our hero from the past, an exemplar we can use to guide us and help us make sense of our experiences. Heidegger proposes that we have a dialogue with this departed hero, thereby gaining insights that were won from his or her own experiences.

So who better for Harry to meet at this critical juncture than the beloved Dumbledore, who himself suffered death not long before and who'd devoted so much of his life to the fight against Voldemort? Not to mention that Dumbledore was, as Harry often says, the greatest wizard of all time.

Such a powerful wizard, one would assume, would be like a king in this place, but it is not so. He is simply kind, witty, patient Dumbledore. Dumbledore had once desired power and glory, until he realized, to his chagrin and shame, how dangerous these pursuits are, especially for himself. The Dumbledore we now see is the wise, gentle headmaster that we all know and love, who, by his own admission, is the better Dumbledore.

This mysterious way-station King's Cross evokes the image of Purgatory, the place of postmortem penitence, penal retribution, and spiritual growth in Catholic doctrine. As Dumbledore patiently catches Harry up on everything that was involved in Dumbledore's battle-plan against Voldemort, we see more than just answers to riddles; we see repentance and atonement. "For the first time since Harry had met Dumbledore, he looked less than an old man, much less. He looked fleetingly like a small boy caught in wrongdoing."[5] We also witness a full-fledged apology and confession from Dumbledore, tears and all. It is not that Dumbledore himself was wicked, or that he is now being caught in some great lie or misdeed. But Dumbledore had been imperfect, and his mistakes, mainly those of his youth, had caused great harm. Now, in death, Dumbledore has come to terms with his past misdeeds, and has grown wiser and merrier as a result.

In stark contrast to Dumbledore in the King's Cross scene is the hideous Voldemort creature. One can only assume that the revolting, deformed atrocity present in the train station is the image of the vanquished bit of Voldemort's soul. It seems that the decisions made by Voldemort have rendered his soul quite beyond repair, as Dumbledore points out in the following exchange.

> "Harry glanced over his shoulder to where the small, maimed creature trembled under the chair."
> "What is that, Professor?"
> "Something that is beyond either of our help," said Dumbledore.[6]

Dumbledore puts it into even plainer words as he and Harry discuss whether Harry will return to the living to finish his work or simply go on to the mysterious beyond:

---

[5] *Deathly Hallows*, pp. 712–13.
[6] *Deathly Hallows*, p. 708.

"I think," said Dumbledore, "that if you choose to return, there is a chance that he [Voldemort] may be finished for good. I cannot promise it. But I know this, Harry, that you have a lot less to fear from returning here than he does."[7]

Ironically, it is Voldemort's misguided fear of death that has driven him to the unspeakable acts that have obliterated any trace of goodness within him, but it is *because* of these choices that Voldemort now *actually* has reason to fear death.

It's worth noting that J. R. R. Tolkien's *Lord of the Rings*, which ranks with *Harry Potter* as one of the most popular fantasy epics of all time, echoes this quest-for-immortality motif. As Tolkien notes in his *Letters*, the real theme of *The Lord of the Rings* is not power or heroic resistance to evil, but "Death and the desire for deathlessness."[8] Sauron, the Dark Lord, pours a good part of his life-force into the One Ring, tying his own incarnate existence irreversibly to the Ring. This ring is the catalyst for much evil, and eventually must be destroyed. Let's see what this motif represents and what insight it may have for our own lives.

Reap a Destiny

It's said that the great American psychologist and philosopher William James (1842–1910) once wrote in the margin of a copy of his *Psychology: Briefer Course* the following lines: "Sow a thought, reap an action; sow an action, reap a habit; sow a habit, reap a character; sow a character, reap a destiny." The idea is that it starts small and ends big; our thoughts lead to actions, which upon becoming habit yield a character and ultimately a destiny. Voldemort's destiny, as revealed in the King's Cross scene, is the result of a lifetime of choices that put him on a fatal trajectory to destruction.

This scene raises a possibility that would be quite foreign to Heidegger. After being raised a Catholic and seriously considering the priesthood, Heidegger embraced atheism, abandoning belief in the afterlife. He once described his philosophy as a "waiting for God," a phrase that inspired Samuel Beckett's famous play "Waiting for Godot." Heidegger, far from thinking that atheism empties life of meaning or significance, thought that our mortality made choosing how we live this life all-important. As he saw it, death represents both the ultimate individuating event and the culmination of the process by which each of us forms our essence through our choices, since each of us must go through death's door alone.

---

[7] *Deathly Hallows*, p. 722.

[8] *The Letters of J.R.R. Tolkien*, ed. Humphrey Carpenter (Boston: Houghton Mifflin, 1980), p. 262. Perhaps the clearest example of the quest for immortality in Tolkien's writings is the invasion of Aman, the Blessed Realm, by Ar-Pharazôn and the men of Númenor in *The Silmarillion* (London: George Allen & Unwin, 1977), p. 279. The Númernoreans sought to wrest immortality from the gods (the Valar), and were destroyed for their impiety. For an insightful discussion of this theme in Tolkien's writings, see Bill Davis, "Choosing to Die: The Gift of Immortality in Middle-earth," in The Lord of the Rings *and Philosophy: One Book to Rule Them All*, ed. Gregory Bassham and Eric Bronson (Chicago: Open Court, 2003), pp. 123–36.

Rowling's view is both similar and different. The Voldemort creature at the station is saddled with an unchanging destiny. It represents the culmination of his development of character, a process that is complete. Voldemort no longer merely did evil; he had become evil. He is, as Dumbledore says, beyond help. He's chosen his fate, and it's ugly. As William James would have put it, Voldemort's thoughts led to actions, then habits, then a character, and finally a destiny. Aristotle notes how our actions put us on a trajectory, turning us gradually into particular kinds of people, each choice incrementally shaping our soul. Rowling's portrayal of Voldemort's terrifying fate represents the ultimate culmination of such a process, if, contrary to Heidegger's view, we don't cease to exist at death but instead must continue to live with the consequences of who we have become.

To put it another way, we might say that in death we will *fully* become who we were in the process of becoming, and now we must live with our chosen selves forever. Dumbledore was imperfect, but he showed remorse for his mistakes and was freed from their harmful effects. In a similar way, the ghostly images of Harry's loved ones who walk with him to the Forbidden Forest also reflect the good-natured, loving people they had been in life, something apparent in their appearance and conduct. Lily is nurturing; James and Lupin are reassuring; Sirius is casual and even a bit flippant, just as we remember him.

Voldemort, by contrast, obstinately refuses to turn from his self-imposed path to perdition, all the way to the very end – and it is not as if Voldemort didn't have his chances. Right down to the waning minutes of his life, Voldemort willfully rejects the one thing that can save him: remorse. Facing a terrible yet vulnerable Voldemort, Harry tries to offer a path of redemption still:

> But before you try to kill me, I'd advise you to think about what you've done . . . Think, and try for some remorse, Riddle . . . It's your one last chance . . . It's all you've got left . . . *I've seen what you'll be otherwise* . . . Be a man . . . try . . . Try for some remorse.[9]

Of course, remorse is not something Voldemort can muster, and this is his undoing. He may have retained his freedom to show remorse even at that last stage, but undoubtedly the pattern of behavior that had recurred so often made it exponentially harder for him to do so. For if Aristotle is right, repeated wrong behavior makes us yet more likely to continue in it, and makes it harder for us to resist. Willful choices of evil in the end, then, detract from freedom, if Aristotle's philosophy and Rowling's fiction is right. If such a picture of the human condition and our moral development is accurate, our choices bring certain truths into being and forge our characters. William James was a firm believer that we are free, an assumption Heidegger made as well. James stressed that this freedom, this liberation from a **deterministic** universe, is the most intimate picture each of us has of "truth in the making":

---

[9] *Deathly Hallows*, p. 741.

> Our acts, our turning-places, where we seem to ourselves to make ourselves and grow, are the parts of the world to which we are closest, the parts of which our knowledge is the most intimate and complete. Why should we not take them at their face-value? Why may they not be the actual turning-places and growing-places which they seem to be, of the world – why not the workshop of being, where we catch fact in the making?[10]

Such freedom, if it exists, is truly one of life's great mysteries, for it would enable us to make decisions on the basis of reasons that aren't causes; we would be morally and **metaphysically** free agents whose decisions shape our destinies but whose choices aren't written in stone. Such a view of human freedom need not require a denial that all events are caused, but it demands that some events are caused not by other events, like the physical processes of our brains, but by us, by persons.

On this view, our actions don't merely reflect who we are, they shape who we are becoming. To the last, Voldemort retains the capacity, however diminished, to show remorse, but he refuses and thereby seals his fate and grows literally beyond redemption. Plato said that evil is only done out of ignorance. But might some people actually prefer the darkness to light, because they've cultivated appetites that only vice can satisfy? Voldemort's fate raises just such a question.

How we live and what the significance of death is, are importantly connected to questions of whether, as Heidegger believed, death is indeed the end or, as Rowling's fiction depicts, there is life after death. Both Rowling and Heidegger highlight the Jamesian point that our choices here shape our destiny: either our completed human essence at the time of our deaths in Heidegger's case, or the part of ourselves that we take to the next life if death isn't the final end. The philosopher John Locke (1632–1704) suggested that the things that give us our most real identity are our memories and character. Locke's view of personal identity as inextricably connected to our characters, together with the possibility that death may not be our end, ratchets up the importance of developing the right character to literally infinite significance. For this will be a character with which we might be stuck for more than three-score and ten, a character that is the result of our own contingent choices rather than something inevitable or unavoidable.

In one of his most famous **arguments**, the German philosopher Immanuel Kant claimed that, to ensure the ultimate harmony of virtue and happiness, we have to assume the existence of an afterlife. Before him, the French philosopher Blaise Pascal (1623–62) was astonished at how many people draw up their ethics and carry on their lives indifferent to the question of whether there's an afterlife:

> The immortality of the soul is something of such vital importance to us, affecting us so deeply, that one must have lost all feeling not to care about knowing the facts of

---

[10]   This is a quote from James's last lecture at Harvard, given on December 6, 1906. Quoted in Robert D. Richardson, *William James in the Maelstrom of American Modernism* (New York: Houghton Mifflin Company, 2007), p. 287.

the matter. All our actions and thoughts must follow such different paths, according to whether there is hope of eternal blessing or not, that the only possible way of acting with sense and judgment is to decide our course in the light of this point, which ought to be our ultimate objective.[11]

Heidegger rightly sees that, if death is the end of us forever, that has implications for meaning and morality. The flip side of the same coin is that if death is *not* the end, but just the beginning, even bigger implications follow.

In the early volumes of her series, Rowling left it ambiguous whether death is the end or just the beginning in her fictional world. In *Sorcerer's Stone*, Dumbledore, in a trademark showcase of wisdom and foreknowledge, tells Harry that "to the well-organized mind, death is but the next great adventure."[12] But it remained unclear just what the great adventure consisted of and whether it included life beyond the grave. Now, however, the scope of the adventure has been brought more fully to light.

One of the most gripping aspects of Rowling's magical fiction is its compelling character development. Imperfect and morally flawed characters tangling with profound choices between what's good and what's easy provide insight into the "moral fiber" of characters we've come to care about. Adding to the drama and lending more potency to watching these characters progress or digress into what they will ultimately be is Rowling's sober recognition of human mortality. Even beyond that Heidegerrian focus, though, is this: if Rowling's fictional portrayal of the afterlife captures an aspect of reality, the choices we make in this life may be vastly more consequential than we could imagine if death, the last enemy, were never destroyed.

---

[11] Blaise Pascal, *Pensées*, trans. by A.J. Krailsheimer (London: Penguin, 1966), p. 427.
[12] *Sorcerer's Stone*, p. 297.

33

Selfish, Base Animals Crawling Across the Earth

House and the Meaning of Life

Henry Jacoby

Summary

Do our lives have meaning? And, if so, does such meaning require a divine plan or a relationship to such a plan? This chapter looks at these questions and defends the Socratic tradition, fully articulated in Aristotle, that the examined life, the life of reason, is the only meaningful one. Dr. Gregory House in fact exemplifies such a life, despite his claims that we are merely "selfish, base animals crawling across the earth" and that life is meaningless.

> *We are selfish, base animals crawling across the Earth. Because we got brains, we try real hard, and we occasionally aspire to something that is less than pure evil.*
> – "One Day, One Room"

So says Gregory House. It doesn't sound like he thinks life has any meaning, does it? Yet our Dr. House is leading what Socrates called "the examined life," and what Aristotle called "a life of reason," and such a life *is* a meaningful one. But how can this be? Could someone like House, who apparently thinks that life has no meaning, lead a meaningful life? And does House actually believe that our lives are meaningless?

"If You Talk to God, You're Religious; If God Talks to You, You're Psychotic"

Many people think that if there were no God, then life would have no meaning. So let's start there. Let's assume that our lives have meaning because we are fulfilling God's plan. In this case, meaning is constituted by a certain relationship with a spiritual being. If God does not exist, then our lives are meaningless. Or even if God does exist, but we're not related to Him in the right way, then again our lives are meaningless.

Perhaps God has a plan, and your life is meaningful to the extent that you help God realize that plan. For example, in the Kabbalah, the mystical writings of Judaism, we're supposed to be helping God repair the universe. This is a good example of what I mean; we're supposed to be helping God's plan succeed. A person who does this by doing good deeds and the like is thereby leading a meaningful life. Notice that someone could, in this view, lead a meaningful life, even if he believed that life had no meaning. Such a person might be doing God's work without realizing it. Could this be the sense in which House is leading a meaningful life?

Well, House doesn't believe in God; that's pretty clear. He consistently abuses those who do – for example, the Mormon doctor he calls "Big Love" in season four. In the season one episode "Damned If You Do," the patient, Sister Augustine, is a hypochondriac. As another Sister explains to House that "Sister Augustine believes in things that aren't real," House quips, "I thought that was a job requirement for you people." As another example, in "Family" House finds Foreman in the hospital chapel (Foreman is feeling remorse after having lost a patient), and he whispers, "You done talking to your imaginary friend? 'Cause I thought maybe you could do your job."

House's distaste for religion mostly stems from the lack of **reason** and **logic** behind religious **belief**. When Sister Augustine asks House, "Why is it so difficult for you to believe in God?" he says, "What I have difficulty with is the whole **concept** of belief; faith isn't based on logic and experience." A further example occurs in season four ("The Right Stuff") when "Big Love" agrees to participate in an experiment that may save a patient's life. The experiment requires him to drink alcohol, which conflicts with his religious beliefs. He tells House that he was eventually persuaded by the reasoning behind House's request. "You made a good **argument**," he says. House is both impressed and surprised. "Rational arguments usually don't work on religious people," he says, "otherwise, there wouldn't be any religious people."

Reason, not faith, gets results in the real world. Again in "Damned If You Do," House berates Sister Augustine when she refuses medical treatment, preferring to leave her life in God's hands. "Are you trying to talk me out of my faith?" she asks. House responds: "You can have all the faith you want in spirits, and the afterlife, heaven and hell; but when it comes to this world, don't be an idiot. Because you can tell me that you put your faith in God to get you through the day, but when it comes time to cross the road I know you look both ways." Here House is hammering home the point that faith might provide comfort or make us feel good, but practical matters require reason and evidence.

Unlike many, House doesn't find religious belief – specifically, the idea of an afterlife – all that comforting. At one point he says, "I find it more comforting to believe that this [life] *isn't* simply a test" ("Three Stories").

Even putting aside House's views for the moment, there are serious problems with the idea that God dictates the meaning of our lives. Think of great scientists, who better our lives with their discoveries. Or humanitarians, who tirelessly work to improve the world. Or entertainers even – like Hugh Laurie! – who make our lives more enjoyable. Do we really want to say that if there's no God, then these accomplishments and goods don't count?

A further and fatal problem (first presented about a similar idea in Plato's dialogue *Euthyphro*, from which I now shamelessly borrow) is this: What makes God's plan meaningful in the first place? Is it meaningful simply *because* it's God's plan, or does God plan it *because it's meaningful*? If it's the former, then the plan is simply arbitrary. There's no reason behind it, and therefore it could just as easily have been the opposite! But this doesn't sit well. Surely not just any old thing could be meaningful.

Instead most would say God's plan is as it is *because God sees that such a course of events would be meaningful*. But if this is right, then something else (besides God's will) makes the plan meaningful. So the meaning in our lives has nothing to do with God. House is right about that (whether or not God exists).

Eternity, Anyone?

Perhaps just the fact that we have souls gives us intrinsic value and makes our lives meaningful. Or perhaps it has something to do with the idea that souls are supposed to be immortal and live on in an afterlife. If there is an afterlife, then *this life* is meaningful *because it's leading somewhere*.

But House no more believes in the soul than he does in God; and he's convinced there's no afterlife as well. No evidence, right? What about so-called near-death experiences? Do they provide evidence for the afterlife?

In the season four episode "97 Seconds," a patient tries to kill himself because he believes in the afterlife and wants to be there. He has already been clinically dead and brought back, and while "dead," he had "experiences" in a beautiful, peaceful afterlife. He says, "The paramedics said I was technically dead for 97 seconds. It was *the* best 97 seconds of my life." House, of course, won't stand for any of this. He tells the patient: "Okay, here's what happened. Your oxygen-deprived brain shutting down, flooded endorphins, serotonin, and gave you the visions."

In the same episode the afterlife theme comes up again as a dying cancer patient refuses the treatment that would prolong his painful life. He prefers death, and tells House and Wilson, "I've been trapped in this useless body long enough. It'd be nice to finally get out." House blasts back: "Get out and go where? You think you're gonna sprout wings and start flying around with the other angels? Don't be an idiot. There's no after, there is just this." Wilson and House then leave and have this wonderful exchange:

WILSON: You can't let a dying man take solace in his beliefs?
HOUSE: His beliefs are stupid.
WILSON: Why can't you just let him have his fairy tale if it gives him comfort to imagine beaches, and loved ones, and life outside a wheelchair?
HOUSE: There's 72 virgins, too?
WILSON: It's over. He's got days, maybe hours left. What pain does it cause him if he spends that time with a peaceful smile? What sick pleasure do you get in making damn sure he's filled with fear and dread?

HOUSE: He shouldn't be making a decision based on a lie. Misery is better than
          nothing.
WILSON: You don't know there's nothing; you haven't been there!
HOUSE: (rolls his eyes) Oh God, I'm tired of that argument. I don't have to go to
          Detroit to know that it smells!

But House, ever the scientist, wants **proof**. He's going to see for himself! He
arranges to kill himself and is clinically dead for a short time before being brought
back. At the end of the episode, he stands over the body of the patient, who has
since died, and says, "I'm sorry to say . . . I told you so." What would House have
said if there were an afterlife and God called him to account? Probably, "You should
have given more evidence."[1]

Whether House's little experiment proved anything or not, what should we say
about meaning and eternity? House, the philosopher, disagrees with the sentiment
that life has to be leading somewhere to give it meaning. Consider this exchange
between House and his patient Eve, who was raped, in the brilliant episode "One
Day, One Room":

HOUSE: If you believe in eternity, then life is irrelevant – the same as a bug is
          irrelevant in comparison to the universe.
EVE: If you don't believe in eternity, then what you do here is irrelevant.
HOUSE: Your acts here are all that matters.
EVE: Then nothing matters. There's no ultimate consequences.

The patient expresses the idea that if this is all there is, then what's the point?
But for House, if this is all there is, then what we do here is the only thing that
matters. In fact, it makes it matter all that much more.

"If Her DNA Was Off by One Percentage Point, She'd Be a Dolphin"

Maybe our lives have no meaning. Maybe we *are* just crawling across the Earth, and
nothing more. Someone could arrive at this conclusion two different ways. First, if
meaning depends on God, the soul, or the afterlife, and none of these is real, then
the conclusion follows. But also, if our lives are eternal, then, as House says, what we
do in this limited time on Earth is diminished to the point of insignificance. From
the point of view of an infinite universe, moreover, how can our little scurryings
about amount to much of anything?

Philosophers who think that life is meaningless are called nihilists. To avoid
nihilism, it seems we should stop worrying about God and the afterlife – and House,

---

[1] This is what Bertrand Russell said in a famous anecdote. I imagine House might add: "And as long
as we're here, how come bad things happen to puppies? Cameron wants to know."

remember, rejects these anyway – and instead try to find meaning in our finite lives in the natural world. As House says, "Our actions here are all that matters."

How about how we *feel* about our actions? Does that matter? If a person feels that she's not accomplishing her goals, for example, or not having a positive impact on society, she might feel that her life has little or no meaning. But if she feels good about what she's doing, if it matters *to her*, might we not say that she's leading a meaningful life?

No, this is too easy. A person might be getting everything he wants, but if those wants are trivial, irrational, or evil, then it's hard to see this adding up to a meaningful life. For example, imagine someone like House who only watched soaps and played video games, but was not also a brilliant diagnostician busy saving lives. That would be a life without much meaning, even though our non-doctor version of House here might be perfectly content with his life.

Not only does "meaningful" not equal "getting what you want," but "meaningless" isn't the same as "not getting what you want." We might again imagine someone like House or even the real House himself: a terrific doctor helping a lot of people and saving lives, yet miserable, and not getting what he wants out of life at all. Yet, his life would still be meaningful and important because of its accomplishments, even though it didn't "feel" that way to him.

Now what if you care about things that are not trivial, irrational, or evil? Then, perhaps, your life could be meaningful to you – *subjectively*, as philosophers say – and at the same time be meaningful in the world, apart from your feelings, or *objectively*. So the question becomes this: What sort of life can we lead that produces meaning in both of these senses? And is our Dr. House leading such a life?

"You Could Think I'm Wrong, but That's No Reason to Stop Thinking"

Socrates (469–399 BCE), the first great hero of Western philosophy, was found guilty of corrupting the youth of Athens and not believing in the gods. For his crimes he was condemned to death. In actuality, Socrates was being punished for his habit of questioning others and exposing their ignorance in his search for truth. The jury would've been happy just to have him leave Athens, but Socrates declined that possibility, because he knew that his way of life would continue wherever he was.

Well, why not just change, then? In Plato's dialogue *Apology*, which describes the trial of Socrates, we hear Socrates utter the famous phrase "The unexamined life is not worth living." Socrates was telling us that he would rather die than give up his lifestyle. Why? What *is* an examined life anyway?

An examined life is one in which you seek the truth. You are curious. You want to understand. You do not just accept ideas because they are popular or traditional; you are not afraid to ask questions. This is the life of the philosopher.

The great British philosopher Bertrand Russell (1872–1970) described the value of this lifestyle and the value of philosophy in general when he wrote:

Philosophy is to be studied, not for the sake of any definite answers to its questions, since no definite answers can, as a rule, be known to be true, but rather for the sake of the questions themselves; because these questions enlarge our conception of what is possible, enrich our intellectual imagination and diminish the **dogmatic** assurance which closes the mind against speculation.[2]

Surely House agrees with this. In the episode "Resignation" House finally figures out what's killing a young girl, and he tries to tell her. Since this information will not change the fact that she's going to die, she has no interest in hearing what he has to say. "I don't want to hear it," she says. House is incredulous: "This is what's killing you; you're not interested in what's killing you?" As her parents make him leave the room, he says, "What's the point in living without curiosity?" Sounds a lot like Socrates.

Now maybe a life of curiosity – the philosopher's life (or the scientist who's interested in knowledge for its own sake) – is a valuable life, and maybe it's better than "an unexamined life." But that hardly means that an unexamined life isn't worth living at all. Why does Socrates think that? And why does House imply that such a life is pointless?

The examined life is the life of the philosopher, a life of reason. And reason is what is distinctive about humans. When Aristotle (384–322 BCE) said that "man is a rational animal," he didn't mean that we are always rational and never emotional or instinctive. He meant that humans alone have the *capacity* for reason. I think Socrates's point, then, is that a person who doesn't use reason, who doesn't lead an examined life, isn't realizing his potential as a human being. A life without reason and curiosity, a life where one doesn't seek the truth, is therefore a life no greater than the life of a lower animal.

House probably wouldn't put it quite like that. Remember, he thinks that "humanity is overrated." Still, a life where his puzzle-solving skills are put to no good use would be a life he would find incredibly dull and pointless.

House and the Life of Reason

It may be true that the unexamined life is a life without meaning and, therefore, not worth living, but that doesn't mean that *the examined life is meaningful* (and worth living). After all, the nihilists could be right. Maybe no life is ever really meaningful. Maybe no life is ever really worth living. How can we decide?

To answer this, we must return to the question of what makes a life meaningful. We must explain the properties that a meaningful life has, and then show that the Socratic examined life has those properties. From what we've seen so far, and especially where House is concerned, these properties have nothing to do with God, the soul, or the afterlife. They may, however, have something to do with how one feels about one's life, as long as those feelings match up with what we ought to care about, what we ought to feel is important.

---

[2] Bertrand Russell, *The Problems of Philosophy* (Oxford: Oxford Univ. Press, 1976), 161.

House's life is meaningful because he, for the most part, brings about desirable consequences. He saves lives. But the problem is, he doesn't seem to care that much about the lives he saves. For him, it's more about solving the puzzle. Why? Because that satisfies him? And it takes away his pain?

It's more than that. By solving puzzles, and thereby saving lives, House is exemplifying the life of reason. And this is what Aristotle deemed to be our proper function.

Aristotle was trying to answer the question "What is the good life?" For him, *good* is defined by a thing's proper function. For example, a good cane would be one that was easy to grip, helped you keep your balance, and kept you from further injury and pain while walking; a good doctor would be a doctor who was able to properly and efficiently diagnose and treat diseases (among other things). A good life then would be the kind of life that a good person would lead. So what is a good person? What is humanity's proper function?

We've already seen the answer: it comes from leading the life of reason. For Aristotle, this amounts to the rational part of us controlling the irrational part. The irrational part of us contains our desires; it tells us what we want and what we don't want. I like Thai food; I hate lima beans. This is how it works. But it doesn't tell us how much or how often we should want what we want. The irrational part, says Aristotle, contains no principle of measurement.

Reason, however, can measure, can discern proper amounts. These "proper amounts" are the virtues. For example, consider courage. Someone who is easily angered and always ready to fight does not possess courage. But neither does the coward. Courage is, as Plato had already noted, "knowing when to fight and when not to." Wilson, for example, often displays courage in his dealings with House, his friend. He knows when to stand up to him, but he also knows when to say nothing and avoid anger.

Just using reason in any old way is, of course, not the same as leading a rational life. Solving sudoku puzzles certainly requires logic and reasoning skills, but someone who did nothing else with his life would not thereby be living rationally. House's prodigious puzzle-solving skills, on the other hand, *are* meaningful and important, because of the results that they help to produce. Reason must be properly tied to action; House understands this. Again from "One Day, One Room" when Eve, the rape victim, says, "Time changes everything," House replies, "It's what people say; it's not true. Doing things changes things; not doing things leaves things exactly as they were."

Living the life of reason is, finally, of ultimate importance, according to Aristotle, because it leads to happiness or well-being – what the Greeks termed *eudaimonia*. So even if House usually seems to care more about solving the puzzles than the results that ensue, solving the puzzles must contribute to some sense of internal well-being for him, if I am right that he's living the examined life, the life of reason.

Some people would no doubt disagree with this conclusion. House, after all, they might say, seems to be miserable. Paraphrasing the sexy nutritionist from season three's "Resignation," I say to them: How miserable can he be saving lives, sleeping around, and doing drugs? Pass Aristotle the Vicodin.

Glossary

accuracy: a way of getting beliefs is accurate if it minimizes the risk of getting false beliefs. Accuracy is not the same as *informativeness*.

argument: a way of giving a reason for believing something by starting with some assumptions and showing step by step how the conclusion you want to be believed follows from them.

belief: thinking that something is true. Most of us believe that $2 + 2 = 4$, that cats give birth to kittens, that the flu is caused by a virus. So there is a great range and variety of our beliefs.

burden of proof: the obligation to provide evidence. In a disagreement, the burden of proof falls on the person making the most contentious claim. Most often, this is the person who is claming something contrary to verified fact or who is claiming to believe in the existence of some extra entity or entities. For example, if you believe in ghosts, the burden of proof is on you to provide evidence for their existence.

categorical imperative: the moral principle that you should always act in accordance with some general rule which could apply to everyone's actions all the time. It is the main principle of *Kant's* ethics. Kant also described it in quite different ways. See also *deontology, impartiality principle*.

compatibilism: the claim that people's actions can be freely chosen and also at the same time determined by physical laws. See *determinism*.

concept: You have a concept when you have a way of thinking about a kind of thing. For example, you have the concept of a cat if you understand the word "cat" or if you have some other way of thinking "that's a cat" when you see one. Concepts are needed for *beliefs*, because in order to believe, for example, that cats eat mice, you have to have the concept of a cat, the concept of a mouse, and the concept of eating.

consequentialism: a way of judging the moral value of actions by weighing up their good and bad consequences. An action is more morally valuable if it leads to more good and fewer bad effects. Different kinds of consequentialism use different concepts of good and bad consequence.

counterexample: a counterexample to a general claim is a single case that shows that the claim is false. For example, if someone says "all cats eat mice" then a vegetarian cat would be a counterexample to that statement. A counterexample to an *argument* is a single case which shows that the assumptions of the argument could be true while the conclusion was false. Suppose, for example, that someone argues "all daughters have mothers, therefore all mothers have daughters." A counterexample to this argument would be a family in which there are two sisters, one of whom has three girls and the other two boys. Then in this family all the daughters have mothers but it is not true that all the mothers have daughters.

deduction: a branch of logic. A person presents a deductive argument when they believe that the truth of their premises would guarantee the truth of their conclusion. Of course, they might be wong. If the their premises would not guarantee their conclusion, their deductive argument is said to be "invalid." Contrast this with *induction*.

deontology: a moral theory which classifies some actions as forbidden or permissible however good or bad their consequences. Most deontological theories, for example, will hold that it is forbidden to kill an innocent person even if killing them is the only way to prevent other people dying.

determinism: the theory that everything that happens is caused to happen in a way that makes it impossible for it to happen any other way. According to determinism, for example, if you scratch your nose at a particular time then given the state of the universe at an earlier time you could not have scratched your chin instead, or scratched your nose a moment later.

dogmatism: the view that some beliefs can be taken for granted and should not be challenged. For example, a religious dogmatist might think that it was obvious that the beliefs of his or her religion were true, and react with anger to anyone who doubted them.

dualism: the view that there are two basic kinds of thing. Most often, it refers to the theory that there are two kinds of substances – mental substance and physical substance.

eliminative materialism: the view that there are no minds, and that we should learn to think of ourselves entirely in terms of the operations of our brains. Eliminative materialists think that *folk psychology* is false.

empirical evidence: evidence drawn from experience to support a theory or belief. For example, empirical evidence for the theory of gravity includes evidence of how fast objects fall downwards near the earth. Note that empirical evidence never proves a theory beyond a doubt; it can only give good reasons for believing it.

existentialism: the view that people face basic choices in life about what kinds of people they are to be, and what they are to consider right and wrong, and that there is no way of being guided through these choices. You just have to face the possibilities, make your choice of who you are to be, and then live with it.

fallibilism: the view that any belief could turn out to be false. This does not mean that there is not a difference between beliefs which we have good reasons to hold and beliefs which we hold just because of, for example, superstition or laziness. But even if you have the best reasons for believing something you may later discover that it is false.

fatalism: the view that for any given thing that does happen, that thing had to happen (that is, it could not have failed to happen). Determinism is fatalist theory. Those who subscribe to it think that the past casually determines the future, and since the past has already happened, the future cannot happen any other way than it will. But one might also think that events are fated for other reaons – for example, one might think that God predetermines the occurrence of all events.

folk psychology: the beliefs about human minds, and why people do what they do, that we normally use to understand ourselves and others. For example, folk psychology holds that people normally act in order to satisfy their desires, choosing acts in accordance with their beliefs. *Eliminative materialism* holds that folk psychology is mostly false.

idea: according to *British Empiricism,* the basic building blocks of our thought are sensations we get when we experience the world through our senses. These are simple ideas (or "impressions"), and they get joined together to make the complex ideas which make up our thoughts.

identity theory: the identity theory of mind and body holds that what happens in our minds is part of what happens in our brains. So a person's thought or imagination is really something happening in their brain.

induction: a branch of logic. A person presents an inductive argument when they believe that the truth of their premises provides good support (but does not guarantee) the truth of their conclusion. Of course, they might be wrong. If the their premises do not provide good support for their conclusion, their inductive argument is said to be "weak." Contrast this with *deduction.*

instrumentalism: instrumentalism about scientific theories is the view that they are devices (instruments) for predicting observations. If two theories are just as good as each other at predicting what will be observed then neither is a better theory than the other.

libertarianism: the view that since many human actions are freely chosen *determinism* is false.

logic: the study of good and bad reasoning. See *deduction* and *induction.*

materialism: the view that everything that exists consists of matter.

metaphysics: the study of what exists, especially in terms of how the human mind can know it.

moral relativism: the view that moral truths are relative to something (for example, to individuals or societies). If one believes that moral truths are relative to societies, then one determines the rightness or wrongness of an individual's action by whether that action lines up with the moral codes of the society the individual lives in.

paradox: a very hard to believe conclusion based on assumptions which it is hard not to believe. "Paradox" can also refer to the puzzle presented when one believes (or is forced to conclude) two different things that seem not to be able to both be true together.

prisoners' dilemma: a situation in which two or more people can choose between a cooperative and an uncooperative action. If they both choose the cooperative action they both do quite well, but not as well as each person will if they choose the uncooperative action and the other chooses the cooperative one.

proof: an argument which attempts to show that its conclusion must be true.

realism: realism about science is the view that scientific theories can be true or false of real objects and real aspects of the world. So, unlike *instrumentalism*, scientific realism holds that a theory that makes accurate predictions may still not be a perfect theory, because it may be false.

reason: the capacity to think and decide, using evidence, memory, and logic to discover what is true and what we should do.

skepticism: the view that we can know very little.

state of nature: the imaginary situation in which people have no social rules and each person struggles against each other for survival and gain. It is discussed by Thomas *Hobbes*.

unfalsifiable: An unfalsifiable belief is a belief that nothing could prove false – no evidence could count against it. Although this may sound like a good thing, philosopohers have shown that unfalsifiable beliefs are often "devoid of content" and that holding them to be true is irrational. For example, conspiracy theories are most often unfalsifiable.

utilitarianism: the view that an action is right when it produces the greatest balance of pleasure over pain among all people it affects. See *consequentialism, deontology.*

utility: the balance of good over bad effects of an action. See *utilitarianism, consequentialism.*

Notes on Contributors

Don Adams received his BA from Reed College in 1983 and his PhD in Philosophy from Cornell University in 1988. He has taught philosophy at several colleges and universities across the United States, including California State University at San Bernardino, Middlebury College in Vermont, Hobart and William Smith Colleges in Geneva, New York, and Bentley College in the Boston area. Since 1998 he has been at Central Connecticut State University. His primary area of expertise and publication is ancient Greek Philosophy, especially the ethics of Socrates and Plato. He has also published work on the medieval philosophy of St Thomas Aquinas, and more recently has been analyzing elements of ancient philosophy in modern American popular culture.

Robert Arp has a PhD in philosophy from Saint Louis University and has interests in philosophy and pop culture, philosophy of biology, and ontology in the information science sense. He works as a contractor building ontologies for the Next Generation Air Transportation System through the Joint Planning and Development Office of the United States.

Jeremy Barris is professor of philosophy at Marshall University, in Huntington, West Virginia. As a philosopher, he is mainly interested in the relations between reality, thinking, style of expression, humour, and justice. His publications include *Paradox and the Possibility of Knowledge: The Example of Psychoanalysis* and *The Crane's Walk; Plato, Pluralism, and the Inconstancy of Truth*.

Michael Bray is an Assistant Professor of Philosophy at Southwestern University. He has published essays on Thomas Hobbes, C. B. Macpherson, Adam Smith, and Theodor Adorno and is at work on issues in film technology, and society.

Richard Davies read Philosophy at Trinity College, Cambridge (PhD 1992). He now lives in Italy, where he teaches Theoretical Philosophy and History of Philosophy at the University of Bergamo. He has written books on Descartes and a compendium of traditional and symbolic logic, as well as publishing articles on ontology, the philosophy of time, ethics, intellectual property, and the status of literary criticism; he is currently working on a defense of hedonism.

Jason T. Eberl is Associate Professor of Philosophy at Indiana University-Purdue University Indianapolis where he teaches bioethics, medieval philosophy, and metaphysics. He's the editor of *Battlestar Galactica and Philosophy* (2008), and co-editor (with Kevin Decker) of *Star Wars and Philosophy* (2005) and *Star Trek and Philosophy* (2008). He has contributed essays to similar books on *Terminator*, *Metallica*, *Harry Potter*, and Stanley Kubrick.

Peter S. Fosl is Professor of Philosophy at Transylvania University in Lexington, Kentucky. Co-author of *The Philosopher's Toolkit* (2nd ed. 2010) and co-editor of *Philosophy: The Classic Readings* (2009), Fosl, when not reading or writing philosophy, can be found where the gods are silent and the music is loud.

Daniel B. Gallagher has authored numerous articles in metaphysics, aesthetics, and Thomistic philosophy, and is the editor of the Values in Italian Philosophy series (Rodopi Press). He has previously contributed to *Basketball and Philosophy: Thinking Outside the Paint*, and *Football and Philosophy: Going Deep*. Father Gallagher, a catholic priest, currently serves at the Vatican.

David M. Hart is a graduate student in the English department of the University of Memphis, where he previously earned his BA in philosophy. His current research interests include Marxism, psychoanalysis, and the political history of fiction. More generally, his work is oriented by the intersections between phenomenology, ethics, and politics, particularly as they are demonstrated in the thought of Marin Heidegger, Emmanuel Levinas, and Alain Badiou.

William Irwin is professor of Philosophy and Director of the Honors Program at King's College in Pennsylvania. In addition to publishing in leading scholarly journals such as *Philosophy and Literature* and *The Journal of Aesthetics and Art Criticism*, Irwin originated the philosophy and popular culture genre of books with *Seinfeld and Philosophy* in 1999. Irwin has also co-edited *The Simpsons and Philosophy* and edited *The Matrix and Philosophy* and *Metallica and Philosophy*. He is currently the General Editor of The Blackwell Philosophy and Pop Culture series.

Henry Jacoby teaches philosophy at East Carolina University in Greenville, North Carolina. He has published articles on philosophy of mind, language, and religion, and on the nature of moral perception. He is the editor of *House and Philosophy, Everybody Lies* (Wiley-Blackwell, 2009).

David Kyle Johnson is currently an assistant professor of philosophy at King's College in Wilkes-Barre, Pennsylvania. His philosophical specializations include philosophy of religion, logic, and metaphysics. He has written extensively on the interaction between philosophy and popular culture, including a book on NBC's *Heroes,* and chapters on *South Park, Family Guy, The Office, Battlestar Galactica, Quentin Tarantino, Johnny Cash, Batman, The Colbert Report, The Hobbit, The Onion,*

Doctor Who, and Christmas. He also regularly teaches a philosophy and pop culture course and critical thinking/reading classes on weird myths (e.g., UFOs), the bizarre brain, and the history of Christmas and Santa Claus.

Renee Kyle is an associate research fellow in the philosophy program at the University of Wollongong, Australia. Her research interests include feminist philosophy, moral psychology, trauma-related disorders, embodiment, and women's health. She is currently researching the ethical implications of nanotechnology.

Matt Lawrence is Professor of Philosophy at Long Beach City College in Long Beach California. He is author of *Like a Splinter in Your Mind: The Philosophy Behind the Matrix Trilogy* (Wiley-Blackwell, 2004), and the forthcoming *Philosophy on Tap: Pint-Sized Puzzles for Pub Philosophers* (Wiley-Blackwell, 2011). The latter guides the beer-loving philosopher (or philosophy-loving beer drinker) through 48 philosophical conundrums over the course of 48 exceptional international and craft brews. Matt's motto is: "Drink in Moderation. Think in excess."

Greg Littmann is an Assistant Professor at Southern Illinois University Edwardsville. His main interests are philosophy of logic, metaphysics, philosophy of mind, and ethics. He has published in philosophy of logic and has written philosophy and popular culture chapters for *Doctor Who and Philosophy*, *Dune and Philosophy*, *Final Fantasy and Philosophy*, *Terminator and Philosophy*, and *The Onion and Philosophy*. He teaches courses in metaphysics, philosophy of mind, media ethics, and critical thinking.

J. Robert Loftis is an assistant professor of philosophy at Lorain County Community College. He has published articles in environmental and medical ethics. He has also written for the *Battlestar Galactica and Philosophy* volume of Wiley-Blackwell's Philosophy and Pop Culture series.

Sean McAleer is Associate Professor of Philosophy at the University of Wisconsin-Eau Claire. His work focuses on ethical theory, the history of ethics, and the philosophy of film.

Bonnie Mann is an Associate Professor of Philosophy at the University of Oregon in Eugene, Oregon. She is the author of *Women's Liberation and the Sublime: Feminism, Postmodernism, Environment* (Oxford Universality Press, 2006), the co-founder and co-director of the Society for Interdisciplinary Feminist Phenomenology, and the mother of four adolescent girls.

James McRae is an Assistant Professor of Asian Philosophy and Religion and the Coordinator for Asian Studies at Westminster College in Fulton, Missouri. He earned his PhD from the University of Hawaii at Manoa in 2006, with specializations in both Japanese philosophy and ethics. His publications include the book, *Environmental Philosophy in the Asian Traditions of Thought* (with J. Baird Callicott, forthcoming).

Matthew P. Meyer is a Lecturer in Philosophy at the University of Wisconsin-Eau Claire. He also teaches classes at the University of St Thomas. He has published in the *International Journal of Listening*.

Dónal P. O'Mathúna is Senior Lecturer in Ethics, Decision-Making and Evidence at Dublin City University, Ireland. His research interests included human dignity and bioethics. His most recent book, *Nanoethics: Big Ethical Issues with Small Technology* (Continuum, 2009), explores the intersection between bioethics, nanotechnology, and science fiction.

Jeremy Pierce is writing a dissertation on the metaphysics of race at Syracuse University and is an adjunct instructor at LeMoyne College. He also has strong interests in metaphysics and philosophy of religion.

Jeffrey C. Ruff is a professor of religious studies at Marshall University in Huntington, West Virginia. As a scholar, he is interested in meditation traditions (especially Zen and Yoga) and mystical and poetic visionary experiences (and the rhetoric one uses to talk about such things). Both as an artist and a scholar, he is generally interested in creativity, processes and methods – generally how human beings think about, talk about, and practice creative, imaginative, or intellectual work.

Greg J. Schneider is an Assistant Professor at Kettering University where he teaches technical communication. His current research centers on the rhetoric of science and technology and the way that museums communicate science to the public.

Robert Sharp is an Assistant Professor of Philosophy at Muskingum University in New Concord, Ohio. His specialty is ethics, especially moral dilemmas and conflicts of value. However, he teaches on a wide range of topics, from Ancient Philosophy to Advanced Moral Theory. He has contributed chapters to the *Family Guy* and *Battlestar Galactica* books in the Wiley-Blackwell Philosophy and Pop Culture Series.

Eric J. Silverman is Assistant Professor of Philosophy and Religious Studies at Christopher Newport University. His research interests include medieval philosophy, ethics, epistemology, and philosophy of religion. He has written several articles and has recently written his first book, *The Prudence of Love: How Possessing the Virtue of Love Benefits the Lover*.

Jason Southworth is an ABD graduate student in philosophy at the University of Oklahoma, Norman, a philosophy instructor at Fort Hays State University, Hays, KS and an adjunct instructor at Barry University in Miami Shores. His research interests include philosophy of language and philosophy of mind. He has contributed chapters to many pop culture and philosophy volumes, including *Batman and Philosophy*, *Heroes and Philosophy*, *X-Men and Philosophy*, and *Steven Colbert and Philosophy*.

Jennifer A. Vines earned a BA in Philosophy from Florida State University. She's currently Assistant Director of Graduate Financial Aid at Indiana University-Purdue University Indianapolis.

Jerry L. Walls is a research fellow in The Center for Philosophy of Religion at Notre Dame. He is writing a book on purgatory to complete a trilogy on the afterlife, along with his books *Hell: The Logic of Damnation* (University of Notre Dame Press) and *Heaven: The Logic of Eternal Joy* (Oxford University Press).

Jonathan L. Walls, Jerry's son, is a former musician and an aspiring filmmaker who switched to his current career path after repeated rejections from the Weird Sisters. He will be finishing film school soon, and he is also somewhat of a Potter proselytizer, having led many people to the joys of Rowling's series.

Mark D. White is Professor in the Department of Political Science, Economics, and Philosophy at the College of Staten Island/CUNY, where he teaches courses combining economics, philosophy, and law. He has written dozens of book chapters and journal articles in the interesections between these topics. His edited books include *The Thief of Time: Philosophical Essays on Procrastination* (with Chrisoula Andreou; Oxford University Press, 2010), *Iron Man and Philosophy* (Wiley-Blackwell, 2010), *Ethics and Economics: New Perspectives* (with Irene van Staveren; Routledge, 2009), *Watchmen and Philosophy* (Wiley-Blackwell, 2009), *Theoretical Foundations of Law and Economics* (Cambridge University Press, 2009), and *Batman and Philosophy* (with Robert Arp; Wiley-Blackwell, 2008)

J. Jeremy Wisnewski teaches philosophy at Hartwick College. He has published widely in moral and political philosophy, and occasionally in phenomenology and philosophy of science. He is the author of *Wittgenstein and Ethical Inquiry* (Continuum, 2007), *The Politics of Agency* (Ashgate, 2008), *The Ethics of Torture* (co-authored with R. D. Emerick, Continuum, 2009), *Understanding Torture* (Edinburgh University Press, 2010), and *Heidegger: A Beginner's Guide* (One World Press, forthcoming). He has also edited several volumes in Wiley-Blackwell's Philosophy and Pop Culture series, including *Family Guy and Philosophy* (2007), *The Office and Philosophy* (2008), *X-Men and Philosophy* and *Twilight and Philosophy* (2009, both with Rebecca Housel).

William Young III is Associate Professor of Humanities at Endicott College. He has published essays on popular culture, friendship, continental philosophy, and the interpretation of scripture. He is the author of two books, *The Politics of Praise: Naming God and Friendship in Aquinas and Derrida* (Ashgate, 2007) and *Uncommon Friendships: An Amicable History of Modern Religious Thought* (Wipf & Stock, 2009). He lives in Beverly, Massachusetts with his wife and daughter.

Sources

The editors and publisher gratefully acknowledge the permission granted to reproduce the copyright material in this book.

1 Young, William W., III, "Flatulence and Philosophy: A Lot of Hot Air, or the Corruption of Youth?," from Arp, Robert (ed.) South Park *and Philosophy: You Know, I Learned Something Today.* (Oxford: Wiley-Blackwell, 2006), pp. 5–16. Reprinted by permission of Blackwell Publishing Ltd.

2 Arp, Robert, "The Chewbacca Defense: A *South Park* Logic Lesson," from Arp, Robert (ed.) South Park *and Philosophy: You Know, I Learned Something Today.* (Oxford: Wiley-Blackwell, 2006), pp. 40–53. Reprinted by permission of Blackwell Publishing Ltd.

4 Jacoby, Henry, "You Know, I Learned Something Today: Stan Marsh and the Ethics of Belief," from Arp, Robert (ed.), South Park *and Philosophy: You Know, I Learned Something Today.* (Oxford: Wiley-Blackwell, 2006), pp. 57–65. Reprinted by permission of Blackwell Publishing Ltd.

5 Lawrence, Matt, "Tumbling Down the Rabbit Hole: Knowledge, Reality, and the Pit of Skepticism," from Lawrence, Matt (ed.), *Like a Splinter in Your Mind: The Philosophy Behind the Matrix Triliogy.* (Oxford: Wiley-Blackwell, 2004), pp. 20–31. Reprinted by permission of Blackwell Publishing Ltd.

6 Silverman, Eric J., "Adama's True Lie: Earth and the Problem of Knowledge," from Eberl, Jason T. (ed.), Battlestar Galactica *and Philosophy: Knowledge Here Begins Out There.* (Oxford: Wiley-Blackwell, 2008), pp. 192–202. Reprinted by permission of Blackwell Publishing Ltd.

7 Lawrence, Matt, "Mind and Body in Zion," from Eberl, Jason T. (ed.), Battlestar Galactica *and Philosophy: Knowledge Here Begins Out There.* (Oxford: Wiley-Blackwell, 2008), pp. 32–46. Reprinted by permission of Blackwell Publishing Ltd.

8 Southworth, Jason, "Amnesia, Personal Identity and the Many Lives of Wolverine," from Irwin, William, Housel, Rebecca, and Wisnewski, J. Jeremy, (eds.), X-Men *and Philosophy: Astonishing Insight and Uncanny Argument in the Mutant X-Verse.* (Hoboken, NJ: Wiley, 2009), pp. 17–26. Reprinted by permission of John Wiley & Sons, Inc.

9 Pierce, Jeremy, "Destiny in the Wizarding World," from Irwin, William and Bassham, Gregory (eds.), *The Ultimate Harry Potter and Philosophy: Hogwarts for Muggles.* (Hoboken, NJ: Wiley, 2010). Reprinted by permission of John Wiley & Sons, Inc.

10 Littmann, Greg, "The Terminator Wins: Is the Extinction of the Human Race the End of People, or Just the Beginning?," from Irwin, William, Brown, Richard and Decker, Kevin S. (eds.), *Terminator and Philosophy: I'll Be Back, Therefore I Am.* (Hoboken, NJ: Wiley), pp. 7–20. Reprinted by permission of John Wiley & Sons, Inc.

11 Johnson, David Kyle, "Cartmanland and the Problem of Evil," from Arp, Robert (ed.), South Park *and Philosophy: You Know, I Learned Something Today.* (Oxford: Wiley-Blackwell, 2006), pp. 213–23. Reprinted by permission of Blackwell Publishing Ltd.

12 Gallagher, Daniel B., "Aquinas and Rose on Faith and Reason," from Kaye, Sharon (ed). Lost *and Philosophy: The Island Has Its Reasons.* (Oxford: Wiley-Blackwell, 2007), pp. 241–52. Reprinted by permission of Blackwell Publishing Ltd.

13 Eberl, Jason T. and Vines, Jennifer A., " 'I Am an Instrument of God': Religious Belief, Atheism, and Meaning," from Eberl, Jason T. (ed.), Battlestar Galactica *and Philosophy: Knowledge Here Begins Out There.* (Oxfod: Wiley-Blackwell, 2008). pp. 155–68. Reprinted by permission of Blackwell Publishing Ltd.

14 Adams, Don, "Plato on Gyges' Ring of Invisibility: The Power of *Heroes* and the Value of Virtue," from Irwin, William and Johnson, David K. (eds.), Heroes *and Philosophy: Buy the Book, Save the World.* (Hoboken, NJ: Wiley, 2009), pp. 93–108. Reprinted by permission of John Wiley & Sons, Inc.

15 McAleer, Sean, "The Virtues of Humor: What *The Office* Can Teach Us About Aristotle's Ethics," from Wisnewski, J. Jeremy (ed.), The Office *and Philosophy: Scenes from the Unexamined Life.* (Oxford: Wiley-Blackwell, 2008), pp. 49–64. Reprinted by permission of Blackwell Publishing Ltd.

16 White, Mark D., "Why Doesn't Batman Kill the Joker?," from Irwin, William, White, Mark D., and Arp, Robert (eds.), *Batman and Philosophy: The Dark Knight of the Soul.* (Hoboken, NJ: Wiley, 2008), pp. 5–16. Reprinted by permission of John Wiley & Sons, Inc.

17 Loftis, J. Robert, "Means, Ends, and the Critique of Pure Superheroes," from Irwin, William and White, Mark D. (eds.), Watchmen *and Philosophy: A Rorschach Test.* (Hoboken, NJ: Wiley, 2009), pp. 63–77. Reprinted by permission of John Wiley & Sons, Inc.

18 Fosl, Peter S., "Metallica, Nietzsche, and Marx: The Immorality of Morality," from Irwin, William (ed.), *Metallica and Philosophy: A Crash Course in Brain*

Surgery. (Oxford: Wiley-Blackwell, 2007), pp. 74–84. Reprinted by permission of Blackwell Publishing Ltd.

19 Sharp, Robert, "When Machines Get Souls: Nietzsche on the Cylon Uprising," from Eberl, Jason T. (ed.), Battlestar Galactica *and Philosophy: Knowledge Here Begins Out There.* (Oxford: Wiley-Blackwell, 2008), pp. 15–28. Reprinted by permission of Blackwell Publishing Ltd.

20 Meyer, Matthew P. and Schneider, Greg J., "Being-in-*The Office*: Sartre, the Look, and the Viewer," from Wisnewski, J. Jeremy (ed.), The Office *and Philosophy: Scenes from the Unexamined Life.* (Oxford: Wiley-Blackwell, 2008), pp. 130–40. Reprinted by permission of Blackwell Publishing Ltd.

21 Hart, David M., "Batman's Confrontation with Death, Angst, and Freedom," from Irwin, William, White, Mark D., and Arp, Robert (eds.), *Batman and Philosophy: The Dark Knight of the Soul.* (Hoboken, NJ: Wiley, 2008). pp. 212–24. Reprinted by permission of John Wiley & Sons, Inc.

22 Kyle, Renee, " 'You care for everybody': Cameron's Ethics of Care," from Irwin, William and Jacoby, Henry (eds.), *House and Philosophy: Everybody Lies.* (Hoboken, NJ: Wiley, 2008), pp. 125–36. Reprinted by permission of John Wiley & Sons, Inc.

23 Mann, Bonnie, "Vampire Love: The Second Sex Negotiates the 21st Century," from Irwin, William, Housel, Rebecca, and Wisnewski, J. Jeremy (eds.), *Twilight and Philosophy: Vampires, Vegetarians, and the Pursuit of Immortality.* (Hoboken, NJ: Wiley, 2009), pp. 131–45. Reprinted by permission of John Wiley & Sons, Inc.

24 Wisnewski, J. Jeremy, "Killing the Griffins: A Murderous Exposition of Postmodernism," from Wisnewski, J. Jeremy (ed.), *Family Guy and Philosophy.* (Oxford: Wiley-Blackwell, 2007). pp. 5–15. Reprinted by permission of Blackwell Publishing Ltd.

25 Davies, Richard, "*Lost*'s State of Nature," from Kaye, Sharon (ed.), Lost *and Philosophy: The Island Has Its Reasons.* (Oxford: Wiley-Blackwell, 2007), pp. 177–90. Reprinted by permission of Blackwell Publishing Ltd.

26 Bray, Michael, "Laughter between Distraction and Awakening: Marxist Themes in *The Office*," from Wisnewski, J. Jeremy. The Office *and Philosophy: Scenes from the Unexamined Life.* (Oxford: Wiley-Blackwell, 2008), pp. 119–29. Reprinted by permission of Blackwell Publishing Ltd.

27 O'Mathúna, Dónal P., "The Ethics of Torture in *24*: Shockingly Banal," from Weed, Jennifer Hart, Davis, Richard Brian, and Weed, Ronald (eds.), 24 *and Philosophy: The World According to Jack.* (Oxford: Wiley-Blackwell, 2007), pp. 91–104. Reprinted by permission of Blackwell Publishing Ltd.

28 Pierce, Jeremy, "Mutants and the Metaphysics of Race," from Irwin, William, Housel, Rebecca, and Wisnewski Jeremy (eds.) X-*Men and Philosophy: Astonishing Insight and Uncanny Argument in the Mutant X-Verse.* (Hoboken, NJ: Wiley, 2009). pp. 183–93. Reprinted by permission of John Wiley & Sons, Inc.

29 McRae, James, "Zen and the Art of Cylon Maintenance," from Eberl, Jason T. (ed.), *Battlestar Galactica and Philosophy: Knowledge Here Begins Out There.*

(Oxford: Wiley-Blackwell, 2008), pp. 205–17. Reprinted by permission of Blackwell Publishing Ltd.

30 Ruff, Jeffrey C., and Barris, Jeremy, "The Sound of One House Clapping: The Unmannerly Doctor as Zen Rhetorician," from Irwin, William and Jacoby Henry (eds.) *House and Philosophy: Everybody Lies.* (Hoboken, NJ: Wiley, 2008), pp. 84–97. Reprinted by permission of John Wiley & Sons, Inc.

31 White, Mark D., "The Tao of the Bat," from Irwin, William, White, Mark D., and Arp, Robert (eds.) *Batman and Philosophy: The Dark Knight of the Soul.* (Hoboken, NJ: Wiley, 2008), pp. 267–78. Reprinted by permission of John Wiley & Sons, Inc.

32 Walls, Jonathan L. and Walls, Jerry L., "Beyond Godric's Hollow: Life after Death and the Search for Meaning," from Irwin, William and Bassham, Gregory (eds.), *The Ultimate Harry Potter and Philosophy: Hogwarts for Muggles.* (Hoboken, NJ: Wiley, 2010). Reprinted by permission of John Wiley & Sons, Inc.

33 Jacoby, Henry, "Selfish, Base Animals Crawling Across the Earth: House and the Meaning of Life," from Irwin, William and Jacoby, Henry (eds.), *House and Philosophy: Everybody Lies.* (Hoboken, NJ: Wiley, 2008), pp. 5–16. Reprinted by permission of John Wiley & Sons, Inc.

Index

Note: page numbers in bold refer to glossary entries

abortion 28, 232n17
Abu Ghraib 276, 279
accuracy 61, 235, **334**
acedia 119, 122–3, 126
Achilles 196, 198
ad hominem fallacy 23
Adams, Don 139
Adams, Marilyn 118n7
Adams, Robert 118n7
ADD (Attention Deficit Disorder) 40, 44
adolescence 230, 231, 233, 234–5
affirmative action 31
afterlife 319
  Harry Potter 317
  House 329–30
  Kant 325
  Pascal 325–6
  Rowling 326
  soul 329
agent-specific rules 166–7, 167n13, 169
agnosticism 32, 36, 64
Ajax 148
Alexander of Aphrodisias 93–4
Alfred, the Butler: *see* Batman
alienation 191
Allhoff, Fritz 274
altruism 251
Alzheimer's disease 73

amnesia 82
anger 142–3, 145
angiotensin 78
Angst 218–20, 321
The Animatrix 50n4
Apocalypse 188
Apollo 93–4
appearances 55, 215–16
appetite 139, 144, 145–7
Appiah, K. Anthony 281n1
appropriateness of wit 151, 154, 155–6
Aquinas, Saint Thomas 110, 119–20
  faith 120–1, 125, 127
  five ways 128
  God 124, 129–31, 130n3
  intelligent design 131
  knowledge 124
  praeambula ad articulos 125
Archimedes 53
Arendt, Hannah 10
  Eichmann in Jerusalem 7–8
  Responsibility and Judgment 10n4–5
argument 17, 18, 19–20, **334**
  beliefs 39
  conclusion 14
  evidence 36
  existence of God 129
  logic 16–18, 25

argument (*cont'd*)
  premise 14
  proof 54
  prudential 43
  for virtue 142
Aristotle
  ethics/politics 151, 247
  flourishing 152–3, 154–5, 317
  future events 90
  good life 333
  happiness 333
  humor 151–2, 154–6
  man as social animal 252n4
  the mean 153, 157, 162
  morality 154–5
  Nicomachean Ethics 9n3, 152–3,
    153n4, 155
  The Office 139, 151
  primary source 124
  purpose 317
  rationality 327, 332, 333
  ready-wittedness 155, 161
  reflection 8, 9
  shame 158
  soul 324
  virtue 9, 139, 152–4
  virtue ethics 152–3
  wit/buffoonery/boorishness 155–6, 157
Arnold, Millard W. 276n18
Arp, Robert 4, 40n2, 297n14
Arrigo, Jean Maria 273n11, 276n17,
  277, 278
art 264n4
artificial intelligence 67, 68, 80, 81, 83
artificial life forms 100
  see also machines
Astonishing X-Men 282
atheism 110, 118, 136, 137–8, 183, 323
atoms 56n13
attachment 290–3
Audi, Robert 39n1
Augustine, Saint 116–17, 132, 271
authenticity 320
authoritarianism 173, 180, 181
authority figures 22–3, 40, 222–3

bad faith concept 184, 204, 205–9
Baggett, David 95n17

balance in life 146, 308–9, 310–11
Barnaby Jones 7
Barris, Jeremy 287
Bartky, Sandra Lee 226n5
Bassham, Gregory 95n17
Batman
  and Alfred 164, 214–16, 217, 218, 219,
    314–15
  Angst 219–20
  balance in life 308–9, 310–11
  as crime-fighter 213–14, 311
  and death 217–18, 313
  freedom 214
  Heidegger 183
  as hero 214
  and Joker 140, 163–4, 165, 167–70
  meaning of life 219–20
  moral code 164
  responsibility 168–9
  Robin characters 309, 311–12,
    313–14
  spiritual quest 309–10
  Taoism 288, 308–9, 315
  utilitarianism 140, 164–5
  vengeance 214, 217, 219
  yin-yang 309–10
Batman: Year One 219
Batman Begins 170n17
Batman comics 163n1, 164n5, 164n6,
  168n15, 214, 312n14, 314n22
Batman Confidential 310n9
Battlestar Galactica 37–8
  Buddhism 287, 289–98
  democracy 63–4
  duhkha 290
  enlightenment 293
  epistemology 57
  existence of God 110, 128
  faith 60, 64
  Greek gods 196–7
  impermanence 292
  life-quest 64–5
  relationships 291, 292
  reliability of beliefs 60–1
  slave morality 195–6, 203
  testimony 60–2
  Zen Buddhism 289
  see also Cylons

Battlestar Galactica episodes
  "Bastille Day" 63, 195, 201
  "Colonial Day" 60
  "Crossroads, Part 2" 59, 60, 61
  "Dirty Hands" 196n2, 201
  "Downloaded" 294, 298
  "Exodus, Part 2" 60
  "The Farm" 292, 294
  "Final Cut" 133
  "Flesh and Bone" 60, 134, 197, 290,
    292, 293, 295, 296, 297–8
  "Fragged" 293
  "The Hand of God" 60, 135, 292
  "Hero" 198, 294
  "Home, Part 1" 137
  "Home, Part 2" 59, 137, 200
  "Kobol's Last Gleaming, Part 1" 59,
    136, 293
  "Kobol's Last Gleaming, Part 2" 60,
    63, 295
  "Lay Down Your Burdens, Part 1" 60,
    133
  "Lay Down Your Burdens, Part 2" 64,
    138, 199
  "Maelstrom" 60, 134
  "A Measure of Salvation" 197
  "Miniseries" 60, 129, 197, 198, 200, 296
  "Occupation" 134, 198, 289, 294
  "The Passage" 133
  "Pegasus" 292
  "Precipice" 201
  "Rapture" 196n2, 201, 203
  "Resistance" 61
  "Resurrection Ship, Part 1" 294
  "Resurrection Ship, Part 2" 199
  "Scar" 137, 294
  "Six Degrees of Separation" 129, 135,
    136, 295, 296
  "Taking a Break from All Your Worries"
    135
  "33" 290
  "Torn" 60, 133
  "Valley of Darkness" 293, 297
  "Water" 57, 60
  "The Woman King" 198
Bat-Tzu 308
Baudrillard, Jean 240
  Simulacra and Simulation 240n2

Bauer, Jack: *see 24*
BBC News Survey 271
Beam, Michael A. 26n4
Beauvoir, Simone de 232, 236
  The Second Sex 184, 230–1
Beckett, Samuel: *Waiting for Godot* 323
Begby, Endre 271n4
begging the question 77, 114
behavior 77–8, 102–4, 106, 303–4
being 102–3, 215–16
being-for-itself 206, 210–11
being-in-itself 206, 210–11
being-in-the-world 215
being-toward-death 213
Bekker numbers 153n4
beliefs **334**
  absurdity 14, 44
  accepted uncritically 41, 44–5
  agnosticism 32
  Aquinas 119
  argument 39
  claims 17
  emotional 23–4
  evidence 37, 39–41, 44, 62–5, 72
  faith 121
  in God 128
  good/bad 15
  justification 38, 46–7, 58, 59
  knowledge 38, 57–8, 121–2, 123–4,
    126–7
  logic 39
  normative 242
  opinion 17, 34–5
  reason 24, 58, 129
  slippery slope 21
  South Park 37, 39–41
  truth 27, 57
  see also religious belief
Bella character: *see Twilight*
Benjamin, Walter 267
Bentham, Jeremy 165n7, 174, 207
Bernstein, Carl 180
Bierly, Mandi 35n38
big bang theory 130, 131
Biko, Steve 276n18
bin Laden, Osama, in *Family Guy* 246n10
Bishop, Mark 104n8
Blaine, David 37, 44

Blake, William 286
blame attribution 83–4
bodily security 253
body 73, 83, 84, 231
boorishness 151, 155–6, 158–60
Bordo, Susan 232
　The Male Body 232n17
　Twilight Zones 232n17
　Unbearable Weight 232n17
Bowden, Mark 275n17
Bowie, David 187n4
Boyle, Danny 252
brain 74–5, 78–9, 80, 87
brain damage 73, 75, 87–8
brain stimulation 70, 72, 75, 77
Braverman, Harry 264n5
Bray, Michael 248
Breaking Dawn 228–9
Brent, David: *see The Office*
Buddha 287, 289–90
Buddhism 287
　Battlestar Galactica 287, 289–98
　interdependence 291n2, 298
　karma 294
　Noble Fourfold Truth 290–3
　nondualism 306
　suffering 289–90
　see also Zen Buddhism
Bufacchi, Vittorio 273n11, 278
buffoonery 151, 155–8
Bullock, Sandra 258
burden-of-proof **334**
burning bush story 31
Burnyeat, Myles 58n1
Burton, Cliff 191
Bush, George W., in *Family Guy* 246
business ethics 152

caloric substance 76–7
Calvin, John 109, 114
cannibalism 28
capitalism
　commodities 263
　consumer society 260, 261–2
　labor 248
　Marx 248, 260, 263, 267n8
　surplus value 248, 262–3
　and working class 261

care, ethic of 224
　feminism 184, 221, 226
　moral reasoning 226, 227
　social networks 221, 225
cartoons/self-awareness 240–1
CAT scans 72
Cataclysm 311n12
categorical imperative 179, **334**
Catwoman 310n6
cause and effect 130, 214
Celestials 282
censorship 13
character development 118
character virtues 153
charity, principle of 26, 30
Chateaubriand, François René Auguste
　305
cherry blossom example 291
Chewbacca Defense 14, 15, 16–17, 21
Chinese room experiment 102–3, 104n8
Christianity
　conservatism 190–1
　conversion of pagans 200
　devaluation of world 189
　Golden Rule 148
　Harry Potter 98
　Metallica 192, 193
　Nietzsche 183, 185, 186, 197, 200
　Plato's influence 113
　and Romans 186
　Serenity Prayer 197
　sin 186
　and slavery 197
　soul 197
　transcendence 189
　truth/reality 190
Chuang-Tzu 309, 309n2, 313, 314–15
Churchland, Paul 76–7
　Matter and Consciousness 76n7, 77
Cicero 271
civil society, Locke 255
Claremont, Chris 285
class differences 260–1, 265, 266, 267n7,
　268n9
Clifford, William K. 37, 38, 44, 45, 62–3
　The Ethics of Belief 39n1
　in *The Theory of Knowledge* 63n7
Cochran, Johnnie, in *South Park* 14–15, 20

coercion 271–2
Colbert, Stephen
    breaking character 35–6
    I am America (And So Can You!) 27,
        30, 35
    satire 26
    truthiness 4, 25, 30–3, 36
    on Washington 33
    wikiality 4, 25, 28–30
    WØRDS 30
Collins, Phil 44
color perceptions 55
Comic Relief Day 161–2
Comics Britannia 181
commodification of labor 262–3
commonwealth, Locke 257
communism 202
communitarian philosophy 247
compassion 174, 251
compatibilism 68, 95, **334**
concept 78, 121, 170, **334**
conception 10, 62
conclusion 14, 16, 17, 19, 20, 112
conclusion-indicating words 18
Confucius 287
consciousness 11n6, 78, 79–81, 104–5,
        106–7
consequences 63, 168
consequentialism **334–5**
    and deontology 172
    ends/means 173
    as rationalization of ruling 181
    reasoning 178
    torture 274
    and utilitarianism 174, 175
conservatism 26, 190–1, 238–9
consumer society 260, 261–2
convention/truth 27
Cooper, Anderson 25
cooperation 258
correspondence theory of truth 27
corruption 6, 7, 22, 181
counterexamples 58, **335**
courage 144, 150, 333
coworkers as family 286
Craig, William Lane 130n4
creativity 192
crime prevention 174

critical thinking 44
cruel actions 177
Cruise, Tom 41, 170
Crumley, Jack 39n1
Cullen character: *see Twilight*
cultural paradox 234
cultural relativism 28–30, 270–1
cyborgs 103–5, 106–7
Cylons, *Battlestar Galactica* 197–9
    duhkha 290, 292
    and humanity 199–200, 203
    ignorance/suffering 297–8
    moral character 294–5
    personhood 289, 297–8
    rebirth 294
    religion 197, 198–9
    uprising 183, 194, 197–9

Dahmer, Jefferey, as example 28
The Daily Show 4
Daniels, Greg 266n6
David, Peter 87
Davies, Richard 247–8
Davis, Michael 275n16
Days of Future Past 283, 284–5
DC Comics 214
De Bary, William Theodore 291n4
death
    and Batman 217–18, 313
    Harry Potter stories 320–3
    Heidegger 321, 325, 326
    idea 319–20
    Islam 191
    as next great adventure 321, 326
    Plato 320
    terrorism 277
    see also afterlife
A Death in the Family 163n1
death-wish 191
Deathly Hallows (Rowling) 98, 317,
        320–3
deception 1, 49–50, 51–2, 54, 78
Declaration of Rights 270
deductive argument 4, 14, 18–19, 20,
        59, **335**
dehumanizing process 276, 277
Deliverance 161
democracy 63–4, 180, 201–2

deontology **335**
 agent-specific rules 166–7
 and consequentialism 172
 dichotomous thinking 178–9
 essential moral rules 172, 173
 justifications of means 165–6
 Kant 165n11, 177
 as rationalization 181
 respect for persons 179
 right/good 170–1
 torture 269
 and utilitarianism 140, 166–7
Descartes, René
 cogito ergo sum 53
 deceitful demon 1
 Discourse on Method 53n10
 dualism 71–2
 existence of God 54
 Meditation on First Philosophy 48,
  53n11
 methodical doubt 49
 own existence 52–3
 reality 241
 skepticism 37, 46, 47–8, 52
Deshimaru, Taisen 304
desire 132–3, 230, 231–2, 234, 235
destiny 89, 95, 96, 324, 325
Detective Comics 310n7, 312n14, 312n15
determinism 90, 91, 214, 220, 324, **335**
deviant 244
Devising a Military Code of Conduct 271
Di Caprio, Leonardo, in *South Park* 41
dichotomous thinking 178–9
Dick, Philip K. 170
différance 241, 245
dignity 142–3, 162
 see also human dignity
discrimination 31
Disneyland 239–40
divine providence 98
DNA 281, 330
doctor–patient relationship 221, 222–3,
  224, 302
Dōgen 291, 292–3, 298
dogmatism 332, **335**
downsizing 264–8
doxa 119, 120, 127
dreams 12, 48–50, 265–6

dualism 67, **335**
 capitalism/working class 261
 Descartes 71–2
 and materialism 69
 The Matrix trilogy 70
 subject/object 214–15
duhkha (suffering) 290, 292
duty 151n1, 152
 see also deontology

Eberl, Jason T. 110
Eco, Umberto 178n12
ecstatics 216–17
education 232
Edwards, Jonathan 114–15, 115n3
egalitarianism 174
Eichmann, Adolf 7–8, 10
eidos 120
eliminative materialism 67, 69, 76, **335**
emancipation 292–3
emergentism 67, 69, 78–9
emotion 45, 105, 106, 143, 227
empathy 145n6, 150n11, 225
empirical evidence 72, 129–31, **335**
ends/means 172, 173, 179, 303
enemies 148–9, 150
Enlightenment 60–1, 62
enlightenment 293
enthusiastic people, Locke 31
envy 202
Epicureans 320
Epistēmē 119, 120, 127
epistemology 33, 37–45, 57, 186n1
epithumetikon 139, 144–6
equality 199–203
ethical behavior 299, 301–4
ethics 31, 63, 222
 Arendt 10
 Buddhism 298
 critiqued 183
 duty 151n1
 emotion 227
 friendship 10–11
 gendered 221, 222
 male bias 221
 morality 139
 outcomes 151n1
 politics 151, 247

torture 269

traditional 222

ethics of behavior 303–4

ethics of belief 37

The Ethics of War (Reichberg, Syse and Begby) 271n4

eudaimonia (happiness) 152–3, 333

euthanasia 5

evidence 17

  argument 36

  beliefs 37, 39–41, 44, 62–5, 72

  ethical theory 63

  proof 102

  prudential reason 42–4

evidentialism 62, 118

evil

  banality of 8

  character development 118

  existence of God 109, 112

  free will 111, 117

  God 114–15, 117

  and good 1, 10, 115–17, 194

  moral 132

  natural 111, 117

  problem of 112, 113

  South Park 1, 8, 109, 111–12

  thoughtlessness 5, 8

ex nihilo nihil fit 131

examined life 331–3

excellence 154–5

existence 52–3, 55, 56n13, 215

  see also human existence

existence of God

  Aquinas 124, 130n3

  argument 129

  Battlestar Galactica 110, 128

  demonstration 124

  Descartes 54

  evil 109, 110

  Job 113–14

  South Park 112, 115–17

existentialism **335**

  Angst 321

  de Beauvoir 184

  Heidegger 319

  Kyoto School 295n8

  meaning of life 317

  Nietzsche 183

  Sartre 205

  Watchmen 179

experience

  brain 78

  class differences 265

  consciousness 104–5

  inner 76

  pain 79–80

  perception 53

  virtual 75n5

facts 32, 36

faith

  Aquinas 120–1, 125, 127

  Battleship Galactica 60, 64

  beliefs 121

  Hugh of St Victor 120

  knowledge 109–10, 119, 120–1, 138

  Lost 109–10, 119–20

  misdirected 123

  reason 41–2, 109–10, 119, 328

  supernatural 110

  truth-telling 126

fallacy 15, 16–17, 20–3, 40n2, 178

fallibilism 90, 91, **336**

false dilemma fallacy 22

Family Guy

  conservatism 238–9

  meta-narrative 243

  politics 242–3, 245

  postmodernism 184, 238

  reality 239–41

  religion 242, 245

  self-awareness 240

  seriousness 241–3

  in *South Park* 7

Family Guy episodes

  "Blind Ambition" 244

  "Brian in Love" 242

  "Brian the Bachelor" 244

  "Chitty Chitty Death Bang" 239

  "Death has a Shadow" 239–41

  "A *Family Guy* Freakin' Christmas" 245

  "I Never Met the Dead Man" 239

  "Joehio" 243

  "Lethal Weapons" 240–1, 242n5

  "Let's Go to the Hop" 242

  "North by North Quahog" 240

Family Guy episodes (*cont'd*)
  "Perfect Castaway" 244
  "PTV" 246
Fantastic Four 213
farting 5, 12
fascism 178, 180
fatalism 67–8, 294n7, 324, **336**
Feinberg, Joel 33n28, 163, 164n2
female circumcision 29
femininity 229, 230, 231, 233, 237
feminism 183
  care ethic 184, 221, 226
  moral reasoning 223–4
  vampire love 228
The Flash: The Fastest Man Alive 312n14
flourishing 152–3, 154–5, 317
folk psychology 75, 76, 277, **336**
Foot, Philippa 140, 166
  Virtues and Vices 166n12
foreknowledge 95n17
Fosl, Peter S. 183
Foucault, Michel 184, 207, 244–5
  Discipline and Punish 207n2
  The History of Sexuality 245n7
  Power/Knowledge 245n8
  "The Subject and Power" 245n6
Fox and Friends 32
Fox News 13
free agents 325
free will
  Augustine 132
  compatibilism 95
  determinism 214, 220
  good/evil 111, 116–17, 133
  humans/machines 67
  libertarianism 95
  predetermination 95
  prophecies 68
  truth in the making 324–5
freedom 205, 210–11, 214, 245
freedom of speech 5
Freud, Sigmund 11, 12
  The Interpretation of Dreams 11n6
  Wit and Its Relation to the Unconscious
    12n8
Friend, Tad 260n1
friendship 10–11, 148, 150
functionalism 67, 69, 79–81

future
  actual/possible 91, 95
  Aristotle 90
  fixed time 97
  fixed/mutable 91
  open 95
  unknowable 176

gadfly 3, 11
Gallagher, Daniel B. 109–10
game theory 249
gaze, masculine 231–2
Geivett, R. Douglas 276n20
gender differences 221, 223, 224, 232
gender equality 235–6
generalization, hasty 21, 22
German National Socialism 268n9
Gervais, Ricky 162n10, 266
Gettier, Edmund 38, 58, 59
  "Is Justified True Belief Knowledge?"
    58n2
Giant-Size X-Men 82
Gibbons, Dave 173, 175, 176, 178,
  180, 181
Gibson, Mel 190–1
Gideon 31
Gilligan, Carol: *In a Different Voice* 223–4
Gladwell, Malcolm: *Blink* 32
Global Warming 25
gluttony 146
God
  as Absolute Nothingness 295
  as architect 133
  belief 128
  evil 114–15, 117
  as intelligent being 131
  Jews 131–2
  kenōsis theology 289, 295
  meaning of life 327–8, 329
  Nietzsche 183, 190
  as parent 133–4
  Plan 328
  purpose of life 317
  revelation 31, 125
  trust in 125–6
  see also existence of God
Goldberg, Stanford 102n3–4
Golden Rule 141, 148

Goldman, Alvin 59, 60n4
good
    and evil 1, 10, 115–17, 194
    instrumental/intrinsic 149
    reflective 9
    sharing 11
good actions 293n5
good life 333
good will 179
goods
    desire 132–3
    limited 252–3
Gotham Knights 164n6, 311n12
Gott, J. Richard III 130n5
government, Plato 149
Greeks 196–7
Griffin family 238–9, 240
Gunn, James E. 130n5
gut thinking 25, 30–3
Gyges 139, 141–50, 147

Hackman, Gene, in *South Park* 41
Hajek, Alan 42n3
Hakuin 296
Haldane, J. J. 131, 131n7
Half-Blood Prince (Rowling) 92–3, 319
happiness 139, 152–3, 174, 175–6, 333
Hárdi, Lilla 273n10
Hardin, Garrett 253n5
Haritos-Fatouros, Mika 276n16
Harris, Sam 245n9
Harry Potter (Rowling)
    afterlife 317, 319
    Christian view 98
    death 317, 319
    destiny 89, 95, 96, 320–1, 324–6
    ethereal realm 321–3
    fatalism 67–8
    fixed time 96–8
    prophecy 89–90, 91–4
    time travel 96, 97n21
    *see also Deathly Hallows; Half-Blood
        Prince; Sorcerer's Stone*
Hart, David M. 183
Hawking, Stephen 131n6
healing 299, 306
    see also care, ethic of
hedonism 174

Heidegger, Martin
    Angst 218–19
    atheism 183, 323
    authenticity 320
    Batman 214
    Being and Time 213, 215
    Dasein 215
    death 321, 325, 326
    existentialism 319
    human existence 213, 215, 216–18, 220
    interpretive horizons 215–16
    understanding life 322
Held, Virginia 224n4, 227n6
Hell, doctrine of 114n2
heroes 196
Heroes
    apology 147–9
    Claire character 142, 147–8
    good actions 141–2
    morality 139
    superpowers 146–7
    temperance 144–6
    virtuous characters 142–4, 146–7,
        149–50
Heroes episodes
    "Angels and Monsters" 145
    "The Eclipse: Part II" 145
    "Exposed" 150n10
    "The Fix" 141
    "Genesis" 143
    "The Hard Part" 150
    "Hiros" 141, 143, 146, 148, 149
    "I Am Become Death" 145
    "In One Giant Leap" 142
    "It's Coming" 145
    "The Kindness of Strangers" 141
    "One Giant Leap" 147
    "Our Father" 145
    "The Second Coming" 145
Hesman, Tina 281n3
heterosexuality 234
heterozygosity 281n2
Hetfield, James 186, 187, 188, 191, 193
Hick, John 109, 117–18, 133–4
Hiroshima 178
Hitler, Adolf 8
Hobbes, Thomas 247, 248, 250, 252
    Leviathan 250n1, 254, 255, 258–9

Holmes, Katie 170n17
Homer
  Iliad 196
  Odyssey 198n3
Homo superior 280, 281, 286
homosexuality 302
honor, personal 142–3
hope 119–20
horse training analogy 6–7
House
  afterlife 329–30
  care ethic 184, 221, 224, 225, 226, 227
  doctor-patient relationship 302
  ethics/male bias 221
  gender differences 221, 223
  healing 306
  meaning of life 318, 327, 333
  nihilism 318
  rhetorical style 299, 300, 303, 304, 305,
    306, 307
  skepticism 303
  unethical practices 300
  Zen Buddhism 299–307
House episodes
  "Acceptance" 227
  "Cursed" 300
  "Damned If You Do" 328
  "DNR" 301, 302
  "Family" 328
  "Half-Wit" 225
  "Heavy" 224
  "House *vs.* God" 303
  "Human Error" 307
  "Informed Consent" 224
  "Maternity" 224–5, 226
  "Mob Rules" 302
  "Need to Know" 225
  "97 Seconds" 329
  "One Day, One Room" 327, 330, 333
  "Pilot" 221, 222
  "Que Sera Sera" 222, 225, 227
  "Resignation" 332, 333
  "The Right Stuff" 328
  "Sleeping Dogs Lie" 225, 300
  "Three Stories" 328
House of M 86, 282
Hubbard, L. Ron 41
Hugh of St Victor 120

Hulk 82, 85
human dignity 277–8, 279
human existence
  being-in-the-world 215
  Heidegger 213, 215, 216–18, 220
  as thrown-project 213, 216–17, 218, 219
human genetic material 281–2
human genome 72
human nature 251–2
human rights 175, 278
humanity
  authentic 267
  Cylons 199–200, 203
  democracy 201–2
  and machines 81, 100–2, 195
  mutants 280–1
  saving of 136
  solidarity 137
  soul 198
  workers 264
Hume, David
  benevolent passion 251
  evidence 39
  God as architect 133
  in *The Matrix* trilogy 72n4
  nature, state of 248, 250
  sensory experience 61
  sun 72
  testimony 60–1, 62
  virtue ethics 153n3
humor 151–2, 154–6, 157, 162
  see also wit
Hursthouse, Rosalind 154n5
Hussein, Saddam, in *Family Guy* 243
Husserl, Edmund 231

idea 7, 72, 120, 238, 319–20, **336**
identity
  amnesia 82
  bodily theory of 83n1
  duplication 87
  Locke 67, 84–5, 325
  memory 67, 84–5, 86–7
  mind 84
  Parfit 88
  persistence through time 67, 83–4, 88
  Wolverine 82
Identity Crisis 310n7, 312n14

identity theory 75, 76, **336**
ignorance 35, 40n2, 289, 290–2, 297
immortality, quest for 323
impermanence 291–2
individualism 263
individual/society 247–8
inductive argument 4, 14, 18–19, 59, 72n4
Infinite Crisis 170n19, 309n4, 312n14
innocence 251–2, 256, 258, 259
input-process-output 79–80
insanity defense 164n3, 170
instrumentalism 149, **336**
intellectual virtues 153
intelligent design 131
intemperance 144–5, 147
interdependence 291n2
interpersonal relationships 263–4, 267
interrogation, coercive 271
intertheoretic reduction 75
intimacy 299, 304–5
intolerance 29
intuitionism 4, 30–3
intuitive aptitude 144–5
Iran-Contra scandal 180
Irish people 284
irony 160–2
Irwin, William 247n1
Isaiah 187n4
Islam 190, 191

Jacoby, Henry 37, 318
James, William
    afterlife 319
    beliefs 38, 63
    destiny 323, 324, 325n10
    faith 64
    freedom 324
    Psychology: Briefer Course 323
    skepticism 65
    in *The Theory of Knowledge* 63n8
Jerry Springer 12
Jesus Christ 70n1
Jews 17, 19, 131–2, 197
Job 109, 112–14
John, Gospel of 186
John Paul II, Pope 138
Johnson, David Kyle 4, 109, 294n7
the Joker

and Batman 140, 163–4, 165, 167–70
    insanity defense 164n3, 170
    as murderer 313
Joker: Last Laugh 169n16
jokes 12, 151, 155–6
Judaism 328
Judges 31
justice 146, 150, 184, 223–4
justification
    belief 38, 46–7, 58, 59
    knowledge 33
    means/ends 172
    testimony 60–1
Juvenal 180

Kabbalah 328
kalon 158
Kant, Immanuel 151n1
    afterlife 319, 325
    categorical imperative 179
    deontology 165n11, 177
    ends/means 179
    *Groundwork for the Metaphysics of
        Morals* 179n15
    reason 241
karma 289, 293–4, 293n5
Kasulis, T. P. 296n11
Keene Act 178, 181n22
Keiji, Nishitani 294n6
Kennedy, John F. 180
kenōsis theology 289, 295
Khadafi, Momar, in *Family Guy* 243
killing 164, 166, 167, 168, 169, 169n16
The Killing Joke 163n1
Klein, Shawn E. 95n17
knowledge
    Aquinas 124
    belief 38, 57–8, 121–2, 123–4, 126–7
    deception 1
    faith 109–10, 119, 120–1, 138
    Foucault 244
    and ignorance 35
    justification 33
    nature of 57, 59
    opinion 110, 120
    power 244–5
    sensory perceptions 124
    truth 58

knowledge (*cont'd*)
  as virtue 153
  and wisdom 32–3
  see also epistemology
koans 288, 296, 300
Koller, John M. and Patricia 290n1
Kracauer, Siegfried 261n2, 263, 264, 268n9
Kurtz, Howard 35n38
Kyle, Renee 184
Kyong Ho 299
Kyoto School 295

labor
  capitalism 248
  commodification 262–3
  manual 264, 264n5
  Marx 263
  meaningful 266n6
  mechanization of 263
  office 264n5
  productivity 263
  routinized 264, 267
  white collar 264–5
  see also workers
Lajtai, László 273n10
LaMarre, Heather L. 26n4
Landreville, Kristen D. 26n4
Lao-tzu 287, 309, 310, 311, 312, 314–15
laughter 12
Law and Order 13
Lawrence, Matt 37, 67
Lear, Jonathan 12n7
Lebowitz, Michael 267n8
Lee, Bruce 159
leper messiah figure 187n4
Levinson, Sanford 276n20
Lewis, David 79
libertarianism 68, 95, 95n17, 98, 247,
    284, **336**
lies 57
Limbaugh, Rush 25, 35
Lincoln, Abraham 30
literalism 158–9
Littman, Greg 68
Locke, John
  afterlife 319
  civil society 255
  commonwealth 257

enthusiastic people 31
*An Essay Concerning Human
    Understanding* 30, 31
  identity 67, 84–5, 325
  memory 85
  nature, state of 248, 249–50, 253
  reason 251
  rights 247
  testimony 61, 62
  Treatises 253, 255
Loeb, Jeph 164n5
Loftis, Robert 140
logic **336**
  argument 16–18, 25
  beliefs 39
  conclusion 20
  discussions of 15n1
  Heroes 143
  The Office 262
  problem of evil 132
  religious belief 328
  South Park 4, 14, 15
  truthfulness 58
  violations 14, 15–16
logistikos 139, 143–4
'the Look' 204, 205–9, 210–11, 212
Lost
  chain of truth 122
  faith 109–10, 119–20
  hope 119–20
  Innocence 256, 259
  language 255–6
  medical skill 256–7
  medical supplies 254–5, 257
  nature, state of 247–8, 249
  Other 257
  ownership 254–5
  smoke monster 124
  tit-for-tat 259
  Trust No. 1 252, 254, 255, 256, 258, 259
Lost episodes
  "Born to Run" 122
  "Confidence Man" 254, 255
  "Deus Ex Machina" 122
  "Exodus" 122
  "Fire + Water" 122, 123
  "1st Pilot" 254, 255, 256
  "Homecoming" 123

"House of the Rising Sun" 124
"The Hunting Party" 122
"In Translation" 122
"Man of Science, Man of Faith" 122
"The Moth" 122, 123, 254
"Raised by Another" 122
"2nd Pilot" 254, 255, 256, 257
"SOS" 120, 125, 126
"Tabula Rasa" 122, 254, 256, 257
"The 23rd Psalm" 122, 124
"Walkabout" 124, 257
"Whatever the Case May Be" 123
"White Rabbit" 252, 253, 257
love 230, 234, 236
Luban, David 272n7, 275, 276, 277
Lyotard, François 241
   The Postmodern Condition 241n4

machines
  and humanity 81, 100–2, 195
  personhood 67, 99, 100, 194
  recognition of 195
  souls 197–8
  Terminator movies 101–4
  thinking 100–2
  see also Cylons
McAleer, Sean 139
McRae, James 287
Madigan, Timothy 39n1
Madrox, Jamie (Multipleman) 86–7
Madrox miniseries 86, 87
magic 45, 89–98
Mahaffey, Tracie 297n14
Malcolm, Norman 162n8
The Man Who Laughed 165n10
management-speak 262, 267–8
Mann, Bonnie 184
marriage 28–9, 63
  same-sex 29n13, 286
Marvel Comics Presents 82, 86
Marx, Karl
  alienation 191
  Capital 262n3
  capitalism 248, 260, 263, 267n8
  on Hegel 187n3
  labor 263
  and Metallica 185
  on religion 183, 185, 186–7

socialism 247
surplus value 262
workers' revolution 261–3
Masao Abe 295n9
masculinity stereotypes 178, 229–30
master morality 196, 197
materialism **335**, **336**
  and dualism 69
  eliminative 67, 69, 76–8
  The Matrix trilogy 70, 73, 74
  mind–body 72–4
  reductive 67, 69, 74–5
Matriculated 50n4
The Matrix trilogy 37
  alternative reality 52
  consciousness 80–1
  deception 1, 49–50, 51–2, 54, 56, 78
  dualism 70
  functionalism 80
  materialism 67, 70, 73, 74
  mind/brain 69
  Neo 50–1, 70–1, 73–4, 76
  Oracle 70–1
  Revolution 73–4
  skepticism 40, 48–50
  truth 51–2
  virtual world 69–70
Matthew, Gospel of 202
mean, doctrine of the 153, 157, 162
meaning of life
  Batman 219–20
  examined life 332–3
  existentialism 205, 317
  God 327–8, 329
  Heidegger 322
  House 318, 327, 333
  nihilism 330–1
  The Office 266–7
  self-annihilation 237
  subjective/objective 331
  workers 263–4
  Zen Buddhism 300
means/ends 172, 179, 303
mechanization of labor 263
medical ethics 257
  see also care, ethic of
megalomania 175
melatonin 72n3

memory 60, 67, 72–3, 84–5, 86–7
mental laziness 37, 44
mental states 74–5, 79
Merchant, Stephen 162n10, 266
Metallica 183, 185
   Christianity 192, 193
   defeatism 188
   good/evil reversed 189
   male-centered lyrics 188
   Marx 186–7
   nihilism 189–93
   nostalgia 191–2
   rebellion 188–9
   religion 187, 193
   St. Anger 193
Metallica songs
   "And Justice for All" 192
   "Dyers Eve" 193
   "Escape" 192, 193
   "The Four Horsemen" 188–9, 192
   "The God that Failed" 185
   "Leper Messiah" 185, 187
   "Master of Puppets" 191
   "One" 187–8, 191
   "Phantom Lord" 188
   "To Live is to Die" 191
meta-narrative 241, 242, 243, 245
metaphysics 67, 70, 186n1, 325, **336**
Meyer, Matthew P. 183–4
Meyer, Stephenie 229, 230, 234,
   235, 237
Mill, John Stuart 151n1, 174, 175
Miller, Frank 219
Miller, Seumas 272n6
mind
   body 70, 71–4
   brain 67, 69, 75, 78
   identity 11n6, 84
mindfulness 298
mindlessness 13
Minsky, Marvin 81
miracles 70–1
misogyny 235, 237
modernism 241
Moore, Alan 173, 175, 176, 178, 180,
   181
   V for Vendetta 180n18–19

moral philosophy 151
moral reasoning 223–4, 226, 227
moral relativism 29, **336**
moral right 33–4, 33n28
morality
   Aristotle 154–5
   Batman 164
   Cylons 294–5
   duty 33n28
   ethics 139
   free will 133
   Heroes 139
   humor 162
   identity 83–4
   individual relativism 28
   killing of innocents 167, 168
   master–slave 195–7
   Nazism 29
   Nietzsche 194
   power 186–8, 195–6
   reason 195–6
   religion 185–6, 186n1
   reversed 183
   slave revolt 183, 194
   suffering 113
   superpowered people 141–2, 149–50
Morissette, Alanis 4, 14
Mormons 40, 44
Morrison, Grant 84
Moses 31
Murder by Numbers 258
mutants 83, 280–1, 282–6
mutation 280, 282

Nagasaki 178
naive realism 54, 55
National Socialism: *see* Nazism
nature, state of 247–8, 249–50, 253,
   257–8, **337**
Nazism 10, 29, 268n9
Neo: *see The Matrix* trilogy
neo-Nazi example 28
neural networks 77, 78
neurological states 75, 76
New, Christopher 170n18
New Avengers 88
New Moon 232

New X-Men 84
New York Times 232, 233
The New Yorker 260
Newman, Randy 243
Newtonian physics 130
Nietzsche, Friedrich
    Beyond Good and Evil 186, 196n2, 202
    on Christianity 183, 185, 186, 197, 200
    democracy 202
    The Gay Science 190n7
    The Genealogy of Morals 186, 186n2,
        196n1, 197, 202
    on God 183, 190
    master morality 196
    and Metallica 185
    morality 194
    nihilism 185, 189
    slave morality 195
    transvaluation 189
    Twilight of the Idols 186, 192n9
    "Untimely Meditations" 191n8
    The Will to Power 189n5, 190
Nightwing 169n16
nihilism
    and atheism 137
    House 318
    Islam 190
    meaning of life 330–1
    Metallica 189–93
    Nietzsche 185, 189
    self-destruction 190
nirvana 293n5
Nishida Kitarō 295
Nixon, Richard 180
No Man's Land 163n1, 164n4
Noble Eightfold Path 292–3, 298
Noble Fourfold Truth 290
nondualism 306
no-self 291
nostalgia 191–2
Nova, Cassandra: *see* X-Men

objectification 211
obligation 168
Oedipus story 93–4
The Office
    Aristotelian ethics 139, 151

boorishness 155–6, 158–60
British/American versions 139, 156, 260–1
buffoonery 155–8
capitalism/labor 248
class differences 260–1, 267n7, 268n9
interpersonal relationships 263–4, 267
irony 160–2
literalism 158–9
logic 262
'the look' 184, 204
management-speak 262, 267–8
meaning of life 266–7
Sartre 183–4
wit 139, 155–6, 160–2
The Office episodes
    "Back from Vacation" 207
    "Ben Franklin" 206
    "A Benihana Christmas" 209
    "Boys and Girls" 263, 264, 265
    "Branch Closing" 262, 263, 265
    "Business School" 264, 267
    "Cocktails" 208
    "The Convict" 266
    "The Fire" 265
    "Hot Girl" 204
    "The Injury" 207
    "The Job" 205
    "The Merger" 205–6, 209–10
    "Office Olympics" 266
    "Phyllis' Wedding" 207
    "The Pilot" 266n6
Office of the High Commissioner for
        Human Rights 270n2
O'Mathúna, Dónal P. 248
opinion 17, 33–5, 119, 120, 214
Oravecz, Robert 273n10
organ transplant problem 167–8
Other 206–7, 208–9, 210–11, 257, 259
Outsiders 312n13
ownership 254–5
Ozymandias: *see Watchmen*

paganism 141, 148, 183, 200
pain 79–80, 104–5, 106–7, 272, 297–8
    see also suffering
Palin, Sarah 35, 229
panopticon 207, 208

paradox **337**
  adolescent girls 233
  capitalism 263
  cultural 234
  koans 300
  Lost 121
  objectification 211
  time travel/fixed time 96–7
parental role 134
Parfit, Derek 67, 86–7, 88
Parker, Trey 5, 11, 21
Parsons, Edward 114n2
Pascal, Blaise 37, 42–3, 128–9, 325–6
Pascal's Wager 42–3, 129
The Passion of the Christ 190–1
patriarchy 180
PC to Mac copying analogy 81n11
Peirlott, Matthew 32
perception 36, 53, 56, 92, 157
personhood
  consciousness 104–5, 107
  Cylons 289, 297–8
  gendered power 232
  identity 83–4
  machines 67, 99, 100, 194
  Parfit 87
  persistence over time 82, 83
  slavery 194
  Terminator movies 99–100
  Turing Test 68
Pessin, Andrew 102n3–4
1 Peter 120
Philippians 295
Phillips, Lynn 233, 234
philosophy 1–4, 35–6, 287–8
philosophy of language 186n1
philosophy of religion 109–10
physics 130
Pierce, Jeremy 67–8, 248
pineal gland 72
Pipher, Mary: *Reviving Ophelia* 233
Plantinga, Alvin 61–2
Plato
  and Christianity 113
  courage 333
  critical reflection 8–9
  death 320
  ethics/politics 247

forms 189n6
  government 149
  justice 146
  ring of Gyges 1, 139, 141–50
  sheepdog analogy 149
  virtue 139
  virtue ethics 153n3
Plato, works
  Apology 6, 7, 9–10, 11, 331
  Euthyphro 329
  Phaedo 320n1
  Protagoras 253n5
  The Republic 9n3, 120, 142n1, 148
  Theaetetus 58
Pojman, Louis P. 63n7, 118n7
political philosophy 248, 249–50
politics 201, 242–3, 245, 247
postmodernism 184, 238, 244
power
  authoritarianism 173
  corruption 181
  gendered 232
  knowledge 244–5
  morality 186–8, 195–6
  rationalization of 176
  virtue 142
  Watchmen 181
praeambula ad articulos 125
praesumptio 119, 126
praise attribution 83–4
predetermination 95
prediction 91–2, 94, 96
pregnancy, vampire fetus 235–6
prejudice 21, 284
premise 14, 16, 17, 20, 112
premise-indicating words 18
prepunishment 170
Preston, John 104n8
presumption 119, 126
pride 210–11, 212
Prisoner of Azkaban 96
prisoners' dilemma 258, **337**
probability 19
productivity of labor 263
proletariat 261, 264
proof 40, 54, 102, 124, 330, **337**
property relations 254–5
prophecies

accessing information 90–1
destiny 89, 95
determinism 91
fallible 90, 91–3
fulfillment 98
Harry Potter 67–8
prediction 94
self-fulfilling 93–4
prophets, Old Testament 31
propositions 27
providential approach 98
psychoanalysis 12
psychological states 75, 135
psychotropic drugs 72
Punisher Vol. 3 88
punishment 83–4, 114–15, 147, 174
Purgatory 322
purpose of life 317
see also meaning of life
Putnam, Hilary 53n11

race
as biological category 281, 282–3, 284
as genetic category 248, 281
mutants 285–6
as social category 248, 283–5
stereotypes 284
X-Men 248, 280–6
racism 28
Rand, Ayn: *Atlas Shrugged* 21
rape 147
rational argument 328
rational inquiry 31, 39
rationality 109, 272, 327, 332, 333
see also reason
ready-wittedness 155, 161
Reagan, Ronald 180
realism 54, 55, **337**
reality
alternative 52
appearance 55
Descartes 241
dreams 48–50
existence 55
Family Guy 239–41
Kant 241
majority consensus 28
The Matrix trilogy 46–7

metaphysics 67
perception 56
Platonic forms 189n6
skepticism 54–6
testimony 61
truth 190
reason 139, **337**
belief 24, 58, 129
emotion 45
evidential 42
faith 41–2, 109–10, 119, 328
Kant 241
Locke 251
morality 195–6
postmodernism 238
prudential 42–4
religious belief 138, 328
thumos 144
see also rationality
reasoning 6, 9
bad 114
believing 58
consequentialism 178
dualism 71
logic 14, 15
rebellion 188–9
rebirth 289, 293–4
red-herring fallacy 4, 21
reductive materialism 67, 69, 74–5
reflection 8–9
Reichberg, Gregory M. 271n4
Reiner, Rob, in *South Park* 23
relativism
cultural 28–30, 270–1
individual 27, 28
moral 29, **336**
perspective 55
truth 27–8
wikiality 4
reliabilism 59, 60–1
religion
Cylons 197, 198–9
disrespect 242
epistemology 186n1
Family Guy 242, 245
Marx 183, 185, 186–7
Metallica 187, 193
metaphysics 186n1

religion (*cont'd*)
  morality 185–6, 186n1
  philosophy of 109–10
  philosophy of language 186n1
  rational argument 328
  traditional views 241
religiosity 135
religious belief
  corruption 6
  distaste for 328
  James 63
  Pascal's Wager 43, 129
  problem of evil 132
  and reason 41–2, 64, 109, 138
  unsupported 40
  see also faith
rennin/kidneys 78
Rescher, Nicholas 42n3
responsibility 168–9
Revelation 188
revelation of God 31
rights 33–4, 175, 179, 247, 278
Robin 164n6, 312n15
  see also Batman, Robin characters
Robinson, Walter 296n13
robots 100–2
Romans 186, 197
Rorschach: *see Watchmen*
Rousseau, Jean-Jacques 248, 249–50, 251–2
  Discourse on the Origin of Inequality
    251n2
Rowe, William 118n7
Rowling, J. K.
  afterlife/death 326
  destiny/free will 68, 89, 95, 96, 324, 325
  ethereal realm 321
  see also Harry Potter books
Ruff, Jeffrey 287
rule utilitarianism 174
Russell, Bertrand
  cynical humor 132
  evidence 330n1
  examined life 331–2
  freedom 136
  meaning of world 137
  perceptions 56
  The Problems of Philosophy 332n2
  skepticism 54–5

sacrifice 168, 175, 226, 228
Sacrifice 165n8
sages 314–15
same-sex marriage 29n13
Sartre, Jean-Paul 183–4
  bad faith concept 184, 204
  Being and Nothingness 205n1
  being-in-itself 210
  existentialism 205
  'the Look' 204–5
  meaning of life 205
  Other 206–7, 211
satire 26
Scarry, Elaine 269n1, 273, 277
Scheffler, Samuel 167n13
Schiller, Aaron 32n23–5
Schiller, Friedrich 264n4
Schneider, Greg J. 183–4
Schramm, David N. 130n5
Schwarzenegger, Arnold 50n5
scientific realism **336**
Scientologists 40, 41
Searle, John 78–9, 80, 102–3, 104
Seinfeld 243
self, immaterial 72
self-alienation 236
self-annihilation 237
self-awareness 240–1, 298
self-deception 184
self-defense 166
self-destruction 190, 235, 236
self-emptying: *see kenōsis*
self-importance 159–60
self-respect 154
self-revelation 125
self-sacrifice 229
self-seriousness 159
sensory perceptions 61, 69, 77, 124
Serenity Prayer 197
The 700 Club 13
sexual encounters 234–5
sexuality, male/female 233–4
shame
  Aristotle 158
  buffoonery 157–8
  'the Look' 209–10, 211
  The Office 204, 212
  Other 210

thumos 146, 147
 torture victim 273
shape perceptions 55–6
Schapiro, Rich 26n5
Sharp, Robert 183
sheepdog analogy 149
Sherwin, Susan 222n2
Shue, Henry 273, 275, 277
Sider, Theodore 97n22
sight 60
Silberstein, Michael 97n21
Silverman, Eric J. 37–8
Simpson, O. J. 14
The Simpsons 136n12
sin 186
single-mindedness 213–14
Sisyphus 51n7
skepticism 337
 cynical 64–5
 Descartes 47–8
 House 303
 James 65
 The Matrix 40, 48–50
 pit of 49, 52
 reality 54–6
slave morality 194, 195, 197, 200–3
slavery 29–30, 194, 195, 197
slippery slope fallacy 21–2
sloth 119, 122–3
Smart, J. J. C. 131n7, 135
Smilansky, Saul 170n18
Smith, Adam: *The Wealth of Nations*
 263
Smith, Joseph 40, 42, 44
Smith, Quentin 130n4
social contract theory 247–8
social networks 221, 225
socialism 247
society/individual 247–8
Socrates
 death sentence 7, 9–10, 331
 defense of 6, 7
 examined life 327, 331–2
 as gadfly 3, 11
 horse training analogy 6–7
 knowledge/opinion 120
 and *South Park* 5
 virtue 7

ways of thinking 13
 wisdom 7, 32–3
Soeng, Mu 299n1
solidarity 137
Solomon, Robert 152n2
Some Kind of Monster 193
soothsayers 89, 91
Sophocles 148
Sorcerer's Stone (Rowling) 326
soul 71n2
 afterlife 329
 Aristotle 324
 Christianity 197
 humanity 198
 justice 146
 machines 197–8
 pineal gland 72
 slave morality 199, 200
 torture 273
 virtue 149
soul-making 117–18, 133, 134
sound waves 75
South Park
 belief 37, 39–41
 criticized 5, 6
 evil 1, 8, 109, 111–12
 freedom of speech 5
 gadfly role 11
 God 112, 115–17
 logic 14, 15–16
 moral issues 9
 philosophy 3
 as provocation 13
 red-herring fallacy 4
 Socrates 5
 vulgarity 11, 12
South Park episodes
 "All About the Mormons" 24, 40
 "Are You There God?" 118
 "The Biggest Douche in the Universe"
  44, 45
 "Butt Out" 23
 "Cartmanland" 43, 109, 111–18
 "Chef Aid" 14–24, 113
 "Chef Goes Nanners" 22
 "Chickenlover" 21
 "Clubhouses" 22
 "Death" 5

South Park episodes (*cont'd*)
  "Do the Handicapped Go to Hell?" 23,
    43–4
  "The Entity" 21
  "Here Comes the Neighborhood" 21
  "Ike's Wee Wee" 17
  "Jewbilee" 116
  "Kenny Dies" 114–15
  "Mr. Hankey, The Christmas Poo" 22
  "The Passion of the Jew" 17–18
  "Prehistoric Ice Man" 11
  "Scott Tenorman Must Die" 19, 41–2
  "Super Best Friends" 44
  "Timmy 2000" 44
  "The Tooth Fairy Tats 2000" 18–19
  "Towelie" 19
  "Trapped in The Closet" 41
  "Weight Gain 4000" 21
Southworth, Jason 67
space-time 97
Spanakos, Tony 181n22
species and subspecies 281–2
Spider-Man 213
Spielberg, Steven 170
spirit 71n2, 139, 142n1
spiritual quest 309–10
Spock, Mr. 143
Star Trek 143
state of nature: *see* nature, state of
Steinhoff, Uwe 276n19
stereotypes 1, 21, 229–30, 284
Stone, Matt 5, 11, 21
Streisand, Barbara 117n5
Strong, Samantha 26n5
subject/object dualism 214–15, 216, 220
subordination of women 232–3
suffering 113, 115, 289–92, 297, 298
superheroes 165, 173, 181
Superman 213
supermarket queue example 250–1
superpowered people 141–2, 149–50
surgeon and transplant problem 167
surplus value 248, 262–3
surrogacy, ethics of 222
Sussman, David 272
Suzuki, D. T. 296n11
Suzuki, Shunryu 301, 304, 307
Syse, Henrik 271n4

Tao Te Ching 287, 309n2, 309n3
Taoism 287, 288, 308–9, 314–15
temperance 144–6, 150
Terjesen, Andrew 145n6, 150n11
Terminator movies
  artificial intelligence 68
  Judgment Day 99, 100
  machines 101–7
  personhood 99–100
The Terrance and Philip Show 5, 6, 7, 12,
  13, 16, 22
terrorism 271, 272, 277
testimony 60–2, 122
texture perceptions 55
thanatos 191
Thatcher, Margaret 180
theism 110, 115–16, 132
theodicy 117–18
thinking 10, 13, 100–2, 104
thirst 78–9
Thomson, Judith Jarvis 166, 168
  Rights, Restitution, & Risk 166n12
thoughtlessness 5, 8
thumos 139, 142–3, 144, 146, 147
ticking bomb argument 273–4, 275–6,
  277
time
  cyclical 289
  fixed 96–8
  space-time 97
time travel 96–8
Tinsley, Beatrice M. 130n5
tit-for-tat 258, 259
Tolkien, J. R. R.
  Letters 323n8
  The Lord of the Rings 280, 323
  The Silmarillion 323n8
Tooley, Michael 118n7
torture
  arguments for/against 273–4, 275–8
  banality of 279
  cancer analogy 277
  consequentialism 274
  cultural context 270–1
  debates on 170–1, 248
  defined 271–3
  dehumanizing process 276, 277
  deontology 269

duhkha 290
efficacy of 276–7
ethics 269
etymology 272n9
folk psychology 277
institutionalized 278
legitimate/illegitimate 274, 278
shame of victim 273
shock 275
soul 273
terrorism 271, 272
24 248, 269, 275, 278–9
utilitarianism 270
torturers, training for 276
Total Recall 50n5
Tower Commission Report 180
traditionalism 222, 241
tragedy, beauty of 136
tragedy of the commons 253, 254, 259
transcendence 71, 136, 189
transvaluation 189
trolley problem 166–9
Trotter, W. F. 42n3
Truman, Harry 178
Trust No. 1 252, 254, 255, 256, 258, 259
truth
  becoming 305
  beliefs 27, 57
  chain of 122
  Christian-Platonic idea 192
  correspondence theory 27
  faith 126
  knowledge 58
  The Matrix trilogy 51–2
  philosophy 4
  premise 20
  reality 190
  relativism 27–8
  as social construct 238
  testimony 122
  universal 27
  Zen Buddhism 299
truth in the making 324–5
truthfulness 58, 64
truthiness 4, 25, 30–3, 36
Turing, Alan 101n2
Turing Test 68, 101, 102
Twain, Mark 157

24
  Bauer as hero/torturer 248, 270, 275, 277
  Bauer tortured 269, 270, 276
  coercion 272
  interrogational torture 273, 274, 278–9
  shootings 271
  torture 248, 269, 275, 278–9
28 Days Later 252, 258
Twilight series
  Bella character 184, 228–32, 234–6, 237
  Breaking Dawn 228–9
  Cullen character 229, 234
  New Moon 232
  sacrifice 228

Uncanny X-Men 85
  "Days of Future Past" 83
unfalsifiable **337**
United Nations *Convention Against Torture* 270
universalization test 179
US Constitution 270
utilitarianism **337**
  Batman–Joker 140, 164–5
  and consequentialism 174, 175
  and deontology 166–7
  happiness 175–6
  superheroes 165
  ticking bomb argument 274
  torture 270

vampire women 228, 235–6
Vines, Jennifer A. 110
violence 178, 250
virtual-reality 50
virtue
  Aristotle 9, 139, 152–4
  defined 152, 153
  excellence 154–5
  good 149
  happiness 139, 152–3
  Plato 139
  power 142
  reflective 8
  Socrates 7
  soul 149
  and vices 152, 153
  wit 151, 154–6

virtue ethics 151–2, 270
virtue utilitarianism 174
Voltaire 44, 185
vulgarity 5, 11, 12

Wachowski, Andy and Larry 71
Wainwright, William J. 115n3
Waiting for Godot (Beckett) 323
Waking Life 48n2
Walls, Jonathan 317
War Games Act Three 312n14
Washington, George 33
Watchmen
  alternative universe 180–1
  consequentialism/deontology 172,
    173–4
  existentialism 179
  Keene Act 178
  Ozymandias 172, 173–6, 177–9, 181
  power 181
  Rorschach 172, 173, 174–5, 177, 178,
    181
  watching the watchmen 140, 180
Watergate scandal 180
Watership Down 254
Wayne, Bruce: *see* Batman
Weapon X stories 82
wei-wu-wei (action without action) 288,
  314
White, Mark 140, 288
White House Correspondents Dinner 34
Whyte, Jamie 33n30, 34n32
Wife Swap 12
wikiality 4, 25, 28–30
Wikipedia 28, 30
Wilks, Michael 270n3
Willems, Brian 198n4
Williams, Edward 114n2

Windsor-Smith, Barry 86
wisdom 7, 32–3, 144, 150, 154, 298
  practical 157, 161
Wisnewski, J. Jeremy 184
wit 151, 154–6, 157, 160–2
Wittgenstein, Ludwig 162
Wolverine 82, 84, 85–6, 87–8
Wolverine: Origins 85
Wolverine Vol. 2 86
womanhood 230, 232–3, 234
  see also femininity
women in paid work 232n17
women's right to vote 175, 232n17
Wonder Woman 165n8, 170n19
Woodward, Bob 180
workers 248, 263–4
workers' revolution 261–3
working class 261

Xavier, Charles, in *X-Men* 84
X-Factor 87, 282
X-Gene 281–2
X-Men
  biological race 282–3
  identity through time 67
  mutants as race/species 248, 280–2,
    285–6
  social race 283–5
X-Men: The Last Stand 282

yin-yang symbol 288, 309
Young, William W. III 3, 4

Zalta, Edward N. 118n7
Zapata, Emilio 188
Zazen 304
Zen Buddhism 287–8, 289, 291, 299–307
Zen proverbs 299, 307